Sources of
Korean Tradition

VOLUME I

INTRODUCTION TO ASIAN CIVILIZATIONS

INTRODUCTION TO ASIAN CIVILIZATIONS

Wm. Theodore de Bary, General Editor

Sources of Japanese Tradition
(1958)

Sources of Chinese Tradition
(1960)

Sources of Indian Tradition
(1958, revised 1988)

Sources of
Korean Tradition

VOLUME I

From Early Times Through
the Sixteenth Century

Edited by Peter H. Lee and Wm. Theodore de Bary
with Yongho Ch'oe and Hugh H. W. Kang

COLUMBIA   UNIVERSITY   PRESS   NEW   YORK

Columbia University Press
Publishers Since 1893
New York   Chichester, West Sussex
Copyright © 1997 Columbia University Press
All rights reserved

Grateful acknowledgment is made to the following for permission to reprint previously
published material:
Jonathan W. Best, for material from "Tales of Three Paekche Monks Who Traveled Afar
in Search of the Law," *Harvard Journal of Asiatic Studies* 51:1 (1991).
Cambridge University Press, for Joseph Needham et al., *The Hall of Heavenly Records:
Korean Astronomical Instruments and Clocks, 1380–1780* (1986). © Cambridge Univer-
sity Press 1986.
Harvard University Press, for Peter H. Lee, *Lives of Eminent Korean Monks: The Haedong
Kosŭng Chŏn.* © 1969 by the Harvard Yenching Institute.
Sungbae Park, for excerpt from "Wŏnhyo's Commentaries on the *Awakening of Faith in
Mahāyāna,*" Ph.D. dissertation, University of California, Berkeley, 1979.
Royal Asiatic Society Korea Branch, for Hahm Pyong-choon, *The Korean Political Tradi-
tion: Essays in Korean Law and Legal History.* © 1967 by Royal Asiatic Society Korea
Branch.
University of Hawaii Press, for material from Robert E. Buswell, Jr., *The Korean Approach
to Zen: The Collected Works of Chinul.* © 1983 University of Hawaii Press.

Diagrams on pages 351, 356, 363, and 369 were taken from Michael C. Kalton, trans. and
ed., *To Become a Sage* (New York: Columbia University Press, 1988).

Library of Congress Cataloging-in-Publication Data

Sources of Korean tradition / edited by Peter H. Lee and Wm. Theodore
    de Bary, with Yongho Ch'oe and Hugh H. W. Kang.
        p.   cm. (Introduction to Asian Civilizations)
    Abridged version of: Sourcebook of Korean civilization, vol. 1.
    Includes bibliographical references and index.
    Contents: v. 1. From early times through the sixteenth century

    ISBN 978-0-231-10566-8 (cloth) — ISBN 978-0-231-10567-5 (paper)
    1. Korea—Civilization.   I. Lee, Peter H., 1929–   .   II. De
Bary, William Theodore, 1918–   .   III. Series.
DS904.S69   1997   96–17701
951.9—dc20

Design by Linda Secondari
Casebound editions of Columbia University Press books are printed on permanent and
durable acid-free paper.
Printed in the United States of America
c 10 9 8 7 6 5 4 3 2 1
p 10 9

C O N T E N T S

PREFACE

This book is a selective abridgement of the *Sourcebook of Korean Civilization*, Volume I, published by Columbia University Press in 1993, with substantial deletions from and some significant additions to it. Our purpose is to make accessible a selection from the great array of documentary materials in that *Sourcebook*, in a form roughly comparable to that used in the volumes in the Introduction to Asian Civilizations series, namely, *Sources of Chinese Tradition*, *Sources of Indian Tradition*, and *Sources of Japanese Tradition*. The latter works were prepared as source materials to be read alongside general historical accounts of these civilizations, and to give readers some sense of how major historical and cultural developments were viewed by participants in or observers of them.

The *Sources* have been used for this purpose by students both of individual cultures and of larger cultural configurations such as East Asia, South Asia, and Southeast Asia, the original intention of this series being not simply to advance the study of individual cultures but to promote the inclusion of Asia in general education and, even more specifically, in programs of study designed as part of the core curriculum. Here the concept of core emphasizes not so much breadth as centrality and a concentration on key features. For these purposes, then, our main criterion has been what ideas, practices, and institutions contribute to the process of civilization, especially as they are found in urban life, literate discourse, complex social and economic organization, and the attendant traditions of civility. Hence the focus is more on the social and civic than on the broadly humanistic and literary, and aesthetic matters are therefore only lightly touched upon. In a collection of this kind one cannot do full justice to the wonderful variety of human culture when the principle of selection must be balance rather than comprehensiveness.

Two qualifications may be noted to this general policy. First, the paucity of documents dating from the Three Kingdoms period makes an adequate understanding of its institutional and cultural history difficult, and to offset this, a higher proportion of the extant materials is included for this period.

Second, there is little documentation for Korea's indigenous folk religion. Like the Japanese Shinto, it is a religion without a written scripture. Through random official and unofficial references, we know that ritual specialists called *mu* (the word is usually translated "shamans") existed in the Three Kingdoms period. The rapprochement between shamanism and Buddhism in Silla and Koryŏ illustrates the way in which an official religion attempted to incorporate a folk religion to make itself more appealing to the people. During the Chosŏn dynasty, however, popular religion was denigrated as superstition, and its practitioners were relegated to the lowest stratum of society. Only during the twentieth century have they become a subject of ethnographic study. Their songs, hitherto orally transmitted, reveal a polytheistic pantheon of more than three hundred gods, including some from Buddhism and Taoism. Husbands of ritual specialists became entertainers or singers of tales that later developed into the oral narrative art of *p'ansori*. However, in the Chosŏn period, because literate discourse was so dominated by the scholar-official class and its Neo-Confucian ideology, nothing developed in Korea like the Shinto revival and National Learning movements, which contributed, along with Confucianism, to the rise of nationalist ideology in late Tokugawa–early Meiji Japan. Although Korean culture matured in its own distinctive ways and Koreans had a strong sense of their own identity, the influence of China and Confucianism remained strong, while indigenous religion played little part in the official life of the Chosŏn dynasty.

In most respects the present volume follows the style and format of the *Sourcebook*, and the two should be considered complementary. Indeed, readers with an appetite for more on subjects dealt with only briefly here are urged to pursue their interests further in the *Sourcebook* itself.

When this series was first projected in the late 1940s, it was the intention to include Korea in it as a major contributor to the civilization of East Asia. The long neglect of Korean studies, however, and the paucity of scholars in the field made it difficult to fulfill that intention until now; in fact, had it not been for the initiative and industry of the sponsors, editors, and contributors of the *Sourcebook*, we might still be waiting for the fulfillment of that earlier dream. Though this book carries no personal dedication, we wish to acknowledge here, and pay tribute to, all those in Korea—especially the Korean National Commission for UNESCO and its officers—other parts of East Asia, and the West who together have brought us fifty years later to this happy outcome.

Peter H. Lee
Wm. Theodore de Bary

EXPLANATORY NOTE

The romanization of Korean names follows the McCune-Reischauer system and certain suggestions made in *Korean Studies* 4 (1980): 111–125. The apostrophe to mark two separate sounds (e.g., *han'gŭl*) has been omitted throughout. For Chinese, the Wade-Giles system is used; for Japanese, Kenkyusha's *New Japanese-English Dictionary* (Tokyo: Kenkyusha, 1974).

Dates for rulers of China and Korea are reign dates without *r*. They are preceded by birth and death dates if required.

Names of places or suffixes (mountains, river, monastery) are translated whenever possible. We have, however, attempted to avoid such pleonasms as Pulguk-sa Monastery, except for such cases as Mount Muak.

For the translation of Buddhist terms we have consulted W. E. Soothill and Lewis Hodous, *A Dictionary of Chinese Buddhist Terms, with Sanskrit and English Equivalents and a Sanskrit-Pali Index* (London: Kegan Paul, 1937), and Mochizuki Shinkō, ed., *Bukkyō daijiten* (Tokyo: Sekai seiten kankō kyōkai, 1960–1963). For Sanskrit terms we have followed Sir Monier Monier-Williams, *A Sanskrit-English Dictionary Etymologically and Philologically Arranged with Special Reference to Cognate Indo-European Languages* (Oxford: Clarendon Press, 1899), and Franklin Edgerton, *Buddhist Hybrid Sanskrit Dictionary* (New Haven: Yale University Press, 1953). For Sanskrit titles of works in the Buddhist canonical collections, we have also consulted Hajime Nakamura, *Indian Buddhism: A Survey with Bibliographical Notes* (Delhi: Motilal Banarsidass, 1987).

The translation of Chinese institutional titles generally follows Charles O. Hucker, *A Dictionary of Official Titles in Imperial China* (Stanford: Stanford University Press, 1985). The translation of Korean institutional titles, together with Korean names of distance, area, and linear measure, generally follows Ki-baik Lee, *A New History of Korea*, trans. Edward W. Wagner with Edward J. Shultz (Cambridge: Harvard University Press, 1984).

We have avoided using brackets in the translations where possible for the sake of fluency. The sources, after the first mention of a person by his full name, subsequently identify him, not by the full name, but by the given name, polite name *(cha)*, pen name *(ho)*, posthumous epithet *(si)*, or some other sobriquet. Believing that this practice could prove confusing to the modern reader unfamiliar with the texts (and with East Asian patterns of nomenclature), we have given the full names of people on subsequent mention but have omitted the brackets around them to avoid cluttering the text. Allusions to the Chinese canonical texts and histories are worked into the translations whenever possible, and sources are indicated in notes. Contentious points are also explained in notes.

Brackets are retained for interpolated dates in the translations. They are also used around the original term supplied along with its translation—for example, "The Wa marauders *[Woegu]* were utterly defeated." When so used, the brackets are italicized. In one or two selections, material missing from the original has been reconstructed by the translators; in these cases the reconstructed text is given in italic within roman (nonitalic) brackets, thus: "Thereupon [*having taken possession of*] fifty-eight towns and seven hundred villages. . . ." Editorial interpolations supplied for clarity or English idiom, however, are set roman within roman brackets.

Works frequently cited in the notes have been abbreviated according to the list below:

HKC   *Haedong kosŭng chŏn* (*T.* 50, no. 2065)
HKSC   *Hsü kao-seng chuan* (*T.* 50, no. 2060)
HPC   *Hanguk pulgyo chŏnsŏ*
HTC   *Hsü Tsang-ching* (Hong Kong reprint of *Dai-Nihon zokuzōkyō*)
KRS   *Koryŏ sa* (Yŏnse taehakkyo, Tongbanghak yŏnguso edition)
KSGN   *Kŭmgang smmaegyŏng non* (*T.* 34, no. 1730)
KT   *Korean Tripiṭaka* (Koryŏ taejanggyŏng)
Legge   James Legge, *The Chinese Classics*, 5 vols.

SGSG	*Samguk sagi* (Yi Pyŏngdo edition)
SGYS	*Samguk yusa* (Ch'oe Namsŏn edition)
SKC	*Sourcebook of Korean Civilization*, vol. 1
SKSC	*Sung kao-seng chuan* (T. 50, no. 2061)
SPPY	*Ssu-pu pei-yao*
SPTK	*Ssu-pu ts'ung-k'an*
T	*Taishō shinshū daizōkyō*
VS	*Vajrasamādhi sūtra* (T. 9, no. 273)

C O N T R I B U T O R S

The translator's initials follow each translated passage.

DC	Donald N. Clark, Trinity University
ES	Edward J. Shultz, West Oahu College
HK	Hugh H. W. Kang, University of Hawaii at Manoa
JB	Jonathan W. Best, Wesleyan University
JD	John B. Duncan, University of California, Los Angeles
JJ	John C. Jamieson, University of California, Berkeley
JW	Jinwol Lee, University of Hawaii at Manoa
MD	Martina Deuchler, University of London
MK	Michael Kalton, University of Washington at Tacoma
MR	Michael C. Rogers, University of California, Berkeley
PL	Peter H. Lee, University of California, Los Angeles
RB	Robert E. Buswell, Jr., University of California, Los Angeles
SP	Sungbae Park, State University of New York, Stony Brook
YC	Yongho Ch'oe, University of Hawaii at Manoa

Sources of
Korean Tradition

VOLUME I

PART ONE

Three Kingdoms and Unified Silla

C H A P T E R   O N E

Origins of Korean Culture

The history of human activity in Korea can be traced far into the ancient past. Some of the earliest archaeological finds include Paleolithic remains at Sŏkchang-ni (South Ch'ungch'ŏng), Kulp'ori (Unggi in North Hamgyŏng), Sangwŏn, Haesang-ni, Tŏkch'ŏn (South P'yŏngan), Chech'ŏn (North Ch'ungch'ŏng), and Chŏngok (Kyŏnggi). These finds include mammal bone fossils, scrapers, choppers, and chopping tools. Radiocarbon dating indicates that habitation began between 40,000 and 30,000 B.C. The oldest Neolithic artifacts are primitive pottery found in the lower layer of Tongsamdong, near Pusan, and Unggi in North Hamgyŏng. The use of comb-pattern pottery emerged around 4,000 B.C. Both the Neolithic primitive pottery people and the comb-pattern pottery people seem to have been clan peoples engaged in gathering, hunting, and fishing.

They were followed by other clan peoples who farmed, used plain pottery, and lived side by side with fishing people. The influence of the former on the latter can be seen in the remains unearthed in Chit'am-ni, Hwanghae (middle of the comb-pattern pottery period), and Tongsamdong—cultivation and hunting are evidenced by carbonized millet at the first site and by the bones of animals at both sites. Finally, the fishing people seem to have been absorbed by the plain-pottery culture. For example, in Mirim-ri and Ch'ŏngho-ri, northeast of P'yŏngyang on opposite shores of the Taedong

River, plain coarse pottery and stone axes and knives were unearthed at the former site and comb-pattern pottery and stone net sinkers at the latter. Judging from the coexistence of the fishing and farming people, there might have been some form of economic exchange. Conflicts arising from the process of exchange and the amalgamation of the clans into tribes called for some form of arbitration. Further change in this early Korean society came with the influx of metal culture from the Scytho-Siberian and the Han Chinese civilizations.

Farming techniques improved in the Bronze Age, and rich remains such as semilunar stone knives, stone hoes, and stone axes with grooves are found on the slopes overlooking fertile valleys and plains. People continued to use stone tools in the Bronze Age, while bronze itself was reserved for weapons, sacrificial vessels, and ornaments. This practice suggests the existence of a dual social structure in which peoples possessing superior bronze weaponry expropriated the agricultural production of Neolithic peoples. To distinguish themselves from their subordinates, the members of a superior tribe would proclaim themselves "sons of heaven" and build imposing dolmens to display their power. Amid such changes in social relationships, some form of political power began to grow in the peninsula.

THE FOUNDATION MYTH

During the Neolithic period, the Tung-i (Eastern Barbarian) tribes, who lived in an area stretching from the Huai River, Shantung peninsula, and southern Manchuria to the Gulf of Pohai and the Korean peninsula, came under the influence of the Shang and Scytho-Siberian civilizations, the latter coming from Central Asia through northern China. The tribes' close ties with these civilizations helped them develop their own Bronze Age. In addition, those along the Huai and on the Shantung peninsula were in contact with the civilization south of the Yangtze. Included among the Tung-i were the Yemaek and Han tribes that constituted the original nucleus of the Korean people. In their eastward migration, these tribes absorbed or pushed out societies distinguished by their production of comb-pattern pottery and became the core of the patternless-pottery society. Linguistically, they are said to be a branch of the Tungusic tribes and thus belong to the Altaic language family. With agriculture as their economic basis, they absorbed the red-pottery and black-pottery cultures, thus building a broad basis for their own civilization. With the fall of the Shang and the rise of the Chou to the west, tribes migrated from along the Huai River and Shantung peninsula to southern Manchuria and the Korean peninsula. Those who reached the Taedong River basin merged with the inhabitants there and formed Old Chosŏn. The illustrations on the stone slabs in the Wu family shrine in Chia-hsiang hsien in Shantung, built in 147, depict the content of the foundation myth—the Tangun legend—as it is recorded in Iryŏn's *Memorabilia of the Three Kingdoms (Samguk yusa)*.

The superior bronze culture tribes of Old Chosŏn ruled over those who were still in the Neolithic stage and tried to assert the authority of their tradition and heritage. The natives' worship of the gods of the wind, rain, and cloud, together with their totemic belief in the bear and the tiger, gave way to the worship of the god of the sun. According to the Korean foundation myth, Hwanung came down to the world of man and married a she-bear who bore Tangun, the first ruler of the age of theocracy. The bear cult, the core of the Tangun legend, descends from the Paleolithic period and is still prevalent among the Ainu and some tribes in Siberia. The stone slabs in the Wu family shrine are proof that the legend was not formed at the time of the Mongol invasion of Korea, as has been suggested by some Japanese scholars. The Wu family may have been part of the tribe belonging to the Korean people or of a tribe close to the Northeast Asian people.

According to the version in the *Rhymed Record of Emperors and Kings (Chewang ungi)* by Yi Sŭnghyu (1224–1300), the great king Hwanung gave medicine to his granddaughter so that she would change into a human. She married a god of the sandalwood tree and bore Tangun, an indication that the Tangun legend originated in the north and was transmitted to the south, where it absorbed tree worship.

In Iryŏn's *Memorabilia of the Three Kingdoms*, the account of the legend was based on the *Wei shu* and *Old Record (Kogi)*. While such Confucian historians as Kim Pusik (1075–1151) rejected the legend, Great Master Iryŏn's inclusion of it is evidence that Buddhism tried to absorb the autochthonous beliefs during its spread in the peninsula. But even Confucian scholars began to acknowledge the importance of their native tradition, as evinced by Paek Munbo (d. 1374), who pointed out that the year 3600 in the Tangun calendar (1267) marked a year of prosperity.

Tangun

[From *Samguk yusa* 1:33–34]

The *Wei shu* tells us that two thousand years ago, at the time of Emperor Yao, Tangun Wanggŏm chose Asadal as his capital and founded the state of Chosŏn. The *Old Record* notes that in olden times Hwanin's son, Hwanung, wished to descend from Heaven and live in the world of human beings. Knowing his son's desire, Hwanin surveyed the three highest mountains and found Mount T'aebaek the most suitable place for his son to settle and help human beings. Therefore he gave Hwanung three heavenly seals and dispatched him to rule over the people. Hwanung descended with three thousand followers to a spot under a tree by the Holy Altar atop Mount T'aebaek, and he called this place the City of God. He was the Heavenly King Hwanung. Leading the Earl of Wind, the Master of Rain, and the Master of Clouds, he took charge of some three hundred and sixty areas of responsibility, including agriculture, allotted lifespans, illness, punishment, and good and evil, and brought culture to his people.

At that time a bear and a tiger living in the same cave prayed to Holy Hwanung to transform them into human beings. The king gave them a bundle of sacred mugworts and twenty cloves of garlic and said, "If you eat these and shun the sunlight for one hundred days, you will assume human form." Both animals ate the spices and avoided the sun. After twenty-one days the bear became a woman, but the tiger, unable to observe the taboo, remained a tiger. Unable to find a husband, the bear-woman prayed under the altar tree for a child. Hwanung metamorphosed himself, lay with her, and begot a son called Tangun Wanggŏm.

PL

KOREA IN THE CHINESE DYNASTIC HISTORIES

The *Records of the Historian (Shih chi*; ch. 115) records the development of Old Chosŏn and its successor state, Wiman Chosŏn, as well as the establishment of the four Chinese commanderies in northern Korea. A similar account is in the *History of the Former Han (Han shu*; ch. 95). The monograph on geography in the latter (ch. 28) describes the territory of the Han commanderies and tells how native customs changed under the Han administration. The iron culture introduced by the Han colonies resulted in considerable change in the peninsula. While the ruling class had monopolized bronze vessels in the Bronze Age, the iron culture spread rapidly, bringing about pervasive changes in society. The head of a family became the head of a clan; as the number of clans increased, it became more difficult to form a federation strong enough to oppose the ruling power. Since the policy of Han colonies was to obstruct the growth of a leading power in the peninsula, the state of Chin south of the Han River was dissolved, and even the indigenous society, only indirectly controlled by China through trade, could not grow into an independent force.

Thus the ancient Korean states had two aims: to free themselves from

Chinese cultural forces and to remain intact in their struggles against other peoples outside the Great Wall. Internally, they had to build a base for uniting the power of clan chiefs and to find a footing for the establishment of a ruling system. The social conditions during this period of travail are best portrayed in the chapter on the Tung-i in the *History of the Later Han (Hou Han shu)* and *History of the Three Kingdoms (San-kuo chih)*.

Accounts of the Eastern Barbarians

[From *San-kuo chih* 30:840–853]

The *Book of Documents* says, "To the east they envelop the sea, to the west they encompass the drifting sands." One can indeed use such words to describe the system of the Nine Zones of Submission. But if one proceeds, relying on multiple translation of tongues, beyond the Desolate Region (the outermost zone), it isn't worth the trouble to mark on maps the places where cart tracks reach, nor is there anyone who knows about the strange forms of national customs to be found there.

Sometime later, when Koguryŏ became refractory and rebellious, Wei further sent an army detachment to visit chastisement upon them. The army went to the end of the earth in exhaustive pursuit and having trampled upon the encampments of the Suksin, they gazed eastwards upon the great sea.

As our elders tell it, there were people of strange faces, the product of proximity to the sun. Accordingly they surveyed the several states, noting their norms and customs and distinguishing small from great; each had its own name and could be described in detail. Even though there were the principalities of the I and the Ti, the shapes of ritual vessels were retained among them. It would seem that one can indeed have credence in the saying, "When the Middle Kingdom has lost the rites, seek them among the Four Barbarians." Therefore we have placed their states in appropriate order, and have set forth their similarities and differences, in order to supply what the previous histories have not provided.

MR

Puyŏ

Puyŏ [Fu-yü] is north of the Long Wall, a thousand *li* distant from Hsüan-t'u; it is contiguous with Koguryŏ on the south, with the I-lou [Ŭmnu] on the east and the Hsien-pei on the west, while to its north is the Jo [Yak] River. It covers an area some two thousand *li* square, and its households number eight myriads. Its people are sedentary, possessing houses, storehouses, and prisons. With their many tumuli and broad marshes, theirs is the most level and open of the Eastern

Barbarian territories. Their land is suitable for the cultivation of the five grains; they do not produce the five fruits. Their people are coarsely big; by temperament strong and brave, assiduous and generous, they are not prone to brigandage. Their state is ruled by a king, and they name their officials after the six domestic animals: there is the Horse *ka,* the Ox *ka,* the Pig *ka,* and the Dog *ka;* the *taesa,* the *taesaja,* and the *p'aeja.* In their settlements there are brave people; those called "lowly households" can all become slaves. The several *ka* separately rule the roads that extend to the four quarters; those of great domain rule several thousand families, those of small several hundred. In eating and drinking they all use ritual vessels; in their meetings they make ceremonial toasts and wash the goblets; bowing and deferring, they ascend and descend.

They sacrifice to Heaven using the correct month of Yin [Shang]. When there is a great assembly in the state they eat and drink, dance and sing for days on end. Such occasions are called welcoming drums *[yŏnggo].* At this time they decide criminal cases and release prisoners. For their dress within their state they favor white; they have large sleeves, gowns, and trousers, and on their feet they wear leather sandals. When they go out from their state, they favor silken brocades and embroidered fabrics to which the chiefs add the fur of the fox, the badger, the monkey, and the white and black sable, and they decorate their headgear with gold and silver. When their translators transmit the words of a Chinese official, they always squat down and, propped on their hands, speak respectfully. In their use of punishments they are very strict: one who kills another must himself die, and the members of his household are made slaves. Thieves must pay a twelvefold indemnity. When a man and a woman have illicit intercourse or a wife is jealous, all are killed. They especially detest jealousy. Having killed a person guilty of such crimes, they expose her body atop a hill to the south of the community; after it has decomposed and the woman's family wants to retrieve it, they are given it only after having paid for it with cattle and horses. Upon the death of his elder brother, a man takes to wife his former sister-in-law, a custom they share with the Hsiung-nu.

The people of their state are good at raising domestic animals; they also produce famous horses, red jade, sables, and beautiful pearls. The pearls *[chu]* are as large as sour jujubes. For weapons they have bows, arrows, knives, and shields; each household has its own armorer. The elders of the state speak of themselves as alien refugees of long ago. The forts they build are round and have a resemblance to prisons. Old and young, they sing when walking along the road whether it be day or night; all day long the sound of their voices never ceases. In the event of military action they also perform sacrifices to Heaven. They kill an ox and observe its hoof to divine good or bad fortune; for the hoof to fall apart is considered to be bad luck, for it to come together is considered to be good. When facing the enemy the several *ka* themselves do battle; the lower households carry provisions for them to eat and drink. Upon their death, in the months of summer they always use ice for preservation. When they kill people, they expose their bodies, sometimes as many as a hundred or more. They bury their dead, with full ceremony, in an outer coffin and no inner one.   MR

Koguryŏ

Koguryŏ lies a thousand *li* to the east of Liao-tung, being contiguous with Chosŏn and Yemaek on the south, with Okchŏ on the east, and with Puyŏ on the north. They make their capital below Hwando. Their territory is perhaps two thousand *li* on a side, and their households number three myriads. They have many mountains and deep valleys and have no plains or marshes. Accommodating themselves to mountain and valley, the people make do with them for their dwellings and food. With their steep-banked rivers, they lack good fields; and though they plow and till energetically, their efforts are not enough to fill their bellies; their custom is to be sparing of food. They like to build palaces. To the left and right of their dwellings they erect large houses, where they offer sacrifices to ghosts and spirits. They also have rituals for numinous stars and for the spirits of the land and grain. By temperament the people are violent and take delight in brigandage.

As for their placement of officials: when there is a *taero* they do not install a *p'aeja,* and vice versa. In the case of the royal family, their Great *ka* are all called *koch'u ka.* Members of the Yŏnno clan originally were rulers of the state; although they are now no longer kings, their legitimate chieftain can still claim the title *koch'u ka* and can also erect an ancestral temple in which to offer sacrifices to the numinous stars and to the altars of the land and grain. The Chŏllo clan by hereditary custom intermarries with the royal clan and is vested with the title of *koch'u.* The several Great *ka* in like manner install their own *p'aeja* and *choŭi* and *sŏnin;* the latter's names are communicated to the king, like the house vassals of our great ministers. In the sessions of their assemblages, however, they are not permitted to line up on the same level with their counterparts of the royal house. Members of the great houses of their state do not till the fields, and those who thus eat the bread of idleness number more than a myriad. It is the lower households who keep them supplied, bearing rice, grain, fish, and salt from afar.

Their people delight in singing and dancing. In villages throughout the state, men and women gather in groups at nightfall for communal singing and games. They have no great storehouses, each family keeping its own small store, which they call a *pugyŏng.* They rejoice in cleanliness, and they are good at brewing beer. When they kneel to make obeisance, they extend one leg; in this they differ from the Puyŏ. In moving about on foot they all run. In the tenth month they sacrifice to Heaven in a great national assembly which they call *tongmaeng*. In their public gatherings they all wear colorfully brocaded clothing and adorn themselves with gold and silver. The Great *ka* and the *chubu* wear *tse* caps on their heads that are similar to ours but have no additional crown. Their Small *ka* wear "wind-breakers" shaped like *pien* caps. To the east of their state there is a large cave called the Tunnel Cave. At the great national festival of the tenth month they welcome the Su spirit at its return to the east of the state and offer sacrifice to it, placing a Su spirit of wood on the spirit seat. They have no prisons; when a crime is committed the several *ka* deliberate together, then kill the guilty one and take his wife and children as slaves.

As for their marriage customs, after the words of the contract have been fixed, the girl's family builds a small house behind the big house, which they call "the son-in-law's house." In the evening the son-in-law comes to the outside of the girl's family gate and, naming himself, bows in obeisance, begging permission to approach the girl's room. After he has done this two or three times, the girl's parents allow him to approach the small house and spend the night there. He stores his money and valuables on one side, and after his offspring have grown up, he takes his wife and returns to his own house. Such is the lewdness of their customs. After a man and a woman have already been married, they then make some clothing for the burial of their parents. They bury their dead with full ceremony; their treasure of gold and silver is consumed in funeral expenses. They pile up stones to make grave mounds and plant pine and oak trees before them in rows.   *MR*

Eastern Okchŏ

Eastern Okchŏ is located to the east of the great mountains of Kaema in Koguryŏ; its people make their settlements on the shore of the great sea. In shape their land is narrow in the northeast and long in the southwest, where it is perhaps a thousand *li*. It is contiguous on the north with I-lou and Puyŏ, and on the south with Yemaek. Its households number five thousand. They have no supreme ruler, each village having its own hereditary chief. Their language has broad similarity with that of Koguryŏ, though at times there are small differences. Since the chiefs of the Okchŏ's villages all call themselves the Three Elders, one may conclude that their system is that of the prefectures-and-kingdoms of former times. Their state being small and hemmed in between great states, they attach themselves as vassals to Koguryŏ; the latter in turn appoints the Great Man of their midst as *p'aeja*, commissioning him to serve as prime minister to the ruler. They further-more charge the Great *ka* with responsibility for collection of their taxes: cloth, fish, salt, and edibles from the sea; they deliver these after bearing them on their backs for a thousand *li*. They also send their beautiful girls to become maidservants; they are treated as slaves.

Their land is fair and fertile, facing the sea with its back to the mountains. It is well suited to the cultivation of the five grains, and they are good at tilling and planting. The people are simple and direct, strong and brave. Having few oxen and horses, they are adept at fighting on foot, wielding spears. In their eating and drinking, dwelling places, clothing and ritual, they bear resemblance to the people of Koguryŏ. As for their burial practices, they build a great wooden coffin more than ten *chang* in length; opening it at one end, they make a door and therein temporarily bury the newly deceased. They then make a tracing of the body, and when skin and flesh are gone, they take the bones and place them inside the coffin. A whole family shares a single coffin, the wooden surface of which is carved to resemble the living shapes of the dead, as many as are contained inside. They also have tile vessels that they fill with rice and hang on strands beside the coffin door.   MR

Ye

The state of Ye is contiguous with Chinhan on the south, and on the north with Koguryŏ and Okchŏ; on the east it ends at the great sea. The whole region east of present Chosŏn is its territory. Its households number two myriads. In the olden days Chi Tzu (Kija) proceeded to Chosŏn and composed his teachings in eight articles to instruct them; as a result, the people did not steal though doors and gates were not closed.

Their elders have long considered that they are of the same stock as the Koguryŏ. Sincere by nature, they keep their desires to a minimum, have a sense of shame, and do not beg for alms. In language, usages, and customs they are in general the same as the Koguryŏ, but in their clothing there are differences. Men and women both wear pleated collars, and the men plait silver flowers several inches wide for adornment.

Their custom is to give great importance to mountains and rivers, each of which has certain parts into which people are not permitted to wade indiscriminately. Members of the same clan do not intermarry. They have many superstitions and taboos: in the event of illness or death, they always abandon their old dwelling, rebuild, and resettle. They have hemp cloth, as well as silkworms and mulberry trees, with which they make silk. At dawn they observe the stars and lunar stations to learn beforehand whether the year's crop will be abundant or short. They do not consider pearls or jade to be precious. They always use the festival of the tenth month to do ritual service to Heaven; drinking, singing, and dancing day and night, they call this dancing to Heaven *[much'ŏn]*. They also sacrifice to the tiger as to a divine being. If their villages violently transgress upon each other, they are always penalized by exaction of slaves, oxen, and horses; this they call exaction for outrage. One who kills another must die in retribution; there is little robbery among them. They make spears three *chang* in length, sometimes carried by three men at once. They are capable foot soldiers; the "sandalwood bow" of Lo-lang comes from their land. Their sea produces striped fish-skin, and their land abounds in the patterned leopard; they also produce "under the fruit" horses;[1] these were presented as tribute in the time of Emperor Huan of Han.   MR

The Han

Han is south of Tai-fang and on the east and west is bounded by the sea; to the south it is contiguous with the state of Wa (Wae). Its territory is perhaps four thousand *li* square. There are three stocks: the first is called Mahan, the second Chinhan, and the third Pyŏnhan, which is the ancient state of Chin. Mahan is to the west of it. Its people are settled on the land and plant [grains]. They know about silkworms and the mulberry and make silk cloth. Each tribe has its own chief, of whom the great ones call themselves *sinji*, those next in status being called *ŭpch'a*. Scattered between the mountains and the sea, their settlements have no inner or outer walls.

By custom they have few rules and regulations. Their national town has a dominant leader, but the people's settlements are scattered, and they are not readily subject to regulation and control. They do not have the ceremony of kneeling to make obeisance. For their dwellings they make grass-roofed earth-chambers shaped like tumuli; the door is on the top, and a whole family lives together inside, with no distinction as to old or young, male or female. In their burial practice they have an inner coffin but no outer coffin. They do not know about riding oxen and horses, their oxen and horses being used exclusively for accompanying the dead. They consider beads of pearls to have great value, sewing them into their clothing as decoration or hanging them from neck and ears. They do not regard gold, silver, brocades, or silks as precious. They are strong and brave by nature. They wear the "tadpole knot" and leave it bare like a shining fishtail. They wear gowns of rough cloth, and on their feet they wear leather sandals. When there is something to be done within their community up to the point where the authorities have walls built, all the young braves and stalwarts gouge out the skin of their backs to string themselves together with a large rope, or, again, they insert through their shin wooden poles about a *chang* in length. They then chant all day as they work, not because they consider the work painful, but to give themselves encouragement; moreover they consider this to be stalwart behavior.

In the fifth month, when the sowing has been finished, they always sacrifice to their ghosts and spirits. Coming together in groups they sing and dance; they drink wine day and night without ceasing. In their dancing, several tens of men get up together and form a line; looking upward and downward as they stomp the ground, they move hands and feet in concert with a rhythm that is similar to our bell-clapper dance. When the farmwork is finished in the tenth month, they do the same sort of thing again. They have faith in ghosts and spirits. In each town one man is appointed master of ceremonies for worship of the Spirit of Heaven, whom they call Lord of Heaven [ch'ŏngun]. Moreover each commune has a separate town, which they call *sodo*. Here they set up a great tree, from which they hang bells and drums for serving the ghosts and spirits. All manner of refugees who enter there are exempt from extradition. They have a fondness for brigandage. The significance of their setting up *sodo* is similar to that of our Buddhist shrines, but there are differences in the good and evil that they ascribe to what they do. The people of their northern communes that are close to our commandery have a fragmentary awareness of our rites and customs, but those located further away are just like aggregations of prisoners or slaves. They have no rare treasures that are different from ours, and their flora and fauna are about the same as those of the Middle Kingdom. They produce large chestnuts, as big as peaches. They also produce fine-tailed birds whose tails are more than five feet long. Among their men one occasionally sees one who is tattooed. Moreover on the large islands in the sea west of Mahan there are outlanders, very short and small people whose language is not the same as that of the Han. They all bind their hair like the Hsien-pei, but they make their clothing of leather and like to raise oxen and pigs. Their clothing has an upper part but no lower part, and indeed it is almost as if they were naked. They go back and forth by boat, buying and selling in Han.   MR

[*Omitted here are the accounts of Chinhan, Pyŏnhan, and Pyŏnjin. See SKC 1: 22–24.*]

FOUNDERS OF TRIBAL FEDERATIONS

Along with the rise of the tribal federations of Old Chosŏn and Wiman Chosŏn in the north, there had arisen in the south, by the fourth century B.C., a tribal confederation known as Chin. These early entities gave way to the new confederations of Puyŏ, Koguryŏ, and Ye in the north and the Three Han in the south. In addition to breeding cattle and raising crops, the Puyŏ and Koguryŏ were horse-riding people with impressive mobility and combat capability, while the people in the south were sedentary. The migrants from the north at the time of the demise of Old Chosŏn stimulated the indigenous society in the south through the dissemination of their iron culture and through the enlargement of the economic base that was made possible by this active trade among tribes and the fusion of their cultures.

The end of the twentieth century has seen a heightened interest in Kaya history, sparked in part by the excavation of tombs that supply new insights into that country's past. The selection below relates the founding of the Kaya state and the miraculous appearance of the first king, Suro (42–199). It also recounts the arrival of his queen from a distant land, commonly believed to be India.

Kaya also figured prominently in histories written at the start of the twentieth century, when the Japanese military asserted that the Kaya state was actually a Japanese outpost called Mimana during the Yamato period (300–710). There is virtually no evidence to support this contention, but Japanese publicists used it to justify their twentieth-century colonization of Korea.

That Japan and Kaya did have a close relationship cannot be denied, and these early links are emerging quite clearly through the current excavation of Kaya tumuli. The discovery of iron artifacts and horse armor in particular suggests that Kaya was an important iron-producing center with links to China, Puyŏ, Japan (Wa), and the other Korean states. Archaeology also shows that the Kaya state developed in the middle of the third century, but in contention with Silla and Paekche, suffered setbacks in the late fifth century, and was finally absorbed by Silla in A.D. 562. Refugees from this turmoil escaped and settled in Japan.

King Suro

[Samguk yusa 2:108–113]

This account of the founding of Kaya is from a later document compiled by the magistrate of Kŭmgwan (Kimhae), a literatus, during the years of Ta-kang (1075–1084) in the reign of King Munjong (1046–1083).

In the beginning, when this area [of Kaya] had no name as a state, and no formal titles for its officials, there were nine chiefs named Ado, Yŏdo, P'ido, Odo, Yusu, Yuch'ŏn, Sinch'ŏn, Och'ŏn, and Singwi. As chieftains they led the people, who comprised one hundred households, numbering seventy-five thousand persons. Many of them gathered and lived in the mountains and fields, digging wells for drinking and cultivating fields for food.

On the day of the bathing purification rites in the third month of the eighteenth year of Chien-wu [A.D. 42] in the reign of Shih-tsu, Emperor Kwangwu, of the Later Han, there was a strange sound, as of someone calling, on a peak called Turtle Back [Kuji], to the north of where they lived. When a multitude of two hundred to three hundred people gathered there, it sounded more like a person's voice. Although nobody was visible, the voice said, "Is anyone there?" The nine chiefs replied, "We are here." The voice then said, "Where am I?" They replied, "Kuji!" The voice said, "The Heavenly Emperor has instructed me to come to this place to form a new country and become its leader. Therefore I have descended here. You must dig in the ground at the peak of the mountain, singing the verse, 'Turtle, Turtle, push out your head, if you do not, we shall cook and eat you.' If you do sing and dance like this, then you will have a great king with great joy."

The nine chiefs followed this command and sang and danced joyfully. Shortly afterward they looked up and saw a purple rope hanging down from the sky and reaching the ground. At the end of the rope there was a golden bowl wrapped in a red cloth. When they opened it, they found six golden eggs, round like the sun. The people, all in surprise, offered countless bows in joy. Shortly thereafter they rewrapped the eggs and took them in another bowl to the house of Chief Ado. The crowd then dispersed, leaving the bowl on a table.

After twelve days had passed, the people of the area reassembled at sunrise, and uncovering the bowl saw that each of the six eggs had been transformed into infant boys whose appearance was extraordinary. Having them sit on the table, all the people bowed, offering them utmost respect. Daily the boys grew, and after more than ten days they were nine feet tall *[ch'ŏk]*.

They were enthroned on the full moon of that month. The boy who first appeared was named Suro or, some say, "Sunŭng" (his posthumous title). His country was called Great Karak or some call it Kaya state, which was one of the six Kaya states. [Suro] had a temporary palace built and resided there. Simple and frugal, it had an uncut thatched roof and an earthen staircase of three steps.

In spring, the first month of the second year, *kyemyo*, of his reign, the king said, "I want to select a site for a capital." Going to a newly reclaimed field south of the temporary palace, he viewed mountain peaks all over. After determining sites for an outer wall of 1,500 paces in circumference, a palace hall, and government office buildings, armories, and granaries, etc., he returned to his palace.

From throughout the country sturdy adults, laborers and craftsmen, assembled, starting the work from Kŭmyang on the twentieth of the [first] month and completing it on the tenth of the third month. Picking an auspicious day, the king moved to the new palace. [From there] he managed the government diligently, attending to all official duties.

On the twenty-seventh day of the seventh month of the twenty-fourth year, *musin*, of Chien-wu [5 August A.D. 48], the nine chiefs and others in an audience with the king said, "Since Your Majesty has descended to earth, you have not obtained a suitable mate. We hope that you will choose, from among the young ladies presented, the best to enter the palace and become your wife." The king replied, "I came down here at the command of Heaven. That I marry and have a queen shall also depend on the will of Heaven; you do not need to worry."

Later he ordered Chief Yuch'ŏn to take a lightly laden ship and a fine horse and to go to Mangsan Island and wait. He also ordered Chief Singwi to go to Sŭngjŏm. (Mangsan is an island south of the capital, while Sŭngjŏm is a subordinate state.) Suddenly, there was a ship upon the sea, sailing north from the southwest and hoisting a red sail and long red flag. Chief Yuch'ŏn and others first lit a fire on top of the island. Then [the people on the ship] competed [with one another] in hurrying to land. Singwi, observing this, rushed to the palace to report it. Upon hearing the news, the king, with great joy, immediately sent the nine chiefs who held the mast and helm of the finest quality to welcome the ship and escort the passengers to the palace.

The queen [who had been on the vessel] said, "As until now I have never met you, how can I dare frivolously follow you?" Yuch'ŏn returned to report what the queen had said. Acknowledging this, the king, accompanied by his officials, went sixty paces southwest of the palace to the edge of a mountain. There he set up his regal tent and waited. The queen, having her ship tied to a ferry port near the mountain, came ashore to rest on a high hill. As the queen slowly approached the regal tent, the king went out to welcome her, and together they entered the tent. The attending officials, in descending order of rank, greeted them from below the steps and then retired.

Later when the king and queen were alone in the royal bedchamber, the queen quietly said to the king, "I am a princess from Ayut'a [Ayodhyā]. My family name is Hŏ and my personal name Hwangok. I am sixteen years old. In the fifth month of this year, when I was still in my home country, my parents, the King and Queen, said to me, 'Last night in a dream we together saw the Heavenly Emperor, who said to us, "A man called Suro is the founding king of the state of Karak and was sent by Heaven to govern. He is indeed sacred and divine. Governing the new country, however, he has to be matched with a spouse. You should send your daughter to be his wife." When the Heavenly Emperor finished speaking, he

ascended to Heaven. After this dream, the words of the Heavenly Emperor continued to ring in our ears. You must quickly depart from here and go to Karak.' So I
set out to sea, searching for steamed dates and heavenly peaches, and now I
have come to Your Majesty, who has a beautiful appearance." The king replied,
"Since I was born I have foreseen that a princess would come from a distant land.
Even though my officials previously requested that I marry a queen, I did not
heed them. And now that you, a virtuous princess, have come to me on your own,
I am indeed extremely fortunate." Thereafter, they were married and passed two
nights and a day together.

One day the king said to his officials, "Even though the nine chiefs are the
leaders of various officials, their [present] titles and names sound like vulgar
country terms and not those of important officeholders. If they become known
abroad, we certainly will be laughed at." Accordingly Ado's name was changed to
Agung.

Adopting the Silla official system, the king set up the ranks of *Kakkan, Ajilgan,*
and *Kŭpkan*. But for lower offices he borrowed from the precedents of Chou and
the usages of Han. That is how Karak established a government, reforming the old
and adapting itself to the new. Thereupon he ruled his country like his own
household and loved his people like his children. His instructions were not strict
yet carried weight, and his rule was not harsh but fitting. Therefore, the pairing
of the king and queen [as man and wife] was like the pairing of Heaven and
Earth, the sun and moon, and yin and yang.　　　　*HK AND ES*

CHAPTER TWO

The Rise of the Three Kingdoms

From the third century, the Three Kingdoms were aware of the existence of the states of Wei, Shu, and Wu on the mainland. The successive rise and fall of such mainland states and dynasties was strongly felt in the Three Kingdoms, since they related to their own fortunes. Koguryŏ, the first to be aware of its place in international politics, was also the first to grow as a state, and it was politically and culturally superior to Paekche and Silla. When the Kung-sun clan encouraged internal dissension in Koguryŏ during the reign of King Sansang, Koguryŏ obstructed the alliance between Liao-tung and Hsüan-t'u. Thus Koguryŏ was able to withstand a Chinese policy aimed at its dissolution. When Silla and T'ang were at odds, the T'ang attempted a similar policy of fostering internal discord in Silla, as attested by diplomatic papers exchanged between the two. Koguryŏ alone was able to see through China's designs and to take advantage of political divisions on the Chinese mainland. The state's negotiations with peoples outside the Wall are another example of Koguryŏ's aggressive diplomacy. Through expansion Koguryŏ extended its sphere of influence to the Moho and Khitan tribes, and the state became the center of Northeast Asia and the leader in the struggle against China. After the fall of the Sui, the founder of the T'ang wondered if Koguryŏ should be treated as a tributary state.[1]

Paekche and Silla, on the other hand, were able to send emigrants to Japan to establish political authority there but were unable to subjugate the Japanese. Their foreign policy was aimed at stopping the southward advance of Koguryŏ, and during the struggle among the Three Kingdoms, they turned to the Sui and T'ang for help. The unification of China by the Sui and the rise of the T'u-chüeh Turks prompted Koguryŏ to ally itself with the latter to oppose the former. Then Koguryŏ's ally Paekche established ties with people residing in what later became Japan. The north-south pact among the T'u-chüeh, Koguryŏ, Paekche, and Japan was opposed by the alliance between Silla and the Sui. And as leaders of the two opposing forces, Koguryŏ and Sui came to war in 598 and again in 612–614. At this crucial moment in Koguryŏ's history, its foremost general was Ŭlchi Mundŏk.

The four monuments built when King Chinhŭng of Silla inspected the newly conquered territories in the north, south, and west include those at Ch'angnyŏng (A.D. 561), Mount Pukhan (555), Hwangch'o Pass, and Maun Pass (568). PL

King Chinhŭng's Monument at Maun Pass

[From *Samguk yusa,* Appendix 14]

If a benevolent wind does not blow, the way of the world perverts truth. And if moral enlightenment is not set forth, evils will vie with one another. Therefore, emperors and kings established their reign titles, cultivated themselves to the utmost, and brought peace to their subjects. I, however, confronting destiny, inherited the foundation of our progenitor and succeeded to the throne. Cautious and circumspect, I was fearful of going against the Way of Heaven. As I basked in Heaven's favor, good fortunes were manifested, the spirits of Heaven and earth responded, and every enterprise tallied with the norm. Hence, the four quarters entrusted their borders to us, and we gained extensively in territory and population. Neighboring countries pledged their trust, and envoys of peace were exchanged. The court sympathized with the people and nurtured both old and new subjects. The people now say, "The transforming process of the Way extends outward and its favor pervades everywhere."

Thereupon, in the eighth month, autumn, of this year, *muja* [568], I have inspected the territory under my jurisdiction and inquired into popular feelings. I intend to encourage by rewards the loyal and the trustworthy, the sincere and the talented, those who apprehend danger and those who fight with valor and serve with loyalty. They shall be rewarded with rank and title and honored for their loyal services.   PL

DEVELOPMENT OF AGRICULTURE

The use of cattle and farm tools made of iron greatly increased agricultural production in the Three Kingdoms. Moreover, the construction of dams and the establishment of private ownership of land accelerated the growth of landowners among the aristocracy. These landowners increased their holdings by land reclamation or purchase and sale; they built reservoirs and owned the rights to mines. The development of industry and the concentration of the means of production in their hands brought about a major change in society: the division between the aristocracy and the commoners. Thus a rigid class system was born.

The monument erected on the occasion of the completion of a dike in Yŏngch'ŏn sheds light on the living conditions of the villagers, who formed the basic stratum of Silla society, and on the labor mobilization system used by the state. Erected when a reservoir called Luxuriant Dike was built and later repaired, both sides of this monument are inscribed. One side, dated *pyŏngjin*, marks the time of construction, probably 536, the twenty-third year of King Pŏphŭng; the other side, dated Cheng-yüan 14, marks the repair of the reservoir in the fourteenth year of King Wŏnsŏng (798). According to the inscriptions, between the sixth century, when Silla was developing as an ancient state, and the eighth century, when its society began to disintegrate, Silla expended considerable energy implementing irrigation plans. The inscriptions also show the relationship between the central authority and powerful local families, the size of the labor force, and the times of its mobilization. Since the inscription dated 536 is chipped and illegible, the 798 inscription is offered here.   PL

Record of Repair of Luxuriant Dike in Yŏngch'ŏn

[From *Chŭngbo Hanguk kŭmsŏk yumun*, no. 5]

Having repaired Luxuriant Dike, we record it here on the thirteenth day of the fourth month of the fourteenth year of Cheng-yüan, *muin*. Since the bank of the reservoir was damaged, the king dispatched an official with the temporary duty of overseeing the work. The bank's length is thirty-five steps; its height, six steps and three *ch'ŏk;* and its width, twelve steps. The work lasted from the twelfth day of the second month to the thirteenth day of the fourth month, and it was completed during that period. The labor force consisted of 136 axe men and 14,140 soldiers from the Dharma Banner; recruiters from the districts of Chŏrhwa (Yŏngch'ŏn) and Amnyang were—[*here the names are obliterated*]. Overseers were Yŏn, the *sonaesa,* whose local rank was *sanggan* [Rank 6] and court rank was *naemi* [Rank 11]; Sasu, whose court rank was *taesa* [Rank 12]; and Oksun, temporary governor of the district *[kat'aesu]* from Saryang, whose court rank was *naemi.* PL

POLITICAL THOUGHT

A major feature of the political life of the Three Kingdoms was the emergence of hereditary lines of kingship as the three entities evolved from loose tribal confederations into centralized monarchies. These royal lines had to achieve for themselves a position superior to the old aristocracy from which they had emerged. This effort was both shaped by and reflected in the political thought of the time, most notably in Confucianism.

In Silla, as shown in the monument at Maun Pass, royal authority was described in terms of the kingly way in the *Book of Documents* and Confucian political thought in the *Analects* in order to justify Silla's territorial expansion. In his request to the Sui for military aid, Great Master Wŏngwang also cited the kingly way to justify Silla's position. Moreover, reign titles, such as *kŏnwŏn* (Established Prime) for King Pŏphŭng as well as *kaeguk* (Opened State), *t'aech'ang* (Great Glories), and *hongje* (Vast Relief) for King Chinhŭng, were attempts to rationalize the development of a state by means of Confucian ideology.

The advocacy of kingly virtue was a means to curb autocratic rule. The fifth, seventh, and fourteenth rulers of Koguryŏ were deposed because of their cruelty. Minister Ch'ang Chori admonished the fourteenth king, Pongsang, for his extravagance and disregard for the welfare of the people. In his admonition, Ch'ang Chori invoked goodness and loyalty to underscore the importance of elements in the Confucian political system that had become popularly accepted. Likewise in Silla, Kim Hujik (fl. 579–631), the erstwhile minister of war, quoted passages from the *Book of Documents* and *The Way and Its Virtue,* an indication of the influence of Chinese political thought at that time. PL

Ch'ang Chori

[From *Samguk sagi* 49:448]

Ch'ang Chori, a man of Koguryŏ, became prime minister under King Pongsang [292–300]. At that time there were frequent border raids by Mu-jung Hui, and the king asked his ministers, "Mu-jung's force is strong and invades our territory. What shall we do?"

Ch'ang replied, "The *taehyŏng* of the Northern Enclave, Konoja, is wise and brave. If you wish to defend the country from foreign invasions and bring peace to the people, Konoja is the only person to employ." When the king made Konoja the governor of Sinsŏng, Mu-jung's forces did not come again.

In the eighth month of the ninth year [300], the king mobilized all adult males above the age of fifteen to repair the palace complex. Suffering from hunger and fatigue, many began to flee. Ch'ang admonished the king, "Because of repeated national disasters and bad crops, the people have lost their homes. The adult flee to the four directions while the old and the young die in ditches. This is the time to heed Heaven, to concern yourself about the people, to be apprehensive and fearful, and to examine yourself with a view to reform. Unmindful of all this, Your Majesty drives the hungry forth and plagues them with public works, contrary to your role as father to the people. Moreover, we have a strong enemy on our border. Should our enemy seize this opportunity to attack, what will become of our dynasty and our people? I beg Your Majesty to consider my words carefully."

The king retorted angrily, "The people must look up to their king. If the palace is not magnificent, we cannot show our majesty. Now you wish to slander me in order to win the praise of the people."

Ch'ang replied, "If the ruler does not relieve the sufferings of the people, he is not good. If a subject does not offer remonstrance, he is not loyal. Having succeeded to the post of prime minister, I cannot help but speak out. How could I have thought of my own reputation?"

Laughing, the king said, "Do you wish to die for the people? I beg you not to mention it again."

Knowing that the king would not mend his ways, Ch'ang withdrew and planned with other ministers to depose him. The king knew that death was inevitable and hanged himself.   PL

TRIBAL COUNCILS

States were formed through the unification of clan leaders and tribal chiefs, but such a power base also entailed limitations. From their beginnings, each of the Three Kingdoms underwent a similar process, as shown by the five-tribe federation in Koguryŏ and the six-tribe federation in Silla. (There was a five-tribe federation in Puyŏ and a six-tribe federation in Kaya as well, but these were destroyed before they could develop into states.) In Koguryŏ and Silla, the organization of a tribal federation resulted in a ruling power and a hierarchy of official ranks. And the management of a ruling system called for the institution of councils. Silla required unanimous consent for decisions on important matters (*hwabaek*, council of nobles), and such deliberations took place at the four sacred places.   PL

Four Sacred Places (Silla)

[From *Samguk yusa* 1:59–60]

Once during the reign of Queen Chindŏk, Lords Alch'ŏn, Imjong, Suljong, Horim, Yŏmjang, and Kim Yusin gathered at Oji Rock on South Mountain to deliberate affairs of state. Thereupon a huge tiger ran out into the meeting place. The lords all rose up in fright, save Lord Alch'ŏn, who laughed and calmly went on with the discussion while seizing the tiger by the tail and dashing it to death. Lord Alch'ŏn sat at the head of the gathering by virtue of his might, but it was the majesty of Lord Kim Yusin that the others most esteemed.

In Silla there were four sacred spots where ministers might gather to discuss important affairs of the state, and any problem of vital importance could be successfully resolved if discussed at one of these. The sacred places were Mount Ch'ŏngsong in the east, Mount Oji in the south, P'ijŏn in the west, and Mount Kŭmgang in the north [Yŏngch'ŏn in North Kyŏngsang].   PL

KING KWANGGAET'O STELE

King Kwanggaet'o (391–413) was a dynamic Koguryŏ monarch, who rapidly expanded Koguryŏ territory into Manchuria and across the northern part of the Korean peninsula. Many of the king's feats are described in the following inscription, which comes from a monument erected to his memory in the ancient Koguryŏ capital at the mid-point of the Yalu River in southern Manchuria. Sections in italics are the translators' reconstructions of text that has become effaced over time.

When the inscription was discovered in the late nineteenth century, a young Japanese intelligence officer surreptitiously brought to Japan the first copy of a rubbing of the stele, which was then used by the expansion-minded general staff of the Imperial Army to show that the Japanese had ruled the southern part of the Korean peninsula in the fourth century, a claim made to justify Japan's twentieth-century occupation of Korea. Controversy over the inscription has continued to play an important role in revisionist versions of ancient Korean-Japanese relations.

The Kwanggaet'o Inscription

Text in italics within roman (nonitalic) brackets in the following selection has been reconstructed from graphs chipped or eroded on the stone monument.

Of old, when our First Ancestor King Ch'umo laid the foundations of our state, he came forth from Northern Puyŏ as the son of the Celestial Emperor *[Ch'ŏnje]*. His mother, the daughter of the Earl of the River (Habaek), gave birth to him by cracking an egg and bringing her child forth from it. Endowed with heavenly virtue, King Ch'umo *[accepted his mother's command and]* made an imperial tour to the south. His route went by way of Puyŏ's Great Ŏmni River. Gazing over the ford, the king said, "I am King Ch'umo, son of August Heaven and of the daughter of the Earl of the River. Weave together the bullrushes for me so that the turtles will float to the surface." And no sooner had he spoken than [the God of the River] wove the bullrushes so that the turtles floated to the surface, whereupon he crossed over the river. Upon the mountain-fort west of Cholbon in Piryu Valley he established his capital, wherein his family would long enjoy the hereditary position. Accordingly he [ritually] summoned the Yellow Dragon to come down and "meet the king." The King was on the hill east of Cholbon, and the Yellow Dragon took him on its back and ascended to Heaven. He left a testamentary command to his heir apparent, King Yuryu, that he should conduct his government in accordance with the Way. Great King Churyu succeeded to the rule and the throne was handed on, [eventually] to the seventeenth in succession, [who], having ascended the throne at twice-nine [i.e., eighteen], was named Great King Yŏngnak ("Eternal Enjoyment"). His gracious beneficence blended with that of August Heaven; and with his majestic military virtue he encompassed the four seas like a [spreading] willow tree and swept out *[the Nine Tribes of Barbarians (Kui),]* thus bringing tranquillity to his rule. His people flourished in a wealthy state, and the five grains ripened abundantly. But Imperial Heaven was pitiless, and at thirty-nine he expired in majesty, forsaking his realm. On the twenty-ninth day, *ŭryu*, of the ninth month of the *kabin* year [28 October 414] his body was moved to its tumulus, whereupon we erected this stele, with an inscription recording his glorious exploits to make them manifest to later generations. Its words are as follows:

It came to pass in the fifth year of "Eternal Enjoyment" [Yŏngnak] [A.D. 395], *ŭlmi,* that because the Piryŏ [*wouldn't desist from their quarrelling*], the king personally at the head of his army crossed over Pu Mountain and [then another] Pu Mountain. On reaching the bank of the Yŏm River, he smashed their three villages, with six or seven hundred encampments in all; he seized cattle, horses, and sheep too numerous to count. He thereupon turned homeward.

Paekchan [Paekche] and Silla had long been our subject peoples and as such had brought tribute to our court. But the Wa [*a Japanese people and state in Kyūshū*] had, since the *sinmyo* year [391], been coming across the sea to wreak devastation. Paekche [*in concert with them*] invaded Silla and subjected its people. In the sixth year, *pyŏngsin* [396], the king personally led his naval force to chastise Paekche. The army, [*marching by separate routes*], first attacked and took eighteen fortified towns, after which they [*advanced and laid siege to*] that state's capital. The enemy, rather than bring their spirit into submission, dared to come out and fight numerous battles. Flaring up in terrible rage, the king crossed the Ari River. He sent his vanguard to put pressure on the city, and [*with a lateral thrust and frontal assault*] they seized the capital. The Paekche king (Chan wang), in dire straits, proffered a thousand male and female captives and a thousand bolts of fine cloth. Pledging his allegiance to our king, the Paekche king swore a solemn oath: "From this time on I shall forever be your slave-guest." Our great king graciously granted him pardon for his [*earlier*] transgressions and formally recorded the sincerity of his pledge of obedience. Thereupon, [*having taken possession of*] fifty-eight towns and seven hundred villages, he turned his army around and returned to his capital, bringing with him the Paekche king's (Chan wang's) younger brother and ten great officers.

In the ninth year, *kihae,* of Yŏngnak [A.D. 399], Paekchan [Paekche], in violation of its sworn oath, concluded a peace with the Wa. The king responded by making a tour down to P'yŏngyang, where an envoy sent from Silla reported to him, saying "The Wa people have filled our territory and are overwhelming and smashing our walls and moats. Since, as slave-guests, we have become your subject people, we take refuge in Your Majesty and ask for your command." The great king in his benevolence praised the sincerity of their loyalty and sent the envoy home to impart [*a secret plan*] to the Silla king.

In the tenth year, *kyŏngja* [A.D. 400], the king sent five myriads of troops, both foot and horse, to go to the aid of Silla. The whole area from

Namgŏ-sŏng to the Silla capital was filled with Wa people. At the approach of our government troops the Wa enemy retreated. [*Our government troops came following their tracks; attacking the Wa*] from behind, our troops reached Chongbal-sŏng in Imnagara, which forthwith surrendered.

The troops of the Alla people seized the Silla capital. It was full of Wa people, who flooded over the walls [in flight?].

In the fourteenth year, *kapchin* [A.D. 404], the Wa rose up and made an incursion into the territory of Taebang. The king's forces, having waited for them at a critical point, suprised and assaulted them. The Wa marauders [*Woegu*] were utterly defeated, and countless numbers of them had their throats cut.

In the seventeenth year, *chŏngmi* [A.D. 407], the king issued instructions for the dispatch of five myriads of troops, foot and horse, [*to wipe out the Wa marauders once and for all. When the marauders turned back and invaded P'yŏngyang, the royal*] army engaged them in battle, smiting them mightily and wiping them out entirely. MR

SOCIAL STRUCTURE

The organization of the ruling structure issuing from the federation of tribal chiefs took the form of the bone rank system. The system had eight classifications:

Holy Bones ⎫ True Bones ⎭	royal clan	Ranks 1–5
six ⎫ five ⎬ four ⎭	aristocracy	Rank 6 Rank 10 Ranks 12–17
three ⎫ two ⎬ one ⎭	commoners	no rank

This rigid system of social stratification appears to have taken its final form in the early sixth century, probably as a means of distinguishing the royal line while also protecting the aristocratic status and privileges of the various tribal leaders who were being incorporated into a centralized sociopolitical system. The bone rank system set the top two strata, the Holy Bones and the True Bones, far above the rest of society. Members of the Holy Bone class monopolized the throne until the reign of Queen Chindŏk; those of the True Bone class ruled from kings Muyŏl to Kyŏngsun. Members of both classes could reach the highest rank of *ibŏlch'an*, and only they could occupy the top four ranks. Members of the sixth through fourth head ranks (*tup'um*) could occupy the sixth to the last ranks, each with different privileges and restrictions. A special promotion system allowed them, within limits, to rise faster through the ranks. The bone rank system even dictated what kinds of clothes, carriages, daily utensils, and houses members could have.

As King Hŭngdŏk's edict of 834 shows, the state tried to enforce the system. Sŏl Kyedu, however, a member of the Sŏl clan belonging to the sixth head rank, disliked this rigid class system. In 621, he left Silla for China and took part in a war against Koguryŏ. *PL*

King Hŭngdŏk's Edict on Clothing, Carts, and Housing

[From *Samguk sagi* 33:320–326]

There are superior and inferior people, and humble persons, in regard to social status. Names are not alike, for example, and garments too are different. The customs of this society have degenerated day by day owing to the competition among the people for luxuries and alien commodities, because they detest local products. Furthermore, rites have now fallen to a critical stage and customs have retrogressed to those of barbarians. The traditional codes will be revived in order to rectify the situation, and should anyone transgress the prohibition, he will be punished according to the law of the land. *PL*

Sŏl Kyedu

[From *Samguk sagi* 47:436]

Sŏl Kyedu was a descendant of a Silla official. Once he went drinking with his four friends, each of whom revealed his wishes. Sŏl said, "In Silla the bone rank is the key to employment. If one is not of the nobility, no matter what his talents, he cannot achieve a high rank. I wish to travel west to China, display rare resources and perform meritorious deeds, and thereby open a path to glory and splendor so that I might wear the robes and sword of an official and serve close to the Son of Heaven."

In the fourth year, *sinsa,* of Wu-te [621], Sŏl stealthily boarded an oceangoing ship and went to T'ang China. *PL*

ANCIENT CUSTOMS

In the societies established by the Three Kingdoms we see a reemergence of the norms of life prevalent in tribal society. Thus Confucian and Buddhist thought began to be understood in the context of tribal rites and customs. In

Koguryŏ, for example, upon the death of King Kogukch'ŏn, his younger brother, Yŏnu, married the widowed queen and became King Sansang. Thereupon, the deceased king's younger brother Palgi rose in revolt on the pretext that his younger brother could not succeed to the throne before him. But Sansang's levirate marriage to the widowed queen, his sister-in-law, originated from the custom of Puyŏ and could not be censured by Confucian morality.

A major feature of Silla royalty was the tracing of descent through both the paternal and maternal lines. Moreover, endogamy was a common practice among Silla aristocrats. But this Silla custom was likely to invite Chinese censure.

The nature of the social order and value systems based on the Silla kinship and marriage system set limits to Silla's understanding of Confucianism. Confucianism was understood not as a social system but as a political ideology that rationalized the ruler's authority. While Silla accepted the Buddhism of the northern dynasties, which conceived of the king as a Buddha, Buddhist institutions neither rejected conquest and territorial expansion nor came into conflict with Confucianism. In the early state, Buddhism helped foster the concept of the state and aided in the understanding of Confucian political thought. This was possible because in the process of translating scriptures into Chinese, a certain amount of Confucianization was inevitable.

Shamanist beliefs and popular customs in ancient Korea were recorded only after they had lost their functions in upper-class culture. Thus scattered references to the subject not only are fragmentary but have been strongly colored by the Confucian and Buddhist worldviews of later times; information preserved in the Korean and Chinese sources (the *Wei chih*) does not antedate the Neolithic period.

Totemism in the Neolithic period—a belief in the common ancestor of a clan-centered community—may be seen in the worship of the totemic animal: the horse of the Pak clan and the cock of the Kim clan of ancient Silla, for example. Silla's council of nobles (*hwabaek*) and four sacred places, as well as Paekche's council at the Administration Rock (*chŏngsaam*), probably have their origins in ancient clan meetings; Silla's *hwarang* order and Koguryŏ's *kyŏngdang* originate, no doubt, in youth organizations in these states. The harvest thanksgiving festivals in Puyŏ (*yŏnggo;* held in the twelfth month), in Koguryŏ (*tongmaeng*), and in Ye (*much'ŏn*), as well as the Three Han in the tenth month, were survivals of the festivals of clan-centered societies. The clan society achieved a degree of economic self-sufficiency, and its religious rites, marriage customs (marriage within a clan was prohibited), and taboos called for minimal legal regulations, such as the eight articles observed in Old Chosŏn, of which only three—stipulations against murder, bodily injury, and theft—are known today. Puyŏ's legal provisions dealt with murder, thievery, adultery, and jealousy on the part of a wife. Puyŏ's expansion of protections to include the male head of a family may reflect the change from a communal clan to a male-centered family after the introduction of iron. In Koguryŏ, too, a jealous wife was punished with death; for example, Lady Kwanna was placed in a leather sack and thrown into the sea (SGSG 17:158–159). The laws of Koguryŏ, Okchŏ, Eastern Ye, and the Three Han may have contained the same provisions, and they were probably observed until the promulgation of the statutes after the Three Kingdoms adopted a Chinese-style administration.

We have noted certain marriage customs and kinship systems that were viewed as incompatible with Confucian morality. One was levirate marriage (the custom by which the brother or next of kin of a deceased man was bound to marry the widow) as found in Puyŏ and Koguryŏ; another was the offering of one's wife to an esteemed guest (*Han shu* 28A:1657) as practiced in Old Chosŏn and later in Silla until the reign of King Munmu (661–681).

Annual functions originating from prehistoric times were observed in the Three Kingdoms: Koguryŏ's hunting expedition on the third day of the third month, accompanied by the worship of the spirits of great mountains and rivers; Silla's Crow Taboo Day on the fifteenth of the first month, *tano* festival on the fifth of the fifth month, *kawi* on the fifteenth of the eighth month, and thanksgiving festival in the tenth month. Silla's annual rituals originating in agricultural society are still observed today.

Neolithic people believed in animism (shamanism). The most popular among the deified objects of worship were the sun god and the spirits of ancestors. Gods and spirits were either good or evil, the latter bringing misfortune and calamity to human beings. In order to propitiate good ones and exorcise evil ones, rituals evolved that included chanting incantations, healing sickness, expelling evil spirits, and praying for a bountiful harvest. Music and dance accompanied these rituals, and sometimes sacrifices were offered, fortunes divined, the clan chief elected, and criminals executed. Religion in the Bronze Age took the form of theocracy. The first ruler in the theocratic society was Tangun of Old Chosŏn. Religious and political leadership separated in the Iron Age, but the use of such titles as *ch'ach'aung* (shaman or chief shaman; later its derivate *chung* designated a Buddhist monk) or Buddhist-inspired names for king's titles in Silla reflects the influence of the theocratic rule.

The fusion of Buddhism and native beliefs may be seen in the notion of the "manifestation of the original substance." Gods and spirits of sacred mountains and rivers (in Silla and Paekche and, later, in Koryŏ) were viewed as reincarnations of buddhas and bodhisattvas. Such deities were given Buddhist names in order to naturalize Buddhism; for example, the mother goddess of the earth became the Bodhisattva Who Observes the Sounds of the World (Avalokiteśvara, or Bodhisattva Sound Observer). Thus native gods and spirits were regarded as manifestations of the original buddhas and bodhisattvas, and the Bodhisattva Sound Observer was the most popular in the Buddhist pantheon.   PL

King Sansang: The Levirate Custom

[From *Samguk sagi* 16:152–154]

The taboo name of King Sansang [196–227], the younger brother of King Kogukch'ŏn [179–197], was Yŏnu. The *Wei shu* says: "The descendant of Chumong, Wigung, opened his eyes and could see at birth. He was called T'aejo. The present king, his great-grandson, was also able to see at birth. In Koguryŏ similarity is indicated by the word *wi*, hence King Sansang was called Wigung." Because Kogukch'ŏn was heirless, Yŏnu succeeded him.

Upon the death of King Kogukch'ŏn, his queen, formerly named U, kept his death secret and at night went to the house of Palgi, the king's younger brother, and said, "The king has no heir; you should succeed him." Not knowing of the king's death, Palgi said, "Heaven dispenses its favors as it will. Moreover it is indecorous for a lady to travel about at night."

Ashamed, the queen went to Yŏnu, Palgi's younger brother. Yŏnu rose, put on his cap and gown, received the queen at the gate, and gave a banquet in her honor. The queen said, "Now that the king is dead and there is no heir, Palgi should succeed him; but instead he insolently accuses me of treason. That is why I have come."

Thereupon Yŏnu showed more respect and cut his finger while carving the meat. The queen undid her belt and wrapped his injured finger. Before returning to the palace she said, "The night is dark, and I am fearful. Please take me home." Yŏnu complied. The queen then took Yŏnu's hand and drew him into the palace. The following morning at dawn, the queen lied to the officials and convinced them that the late king had wished Yŏnu to succeed him.

Palgi was furious when he heard the news. He surrounded the palace with soldiers and shouted, "It is proper for a younger brother to succeed an elder brother. You have upset the proper order and usurped the throne. This is a grave crime. Come out at once. If not, your wife and children will be put to death."

Yŏnu closed the palace gate for three days, and none of the people followed Palgi. Anticipating a disaster, Palgi, together with his wife and children, took refuge in Liao-tung and reported to the governor Kung-sun Tu, "I am the brother of Nammu [King Kogukch'ŏn], king of Koguryŏ. Nammu died leaving no heir, but my younger brother Yŏnu has plotted with his sister-in-law and ascended the throne. This is a transgression of the eternal ways of man. In my anger I have come to you. I beg you to give me a troop of thirty thousand to attack and suppress the rebel." Kung-sun Tu complied.

Yŏnu had his younger brother Kyesu lead the defending army, and Kyesu routed the Chinese troops. When Kyesu personally led the van and pursued the fleeing enemy, Palgi asked, "Are you trying to kill your older brother?"

Kyesu was not so heartless as to kill his brother. He said, "It is not just for Yŏnu to have accepted the throne, but are you trying to destroy your own state in a fit of temper? How can you face your own father in the underworld?" Ashamed and remorseful, Palgi fled to Paech'ŏn, where he cut his own throat. Kyesu wept bitterly, gave the corpse a hasty burial, and returned.

The king, assailed by mingled feelings of joy and sorrow, received Kyesu in the inner chamber with brotherly rites, saying, "Palgi requested troops from China and invaded our country. His crime was great. You defeated him, but then let him go and spared his life. That was sufficient. But when he committed suicide, you wept bitterly. Are you making of me a ruler without principles?"

Kyesu changed color and holding back his tears replied, "I would like to say a word and beg to be killed."

The king asked, "What is it?"

"Even if the queen made you king with the deceased king's will," Kyesu replied, "you didn't decline it, because you lacked a sense of duty to your brothers. In order to display your virtue I buried Palgi. I did not expect that I would incur your anger. If you answer evil with goodness and bury Palgi with brotherly rites, who will call you unjust? Now that I have voiced my true feelings, death will be the same as life. I beg you to put me to death."

Drawing closer to Kyesu with a mild face, the king praised Kyesu's services. "Being unworthy, I harbored a doubt, but your word makes me realize my error. I beg you not to reproach yourself," he said.

When Kyesu rose and bowed, the king too rose and reciprocated. After sharing their mutual delight to the fullest they parted.

In the ninth month the king ordered Palgi's corpse to be received and interred at Pae Pass with royal rites. Because the king obtained the throne with the former queen's help, he did not remarry but made her his queen.   PL

Kim Yusin: Worship of the Three Guardian Spirits

[From *Samguk yusa* 1:60–61]

The eldest son of *Kakkan* Kim Sŏhyŏn, son of *Igan* Horyŏk, was born in the seventeenth year, *ŭlmyo*, of King Chinp'yŏng [595]. His younger brother was Hŭmsun; his sisters were Pohŭi (Ahae) and Munhŭi (Aji). Gifted from birth with the essence of the sun, the moon, and the five stars, he bore on his back the pattern of the seven stars, and miraculous happenings befell him.

At the age of eighteen he mastered the art of swordsmanship and became a *hwarang*. At the time a certain Paeksŏk [White Stone], whose origins were unknown, had belonged to the *hwarang* institution for a number of years. Knowing that Kim Yusin was making plans day and night to attack Koguryŏ and Paekche, Paeksŏk suggested that they both spy out the enemy before making final plans. Kim was pleased and set out with Paeksŏk one night. When the two were resting atop a hill, two girls appeared and followed Kim. When they arrived at Korhwach'ŏn (now Yŏngch'ŏn), a third girl appeared, and Kim spoke happily with the girls together. The girls presented Kim with delicious fruits, and he spoke without reserve. The girls said, "We already know all that you have told us. Please leave Paeksŏk behind and follow us to the forest, where we shall reveal the situation to you in detail." Kim followed the three girls, whereupon they transformed themselves into spirits. "We are the guardian spirits of the three sacred mountains, Naerim, Hyŏllye, and Korhwa. We came to warn you that you are being lured by an enemy spy and to detain you here." With these words they vanished.

Kim prostrated himself in amazement and gratitude before the spirits and returned to his lodging in Korhwa. Kim spoke to Paeksŏk, "I have neglected to bring along an important missive. Let us return and fetch it." Upon arrival in the capital Kim had Paeksŏk arrested, bound, and interrogated.

Paeksŏk confessed, "I am a man of Koguryŏ. Our officials say that Kim Yusin of Silla is a reincarnation of the Koguryŏ diviner Ch'unam. On the frontier between Silla and Koguryŏ is a river that flows backwards. At the king's request, Ch'unam divined, 'The queen acts against the way of the yin and yang, and the river reflects her misdeeds.' The king was baffled and astonished, while the furious queen declared, 'This is a libel by a cunning fox.' She then suggested to the king that they try Ch'unam once more and put him to death if his words should prove false. Thereupon the queen concealed a rat in a box and asked Ch'unam what was inside. 'It contains one rat, or so you think, but in fact there are eight rats in the box.' 'Your answer is wrong, and you shall die,' the queen said. Ch'unam then vowed, 'After I die I shall be reborn as a general who will destroy Koguryŏ.' Ch'unam was beheaded. When the rat's belly was slit open, it was found to contain seven unborn young. Only then did the king and queen realize that Ch'unam had spoken the truth. On the same night the king dreamt that he saw Ch'unam entering the bosom of the wife of Lord Sŏhyŏn (Kim Yusin's mother). When the king recounted this dream to his ministers they said, 'Ch'unam's vow has turned out to be true,' and they dispatched me to lure you to Koguryŏ."

Kim Yusin beheaded Paeksŏk and offered sacrifices of a hundred delicacies to the three guardian spirits, whereupon they appeared and partook of libations.

PL

CHAPTER THREE

The Introduction of Buddhism

Buddhism was transmitted to each of the Three Kingdoms during their transition from tribal federations to ancient states: to Koguryŏ in 372, to Paekche in 384, and to Silla in 527. During its dissemination Buddhism absorbed the myths, legends, and shamanist beliefs of the tribes and forged a more systematized religion and philosophy. By offering a way for the people to comprehend the conflicts and contradictions in society, it provided the social and spiritual basis for each of the Three Kingdoms to develop into a state.

The introduction of Buddhism meant the importation not only of the religion but also of an advanced Chinese culture because by nature Buddhism was neither closed nor exclusive. The inclusion of monks in the *hwarang* order in Silla indicates that Buddhism provided the social and spiritual basis for the development of Silla into a state.

From its inception Buddhism was allied with the royal authority. But this alliance was most conspicuous in Silla, which had the lowest standard of culture and was the last to develop as a state. In Silla, Buddhism became a force accelerating the growth of the state structure and of royal power. In order to strengthen kingly powers, the ruler was viewed as the wheel-turning emperor of the Kṣatriya caste. The twenty-third to twenty-eighth rulers adopted Buddhist names—for example, King Chinp'yŏng adopted the name of Śuddhodana, his queen became Māyā, and Queen Chindŏk became Śrīmālā.

Although Buddhism in Koguryŏ and Paekche also had a nationalist color, these states were more advanced in their cultural standards, were familiar with Taoist literature, and distinguished the Buddhadharma from royal authority. Koguryŏ, which had contacts with the Chinese mainland and Central Asia, adopted the Buddhism that used the method of *ke-yi* (employing Taoist terms to elucidate Buddhist ideas). Likewise, Paekche had contacts with the Han commanderies and the southern dynasties, and the aristocracy was more powerful than the royal house. Thus the nobles were able to uphold the independence of the Buddhist church. Instead of holding Buddhist ceremonies to pray for the protection of the country, monks in Paekche and Koguryŏ specialized in the study of Buddhist doctrines or disciplinary texts (Vinaya)—in Paekche the *Nirvana Scripture* and the *Perfection of Wisdom Scripture* and in Koguryŏ the Three Treatise school. Active Koguryŏ monks include P'ayak, a disciple of Chih-i, who transmitted the teachings of the T'ien-t'ai school in 596; Sŭngnang, who played a major role in China as a master of the Three Treatise school; and Hyegwan, who founded the same school in Japan.

In Paekche the study of the disciplinary texts flourished; it was founded by Kyŏmik, who had returned from India in 526; three Japanese nuns traveled to Paekche to study it. Studies in the *Nirvana Scripture* continued, judging from the request to the Liang during the reign of King Sŏng (523–554) for commentaries on the text; the Koguryŏ monk Podŏk, who sought refuge in Paekche, further stimulated the study of the same text. Other eminent monks include Hyehyŏn, who did not go to China but whose biography was included in the *Hsü kao-seng chuan (Further Lives of Eminent Monks)*; Kwallŭk and Hyech'ong, who went to Japan as experts on the Three Treatise school; and Tojang, who founded the Tattvasiddhi (Jōjitsu) school in Japan.

Early Buddhism in Silla developed under the influence of Koguryŏ. Hyeryang, an exile from Koguryŏ, was made the national overseer of monks (*kukt'ong*), and Chajang, upon returning from the T'ang, succeeded to the position as great national overseer (*taegukt'ong*). Both contributed to the institutional development of the church and the consolidation of Buddhist thought. Chajang also systematized the belief that Silla was the land of the Buddha—that in Silla, a land supposedly chosen and blessed by former buddhas, Buddhism was not a new religion. PL

KOGURYŎ BUDDHISM

Sŭngnang (end of the fifth to the early sixth century), a native of Yodong (Liao-tung) in Koguryŏ, was a master of the Three Treatise (Mādhyamika) school of Nāgārjuna. After its introduction to China by Kumārajīva (344–413) it reached Koguryŏ, and Sŭngnang is said to have studied it and the Flower Garland school. He traveled to Chiang-nan during the period of Chien-wu (494–497) and stayed at Ts'ao-t'ang Monastery on Bell Mountain, north of Nanking, and later at Ch'i-hsia Monastery on Mount She. He expounded the Three Treatises among the teachers of the *Treatise on the Completion of Truth (Tattvasiddhi)*, but none could challenge him. Thereupon he propagated the Three Treatises. Subsequently Emperor Wu of the Liang had Sŭngnang teach the Three Treatises to ten students (512). His teaching was continued by his disciple Seng-ch'üan (c. 512), and Seng-ch'üan's disciple Fa-lang (507–581), and Fa-lang's disciple Chi-tsang (549–623), author of the *Profound Meaning of the Three Treatises (San-lun hsüan-i*; T. 45, no. 1852).

The teaching was transmitted by Koguryŏ to Japan—first by Hyeja (Eji; d. 623; in Japan 595–615), Hyegwan (Ekan), and Todŭng (in Japan 629–646). Paekche sent Hyech'ong (Eso; in 595) and Kwallŭk (Kanroku; in Japan 602–624). At Hōkō-ji, Hyeja (Eji) gave lectures in the presence of Prince Shōtoku. In the same year Hyech'ong arrived and stayed at the same monastery. Kwallŭk stayed at Gangō-ji, where he became *sōjō* (superintendent). Hyegwan, a disciple of Chi-tsang, also stayed at Gangō-ji, where he expounded the doctrine of emptiness and was appointed *sōjō*.

Ŭiyŏn's Research into a History of Buddhism

[From *Haedong kosŭng chŏn* 1A:1016b–c]

In 576, Prime Minister Wang Kodŏk of Koguryŏ dispatched the monk Ŭiyŏn to the Northern Ch'i. In Yeh, the capital, Ŭiyŏn met Chief of Clerics Fa-shang and learned from him about the history of Buddhism as well as about the authors and the circumstances surrounding the writing of certain Mahāyāna scriptures. Thus in Koguryŏ more precise knowledge of the origin and nature of Buddhism was deemed important to its study. Devotees' knowledge of the *Scripture Concerning the Ten Stages (Daśab-hūmika)*, *Perfection of Wisdom (Prajñāpāramitā)*, *Stages of Bodhisattva Practice (Bodhisattvabhūmi)*, and *Diamond Scripture* indicates that these scholars, who earlier had studied the Three Treatise school (Mādhyamika), now desired to learn about the Consciousness-Only school as well. Excerpts from the biography of Ŭiyŏn in the *Lives of Eminent Korean Monks* follow.

The prime minister of Koguryŏ, Wang Kodŏk, had deep faith in the orthodox doctrine and respected Mahāyāna Buddhism. He desired to spread the influence of Buddhism over this corner of the sea. But because he was ignorant of the origin and development of the religion as well as the reign in which it had been introduced from the west, he listed the following questions and sent Ŭiyŏn to Yeh by sea in order to enlighten him. The general contents of the inquiry were as follows: "How many years has it been since Śākyamuni entered nirvana? How many years passed in India before Buddhism was introduced into China? Who was the emperor when it was first introduced? What was his reign title? And which state, in your opinion, first adopted Buddhism, Ch'i or Ch'en? Please indicate the number of years and emperors since the practice of Buddhism began. Who wrote the treatises on the *Scripture Concerning the Ten Stages, the Perfection of Wisdom, the Stages of Bodhisattva Practice,* and the *Diamond Scripture?* Is there any biography relating who originated or inspired the composition of these scriptures? I have recorded these questions and await your investigation to cast off my doubts."

Fa-shang answered thus: "The Buddha was born in the twenty-fourth year, *kabin* [1027 B.C.], of King Chao of Chou, whose clan name was Chi. He left home at nineteen and became enlightened at thirty. In the twenty-fourth year, *kyemi,* of King Mu of Chou [977 B.C.], the king heard of one from the west who had been transformed into a human being in order to enlighten living beings, and who had then gone to the west and never returned. Judging from this, Śākyamuni was in this world for forty-nine years. From his nirvana to the present, the seventh year, *pyŏngsin* [576], of Wu-p'ing of Ch'i, 1,465 years have elapsed. The scriptures and doctrines of Buddhism were first brought to China during the era Yung-p'ing [58–75 B.C.] of Emperor Ming of the Later Han and handed down through Wei and Chin. But it was not until the arrival of K'ang Seng-hui at Wu during the era Ch'ih-wu [A.D. 238–250] of Sun Ch'üan [222–252] of Wu that the teachings of Buddhism were spread and propagated. Bhiksu Asaṇga received a copy of the *Stages of Bodhisattva Practice* from Maitreya, and during the era Lung-an [397–401] of Emperor An [397–418] of Eastern Chin it was translated by T'an-mo-ch'an [Dharmakṣema, 385–433] at Ku-tsang for the king of Ho-hsi, Chü-ch'ü Meng-hsün [401–433]. The *Mo-ho-yen lun [Great Perfection of Wisdom Treatise]* was written by Bodhisattva Nāgārjuna [c. 100–200] and translated, on the order of Yao Hsing

[394–416], by Kumārajīva [344–413] upon his arrival in Ch'ang-an during the era Lung-an of Chin. The *Treatises on the Scripture Concerning the Ten Stages* and the *Diamond Scripture* were compiled by Asaṇga's brother Vasubandhu and first translated by Bodhiruci [c. 508–535] during the reign of Emperor Hsüan-wu [500–515] of the Northern Wei."

In answering these queries, Fa-shang offered evidence and drew references from a wide range of sources. Here I have recorded only the most important points. Ŭiyŏn did not forget the answers for a moment, had superior skill in leading people, and was versed in the mysterious and arcane. His ability in exegesis was inexhaustible, and his reason could master the secret of the joined circles. Once dispelled, former doubts melted away like ice. Now this new, wonderful doctrine shines brilliantly like the dawn, securing the Wisdom Sun in the west and pouring the fountain of dharma into the east. His teaching, like a gold pendant or a string of gems, is imperishable. Was not our master, then, a "ferry on the sea of suffering" and the "middle beam over the dharma gate?" After he returned to his country and promulgated great wisdom, he skillfully persuaded and led the straying masses. His exposition of the doctrine transcends the past and present, and his name has become most famous. Had the master not been endowed with extraordinary talent and blessed with the favors of both the Time and the Way, how could he have achieved such greatness?   *PL*

PAEKCHE BUDDHISM

Paekche imported the Buddhism of the southern dynasties of China and focused its study on the Disciplinary (Vinaya) school. The key document shedding light on this aspect is the record of events of Mirŭk Pulgwang Monastery. According to this record, Paekche sent the monk Kyŏmik to India to bring back the Sanskrit texts of *Wu-fen lü* and translate and annotate them. This was under King Sŏng (523–554), who adopted the policy of restoring Paekche power and encouraged overseas trade. Kyŏmik entitled his translation, which took seventy-two rolls, *New Vinaya* to show that the Koreans had access to the same texts then current in China.

The Disciplinary school in Paekche enjoyed international authority. In 588, three Japanese nuns studied the rules of discipline for three years in Paekche and upon their return became the founders of the Disciplinary school in Japan. Hyech'ong, a Paekche monk, went to Japan in 590 and transmitted the rules to Soga no Umako. Within Paekche itself, a decree was issued in 599 to prohibit the killing of living beings; it was realized by setting free domestic birds and burning the implements used for hunting and fishing.

Kyŏmik and the Disciplinary School

[From *Chosŏn pulgyo t'ongsa* 1:33–34]

In the fourth year, *pyŏngo,* of King Sŏng of Paekche [526], the monk Kyŏmik resolved to seek the rules of discipline and sailed to central India. He studied Sanskrit for five years at Great Vinaya Monastery in Saṅghāna [*this name and Vedatta, below, are unidentified reconstructions*] and acquired a sound knowledge of the language. He then studied the disciplinary texts thoroughly and solemnly embodied morality [*śīla*] in his heart. He returned together with an Indian monk, Tripiṭaka Master Vedatta, and brought with him the Sanskrit texts of the *Abhidharma Piṭaka* and five recensions of the Discipline. The king of Paekche welcomed the two at the outskirts of the capital with a plume-canopied carriage and drums and pipes and had them reside at Hŭngnyun Monastery. The king also summoned the country's twenty-eight famous monks and, together with Dharma Master Kyŏmik, had them translate seventy-two rolls of the rules of discipline. Thus Kyŏmik became the founder of the Disciplinary school in Paekche. Thereupon Dharma Masters Tamuk and Hyein wrote commentaries on the rules of discipline in thirty-six rolls and presented them to the king. The king composed a preface to the *Abhidharma* and this *New Vinaya,* treasured them in the T'aeyo Hall, and intended to have them carved on wood blocks for dissemination. The king died, however, before he could implement his plan.   PL

Hyŏngwang and the *Lotus Scripture*

[From *Sung kao-seng chuan* 18:820c–821a]

Like Chih-i (538–597), Hyŏngwang (fl. 539–575) was a disciple of Hui-ssu (515–577). Biographies of eminent monks in China call Hyŏngwang a native of Silla, but his life included the period before the demise of Paekche and his activities were centered around Ungju in Paekche. Hence it is proper to consider him a Paekche national. The *Lives of Eminent Monks Compiled during the Sung (Sung kao-seng chuan)* portrays Hyŏngwang as having been praised by Hui-ssu for his grasp of the *Lotus Scripture.* Upon returning home, Hyŏngwang resided on Mount Ong in Ungju, where he practiced the Dharma Blossom *samādhi*[1] and taught the people to believe in the Buddha as a manifestation of the eternal truth and universal salvation. Thus, after Hyŏngwang's return from China, the *Lotus Scripture* was studied and practiced in Paekche during the time of King Mu (600–641). The eminent monk Hyehyŏn made the chanting of the *Lotus* a central Buddhist activity.   PL

The monk Hyŏngwang was a native of Ungju in Korea. As a youth—and one of marked intelligence—he abruptly abandoned the secular life and determined to gain access to a religious teacher of high repute. Thereafter he devoted himself to a pure and celibate existence and when fully grown, he resolved to cross the ocean in order to seek training in the meditative methods of China.

Accordingly, he made a journey to the state of Ch'en, where to his good fortune, he visited Mount Heng and met the Reverend Teacher Hui-ssu, who opened his understanding to the transience of phenomena and brilliantly eluci-dated all the matters they discussed. Master Hui-ssu comprehended Hyŏngwang's reasons for having come there and thoroughly instructed him in the "Method of Ease and Bliss" of the *Lotus Scripture*. Hyŏngwang's progress was like that of a supremely sharp awl that meets no impediment and does not deviate from its course; he was as unblemished as a freshly dyed length of cotton cloth. Having requested and received instruction in the method, he was assiduous and meticu-lous in his practice of it and achieved abrupt entrance into the Lotus Samādhi. When he requested confirmation of this attainment, Hui-ssu verified his accom-plishment, saying: "That which you have experienced is genuine and no delusion. Closely guard and sustain it, and your penetration of the dharma will become fuller and more profound. You should now return to your homeland and there establish this efficacious means. It is well 'to dislodge the *ming-ling* caterpillars from their nests so that they may all be transformed into sphex wasps.' "[2] Hyŏngwang, with tears flowing, did reverence to the master.

Following his return to Korea, Hyŏngwang settled on Mount Ong in Ungju, where initially only a simple hermitage was constructed, but in time this was developed into a full monastery. It is written that "notes of the same key respond to each other,"[3] and so it was that those who wished to attain to the dharma clustered at his gate and opened themselves to his instruction. The carefree and young, those solemnly resolved to adhere to the true Path, even those who still craved the taste of flesh—they all, like ants in a line, sought him. Among these, there was one who ultimately ascended to a position of eminence and was designated as Hyŏngwang's successor. There was also one who achieved the "Fire Radiance Samādhi," two who achieved the "Water Radiance Samādhi," and even some who became proficient in both of these practices. Those who followed him and distinguished themselves were especially celebrated for their attainments in meditation. In fact, his disciples could be likened to the flocks of birds that haunt Mount Sumeru in that they all were of one color. While Hyŏngwang was yet living, he left Mount Ong and disappeared; where he went is not known.

When the patriarch of Nan-yüeh built an image hall, Hyŏngwang's likeness was one of the portraits of twenty-eight honored masters displayed there. His likeness is also to be seen in the Patriarchs' Hall at Kuo-ch'ing Monastery on Mount T'ien-t'ai.

JB

SILLA BUDDHISM

Masters Wŏngwang and Chajang devoted their lives to importing an advanced culture from the continent and establishing Buddhism as the state religion. Wŏngwang's close ties to the monarch and the country's expansionist policy may be seen in his simplified form of the bodhisattva ordination, in which he gave five—rather than ten—commandments to Silla warriors. They contain secular and religious injunctions not to retreat from a battlefield and not to take life indiscriminately. As great national overseer, Chajang set up Buddhist discipline and supervised the order. The nine-story stupa at Hwangnyong Monastery, built at his request, was constructed to unify the peninsula and to encourage the surrender of neighboring enemies. The plan was originally suggested by a guardian of the dharma, who appeared to Chajang during his study tour in China. As a symbol of national protection (and later as one of the three national treasures), the stupa became the focus of a belief in Silla as the land of the former as well as the present and future Buddha, an impregnable fortress designed to frustrate the territorial designs of enemies.

Pŏpkong Declares Buddhism the National Faith

[From *Haedong kosŭng chŏn* 1A:1018c–1019b]

The monk Pŏpkong was the twenty-third king of Silla, Pŏphŭng [514–540]. His secular name was Wŏnjong; he was the first son of King Chijŭng [500–514] and Lady Yŏnje. He was seven feet tall. Generous, he loved the people, and they in turn regarded him as a saint or a sage. Millions of people, therefore, placed confidence in him. In the third year [516] a dragon appeared in the Willow Well. In the fourth year [517] the Ministry of War was established, and in the seventh

year [520] laws and statutes were promulgated together with the official vest-
ments. After his enthronement, whenever the king attempted to spread Buddhism,
his ministers opposed him with much dispute. He felt frustrated, but remembering
Ado's devout vow, he summoned all his officials and said to them: "Our august
ancestor, King Mich'u, together with Ado, propagated Buddhism, but he died
before great merits were accumulated. That the knowledge of the wonderful
transformation of Śākyamuni should be prevented from spreading makes me very
sad. We think we ought to erect monasteries and recast images to continue our
ancestor's fervor. What do you think?" Minister Kongal and others remonstrated
with the king, saying, "In recent years the crops have been scarce, and the people
are restless. Besides, because of frequent border raids from the neighboring state,
our soldiers are still engaged in battle. How can we exhort our people to erect a
useless building at this time?" The king, depressed at the lack of faith among his
subordinates, sighed, saying, "We, lacking moral power, are unworthy of succeeding to the throne. The yin and the yang are disharmonious and the people ill
at ease; therefore you opposed my idea and did not want to follow. Who can
enlighten the strayed people by the wonderful dharma?" For some time no one
answered.

In the fourteenth year [527] the Grand Secretary Pak Yŏmch'ok (Ich'adon or
Kŏch'adon), then twenty-six years old, was an upright man. With a heart that was
sincere and deep, he advanced resolutely for the right cause. Out of willingness
to help the king fulfill his noble vow, he secretly memorialized the throne: "If
Your Majesty desires to establish Buddhism, may I ask Your Majesty to issue a
false decree to this officer, stating that the king desires to initiate Buddhist
activities. Once the ministers learn of this, they will undoubtedly remonstrate.
Your Majesty, declaring that no such decree has been given, will then ask who has
forged the royal order. They will ask Your Majesty to punish my crime, and if their
request is granted, they will submit to Your Majesty's will."

The king said, "Since they are bigoted and haughty, we fear they will not be
satisfied even with your execution." Yŏmch'ok replied, "Even the deities venerate
the religion of the Great Sage. If an officer as unworthy as myself is killed for its
cause, miracles must happen between heaven and earth. If so, who then will dare
to remain bigoted and haughty?" The king answered, "Our basic wish is to further
the advantageous and remove the disadvantageous. But now we have to injure a
loyal subject. Is this not sorrowful?" Yŏmch'ok replied, "Sacrificing his life in
order to accomplish goodness is the great principle of the official. Moreover, if it
means the eternal brightness of the Buddha Sun and the perpetual solidarity of
the kingdom, the day of my death will be the year of my birth." The king, greatly
moved, praised Yŏmch'ok and said, "Though you are a commoner, your mind

harbors thoughts worthy of brocaded and embroidered robes." Thereupon the king and Yŏmch'ok vowed to be true to each other.

Afterward a royal decree was issued, ordering the erection of a monastery in the Forest of the Heavenly Mirror, and officials in charge began construction. The court officials, as expected, denounced it and expostulated with the king. The king remarked, "We did not issue such an order." Thereupon Yŏmch'ok spoke out, "Indeed, I did this purposely, for if we practice Buddhism the whole country will become prosperous and peaceful. As long as it is good for the administration of the realm, what wrong can there be in forging a decree?" Thereupon the king called a meeting and asked the opinion of the officials. All of them remarked, "These days monks bare their heads and wear strange garments. Their discourses are wrong and in violation of the Norm. If we unthinkingly follow their proposals, there may be cause for regret. We dare not obey Your Majesty's order, even if we are threatened with death." Yŏmch'ok spoke with indignation, saying, "All of you are wrong, for there must be an unusual personage before there can be an unusual undertaking. I have heard that the teaching of Buddhism is profound and arcane. We must practice it. How can a sparrow know the great ambition of a swan?" The king said, "The will of the majority is firm and unalterable. You are the only one who takes a different view. I cannot follow two recommendations at the same time." He then ordered the execution of Yŏmch'ok [15 September 527].

Yŏmch'ok then made an oath to Heaven: "I am about to die for the sake of the dharma. I pray that rightness and the benefit of the religion will spread. If the Buddha has a numen, a miracle should occur after my death." When he was decapitated, his head flew to Diamond Mountain, falling on its summit, and white milk gushed forth from the cut, soaring up several hundred feet. The sun darkened, wonderful flowers rained from heaven, and the earth trembled violently. The king, his officials, and the commoners, on the one hand terrified by these strange phenomena and on the other sorrowful for the death of the Grand Secretary who had sacrificed his life for the cause of the dharma, cried aloud and mourned. They buried his body on Diamond Mountain with due ceremony. At the time the king and his officials took an oath: "Hereafter we will worship the Buddha and revere the clergy. If we break this oath, may heaven strike us dead."

In the twenty-first year [534], trees in the Forest of the Heavenly Mirror were felled in order to build a monastery. When the ground was cleared, pillar bases, stone niches, and steps were discovered, proving the site to be that of an old monastery. Materials for beams and pillars came from the forest. The monastery being completed, the king abdicated and became a monk. He changed his name to Pŏpkong, mindful of the three garments and the begging bowl. He aspired to lofty conduct and had compassion for all. Accordingly, the monastery was named

Taewang Hŭngnyun because it was the king's abode. This was the first monastery erected in Silla.

The queen, too, served Buddha by becoming a nun and residing at Yŏnghŭng Monastery. Since the king had patronized a great cause, he was given the posthumous epithet of Pŏphŭng (Promoter of Dharma), which is by no means idle flattery. Thereafter, at every anniversary of Yŏmch'ok's death, an assembly was held at Hŭngnyun Monastery to commemorate his martyrdom.   *PL*

Wŏngwang Goes to China for Study

[From *Haedong kosŭng chŏn* 1B:1020c–1021b]

The monk Wŏngwang's secular name was Sŏl or Pak. He was a resident of the capital of Silla. At the age of thirteen he had his head shaved and became a monk. His Sacred Vessel was free and magnificent, and his understanding beyond the ordinary. He was versed in the works of the Mysterious Learning *[Hsüan-hsüeh]* and Confucianism, and he loved literature. Being lofty in thought, he had great disdain for worldly passions and retired at thirty to a cave on Samgi Mountain. His shadow never appeared outside the cave.

One day a mendicant monk came to a place near the cave and there built a hermitage for religious practice.

One night, while the master was sitting and reciting scriptures, a spirit called to him: "Now, that monk is cultivating black art. I beseech you to persuade him to move away. If he does not follow my advice, there will be a disaster."

The master went to the monk and told him, "You had better move away to avoid disaster. If you stay, it will not be to your advantage."

But the monk replied, "When I undertake to do something opposed by Māra [the Evil One] himself, why should I worry about what a demon has to say?"

The same evening the spirit returned and asked for the monk's answer. The master, fearful of the spirit's anger, said that he had not yet been to the monk but knew the monk would not dare disobey. The spirit, however, remarked, "I have already ascertained the truth. Be quiet and you shall see."

That same night there was a sound as loud as thunder. At dawn the master went out and saw that the hermitage had been crushed under a landslide.

Later the spirit returned and said, "I have lived for several thousand years and possess unequaled power to change things. This is, therefore, nothing to be marveled at."

He advised the master: "Now the master has benefited himself, but he lacks the merit of benefiting others. Why not go to China to obtain the Buddhadharma, which will be of great benefit to future generations?"

"It has been my cherished desire to learn the Path in China," replied the master, "but owing to obstacles on land and sea I am afraid I cannot get there." Thereupon the spirit told him in detail of matters relating to a journey to the west.

In the third month, spring, of the twelfth year of King Chinp'yŏng [590], the master went to Ch'en. He traveled to various lecture halls, was received, and noted subtle instructions. After mastering the essence of the *Treatise on the Completion of Truth [Tattvasiddhi]*, the *Nirvana Scripture*, and several treatises from the *Tripiṭaka*, he went to Hu-ch'iu in Wu, now harboring an ambition that reached to the sky. Upon the request of a believer, the master expounded the *Treatise on the Completion of Truth*, and thenceforth requests from his admirers came one after another like the close ranks of scales on a fish.

Now that he had further cultivated meritorious works, it was incumbent on him to continue the spread of dharma eastward. Our country therefore appealed to Sui, and a decree allowed him to return to his country in the twenty-second year, *kyŏngsin*, of King Chinp'yŏng [600].

In his thirtieth year [608], King Chinp'yŏng, troubled by frequent border raids from Koguryŏ, decided to request help from Sui to retaliate and asked the master to draft the petition for a foreign campaign. The master replied, "To destroy others in order to preserve oneself is not the way of a monk. But since I, a poor monk, live in Your Majesty's territory and waste Your Majesty's clothes and food, I dare not disobey." He then relayed the king's request to Sui.

The master was detached and retiring by nature, but affectionate and loving to all. He always smiled when he spoke and never showed signs of anger. His reports, memorials, memoranda, and correspondence were all composed by himself and were greatly admired throughout the whole country. Power was bestowed on him so that he might govern the provinces, and he used the opportunity to promote Buddhism, setting an example for future generations.

In the thirty-fifth year [613] an Assembly of One Hundred Seats was held in Hwangnyong Monastery to expound the scriptures and harvest the fruits of blessing. The master headed the entire assembly. He used to spend days at Kach'wi Monastery discoursing on the true path.

Kwisan and Ch'uhang from Saryang district came to the master's door and, lifting up their robes, respectfully said, "We are ignorant and without knowledge. Please give us a maxim which will serve to instruct us for the rest of our lives."

The master replied, "There are ten commandments in the bodhisattva ordination. But since you are subjects and sons, I fear you cannot practice all of them. Now, here are five commandments for laymen: serve your sovereign with loyalty; attend your parents with filial piety; treat your friends with sincerity; do not retreat from a battlefield; be discriminating about the taking of life. Exercise care in the performance of them."

Kwisan said, "We accept your wishes with regard to the first four. But what is the meaning of being discriminating about the taking of life?"

The master answered, "Not to kill during the months of spring and summer nor during the six meatless feast days is to choose the time. Not to kill domestic animals such as cows, horses, chickens, dogs, and tiny creatures whose meat is less than a mouthful, is to choose the creatures. Though you may have the need, you should not kill often. These are good rules for laymen." Kwisan and his friend adhered to them without ever breaking them.

Later, when the king was ill and no physician could cure him, the master was invited to the palace to expound the dharma and was given separate quarters there. While expounding the texts and lecturing on the truth, he succeeded in gaining the king's faith. At first watch, the king and his courtiers saw that the master's head was as golden as the disk of the sun. The king's illness was cured immediately.

When the master's monastic years were well advanced, he went to the inner court of the palace by carriage. The king personally took care of the master's clothing and medicine, hoping thus to reserve the merits for himself. Except for his monastic robe and begging bowl, the master gave away all the offerings bestowed upon him to the monasteries in order to glorify the true dharma and to lead both the initiated and the uninitiated. When he was near the end, the king tended him in person. The king received his commission to transmit the dharma after the master's death and thus to save the people. Thereupon the master explained the omens to him in detail.

In the fifty-eighth year of Kŏnbok,[4] seven days after the onset of his illness, the master died, sitting upright, in his residence, giving his last commandments in a lucid, compassionate voice. In the sky northeast of Hwangnyong Monastery music filled the air, and an unusual fragrance pervaded the hall. The whole nation experienced grief mingled with joy. The burial materials and attending rites were the same as those for a king. He was ninety-nine years old.   *PL*

Chajang Establishes the Monk's Discipline

[From *Samguk yusa* 4:191–194]

The venerable Chajang [fl. 636–645], surnamed Kim, was the son of Murim, Rank 3 of the True Bone class and a native of Chinhan. Early on, he lost both his parents and came to abhor the dust and clamor of the world. Renouncing wife and children, he donated fields and gardens to be made into Wŏnnyŏng Monastery and dwelled alone amidst the remote escarpments. He did not run from wolves and tigers and cultivated the meditation on dried bones. Becoming somewhat exhausted and vexed, he then built a small hut and covered the walls with thorns and brambles. He sat inside naked and, if he nodded abruptly, he was pricked and pierced. He tied his head to a beam in the roof in order to ward off stupor.

Chajang lamented to himself that he had been born in a border region, and wished to travel to the west to learn the transforming teaching. Therewith, in the third year, *pyŏngsin*, of Inp'yŏng [636], he received royal permission and together with more than ten of his disciples, such as the monk Sil, traveled west to T'ang, arriving at Ch'ing-liang Mountain.

T'ai-tsung [626–649] sent a messenger to cater to his needs and ensconce him in Sheng-kuang Cloister. Though favors and gifts were richly given, Chajang despised this opulence. Upon his request, he went to Yün-chi Monastery on Chungnan Mountain and used an overhanging cliff on its eastern slope for his dwelling. There he lived for three years. Men and spirits received the precepts, and miracles took place every day. To relate all these would make the narrative complicated, and so they are omitted.

Subsequently, he returned to the capital and again received imperial favors. He was granted two hundred rolls of damask to use as capital for the cost of clothing.

During the seventeenth year, *kyemyo*, of Chen-kuan [643], Queen Sŏndŏk [632–646] sent a letter to T'ai-tsung requesting Chajang's repatriation. Giving his consent, the emperor invited Chajang to enter the palace and granted him one bolt of damask and five hundred of assorted textiles. The heir apparent also granted him two hundred lengths of textiles and other gifts. As there were still many missing scriptures and images in his native kingdom, Chajang begged to be given a set of the *Tripiṭaka* to take back, as well as all types of banners and streamers and flowered canopies, and anything else that could serve as an object of merit.

Once he arrived in Silla, he received the welcome of the entire country and was ordered to dwell in Punhwang Monastery, where he was provided with generous supplies and protection. One summer he was invited to the palace to discourse on the treatises of the Mahāyāna. Furthermore, at Hwangnyong Monastery, he lectured on the *Text of the Bodhisattva Precepts* for seven days and seven nights. The heavens rained sweet showers, and cloudy mists, murky and nebulous, enveloped the lecture hall. All the fourfold congregation[5] marveled at the wonder.

The court deliberated, "Although the eastern flow of Buddhism has continued for hundreds and thousands of years, there has been a lack of rules and regulations concerning its monastic hierarchy. Without any principles of control, there will be nothing to keep the Saṇgha dignified and pure." By royal order Chajang was appointed to be the great national overseer, and it was ordered that all the regulations and plans of the monks and nuns would be the ultimate responsibility of this Saṇgha Overseer.

Chajang used this good opportunity to propagate the religion zealously and encouraged each of the five divisions[6] of the order of Buddhist monks to enhance their earlier training through the following measures: recite the precepts each fortnight; hold comprehensive examinations in winter and summer; establish an administrative post to examine whether monks are keeping or transgressing the precepts; send investigators out on rounds of the outlying monasteries to admonish the monks on their faults, and ensure that they rigorously and regularly maintain the scriptures and images. Thus the protection of the dharma flourished for an entire generation. It was like the time when Confucius, on his return from Wei to Lu, standardized the music of the odes and hymns so that each was thenceforth perfected. At this time, the Silla people who received the precepts and honored the Buddha were eight or nine households out of ten.

Early on, the Korean style of dress was different from that of China. This matter was brought up for discussion in court, and the motion to change to Chinese dress was endorsed. Accordingly, in the third year, *kiyu,* of Queen Chindŏk [649], the caps and gowns of the Chinese court were first worn. The following year, *kyŏngsul* [650], the court adopted the Chinese calendar and for the first time used the T'ang reign title of Yung-hui. From that point on, whenever there was an imperial audience, the Silla envoy was placed at the head of the tributary states. All this was due to the achievements of Chajang.

During his lifetime, Chajang established monasteries and stupas at ten different sites; and as each one was under construction, some strange and auspicious portent perforce appeared. Because of this, laymen who came to offer their services were as numerous as a crowded marketplace, and they would finish these structures in a matter of days. RB

MAITREYA AND ESOTERIC BUDDHISM

The Maitreya cult in Silla was a product of a belief that Silla was the Buddha Land of Maitreya. This version of the Maitreya cult played an important role in Silla Buddhism. Not only was Maitreya ("The Friendly One") the patron saint of the *hwarang,* but members of the *hwarang* class were thought to be reincarnations of Maitreya. Kim Yusin and his group were called "the band of the Dragon Flower tree," a reference to the bodhi tree of Maitreya. By adopting the Buddhist name Pŏbun ("Dharma Cloud"), King Chinhŭng sought to be a wheel-turning king (the ideal Buddhist ruler) in the land of Maitreya. The monk Chinja prayed before an image of Maitreya, asking that the celestial bodhisattva be reborn as a *hwarang* so that he, Chinja, could serve him. Chinja's prayer was answered. The discovery of stone statues of Maitreya at various places, and reincarnations of the dead youth in Silla, underscore the power of the cult over its devotees. In his poem "Song of Tuṣita Heaven," composed in 760, Master Wŏlmyŏng enjoins flowers to serve Maitreya. Chinp'yo received from Maitreya two special sticks to be used in divination ceremonies. The eighth and ninth sticks, two bones from Maitreya's fingers, represent the two Buddha natures: the innate Buddha nature and that realized through religious practices.

Two types of belief in Maitreya existed in Silla. One was a belief that Maitreya would come down to earth when the wheel-turning king ruled, as in the period before the unification. (The *hwarang* Miri was thought to be an incarnation of Maitreya, and Chinja was a member of the clergy who assisted the *hwarang* order.) The other was a belief in rebirth in the Tuṣita Heaven, a prevalent trend after the unification of the Three Kingdoms.

The esoteric teaching that cannot be revealed to the uninitiated was popular just before the unification. The monk Myŏngnang returned from the T'ang in 635 and transmitted the secret incantation. In 671, he set up a secret platform to the south of Mount Nang and was reputedly able to sink the battleships of the invading T'ang forces. The monk Milbon healed the illness of Queen Sŏndŏk (632–647) and Kim Yangdo (SGYS 5:211–212). Healing the sick, once the function of the shaman, was taken over by the Buddhist clergy. PL

Maitreya's Incarnation as a *Hwarang*

[From *Samguk yusa* 3:153–155]

The surname of King Chinhŭng, the twenty-fourth monarch of Silla, was Kim. His given name was Sammaekchong, or Simmaekchong. He ascended the throne in the sixth year, *kyŏngsin,* of Ta-t'ung [540]. In pursuance of the will of his uncle, King Pŏphŭng, he devotedly served the Buddha, erected monasteries, and issued certificates to monks and nuns. Endowed with grace, he respected the *hwarang* and made beautiful girls *wŏnhwa* [female leaders of the *hwarang*]. His purpose was to select persons of character and teach them filial piety, brotherly love, loyalty, and sincerity—the substance of governing the country.

After many years, he thought it best for the health of the country to establish the way of the *hwarang* and ordered a selection of virtuous youths from good families to be its members. At first, the knight Sŏrwŏn was made *hwarang* [*kuksŏn*]—that was the beginning of the *hwarang* institution. Thereafter a monument was erected in Myŏngju, and the king had the people refrain from evil and do good, respect their superiors, and be kind to their inferiors. Thus the five constant ways (humaneness, rightness, ritual decorum, wisdom, and trustworthiness), the six arts (etiquette, music, archery, chariot driving, calligraphy, and mathematics), the three teachers, and the six ministers came into use.

During the reign of Chinji [576–579], the monk Chinja (or Chŏngja) of Hŭngnyun Monastery would make this plea before the image of Maitreya: "O Maitreya, please incarnate yourself as a *hwarang* so that I might be near you and serve you!" His kind sincerity and the fervor of his prayers increased day by day. One night he had a dream in which a monk told him, "If you go to Suwŏn Monastery in Ungch'ŏn (now Kongju), you will behold Maitreya." The stunned Chinja set out, bowing at every step throughout the whole ten days of his journey. Outside the monastery gate a handsome youth welcomed him with a smile and led him through a small gate into a guest room. Chinja went up, bowed, and said, "You don't know me. Why do you treat me so warmly?"

"I too am from the capital. I saw you coming, Master, and merely wished to refresh you," replied the youth. Then he went out of the gate and vanished.

Chinja thought this a coincidence and did not marvel at it. He told the monks about his dream and the purpose of his trip, adding, "If you don't mind, I'd like to wait for Maitreya at the last seat." The monks realized that they were being fooled, but sensing Chinja's sincerity, they said, "Go south and you'll find Mount Ch'ŏn, the traditional abode of the wise, where there have been many responses from the invisible. Why don't you go there?"

So Chinja reached the foot of the mountain, where a mountain god changed into an old man and welcomed him.

"What would you do here?" asked the god.

"I wish to behold Maitreya," Chinja replied.

"You already saw one outside the gate of Suwŏn Monastery. Why do you seek further?"

The stunned Chinja hurriedly returned to the monastery.

After a month, King Chinji heard the story and asked for the facts: "The boy is reported to have said that he was from the capital—and the sage doesn't lie. How is it that he does not visit the city?"

With his followers, Chinja sought the youth in the village and soon caught sight of a handsome youth strolling and amusing himself under a tree northeast of Yŏngmyo Monastery. Chinja approached him and said, "You're Maitreya. Where is your home, and what is your name?"

"My name is Miri, but I don't know my surname, because I lost my parents as a child," the youth replied.

Chinja then conducted the youth to the palace in a palanquin. The king respected and loved him and made him *kuksŏn*. He maintained harmony with other youths, and his decorum and elegant teaching were uncommon. After seven years of a brilliant career, he vanished. Although Chinja was sunk in sorrow, he basked in Miri's favor. Continuing his pure transformation of the group, he cultivated the faith with sincerity. We do not know how he died.

Now, the people call the *hwarang* "Maitreya Sŏnhwa" and a mediator is called *miri*—these are all vestiges of Chinja.   PL

Rapprochement Between Buddhism and Shamanism

The Silla people believed that the holy mother—the mountain goddess and guardian of the country—lived on Mount West, or Mount Fairy Peach, west of the capital. She may have been a composite of a belief in the mountain god and a Taoist immortality cult. Thus Silla's Mount West was likened to a mountain where the Emperor Wu of the Han received the peach of immortality from the Queen Mother of the West. Similar stories recount how Lady Unje, the queen of the second Silla king, became a guardian of Mount Unje in Yŏngil and how Pak Chesang's wife became a guardian of Ch'isul Pass. The fusion of the cult of the earth mother and Buddhism resulted in a belief in the presence of the Bodhisattva Who Observes the Sounds of the World on Mount Nak near T'ongch'ŏn in Kangwŏn, Korea's Mount Potalaka. Similarly, worship of Mount Odae evolved from a belief in Mañjuśrī fused with a popular belief in the five elements.   PL

Holy Mother of Mount Fairy Peach

[From *Samguk yusa* 5:216–217]

During the reign of King Chinp'yŏng [579–632], a nun named Chihye who did many virtuous deeds wished to repair a hall for the Buddha at Anhŭng Monastery, but could not carry out her desire. A beautiful immortal fairy, her hair adorned with ornaments, appeared in the nun's dreams and consoled her: "I'm the holy goddess mother of Mount Fairy Peach [Mount West], and I am pleased that you would repair the Buddha Hall. I offer you ten *kŭn* of gold. Take it from under my seat, decorate the three main honored images, and on the walls paint fifty-three Buddhas, six kinds of supernatural beings,[7] heavenly gods, and gods of the five mountains. On the tenth day of each month in spring and autumn, make it a rule to gather good men and women and hold a divination ceremony for all living beings."

Chihye awoke in amazement, went with her colleagues to the seat beneath the shrine dedicated to the goddess mother, dug up 160 *yang* of gold, and carried out her plan—all according to the guidance of the holy mother. The evidence survives, but the ceremony was eventually abolished.

The holy mother, originally the daughter of a Chinese emperor, was named Saso. Early in her life she learned the art of the immortals and came to live in Korea, where she stayed for a long time. Her father, the emperor, tied a letter to the foot of a hawk, instructing her to build her home wherever the bird perched. Upon reading the letter, Saso set the bird free, and it lighted on Mount Sŏndo, where she came to reside, becoming the mountain spirit. She stayed on the mountain called Sŏyŏn [West Hawk] a long time, protecting the country and performing many wonders. After the founding of Silla, she received one of the three sacrifices, superseding all mountain sacrifices.

King Kyŏngmyŏng, the fifty-fourth monarch, loved hawking. Once, while hunting on this mountain, he lost his hawk and offered prayers to the goddess and promised to enfeoff the hawk should it be found again. Suddenly the hawk returned and perched on the king's desk, whereupon he conferred on it the title of "great king."

When Saso first came to Chinhan, she gave birth to a holy man who became the first ruler of Silla—perhaps he was Hyŏkkŏse, who married Aryŏng. Therefore Chinhan was called Kyeryong, Kyerim—because the cock belongs to the west—and Paengma. Earlier, she had all the fairies weave silk and then dyed it red, made court robes of it, and gave these to her husband. Thus did the people know of her efficacy.

The *Historical Record of the Three Kingdoms* comments: "When Kim Pusik went to the Sung as envoy during the reign of Cheng-ho [1100–1125], he worshiped at the Yu-shen Hall, which enshrined the image of a fairy. The reception official Wang Pu asked, 'Did you know that she is the goddess of your country?' Long ago a Chinese princess drifted to the shores of Chinhan, where she gave birth to a son who became the founder of Korea. She herself became a guardian goddess and resides on Mount Sŏndo. This is her image." When Wang Hsiang, the Sung envoy, came to Korea and offered sacrifices to the holy mother of the east, the prayer read, "She gave birth to a sage who founded a state." Saso donated gold to make a Buddha image, lighted incense for the living beings, and initiated a religion.

How could she be merely one who learned the art of longevity and became a prisoner in the boundless mist?   PL

The Bodhisattva Who Observes the Sounds of the World on Mount Nak

[From *Samguk yusa* 3:159–160]

Ages ago, Dharma Master Ŭisang, upon his return from T'ang China, heard that the abode of the dharma body of the "Great Compassion"[8] was to be found in a cave by the sea, and he called this place Naksan after Mount Potalaka in the Western Regions. The place was also called Small White Blossom after the abode of the true body of the white-clad mahāsattva.

On the seventh day of his purification, the master let his sitting mat float out on the morning tide. The eight kinds of supernatural beings[9] led him into the cave. He then looked up to the sky and worshiped the bodhisattva, and he was given a crystal rosary. The master received it, and as he withdrew, the dragon of the Eastern Sea offered him a fabulous jewel. After another seven days of abstinence, the master entered the cave and beheld the true features of the bodhisattva. The bodhisattva said, "On the mountain peak above my seat you will see a pair of bamboo plants growing. Build there a Buddha Hall." When the master emerged from the cave, two bamboo plants sprouted. There he built the main hall and enshrined the well-rounded and beautiful lifelike image of the bodhisattva, named it Naksan Monastery, and deposited the rosary and jewel there.

Soon thereafter Dharma Master Wŏnhyo wished to make a pilgrimage to the cave. Upon his arrival at the southern outskirts, he saw a white-clad woman harvesting rice in the paddy. The master jokingly asked the woman to give him some rice, to which she replied that it was a lean year. As he went on under a bridge, he met another woman washing her menstrual napkin. When the master asked for drinking water, she scooped up unclean water and gave it to him. Wŏnhyo threw it away, scooped again, and drank. Then a blue bird in a pine tree called to him, "O monk"—but the woman was nowhere to be seen, except for a pair of sandals under the tree. Reaching the monastery, Wŏnhyo noticed under the seat of the Bodhisattva Sound Observer the same pair of sandals he had recently seen; only then did he realize that the woman he had met was the dharma body of the bodhisattva. His contemporaries called the tree the "Sound Observer Pine." Wŏnhyo wished to enter the cave to behold the true form, but a storm forced him to depart before he could do so.   PL

THE HWARANG

The origin of the *hwarang*, Silla's unique social group, may be traced to the "age set" organization of earlier times. Through that group's communal life and rites, young men learned the society's traditional values; through military arts, poetry, and music, they learned mutual understanding and friendship. Generally organized at the village or clan level, this basic social group maintained the fixed social structure. Beginning in the middle of the fourth century, however, as Silla accelerated its development toward statehood, the village- or clan-based group became harder to maintain. Starting in the early sixth century, Silla began to expand its territory, and a transformation of the youth group became inevitable. Under the new conditions, the *hwarang*, now a semiofficial body at the national level, came into being as an organization dedicated to the nurturing of talent.

A *hwarang* group, comprising several hundred young men, was headed by a youth from the True Bone aristocracy and several monks. For a fixed period, they lived together to learn military arts and cultivate virtue. They also toured famous mountains and rivers to nurture love of their country, and they learned the beauty of order and harmony through poetry and music. Together they prayed for the country's peace and development. Monks serving as chaplains were entrusted with their religious education and taught them universalistic Buddhism and loyalty to the king.

Wŏngwang's "Five Commandments for Laymen" best illustrate the content of the *hwarang*'s education: serve the king with loyalty; tend parents with filial piety; treat friends with sincerity; never retreat from the battlefield; be discriminate about the taking of life (SGSG 45:425). Here courage required in the war for unification and the Buddhist concept of compassion were added to the Confucian virtues. Of these, loyalty and sincerity were considered fundamental. Some *hwarang* members went on to study the Confucian classics, the *Record of Rites*, and the *Tso Commentary*.

Willing to lay down his life for the country, the *hwarang* member vowed to serve it in times of need. Such spirit continued to inspire the youth as he came of age and began his career as a politician or soldier. With the firm bases of national morality and spirit established, the *hwarang* became a prime source of Silla's success in wars against its enemies.

After the unification of the Three Kingdoms by Silla military power was accomplished, however, the *hwarang* as a military organization went into decline. With the ensuing peace, Silla's people no longer felt the threat of war, and the virile spirit once manifested by the *hwarang* disappeared. The *hwarang* subsequently came to be known more as a group specializing in poetry, music, and dance—not for moral cultivation but for enjoyment and "play."

PL

Origins of the *Hwarang*

[From *Samguk sagi* 4:40]

The *wŏnhwa* ["original flower"; female leaders of the *hwarang*] were first presented at court in the thirty-seventh year [576] of King Chinhŭng. At first the king and his officials were perplexed by the problem of finding a way to discover talented people. They wished to have people disport themselves in groups so that they could observe their behavior and thus elevate the talented among them to positions of service. Therefore two beautiful girls, Nammo and Chunjŏng, were selected, and a group of some three hundred people gathered around them. But the two girls competed with one another. In the end, Chunjŏng enticed Nammo to her home and, plying her with wine till she was drunk, threw her into a river. Chunjŏng was put to death. The group became discordant and dispersed.

Afterward, handsome youths were chosen instead. Faces made up and beautifully dressed, they were respected as *hwarang,* and men of various sorts gathered around them like clouds. The youths instructed one another in the Way and in rightness, entertained one another with song and music, or went sightseeing to even the most distant mountains and rivers. Much can be learned of a man's character by watching him in these activities. Those who fared well were recommended to the court.

Kim Taemun, in his *Annals of the Hwarang [Hwarang segi],* remarks: "Henceforth able ministers and loyal subjects shall be chosen from them, and good generals and brave soldiers shall be born therefrom."

Kwanch'ang

[From *Samguk sagi* 47:437]

Kwanch'ang (or Kwanjang) was the son of General P'umil of Silla. His appearance was elegant, and he became a *hwarang* as a youth and was on intimate terms with others. At the age of sixteen he was already accomplished in horseback riding and archery. A certain commander [*taegam*] recommended him to King Muyŏl [654–661].

When, in the fifth year, *kyŏngsin,* of Hsien-ch'ing [660], the king sent troops and, together with a T'ang general, attacked Paekche, he made Kwanch'ang an adjunct general. When the two armies met on the plain of Hwangsan [now Nonsan], P'umil said to his son, "You are young, but you have spirit. Now is the time to render brilliant service and rise to wealth and honor. You must show dauntless courage."

"I shall," Kwanch'ang replied. Mounting his horse and couching his lance, he galloped into the enemy line and killed several of the foe. Outnumbered, he was taken prisoner and brought to the Paekche general, Kyebaek. Kyebaek had Kwanch'ang's helmet removed. Kyebaek was greatly moved by the youth and valor of his captive and could not bring himself to kill him. He said with a sigh, "Silla has marvelous knights. Even a youth is like this—how much stronger must their soldiers be?" He then let Kwanch'ang return alive.

Upon returning, Kwanch'ang remarked, "Earlier when I attacked the enemy's position I could not behead the enemy general, nor capture their standard. This is my deepest regret. In my second attack I will be sure to succeed." He scooped up water from a well and drank; he then rushed upon the enemy line and fought desperately. Kyebaek caught him alive, beheaded him, and sent back the head, tied to the saddle of his horse.

P'umil took the head and, wiping the blood with his sleeve, said, "He saved his honor. Now that he has died for the king's cause, I have no regrets." The three armies were moved by this and strengthened their resolve. Beating drums and shouting war cries, they charged the enemy lines and utterly routed the Paekche forces.

King Muyŏl conferred the posthumous title of *kŭpch'an* [Rank 9] on Kwanch'ang and had him buried with full rites. Toward funeral expenses the king sent thirty rolls each of Chinese silk and cotton and one hundred sacks of grain.   PL

Consolidation of the State

UNIFICATION OF THE THREE KINGDOMS

As Koguryŏ pressed hard upon Paekche and Silla, her enemies in the south, Silla turned to China for an alliance. Silla's envoy Kim Ch'unch'u obtained China's agreement that in the event the Silla-T'ang allied army won the war against Koguryŏ, the territory south of P'yŏngyang would belong to Silla. In 660, the combined Chinese and Silla forces destroyed Paekche. But after the conquest, the T'ang ignored the earlier agreement and set up five commanderies in Paekche. When Silla opposed this policy and executed pro-Chinese elements inside Silla, conflicts arose with T'ang China. But as long as Koguryŏ existed in the north, Silla avoided direct confrontation with the Chinese.

Although Koguryŏ repulsed the T'ang invasions, the continuous warfare dissipated its energy. Moreover, the Khitan and Moho tribes under Koguryŏ's control submitted to the Chinese, Koguryŏ's defense line in Liao-tung weakened, and the T'ang navy began to haunt the Yalu. After the fall of Paekche, the navy led by Su Ting-fang entered the Taedong River and laid siege to P'yŏngyang, but without success. At this critical juncture, the Koguryŏ prime minister, Yŏn Kaesomun, died, his two sons feuded with each other, and his younger brother surrendered to Silla. Taking advantage of this internal discord, the T'ang army under Li Chi and the Silla army under Kim Inmun surrounded P'yŏngyang and reduced it in 668, after a fierce month-long battle.

With the fall of Koguryŏ, Silla and the T'ang openly collided. In 670, after the main Chinese forces had left Korea, Silla joined with the loyal forces of Paekche and Koguryŏ and attacked the Chinese army. Although the Chinese mobilized the Khitan and Moho tribes and the navy, they were compelled to withdraw after a number of battles. Finally, Silla was able to control the territory south of the Taedong River and Wŏnsan Bay and to unify the peninsula.

There were three queens among Silla's fifty-five monarchs. Queen Sŏn-dŏk (632–647) came to power at a pivotal time in Silla's history. She and her cousin Queen Chindŏk were the last rulers to be of the prestigious Holy Bone (sŏnggol) lineage, Silla's highest social status. After these two queens all subsequent rulers were of the slightly lower True Bone (chingol) status. Furthermore, during Sŏndŏk's reign the foundations were laid for the ultimate unification of the Korean peninsula. Culturally, Silla and T'ang enjoyed frequent contacts, and the first record of Sŏn Buddhist practices in Korea dates from this reign.

Queen Sŏndŏk's reign also sheds light on the importance of women in Korean society. Besides fulfilling traditional roles, Korean women occupied the highest positions of power and enjoyed elite status. The selection given here also indicates that the queen was considered to possess unique spiritual powers that enabled her to perceive omens and predict the future. Early monarchs were believed to be both shamans and political leaders, and this passage suggests that the queen enjoyed such powers.   *PL*

Account of the Silla-T'ang War

[From *Samguk sagi* 7:75–76]

In the second month of the fifteenth year of King Munmu [675], the T'ang general Liu Jen-kuei defeated the Silla army at the walled town of Ch'ilchung [Chŏksŏng] and returned home with his men. Then the emperor appointed Li Chin-hsing as Commissioner for Pacification of the East to govern the area. Thereafter the Silla king sent an envoy with tribute to beg for forgiveness, whereupon Emperor Kao-tsung forgave him and restored his office and title. Upon hearing the news on his way home from T'ang China, Kim Inmun went back and was enfeoffed as duke of Lin-hai Commandery.

Silla, however, took Paekche's territory as far as the southern borders of Koguryŏ and established provinces and districts of Silla.

At the news of the invasion of the T'ang army, together with Khitan and Moho soldiers, Silla mobilized its nine armies and waited. In the ninth month, using the beheading of Kim Chinju, the father of P'unghun, a Silla student and imperial guard in T'ang China, as a pretext, the T'ang general Hsüeh Jen-kuei, with P'unghun as a guide, attacked the walled town of Paeksu. The Silla general Munhun and others met the attack and won the battle, beheading fourteen hundred of the enemy and taking forty war vessels. The Silla army also took a thousand war horses as Hsüeh raised his siege and fled.

On the twenty-ninth day of the ninth month, Li Chin-hsing stationed two hundred thousand men in Maech'o Walled Town [Yangju], but the Silla forces again routed them, capturing 30,380 horses and weapons in the process. Silla built a garrison along the Anbuk River [north of Tŏgwŏn] and built the Ch'ŏlgwan wall [Tŏgwŏn].

The Moho attacked the walled town of Adal and plundered it; the Silla commander Sona was killed in action.

The T'ang army, together with Khitan and Moho soldiers, besieged the walled town of Ch'ilchung, but could not take it. The Silla official Yudong died in battle.

The Moho again besieged and reduced the walled town of Chŏngmok; the magistrate T'algi led his people in a heroic resistance, but all of them died. Again, T'ang troops took the walled town of Sŏkhyŏn after a siege. Magistrates Sŏnbaek and Silmo and others died in battle.

The Silla forces won all their eighteen engagements with the T'ang, large and small alike, beheading 6,047 of the enemy troops and capturing 200 warhorses.

In the seventh month of the sixteenth year [676], the T'ang army attacked and took Torim Walled Town [T'ongch'ŏn]; the magistrate Kŏsiji died in action.

In the eleventh month, the fleet of *Sach'an* [Rank 8] Sidŭk unsuccessfully fought the T'ang general Hsüeh in Kibŏlp'o [Changhang] in Soburi province [Puyŏ]. Sidŭk finally won a victory, however, killing four thousand of the enemy in twenty-two engagements large and small.   *PL*

The Life of Kim Yusin

[From *Samguk sagi* 41:394]

His lordship became a *hwarang* at the age of fifteen. His contemporaries, to a man, followed him as leader and styled him *Yonghwa hyangdo* ["Dragon Flower Disciple of Fragrance"].

In the twenty-eighth year, *sinmi* of Kŏnbok, of King Chinp'yŏng [611], his lordship was seventeen. Seeing his country's border territory being invaded and attacked by Koguryŏ, Paekche, and the Moho, he was aroused in determination to defeat the brigands.

During the forty-sixth year, *kich'uk,* of Kŏnbok [629], in autumn, the eighth month, the king sent *Ich'an* [Rank 2] Imyŏngni, *P'ajinch'an* [Rank 4] Yongch'un and Paengnyong, and the *Sop'an* [Rank 3] Taein and Sŏhyŏn and others at the head of troops in an attack on Koguryŏ's Nangbi Fortress. The Koguryŏans sent out a counterforce, and the situation turned against our men, with numerous deaths suffered and a breakdown in spirit to the point that none would fight on. Yusin was a commander of the Central Banner at that time. He came forward to his father, stripped off his helmet, and announced, "They've defeated us. But my life has been guided by loyalty and filial devotion, and I must be courageous in the face of battle. We hear the saying, 'Shake a coat by its collar and all the fur will fall smooth; lift up the headrope and the whole net will open.' Can't I be the collar or headrope now?" Then he mounted his horse, drew his sword, and leapt over a trench into the enemy's ranks, where he beheaded the general. He came back holding the head up high, and when our army saw this, they struck out in attack to take advantage of his victory. Over five thousand enemy men were killed and beheaded, and a thousand were taken alive. The beasts inside the fortress, too frightened to resist, all came out in surrender.   JJ

During Great King T'aejong's seventh year, *kyŏngsin* [660], in summer, the sixth month, the great king and Crown Prince Pŏmmin moved out with a huge army to attack Paekche, pitching camp at Namch'ŏn. At the same time, the *p'ajinch'an* Kim Inmun, who had gone to T'ang to request troop support, came along with the T'ang Great Generals Su Ting-fang and Liu Po-ying at the head of one hundred thirty thousand troops, crossing the sea and landing at Tŏngmul Island. They had first sent an attendant, Munch'ŏn, on ahead to announce their arrival; and with receipt of this news, the king ordered the crown prince, Generals Yusin, Chinju, and Ch'ŏnjon, and others to take a hundred large vessels laden with troops to meet them. . . . [Thus] T'ang and Silla joined in the attack on Paekche. They destroyed her.

Throughout that campaign, it was Yusin's merit that was greatest, and when the emperor of T'ang heard of it, he sent an emissary to praise and compliment him. General Su Ting-fang said to Yusin, Inmun, and Yangdo, "My command allows me to exercise authority as conditions dictate, so I will now present to you as maintenance lands all of Paekche's territory that has been acquired, this as reward for your merit. How would that be?" Yusin answered, "You came with Heavenly

Troops, Great General, to help realize our unworthy prince's wish to avenge our small nation, and from our unworthy prince on down to all officials and people throughout the nation there is endless rejoicing. How could it be just for the three of us alone to enrich ourselves by accepting such a gift?" They did not accept it. [*SGSG* 42:400–401]

JJ

In the first year, *mujin*, of Tsung-chang [668], the T'ang emperor appointed the state duke of Ying, Li Chi, to marshal a force to attack Koguryŏ. Aid was thus requested of us. Preparing to set out with troops in response, Great King Munmu ordered Hŭmsun and Inmun to serve as generals. Hŭmsun said in his report to the king, "I fear we'll regret it if Yusin does not march out together with us." The king responded, "You three are our dynastic treasures. Should you all go into enemy territory and some mishap occur that prevented your return, what then of the state? My wish is to keep Yusin here to protect our state. With him as imposing as a great wall we will be free from concern."

Hŭmsun was Yusin's younger brother and Inmun the son of his sister, so that they paid him great respect and never dared defy him. They reported to him then, saying, "We, who are not equal to the task, are about to go with the great king on an uncharted course and know not what to do. We are desirous of your counsel." He responded, saying, "The general serves as shield and wall of the people and as his prince's talons and fangs. It is in the midst of rocks and arrows that he determines victory or defeat. Only when he is in command of the Way of Heaven on high, of the figurations of the land below, and of the minds of men before him can he command success. Our country survives today because of its loyalty and trust, while Paekche and Koguryŏ have perished through conceit and arrogance. We achieve our purpose at this time by simply striking with our uprightness at their deviousness, but how infinitely more secure we are with the support of the august power of the Great State's brilliant Son of Heaven! Go now and strive your utmost. Don't fail your charge." The two bowed and said, "Your instructions have been respectfully received and will be carried into practice. We dare not slip or weaken." [*SGSG* 43:405–406]

JJ

The Three Prophecies of Queen Sŏndŏk

[*Samguk yusa* 1:58–59]

The twenty-seventh monarch of Silla, known as Tŏngman, was posthumously called Great Queen Sŏndŏk. Her family name was Kim and her father was King

Chinp'yŏng [579–632]. She ascended the throne in the sixth year of Chen-kuan [632] and reigned for sixteen years, during which she made three prophecies.

The first was when T'ai-tsung [627–649] of T'ang sent a painting of peonies in three different colors, red, white, and purple, together with three *toe* measures of seeds. The queen saw the painted flowers and said, "These flowers are probably the kind with no fragrance." She ordered the seeds to be planted in a garden. From when the flowers bloomed until the petals dropped, it was just as she had said [there was no fragrance].

The second prophecy was in the winter months, when many frogs gathered at Jade Gate Pond [Ongmun] at Yŏngmyo Monastery and croaked for three or four days. The people, believing this to be strange, asked the queen about it. The queen immediately ordered Kakkan [highest honorary title of rank] Alch'ŏn and P'ilt'an and others to muster two thousand elite troops and rush them to the western suburbs, saying that if they searchd Woman's Root Valley [Yŏgŭn], they would discover enemy soldiers whom they should take [by surprise] and kill. Upon receiving this order, the two *kakkan,* each leading one thousand men, searched the western suburbs. Beneath Mount Pu they found five hundred Paekche soldiers hiding in Yŏgŭn valley. So they captured and killed all of them.

The third occasion was when the queen was [still] in good health, and confided to her courtiers, saying, "As I will die on such and such day of such and such month in such and such year, please bury me on Torich'ŏn." [*This is the second of the six Buddhist heavens of desire, and in turn has thirty-three sub-heavens.*] The courtiers, not knowing the location of such a place, asked where it was. The queen replied, "It is south of Wolf Mountain." When that date came, the queen, as she had predicted, died, and the courtiers buried her south of Wolf Mountain. More than ten years later King Munmu (661–681) constructed Four Deva Kings [*the heavenly guardians of the four directions, hence the guardians of the state in Buddhism*] Monastery below the queen's tomb. According to Buddhist scriptures, above the heaven of the four heavenly guardians are the heavens of the Thirty-three Devas *[Trayastriṁśā].* This indicates the great queen's spiritual holiness.

Once the officials asked the queen, "How did you know about the flowers and the frogs?" The queen replied, "Because in the painting of the flowers there were no butterflies, I knew there would be no fragrance. This was the T'ang emperor teasing me for having no husband. Frogs having an angry appearance indicates many enemy troops. The Jade Gate [Ongmun] is the female genital organ *[yŏgŭn].* Women carry the *yin* element, which is represented by the color white, and white stands for the western direction. Therefore I knew there were enemy soldiers in the western direction. When the male genital enters the female genital it will certainly die [i.e. lose its erection]. Therefore I knew it would be easy to defeat [the enemy]. Thereupon the courtiers all admired her divine wisdom."

HK AND ES

CONFUCIAN POLITICAL THOUGHT

King Muyŏl, unifier of the Three Kingdoms, was not of the Holy Bone but of the True Bone class. He suppressed the revolts of Pidam and Alch'ŏn and emerged victorious. He took his wife not from the Pak clan, which had hitherto supplied queens, but from the Kim clan, of Kaya origin. He also abandoned Buddhist names and adopted Chinese-style nomenclature. Thus he inaugurated the middle period of Silla, during which the realm was ruled by his direct descendants until King Hyegong (765–779). This period was marked by the weakening of the aristocracy and the strengthening of royal authority. The *chipsabu* (state secretariat) became the principal administrative office, supplanting the *hwabaek* council. By the time of King Sinmun, the government consisted of six ministries. Local administration was also expanded to govern the conquered territory; King Sinmun set up nine prefectures and five subsidiary capitals. Likewise the army, consisting of nine banners *(sŏdang)* and ten garrisons *(chŏng,* stationed in the provinces), defended the country. With the central and local administration firmly in place, Silla felt a strong need for an ideology such as Confucian political thought to buttress the country's administrative structure. *PL*

Posthumous Epithet for King Muyŏl

[From *Samguk sagi* 8:82]

In the spring of the twelfth year of King Sinmun [692], Emperor Chung-tsung [684–710] sent an envoy who orally communicated the emperor's edict: "As for our T'ai-tsung, the Cultured Emperor [626–649], his merit and virtue were matchless. Upon his death, therefore, he received the temple name of T'ai-tsung [Grand Ancestor]. To accord the same temple name to your former king Kim Ch'unch'u [Muyŏl, 661–681] is to overstep the established norms. You should rename him at once."

After consulting his ministers, the king replied, "The posthumous epithet of our former king Kim Ch'unch'u happens to be the same as the temple name of T'ai-tsung, and so you order us to change it. How dare we not follow your command? Upon consideration, our former king too had in a high degree wise virtues. During his lifetime he obtained a good minister, Kim Yusin, cooperated with him in good administration, and unified Korea. His merit was indeed great. At the time of his death, therefore, our people, cherishing the dear memory of him, honored him with the name T'aejŏng, unaware that this was a violation of decorum. We have been appropriately chastened by your edict. I hope that Your Majesty's envoy will duly report our deliberations to Your Majesty."

No further edict on the subject was ever received. *PL*

King Sinmun's Proclamation of His Accession

[From *Samguk sagi* 8:79–80]

On the eighth day of the eighth month of the first year of King Sinmun [25 September 681], *Sop'an* [Rank 3] Kim Hŭmdol, *P'ajinch'an* [Rank 4] Hŭngwŏn, and *Taeach'an* [Rank 5] Chingong and others were put to death for plotting treason.

Thirteenth day [30 September 681]: King Podŏk (An Sŭng) sent as envoy *Sohyŏng* [Rank 3 or 4, depending on which of the Chinese sources is cited] Sudŏkkae to offer congratulations on the suppression of the rebels.

Sixteenth day [3 October 681]: The king issued a proclamation: "To honor the meritorious is a worthy admonition of the former sages; to punish the criminal is the law of the former kings. With my own insignificant body and negligible virtue I have inherited a great undertaking. I have gone without meals, risen early, retired late. Together with my ministers I have wished to bring peace to the country. How could I have imagined that while I was in mourning a rebellion would arise in the capital? The rebel leaders, Hŭmdol, Hŭngwŏn, and Chingong, had obtained their positions not through talent but by royal favor. Being incapable of prudence and thrift, they plotted to aggrandize themselves by their iniquities. They insulted the officials and deceived those in high position and low. Each day gave new proof of their insatiable ambition, as they perpetrated various outrages, invited the wicked to their board, and associated with the petty officials in the palace. Misfortune spread within and without, and the evildoers banded together and set the date for their revolt. Luckily, I have relied on the help of Heaven and earth from above and have received the help of my royal ancestors from below, and the plot of those who planned yet more grievous sins was brought to light. This indeed shows that they were abandoned by men and gods and were unacceptable to Heaven and earth. Never before have there been more blatant violations of justice or such injury to public good. Therefore I assembled the troops, intending to do away with the disloyal ones. Some of these fled to the mountain valleys, while others surrendered in the palace courtyard. We hunted down the stragglers and wiped them out. In three or four days, we were done with the criminals; there could have been no other outcome. I alarmed the officials because of this matter, and I cannot quiet my conscience morning or evening. Now that this evil band has been purged, no threat exists near or far. Quickly let the mustered soldiers and cavalry return and proclaim my wishes to the four quarters."

Twenty-eighth day [15 October 681]: The *Ich'an* Kungwan is put to death. The royal message reads: "The basis in serving one's master is loyalty, and the just cause of officialdom is constancy. The minister of war, *Ich'an* Kungwan, rose to his position through the regular channels. But being unable to repair his own omissions, he could not do his part at court or devote his very life to the cause of the state. Instead he associated with the rebel Hŭmdol and others and kept his treasonous secrets for him. Kungwan had neither patriotic concern for the welfare of the country nor public spirit. How could he as minister recklessly confuse the laws of the state? We will treat him as a common criminal as a warning to others like him. We will allow him and his one son by his legal wife to commit suicide. Let this proclamation be known far and near."   *PL*

CONFUCIAN LEARNING

When an ideology was needed to manage the society and politics of Silla, King Sinmun established the Royal Confucian Academy and had scholars teach Confucianism and the classics. The establishment of institutions had already inspired interest in Confucian political thought, as evinced by the "Five Commandments for Laymen" and the "Record of the Oath Made in the Year *Imsin*." Thus in 636, even before the foundation of the Royal Confucian Academy, Queen Chindŏk had appointed scholars to teach Chinese learning. With the establishment of the Royal Confucian Academy in 682, the core curriculum consisted of the *Analects* and the *Book of Filial Piety* and specialization in one of the following: the *Book of Odes*, the *Book of Changes*, the *Book of Documents*, the *Record of Rites*, the *Tso Commentary*, or the *Anthology of Refined Literature (Wen hsüan)*. Students ranged in age from fifteen to thirty. In 788, a state examination system was instituted whereby students were classified into three classes. This system lasted only briefly, however, and never truly challenged the hereditary bone rank order.

The Royal Confucian Academy

[From *Samguk sagi* 38:366–367]

The Royal Confucian Academy belongs to the Ministry of Rites. Established in the second year of King Sinmun [682], the academy was called *Taehakkam* by King

Kyŏngdŏk [742–765] but was again called *Kukhak* by King Hyegong [765–780]. There was one director, which King Kyŏngdŏk called *saŏp* but which King Hyegong renamed *kyŏng*. The director's rank was the same as that of other directors. Erudites *[paksa]* and instructors were appointed in 651 as well as two holding the rank of *taesa*, who were called *chubu* by King Kyŏngdŏk but were again called *taesa* by King Hyegong. The ranks ranged from *saji* to *naema*. There were two erudites of history, and two more were added by King Hyegong.

The curriculum included the *Book of Changes*, the *Book of Documents*, the *Book of Odes [Mao shih]*, the *Record of Rites [Li chi]*, the *Spring and Autumn Annals*, the *Tso Commentary*, and the *Anthology of Refined Literature*. One erudite or instructor taught in each of the three areas of study: (1) the *Record of Rites*, the *Book of Odes*, the *Book of Changes*, the *Analects*, the *Book of Filial Piety*; (2) the *Spring and Autumn Annals*, the *Tso Commentary*, the *Book of Odes*, the *Analects*, the *Book of Filial Piety*; (3) the *Book of Documents*, the *Analects*, the *Book of Filial Piety*, and the *Anthology of Refined Literature*.

Students graduated in three ranks. Those proficient in the *Spring and Autumn Annals*, the *Tso Commentary*, the *Record of Rites*, and the *Anthology of Refined Literature*, as well as the *Analects* and the *Book of Filial Piety*, were assigned to the top rank. Those who had read the "Various Rites" *[Chü li]*, the *Analects*, and the *Book of Filial Piety* were middle-ranking students. Those who had read the "Various Rites" and the *Book of Filial Piety* were ranked lowest. A student who was versed in the Five Classics, the Three Histories, and the various schools of Chinese philosophy was elevated a rank for employment. One erudite or instructor of mathematics was made to teach the *Chui ching*, the *San-k'ai*, the *Nine Chapters on the Art of Mathematics*, and the *Six Chapters on the Art of Mathematics*. The ranks of the students ranged from *taesa* to no rank, and their ages ranged from fifteen to thirty. The period of study was nine years. Simple, dull, and otherwise unpromising students were dismissed, but those who showed undoubted potential while still failing to complete the curriculum were allowed to remain beyond the standard nine-year period. Students were allowed to leave the academy only after attaining the rank of *taenaema* or *naema*.   PL

CHINESE LEARNING AND THE GROWTH
OF THE EDUCATED CLASS

Koguryŏ used Chinese script from early times. Under King Sosurim (371–384) a Chinese-style state university was established, and the learned class studied the Five Classics, histories, and the *Anthology of Refined Literature*. There were also private schools *(kyŏngdang)* that taught Chinese and archery. The representative example of writing from Koguryŏ is the inscription on the monument erected in honor of King Kwanggaet'o, which uses the Korean style of calligraphy. Paekche had erudites of the Five Classics, medicine, and the calendar, and it was they who transmitted Chinese writing to Japan. An example of Paekche writing is the state paper King Kaero (455–475) sent to the Northern Wei in 472, preserved in the *Wei shu*, and the monument of Sat'aek Chijŏk. Monuments erected at the sites of King Chinhŭng's tours of inspection show the mastery of written Chinese in Silla. Beginning with the time of King Chinhŭng, Confucianism was actively studied, especially by monks.

Proficiency in Chinese enabled the compilation of dynastic history in the Three Kingdoms: Yi Munjin condensed a history of one hundred chapters into five chapters in Koguryŏ (600); Kohŭng wrote one or more histories in Paekche (375), and, judging from the quotations in the *Nihon shoki*, other historical material also existed; Kŏch'ilbu (fl. 545–576) compiled a history in Silla. The compilation of histories in Paekche and Silla coincided with their territorial expansion and may be said to reflect their national consciousness.

When Confucian rule was proclaimed at the time of unification, studies in Chinese literature began to proliferate. Among the six writers famous at the time, Kangsu was known for his talent in drafting diplomatic papers. Then came Sŏl Ch'ong (c. 660–730), who used the *idu* transcription system to facilitate the reading of Chinese classics. With the emergence of Kim Taemun (fl. 704), the author of historical and geographical works, Silla no longer imitated Chinese models. Moreover, the number of students studying in China, officially or privately, increased, and among them were Kim Ungyŏng (fl. 821), Kim Kagi (d. 859), and Ch'oe Ch'iwŏn.

There were three styles in Chinese writing: the *hyangch'al* system used in the *hyangga* (see ch. 6); the simple style used by monks, village chiefs, and lower officials; and Buddhist Chinese. When the central authority declined in the latter period of Silla, the students going abroad consisted mainly of the sixth head-rank class. Among them were Wang Kŏin and Ch'oe Ch'iwŏn, who criticized the central government from the viewpoint of the learned class, and Ch'oe Ŏnwi (868–944) and Ch'oe Sŭngu (fl. 890–918), who aligned themselves with such local chiefs as Wang Kŏn and Kyŏnhwŏn (d. 936).

PL

Kangsu

[From *Samguk sagi* 46:428–429]

Kangsu [d. 692] was a man of the Saryang district in Chungwŏn Capital (now Ch'ungju). His father was *Naema* Sŏkch'e. Kangsu's mother conceived him after dreaming of a man with a horn on his head. When he was born, Kangsu had a piece of bone protruding from the rear of his skull. Sŏkch'e took his son to the acknowledged worthy of the day and asked, "What is the reason for his skull bone so shaped?"

"I have heard that Fu-hsi had the frame of a tiger," the worthy replied, "Nü-kua the body of a snake, Shen-nung the head of an ox, and Kao-yao the mouth of a horse. The wise and worthy are of the same kind, but their physiognomy differs from that of the ordinary. Your son also has a black mole on his head. According to the art of physiognomy, a black mole in the face is not good, but that on the head is not bad. This must be a marvelous sign."

Returning home, Sŏkch'e told his wife, "Your son is extraordinary. If you rear him well, he will one day become a leading scholar, esteemed by all."

As an adult, Kangsu had taught himself to read, and he understood the meaning of what he had read. To test him Sŏkch'e asked, "Will you study the way of the Buddha or that of Confucius?"

Kangsu replied, "I have heard that Buddhism is a teaching that does not concern this world. Since I am a man of this world, how could I study Buddha's path? I wish to study of the way of Confucius."

"Do as you please," Sŏkch'e replied.

With a tutor Kangsu studied the *Book of Filial Piety*, the "Various Rites," the *Erh ya*—a lexical work comprising glosses on words in the classics—and the *Anthology of Refined Literature*. Though what he heard was mean and near at hand, what he attained was lofty and distant. Thus he became a giant among the learned of the day. At last he entered officialdom, served in various posts, and became famous.

Earlier Kangsu had had an illicit affair with the daughter of a metalworker and greatly loved the girl. When at the age of twenty his parents wished to arrange a marriage with a village woman of good bearing and conduct, Kangsu declined on the ground that he could not marry twice.

"You are well known and well thought of by all. Would it not be a pity to wed a woman of lowly birth?" his father replied angrily.

Kangsu bowed twice and replied, "To be poor and humble is not a thing to be ashamed of. What is shameful is to fail to put into practice what one has learned. The ancients say: 'The wife who has shared one's poverty must not be put aside in times of prosperity, and a friendship formed when one is poor and mean should not be forgotten later.' I cannot bear to abandon my love just because of her lowly origins."

When King Muyŏl ascended the throne [654], the T'ang envoy came with an edict that contained difficult passages. The king summoned Kangsu, who after one reading explained everything without hesitating or stumbling. Amazed and delighted, the king regretted having met him so late and asked his name. Kangsu replied, "Your subject is from Imna Kara (Tae Kaya) by origin, and his name is Chadu." The king said, "Judging from your skull bone, your are worthy to be called Master Strong-Head [Kangsu]." The king asked Kangsu to draft a memorial of thanks to the emperor. The memorial was well wrought and its import deep. Marveling all the more, the king no longer called his subject by his name Kangsu, but only by the name of "Mr. Im of Imna Kara."

Unconcerned about his livelihood, Kangsu was poor but serene. The king ordered an office to grant him one hundred bags of tax grain from Sinsŏng.

King Munmu said, "Kangsu accepted the responsibility of a scribe, conveying our wishes in letters to China, Koguryŏ, and Paekche, and succeeded in establishing friendly relations with neighboring countries. With military aid from T'ang China, our former king pacified Koguryŏ and Paekche. His military feats owe also to the help given by Kangsu's literary ability. Kangsu's achievements cannot be overlooked." The king conferred on Kangsu the title of *sach'an* and increased his stipend to two hundred bags of tax grain annually. Kangsu died during the reign of King Sinmun [681–692]. The state provided funeral expenses and furnished an abundance of raiment, cloth, and other necessities. These the family offered to the Buddha.

When Kangsu's widow was about to return to her village because of a shortage of food, a minister heard of it and petitioned the throne to grant her a hundred bags of tax grain. She declined, saying, "As a humble person, I used to depend for food and clothing on my late husband and received many favors from the court. Now that I am alone, how dare I receive your kind present?" She then retired to her home village. *PL*

Nokchin

[From *Samguk sagi* 45:420–421]

The clan and polite names of Nokchin are uncertain, but he was the son of *Ilgilch'an* Subong. He first took office at the age of twenty-three, and after filling various court and provincial posts, he became vice-minister of state in the tenth year, *musul*, of King Hŏndŏk [818]. In the fourteenth year the king, being without an heir, appointed his younger brother Sujong heir apparent and had him reside in Wŏlchi Palace. Thereupon *Kakkan* Ch'unggong became prime minister and presided in the administration hall over the selection of officials for service in the court and the provinces. After his withdrawal, Ch'unggong fell ill. The official physician took his pulse and said, "Your sickness is of the heart. You need dragon-tooth medicine."

Ch'unggong obtained a twenty-one-day leave. He closed his gate and would receive no guests. When Nokchin wished to see Ch'unggong, the gatekeeper refused him. Nokchin said, "I know that the minister refuses visitors because of his illness. But I should like to say a word to dispel his melancholy. I cannot withdraw without seeing him." In the end, the gatekeeper let Nokchin in.

To Ch'unggong Nokchin said, "I have heard that you are not well. Is this because you go to office early and retire late, exposed to the wind and the dew, and have impaired your circulation and injured your four limbs?"

"My ailment is not that bad," Ch'unggong replied. "I feel slightly dazed and cheerless."

"If so, your illness requires neither medicine nor needle; it can be dispelled by reasonable speech and lofty discussion. Would you listen to what I have to say?"

"You have not abandoned me, but rather you have honored me with your company. I beg to be allowed to hear you out, so that I might unburden my heart," replied Ch'unggong.

"When a carpenter builds a home," Nokchin said, "he uses hefty pieces of lumber for beams and pillars and smaller ones for rafters. Only after crooked and straight pieces are placed in the right spots will you have a great house. Since olden times, has the wise government of a state ever been any different? If you place men of great talent in high positions and men of lesser talent in low positions, then from the six ministers and one hundred officials at court down to provincial governors and local magistrates, no position will be unfilled and none will be occupied by an unqualified person. There will be then perfect order high and low, and the wise and the incompetent will be kept apart. Only then will you achieve a royal rule. But it is not so today. Now favoritism undermines the public good, and offices are chosen for men. Even the unfit are awarded high positions if they are well linked; and even the capable are made to grovel in the ditch if they are in disfavor. Thus you are at a loss for a solution, and your ability to distinguish right from wrong is lessened. Thus the affairs of the state are muddled, and a statesman becomes weary and ill. If one is impeccable in the performance of his duties, the gate will be shut to bribery and special pleading. Promotion and demotion should depend on one's relative intelligence, and giving and taking should not depend on individual love or hatred. Like a scale, one will be able to assess the gravity of the matter; like a plumb line, one will be able to distinguish right from wrong. Then the laws and government will be worthy of trust and the country will be at peace. You may then open the gate like Kung-sun Hung[1] and serve wine like Ts'ao Ts'an,[2] chatting cheerfully and enjoying yourself with old friends. How could you then worry about medicine, idle away your time, and discontinue your work?"

"I heard Nokchin's words which were like medicine and acupuncture needles combined. His method was by no means merely a matter of taking dragon-tooth medicine." Ch'unggong then recounted everything to the king.

The king said, "I have been your ruler, and you my prime minister. What a delight to have one who will admonish me honestly! You must report this to the heir apparent. Go to the Wŏlchi Palace!"

Upon listening to Ch'unggong, the heir apparent congratulated the king. "I have heard that if the ruler is bright, the subjects will be honest. This indeed is a praiseworthy matter," he said.

Later, when Hŏnch'ang, governor of Ungch'ŏn province, rebelled, the king took up arms to put down the revolt, and Nokchin served the king and distinguished himself. The king offered Nokchin the title of *taeach'an,* but he declined.   PL

Ch'oe Ch'iwŏn

[From *Samguk sagi* 46:429–431]

Ch'oe Ch'iwŏn, whose polite name was Koun, was from the Saryang district of the capital of Silla. Since historical records have been destroyed, we know nothing of his genealogy. From his youth onward he was precocious and capable and loved learning. When, at the age of twelve [868], he went to board a ship to study in T'ang China, his father said to him, "If you cannot pass the examination in ten years, you are not a worthy son of mine. Go and study hard!" Once in China he studied diligently under a teacher.

In the first year, *kabo,* of Ch'ien-fu [874], the examiner Pei Ts'an, vice president of the Ministry of Rites, passed Ch'oe on his first attempt, and Ch'oe was appointed chief of personnel (or comptroller) in Liao-shui county. After a periodic review of his work, he was made secretary and censor in attendance and received a purple pouch with a golden fish tally. At that time the Huang Ch'ao rebellion broke out [874], and Kao P'ien [d. 887] was appointed circuit field commander. Kao appointed Ch'oe his secretary, and the memorials, letters, and manifestos that Ch'oe wrote at that time are still extant.

At the age of twenty-eight Ch'oe wished to return home. Learning of his desire, Emperor Hui-tsung [873–888] sent him to Korea as envoy with an imperial edict in the first year of Kuang-ch'i [885]. He was then appointed reader in attendance, Hallim academician, vice-minister of war, and *Chi Sŏsŏgam.* Ch'oe had benefited greatly from his study in China. Upon returning to Korea he wished to realize his ideals, but those were decadent times, and, an object of suspicion and envy, he was not accepted. He then became the magistrate of Taesan prefecture.

The monograph on literature in the *New History of the T'ang* says: "Ch'oe Ch'iwŏn has written a chapter of parallel prose and twenty chapters of works called *Kyewŏn p'ilgyŏng*." A note reads: "Ch'oe Ch'iwŏn is from Silla. He passed the examination for foreigners and served under Kao P'ien." Thus his name was well known in China. His works in thirty chapters are extant.   PL

Preface to the *Kyewŏn p'ilgyŏng chip*

[From *Ssu-pu ts'ung-k'an* ed.:1a–2a]

Your subject Ch'oe Ch'iwŏn, the envoy who carried an imperial edict on his way home from Huai-nan and who as inspector under the commander, secretary, and censor in attendance was granted a pouch with the fish tally, presents to Your Majesty his miscellaneous poems, rhyme-prose, memorials, and proposals in twenty-eight chapters, which comprise modern-style verse, five pieces in one chapter; penta- and heptasyllabic modern-style verse, one hundred pieces in one chapter; miscellaneous poems and rhyme-prose, thirty pieces in one chapter; *Chungsan pokkwe chip* in five chapters; *Kyewŏn p'ilgyŏng chip* in twenty chapters.

When at the age of twelve your subject was about to leave home and board a ship for China, his late father admonished him, "If you cannot obtain the *chin-shih* degree within ten years, then you are not worthy to be my son, and I shall tell people that I have no son. Study hard while you are in China." Your subject was bound by his father's strict injunction and studied earnestly, exerting himself to the utmost to fulfill his father's wishes. After six years his name was entered at the end of a roster of successful candidates. At that time he expressed feelings in song and wrote metaphorical verse. His rhyme-prose and verse began to accumulate, but in a grown man such childish efforts could only inspire shame. After receiving the fish tally pouch, he put his writings aside. He then traveled to Lo-yang, the Eastern Capital, where he earned his livelihood by writing. Finally he compiled a three-volume anthology of five rhyme-prose works, one hundred poems, and thirty pieces of miscellaneous verse.

Your subject then lived through a rebellion and slept, ate, and drank in an armed encampment. Accordingly he titled his works *P'ilgyŏng* ["Plowing with a Writing Brush"], taking the words of Wang Shao[3] as a precedent. Although he has not realized his aspirations and is ashamed of his lowly position, he has already plowed and weeded the fields of his mind and cannot bear to discard the harvest.

Earnestly hoping that they may reach Your Majesty's inspection, he respectfully presents twenty-eight chapters of poetry, rhyme-prose, memorials, and memorials to express thanks for favors received *[chang]*, together with the preface.   PL

Record of the Mañjuśrī Stupa at Haein Monastery

[From *Chŭngbo Hanguk kŭmsŏk yumun*, no. 61]

This stupa was erected as a memorial to those killed during the seven years of armed revolt that ravaged Silla about 895. The author of the record, Ch'oe Ch'iwŏn, says that the war and famine that raged during the Huang Ch'ao rebellion in China moved to Silla. In 888, Wŏnjong and Aeno rose in revolt in Sabŏl province (Sangju); in 890, Yanggil rose in Pugwŏn (Wŏnju); in 891, Kyŏnhwŏn called his state Later Paekche in Wansan; and in 893, Kungye marched to Asŭlla (Samch'ŏk), and established his power in the north the following year. Ch'oe Ch'iwŏn himself later retired to Haein Monastery to spend his remaining years there.

When the nineteenth ruler of T'ang China was about to be restored, the two calamities of war and famine ceased in the west but came to the east. With one misfortune following another, no place was unaffected. The bodies of those who had starved to death or fallen in action were scattered about the plain like stars. Out of intense grief, therefore, the venerable Hunjin of Haein Monastery, confirmed in another city as the leading master, called forth the hearts of the people, and had each donate a sheaf of rice. Together with others, the master built a three-story white stone stupa. The protection of the state generally forms the core of the Buddhist Path of the vow-wheel, whose special function is to save the souls of those who have died resentfully and violently. I record that the offering of sacrifice for their repose shall continue without end. The time I write is after the full moon in the seventh month of the second year of Ch'ien-ning [895].

PL

TAOISM

Records are scarce on the subject of Taoism in the Three Kingdoms, but it appears that the aristocracy was attracted to its tenets. In his heptasyllabic quatrain sent to Yü Chung-wen, Ŭlchi Mundŏk cites a line from the *Lao Tzu*. The cult of immortality, as evinced in the murals of Koguryŏ tombs, merged with popular beliefs in prognostication. After the transfer of the capital to P'yŏngyang, Koguryŏ had close contacts with the Northern Wei and must have learned about Taoism. Upon entering diplomatic relations with Koguryŏ, Emperor Kao-tsu sent Taoist priests and images in 624, and in the following year Koguryŏ envoys were dispatched to China to study Buddhism and Taoism. In 643, at the request of Yŏn Kaesomun (d. 665), T'ai-tsung sent eight Taoist priests. Yŏn's promotion of Taoism was felt strongly by the Buddhist clergy: the monk Podŏk sought refuge in Paekche in 650.

We do not know when Taoism was first transmitted to Paekche, but it seems to have been quite early in the history of the kingdom. In its developmental stage, Paekche absorbed the civilization of Lo-lang and Tai-fang, the Chinese commanderies in the north, and later received the refined aristocratic culture of the southern dynasties in China. The earliest historical mention of Taoism in Paekche dates from the first year (214) of King Kŭn-gusu. When the Paekche army was about to pursue the fleeing army of Koguryŏ, General Makkohae admonished Kŭngusu, then heir apparent, with a quotation from the *Lao Tzu* (ch. 46): "There is no disorder greater than not being content; there is no misfortune greater than being covetous. Hence in being content, one will always have enough." By the time of King Kŭngusu, the *Lao Tzu* and *Chuang Tzu* were widely read among the educated.

When a lake was dug in his palace, King Mu had an island built in the lake and called it Fang-chang (fairyland; a sacred mountain); the monk Kwallŭk, who went to Japan in 602, is said to have been a master of *tun-chia* (a method of prognostication and making oneself invisible). The inscription of Sat'aek Chijŏk (654) presented here is another indication of the understanding of Taoist philosophy among the aristocracy.

We do not know when Taoism was transmitted to Silla, either, but Taoist texts were known among the educated during the Three Kingdoms period. In his admonition to King Chinp'yŏng, who loved to hunt, Kim Hujik cited a passage from the *Lao Tzu* and the *Book of Documents*. Kim Inmun is said to have studied not only the Confucian classics but also the *Lao Tzu*, the *Chuang Tzu*, and Buddhist scriptures. The official transmission of the *Lao Tzu* is dated 738, when the T'ang envoy Hsing Tao presented King Hyosŏng with a copy, but inscriptions for the images at Kamsan Monastery (discovered in 1915), built by Kim Chisŏng (Kim Chijŏn in the inscription below) in 719, show the merging of Yogācāra philosophy and Taoism. Those who were disillusioned with the True Bone class, or had lost their struggles against it, lived in exile, voluntary or enforced, and espoused Taoist tenets. Kim Kagi died as a Taoist priest in T'ang China. PL

Yŏn Kaesomun (Koguryŏ)

[From *Samguk sagi* 49:448–450]

The clan name of Yŏn Kaesomun [d. 665] was Ch'ŏn. He seduced the people by claiming that he was born under water. He had an imposing presence and was broad-minded. Upon the death of his father, who held the rank of chief of the Eastern Province and chief minister *[taedaero]*, the people stopped Kaesomun from inheriting the position because they hated his cold-bloodedness. Thereupon Kaesomun kowtowed and apologized and begged to be allowed to take over the position, saying, "You may depose me if I fail. I will not complain." The people sympathized with Yŏn and permitted him to succeed to his father's post.

Yŏn reported to the king, "I have heard that in China the three ways of thought exist side by side, but in our country Taoism is unknown. I suggest that we send an envoy to T'ang China to obtain this learning for us." When the king sent a memorial to that effect, the T'ang court sent a Taoist adept, Shu-ta, with seven other envoys and a copy of *Tao Te Ching* [*The Way and Its Virtue*]. A Buddhist monastery was made into a Taoist temple. PL

Podŏk (Koguryŏ)

[From *Samguk yusa* 3:130–132]

According to the basic annals of Koguryŏ, toward the end of that kingdom [618–627] the Koguryŏ people strove to demonstrate their belief in Taoism. Emperor Kao-tsu of the T'ang heard of this and sent a Taoist priest to Koguryŏ with the images of Lao Tzu to lecture on *The Way and Its Virtue*. King Yŏngnyu and his people attended the lecture—it was the seventh year of Wu-te [624]. The following year the king sent an envoy to the T'ang court to obtain books on Buddhism and Taoism, a wish the emperor granted.

Upon his accession to the throne, King Pojang [642] wished to see Buddhism, Taoism, and Confucianism flourish in his country. At the time, his favorite minister, Yŏn Kaesomun, said, "Confucianism and Buddhism flourish now, but not Taoism. We should send a mission to China to seek knowledge of Taoism."

The Koguryŏ monk Podŏk of Pallyong Monastery (in Yonggang) lamented the danger to the country's fortunes if a conflict between Taoism and Buddhism should arise and remonstrated with the king without success. By supernatural power he flew with his hermitage to Mount Kodae (or Kodal) in Wansan province (now Chŏnju)—it was in the sixth month of the first year, *kyŏngsul*, of Yung-hui [650]. Soon thereafter, Koguryŏ was destroyed. It is said that the flying hermitage in Kyŏngbok Monastery is Podŏk's.

In the eighth year, *sinmi*, of Ta-an [1092], the chief of clerics, Ŭich'ŏn, went to Podŏk's hermitage, bowed to his portrait, and composed a poem: "The teachings of universal nirvana were transmitted to Korea by him. Alas, after he flew with his hermitage to Mount Kodae, Koguryŏ was on the verge of ruin." The postscript reads: "King Pojang of Koguryŏ was deluded by Taoism and abandoned Buddhism. Hence the master flew south with his hermitage and landed on Mount Kodae. Later, a guardian of the dharma appeared on Horse Ridge in Koguryŏ and said, 'Soon your country will be destroyed.' " This story is exactly like the one recorded in the national history, and the rest is in the original record and the lives of eminent monks. *PL*

Inscription on an Image at Kamsan Monastery (Silla)

[From *Chōsen kinseki sōran* 1:36]

Among the sources indicating the spread of Taoism among the nobility are the inscriptions composed upon the completion of the images of the Bodhisattva Maitreya and Amitābha the Thus Come One in Kamsan Monastery. Upon his retirement, Kim Chisŏng (or Kim Chijŏn, died c. 720), who held the rank of vice-minister of state (*chipsabu sirang*), had these two images cast to aid the souls of his parents. Upon retirement, the inscription says, Kim read the *Compendium of Mahāyāna* (*Mahāyānasaṅ-graha*), the *Stages of Yoga Practice* (*Yogācārabhūmi*), the *Lao Tzu*, and the "Free and Easy Wandering" chapter from the *Chuang Tzu*. Of two inscriptions at Kamsan, one of them, written by Sŏl Ch'ong to mark the casting of the image of the Thus Come One of Infinite Life, is given here.

Chungach'an Kim Chijŏn was born in a blessed land and received the power of the stars. His nature was in harmony with the clouds and mist; his emotion befriended the mountains and waters. Equipped with outstanding ability, his name was known to his generation; carrying wise strategies in his heart, he assisted his time. He went to China as envoy, and the Son of Heaven bestowed on him the title of *shang-she feng-yü* [chief steward in the palace administration]. Upon returning to Silla, he was granted the important post of minister of state *[chipsa sirang].* At age sixty-seven he withdrew and, shunning the world, lived in seclusion. He emulated the lofty magnanimity of the Four White Heads, declined glory, and nourished his nature. Like brothers Shu Kuang and his nephew Shu Shou,[4] he retired at an opportune time.

Looking up with respect to the true teaching of Asaṅga [fourth century], he read the *Stages of Yoga Practice* from time to time. In addition, he loved the dark and mysterious way of *Chuang Tzu* and read the "Free and Easy Wandering" chapter. He intended to repay his parents' love thereby, but it could not match the power of the Buddha. He wanted to repay the favor of his king, but it could not equal the primary cause of the Three Jewels: the Buddha, the Dharma, and the Order.   *PL*

The Rise of Buddhism

About the time of the unification of the Three Kingdoms, the learned Silla monks Wŏnhyo, Wŏnch'ŭk, and Ŭisang began to study Buddhist philosophy and popularize the faith. The epochal development of Silla Buddhism at this time, almost a century after its introduction, was made possible by political and ideological factors that facilitated the study and understanding of Buddhist thought. Although Silla received Buddhism from Koguryŏ and Paekche, it may have come into direct contact with Chinese Buddhism when the Liang monk Yüan-piao arrived as an envoy. Beginning with the time of King Chinhŭng (540–576), Silla monks studying abroad began to return home, bringing with them Buddhist images and scriptures. Thus toward the end of the seventh century, most scriptures translated into Chinese were known in Silla, as evinced by Wŏnhyo, who never went to China but was able to establish his own unique system of Buddhist philosophy based on translated scriptures.

Earlier Silla Buddhism may have leaned toward the *ke-yi* ("matching the meaning") technique used by translators of the Prajñā scriptures, but the influx of Mahāyāna texts enabled Silla to better understand the Great Vehicle—that is, the vehicle of the bodhisattva leading to Buddhahood. Although the doctrines of the Three Treatise school (as propagated in Koguryŏ) and the T'ien-t'ai school (as propagated in Paekche) were little known, the efforts of Wŏngwang (d. 640) and Chajang (fl. 636–645) enabled Silla monks to understand the tenets of the *Compendium of Mahāyāna* of the Conscious-ness-Only school and, later, those of Flower Garland metaphysics.

The impetus for the development of Buddhist philosophy in Silla was the unification of the Three Kingdoms, which also entailed the absorption of Koguryŏ and Paekche Buddhism. Opposing the state's adoption of Taoism, the Koguryŏ monk Podŏk lectured on the *Nirvana Scripture* and finally moved to Wansan prefecture (now Chŏnju) in Paekche (650). His eleven disciples built monasteries and lectured on the *Nirvana Scripture*, and Wŏn-hyo and Ŭisang are said to have attended Podŏk's lecture. Wŏnhyo wrote a commentary on the text, and other commentaries followed—an indication of Koguryŏ influence on the formation of the Nirvana school in Silla. Likewise, the transmission of the Three Treatise school may have helped make Silla monks aware of the doctrinal differences between Mādhyamika and Vijñānavāda (or Yogācāra).

In China, Chih-i (538–597) established the T'ien-t'ai school; Hsüan-tsang (c. 596–664) translated the texts of the Consciousness-Only school that he had brought from India; and K'uei-chi (632–682) founded the idealistic Fa-hsiang ("dharma-characteristics") school. Thus the polemics between the Mādhyamika and Yogācāra schools were intensified—one upholding the truth of emptiness [*śūnyatā*] and the other expounding that everything exists in consciousness only. A new doctrinal system that could overcome these two opposing philosophies was Hua-yen (Flower Garland) metaphysics. As Silla pursued active diplomatic relations with the Sui and T'ang, trends in doctrinal studies in China were introduced and became the subject of inquiry for Silla monks. Mutual stimulation and development in T'ang and Silla testify to a close interaction between the two countries. Wŏnhyo, for example, wished to study and transmit the Consciousness-Only philosophy from Hsüan-tsang but remained in Silla all his life to develop his own system of Buddhist philosophy. Indeed, by abandoning his studies abroad he became the most original and prolific Buddhist philosopher in Korea and East Asia at that time. Wŏnhyo's accomplishments were transmitted to T'ang, where they stimulated the development of Hua-yen metaphysics—for exam-ple, Wŏnhyo's commentary on the *Awakening of Faith* inspired a similar work by Fa-tsang. Conversely, T'ang developments in Consciousness-Only and Flower Garland philosophy influenced the formation of these schools in Silla, and Silla's contributions to the two schools were transmitted to T'ang (see Fa-tsang's letter to Ŭisang).

With the development of royal authority in Silla came an awareness of the limits and contradictions of a Buddhism established and legitimized as a bulwark of the state. In its effort to consolidate power within and without,

Silla used Buddhism to enhance the privilege and status of the ruling house and to foster enthusiasm for unification. Until unification occurred, Buddhism was regarded primarily not as a religion but as a political-religious ideology that furthered the secular objectives of the state, and the faith was thereby deprived of its religious autonomy. With unification an accomplished fact, however, Silla Buddhism aspired to a new dimension: the abolition of conflict between the state's earthly objectives and the religion's otherworldly outlook, as well as the separation of church and state.

Meanwhile, in response to the consolidation of the administrative machinery after unification, Confucianism began to replace Buddhism as a political ideology. As Buddhism separated itself from politics, its political influence began to decline. The king was no longer considered a Buddha (as King Chinhŭng had been) but instead was accorded a Chinese-style posthumous epithet. Similarly, the state sought Buddhism's aid not through eminent monks but through the Buddhist community.

Such Confucian scholars as Kangsu and Sŏl Ch'ong emerged to play a major role in importing Chinese civilization, drafting diplomatic papers, and functioning as political advisers, roles hitherto reserved for eminent monks. They also began to criticize a Buddhism that had forgotten its primary religious function, as the remarks attributed to Kangsu show. King Munmu, who wished to adopt Confucian political thought, banned contributions of land and money to monasteries in 664. Aware of the contradiction inherent in upholding Buddhism with its magic and incantations as the state religion, he intended to curtail a drain on the kingdom's economic resources. In his attempts to point out a new direction for Buddhism, King Munmu ordered Ŭisang, who had just returned from China, to construct Pusŏk Monastery as the major place of worship for the Flower Garland school. In his will, he recommended Kyŏnghŭng, the master of the Consciousness-Only school, as national preceptor.

The outstanding questions around the time of unification, then, were the reconciliation of the tenets of the Mādhyamika and Yogācāra schools and a blending of the state's secular aims with the otherworldly goals of Buddhism. The solutions to these problems took the form of research into Buddhist doctrine and popularization of the faith.   *PL*

WŎNHYO'S BUDDHIST PHILOSOPHY

Toward the end of the seventh century, Silla Buddhism made great strides in establishing a unique version of Buddhist philosophy through the efforts of Great Master Wŏnhyo (617–686). Posthumously honored as the "National

Preceptor Who Harmonizes Disputes," he systematized different schools of Buddhism and established a basis on which the people of Silla might understand them. Wŏnhyo had no special teacher, nor did he travel to China. He read widely and interpreted every text he could find, regardless of its doctrinal affiliation. His works indicate the scope of his broad reading and acute comprehension of Mahāyāna texts.

Focusing on the *Flower Garland Scripture* and the *Awakening of Faith*, Wŏnhyo was able to establish his unique universalistic and syncretic Buddhist philosophy, a harmonization of nature and characteristics. He traced various texts to their origins and periods of formation. His *Treatise on Ten Approaches to the Reconciliation of Doctrinal Controversy (Simmun hwajaeng non)* offers a logical basis for overcoming doctrinal inconsistencies and differences. Thus while Chih-i classified and rated the Buddha's teachings by periods, methods, and modes of doctrine, Wŏnhyo harmonized them and established their essential equality and unity.

Wŏnhyo's works were transmitted to China and Japan, where they exerted considerable influence. Known as the *Korean Commentary (Haedong so)*, his commentary on the *Awakening of Faith*, which offers a theoretical system resolving the controversy between Mādhyamika and Yogācāra, is one of the three great commentaries on that text. His commentary on the *Adamantine Absorption Scripture*, which presents the practical theory of his Buddhism, was elevated to the status of *non* (treatise), indicating that the author was a bodhisattva, not just a mortal man; his *Treatise on Ten Approaches*, together with the *Meaning of Two Obstructions (Ijangŭi)*, influenced Fa-tsang's *Wu-chiao chang* and was said to have been carried to India to be translated into Sanskrit. Chinese masters who were influenced by Wŏnhyo include Fa-tsang (643–712), Li T'ung-hsüan (635–730 or 646–740), and Ch'eng-kuan (738–839). The Japanese monks Gyōnen (1240–1321) of the Flower Garland school and Zenshu (723–797) and Jōtō (740–815) of the Fa-hsiang school were also influenced by him. Furthermore, Wŏnhyo visited Ŭisang at the Avalokiteśvara Cave on Mount Nak and discussed with him his *Diagram of the Dharmadhātu (Ilsŭng pŏpkye to; 668)*, an indication that he maintained close ties with Ŭisang after the latter's return from China. Unlike Ŭisang, however, Wŏnhyo had no intention of founding a school or nurturing disciples. Hence he failed to form a school of his own, was accorded less esteem in Silla than in China, and had fewer disciples than Ŭisang. Only Ŭich'ŏn (1055–1101) was able to appreciate Wŏnhyo's contribution. Wŏnhyo's works were quoted by Silla monks but received no serious study—in sharp contrast to a host of later studies on Ŭisang's diagram.

Wŏnhyo, perhaps the most seminal Buddhist thinker in Korea, contributed greatly to the development of a distinctively Korean style of Buddhist philosophy and practice. His range of scholarly endeavor spanned the whole of East Asian Buddhist materials, and some one hundred works are attributed to him. Wŏnhyo was a master of Chinese prose. The prefaces to his commentaries on various Mahāyāna scriptures are known for their concision and clarity, and he had a gift for summarizing the doctrine presented in various scriptures. Presented here are his introduction to *Exposition of the "Adamantine Absorption Scripture," Arouse Your Mind and Practice!*, and the beginning section of his commentary on the *Awakening of Faith*, which greatly influenced Fa-tsang's commentary on the same text.   PL

Introduction to *Exposition of the "Adamantine Absorption Scripture"*

[From *Taishō Tripiṭaka* 34:961a–963a]

Wŏnhyo's introduction to his *Exposition of the "Adamantine Absorption Scripture,"* portions of which are translated here, is one of the principal statements of his ecumenical approach to Buddhist thought and practice. The adamantine absorption *(vajrasamādhi)* is a special type of meditative concentration that is said to catalyze the final experience of enlightenment. Just as adamant, or diamond, shatters all other minerals, so too the adamantine absorption destroys all forms of clinging, initiating the radical nonattachment that is nirvana. In this treatise, Wŏnhyo seeks to treat the *vajrasamādhi* as not only consummating all the progressive stages of the Buddhist path of religious training but as in fact subsuming those stages. He therefore uses this absorption as a tool for effecting his syncretic vision, especially with respect to Buddhist practice. There is, briefly, a fourfold structure to the explication of this scripture: a narration of its principal ideas, an analysis of its theme, an explanation of its title, and an explication of the meaning of passages in the text.

Narration of Its Principal Ideas

Now, the fountainhead of the one mind, which is distinct from existence and nonexistence, is independently pure. The sea of the three voidnesses,[1] which amalgamates absolute and mundane, is calm and clear. Calm and clear, it amalgamates duality and yet is not unitary. Independently pure, it is far from the extremes and yet is not located at the middle. It is not located at the middle and yet is far from the extremes: hence, a phenomenon that does not exist does not just abide in nonexistence; a characteristic that does not nonexist does not just abide in existence. It is not unitary, and yet it amalgamates duality: hence, its nonabsolute dharmas have not once been mundane; its nonmundane principle has not once been absolute. It amalgamates duality and yet is not unitary: hence, there are none of its absolute or mundane natures that have never been established; there are none of its tainted or pure characteristics with which it has not been furnished. It is far from the extremes and yet is not located at the middle; hence, there are none of the existing or nonexisting dharmas that do not function; there are none of their positive or negative aspects with which it is not equipped. Accordingly, while nothing is negated, there is nothing not negated; while nothing is established, there is nothing not established. This can be called the ultimate principle that is free from principles, the great thusness that is not thus. These are said to be the principal ideas of this scripture.

Analysis of the Theme

The thematic essentials of this scripture have an analytic and a synthetic aspect. From a synthetic standpoint, its essential point is the contemplation practice that has but a single taste. From an analytic standpoint, its fundamental doctrine involves ten types of approaches to dharma.

SYNTHETIC STANDPOINT

In the approach to contemplation outlined in this scripture, there are six practices established—from initial resolute faith through equal enlightenment. When the six practices are completed, the ninth consciousness appears by way of an evolutionary process. The manifestation of this immaculate consciousness is the pure dharma realm. The other eight consciousnesses evolve into the four wisdoms.[2] Once these five dharmas are perfected, one is then furnished with the three bodies.[3] In this wise, cause and fruition are not separate from phenomenal objects and wisdom. Since phenomenal objects and wisdom are free from duality, there is only a single taste. Thus, the contemplation practice that has but a single taste is considered to be the theme of this scripture.

ANALYTIC STANDPOINT

From an analytic standpoint, the themes of this scripture can be explained through ten approaches—that is to say, from an approach based on monads to an approach based on decades.

What is the approach based on monads? Within the one mind, one thought develops and conforms with the one reality. There is cultivation of one practice, entrance into the one vehicle, abiding in the one path, putting to use the one enlightenment, and awakening to the one taste.

What is the approach based on dyads? Not abiding on either of the two shores of samsara or nirvana, one accordingly abandons the two assemblies of ordinary people and Hīnayānists. Not grasping at the two kinds of selfhood, of person and dharmas, one accordingly leaves behind the two extremes of eternality and annihilationism. Penetrating to the twofold voidness of person and dharmas, one does not drop to the level of the two vehicles of śrāvakas and pratyekabuddhas. Assimilating both of the two truths, absolute and mundane, one does not turn away from the two accesses of principle and practice.

What is the approach based on triads? Taking refuge oneself with the three buddhas as above, one receives the three moral codes.[4] One conforms with the three great truths[5] and gains the three liberations,[6] the three levels of equal enlightenment,[7] and the three bodies of sublime enlightenment.[8] One accesses the three groups of voidness as above and annihilates the minds of the three existences.[9] What is the approach based on tetrads? One cultivates the four right efforts[10] and enters the four bases of supranormal powers.[11] Through the power of the four great conditions,[12] the four postures are constantly benefited. One transcends the four stages of meditative absorption and leaves far behind the four types of slander.[13] The four wisdoms flow out from its four vast grounds.

What is the approach based on pentads? With the arising of the five *skandhas*,[14] one comes into possession of fifty evils.[15] For this reason, while planting the five spiritual faculties[16] one can develop the five powers.[17] One wades through the sea of the five voidnesses,[18] topples the five levels,[19] gains the five pure dharmas, ferries across the beings of the five destinies,[20] and so on.

What are the approaches based on hextads, heptads, octads, enneads, and so forth? Perfecting the cultivation of the six perfections,[21] one forever abandons the six sense-bases.[22] Practicing the seven branches of enlightenment,[23] one annihilates the sevenfold matrix of meaning.[24] "Its sea of the eighth consciousness is limpid, and the flow of its ninth consciousness is pure." From the ten faiths up through the ten stages, the hundreds of practices are completely accomplished and the myriads of meritorious qualities are fully perfected. In this wise, all of these approaches are the themes of this scripture. They all appear in the text of the scripture and will be explained in the commentary to that particular passage in the text.

Nevertheless, these latter nine approaches are all included in the approach based on monads, and the approach based on monads contains all nine; none are distinct from the contemplation of the single taste. Therefore, even if they are explained analytically, they do not add to the one; even if they are explained synthetically, they do not take away from the ten. Neither increase nor decrease is this scripture's thematic essential.

EXPLICATION OF *SAMĀDHI*

The explanation of the term *samādhi* is in two subsections. First will be an explanation of the meaning of the term; second will be an analysis of different types of concentrations.

The explanation of an ancient master says, "In India it is called *samādhi;* here in China it is called correct consideration." The following passages will be given in explanation of this statement.

It is said that when one is in a state of concentration, there is meticulous examination of the external sense spheres; hence, it is called correct consideration. As the *Treatise on the Stages of Yoga Practice* states, "*Samādhi* means that there is meticulous investigation of the external sense spheres; it involves one-pointedness of mind."

QUESTION: Concentration perforce involves tranquillity, and tranquillity means that one is focused on a single point. Why then do you say there is meticulous examination? The functioning of examination perforce involves applied thought and imagination. How then can you say that concentration is examination?

RESPONSE: If you maintain that guarding one-pointedness is concentration, then concentration would even mean the one-pointedness of sloth and torpor. If correct examination is the same as thought and imagination, then examination conducted by means of perverse wisdom would not involve thought and imagination. It should be understood that examination is of two types. If examination refers to a faculty that is associated with both perverse and correct mental and verbal discrimination, then it involves both thought and imagination and is thus just discrimination. But if examination refers to a faculty that meticulously observes the external sense spheres, then it is precisely the functioning of concentration and is neither thought nor imagination. Concentration, on the other hand, applies both within discrimination and nondiscrimination; hence, it meticulously analyzes that thought and imagination.

Furthermore, one-pointedness is also of two types. If a person is one-pointed while being slothful, dull, and deluded, and he is not able to investigate carefully, then this is simply sloth and torpor. If a person is one-pointed while being neither torporific nor distracted, and he investigates meticulously, then this is called concentration. For this reason, investigation is different from sloth and torpor. Hence, it should be understood that one should not judge the difference between concentration and distraction solely on the distinction between the one-pointedness of and the aberrations in a particular thought process. Why is this?

Although opinions that are hastily arrived at might develop rapidly, they still involve concentration; although a dull mind might abide for long periods on one object, its thought proecesses still involve distraction. Now the reason that this adamantine absorption is said to be correct investigation is because it is neither correct nor incorrect; it is neither consideration nor nonconsideration. It is instead to be differentiated from discrimination and perverted thoughts. Furthermore, it is not the same as empty space or aphasia [acittaka]. Therefore, correct consideration is the label we force upon it. The term samādhi can be explained briefly in this manner.

EXPLICATION OF THE TEXT

The beginningless churnings of all deluded thoughts ordinarily result from nothing more than the affliction of discrimination, which derives from clinging to signs. Now, wishing to reverse this churning in order to return to the fountainhead, one must first negate all these signs. It is for this reason that the scripture first explains the contemplation of the signless dharma.

But while all these signs may have been annihilated, if one conserves the mind that contemplates, then the mind that contemplates will continue to arise, and one will not experience original enlightenment. Consequently, one must annihilate the arising of the mind. Therefore, this second chapter of the main body of the text illumines the practice of nonproduction.

Once one's practice produces nothing, one then experiences original enlightenment. Drawing from this experience, one transforms beings and prompts them to gain the original inspiration. If, while relying on original enlightenment, one inspires sentient beings, then those sentient beings in fact can leave behind falsity and access reality. One's internal practice is in fact signless and unproduced. External proselytism is in fact the original inspiration's accessing of reality. In this wise, the two types of benefit (of oneself and others) are replete with the myriads of spiritual practices. These all derive from the true nature and all conform to true voidness. Relying on this true nature, the myriads of spiritual practices are perfected. One accesses the tathāgatagarbha's fountainhead, which has a single taste. Since one has returned to the fountainhead of the mind, one then has nothing more to do. As there is nothing more to do, there is nothing that is not done. Furthermore, there is an alternative interpretation of these six chapters. The first chapter explains the dharma that is contemplated—dharma being the essence of the tathāgatagarbha of the one mind. The second chapter elucidates the practices that are the agents of contemplation—practices being the nondiscriminative contemplation that takes place on the six stages of practice. The third chapter, the "Inspiration of Original Enlightenment," illumines the arising-and-ceasing aspect of the one mind, while the fourth chapter, "Approaching the Edge of Reality," illumines the true-thusness aspect of the one mind. The fifth chapter, the "Voidness of the True Nature," negates both absolute and mundane without subverting the two truths. The sixth chapter, the "Tathāgatagarbha," completely assimilates all of these approaches and shows that they all have but a single taste.

Why is it that these six chapters have but a single taste? Signs and production are devoid of nature. Original enlightenment is devoid of origin. The edge of reality leaves behind all limits. The true nature is also void. So how does one gain the nature of the *tathāgatagarbha?* As is explained below in the "Tathāgatagarbha" chapter: "The consciousnesses are perpetually calm and extinct; but that calm extinction is also calm and extinct." The "Codes" chapter states: "The seventh consciousness and the five sensory consciousnesses are unproduced. The eighth and sixth consciousnesses are calm and extinct. The characteristic of the ninth consciousness is to be void and nonexistent." In this wise, the one taste that is unascertainable is exactly the essential point of the theme of this scripture. It is merely because there is nothing to obtain that there is nothing that is not obtained. Therefore, as there are no approaches that are not opened through the scripture, it presents a theme that has innumerable meanings.   *RB*

Arouse Your Mind and Practice!

[From *Hanguk pulgyo chŏnsŏ* 1:841a-c]

In addition to his exegetical writings, Wŏnhyo made a profound personal commitment to disseminating Buddhism among the people of Silla Korea. His Korean biographer, Iryŏn, tells us that Wŏnhyo "composed a song that circulated throughout the land. He used to sing and dance his way through thousands of villages and myriads of hamlets, touring while proselytizing in song." Wŏnhyo's *Arouse Your Mind* probably dates from between 677 and 684. It is Wŏnhyo's most edifying work and one of the strongest admonitions about the urgency of religious practice to be found in all of Buddhist literature. Even today it is among the first works read by Korean postulants who have just joined the Buddhist monastic community.

Now all the buddhas adorn the palace of tranquil extinction, nirvana, because they have renounced desires and practiced austerities on the sea of numerous kalpas. All sentient beings whirl through the door of the burning house of samsara because they have not renounced craving and sensuality during lifetimes without measure. Though the heavenly mansions are unobstructed, few are those who go there; for people take the three poisons (greed, hatred, and delusion) as their family wealth. Though no one entices others to evil destinies, many are those who go there; for people consider the four snakes and the five desires to be precious to their deluded minds.

Who among human beings would not wish to enter the mountains and cultivate the path? But fettered by lust and desires, no one proceeds. But even though people do not return to mountain fastnesses to cultivate the mind, as far as they are able they should not abandon wholesome practices. Those who can abandon their own sensual pleasures will be venerated like saints. Those who practice what is difficult to practice will be revered like buddhas. Those who covet things join Māra's entourage, while those who give with love and compassion are the children of the King of Dharma himself.

High peaks and lofty crags are where the wise dwell. Green pines and deep valleys are where practitioners sojourn. When hungry, they eat tree fruits to satisfy their famished belly. When thirsty, they drink the flowing streams to quench their feeling of thirst. Though one feeds it with sweets and tenderly cares for it, this body is certain to decay. Though one softly clothes it and carefully protects it, this life force must come to an end. Thus the wise regard the grottoes and caves where echoes resound as a hall for recollecting the Buddha's name. They take the wild geese, plaintively calling, as their closest of friends. Though their knees bent in prostration are frozen like ice, they have no longing for warmth. Though their starving bellies feel as if cut by knives, they have no thoughts to search for food.

Suddenly a hundred years will be past; how then can we not practice? How much longer will this life last? Yet still we do not practice, but remain heedless. Those who leave behind the lusts within the mind are called mendicants. Those who do not long for the mundane are called those gone forth into homelessness. A practitioner entangled in the net of the six senses is a dog wearing elephant's hide. A person on the path who still longs for the world is a hedgehog entering a rat's den.

Although talented and wise, if a person dwells in the village, all the buddhas feel pity and sadness for him. Though a person does not practice the path, if he dwells in a mountain hut, all the saints are happy with him. Though talented and learned, if a person does not observe the precepts, it is like being directed to a treasure trove but not even starting out. Though practicing diligently, if a person has no wisdom, it is like one who wishes to go east but instead turns toward the west. The way of the wise is to prepare rice by steaming rice grains; the way of the ignorant is to prepare rice by steaming sand.

Everyone knows that eating food soothes the pangs of hunger, but no one knows that studying the dharma corrects the delusions of the mind. Practice and understanding that are both complete are like the two wheels of a cart. Benefiting oneself and benefiting others are like the two wings of a bird. If a person chants prayers when receiving rice gruel but does not understand the meaning, should he not be ashamed before the donors? If one chants when receiving rice but does not tumble to its import, should one not be ashamed before the sages and saints?

There is no benefit in nourishing a useless body that does not practice. Despite clinging to this impermanent, evanescent life, it cannot be preserved. The four great elements will suddenly disperse; they cannot be kept together for long. Today, alas, it is already dusk and we should have been practicing since dawn. The pleasures of the world will only bring suffering later, so how can we crave them? One attempt at forbearance conduces to long happiness, so how could we not cultivate? Craving among persons on the path is a disgrace to cultivators. Wealth among those gone forth into homelessness is mocked by the noble. Despite infinite admonitions, craving and clinging are not ended. Despite infinite resolutions, lust and clinging are not eradicated. Though the affairs of this world are limitless, we still cannot forsake worldly events. Though plans are endless, we still do not have a mind to stop them. Hours after hours continue to pass; swiftly the day and night are gone. Days after days continue to pass; swiftly the end of the month is gone. Months and months continue to pass; suddenly next year has arrived. Years after years continue to pass; unexpectedly we have arrived at the portal of death.

A broken cart cannot move; an old person cannot cultivate. Yet still we humans lie, lazy and indolent; still we humans sit, with minds distracted. How many lives have we not cultivated? Yet still we pass the day and night in vain. How many lives have we spent in our useless bodies? Yet still we do not cultivate in this lifetime either. This life must come to an end; but what of the next? Is this not urgent? Is this not urgent?   RB

Commentary on the *Awakening of Faith*

[From *Hsü Tsang-ching* 71:310a–311a]

On Revealing the Essence of the Doctrine

The essence of the Great Vehicle is described as being completely empty and very mysterious. But no matter how mysterious it may be, how could it be anywhere but in the world of myriad phenomena? No matter how empty it may be, it is still present in the conversation of the people. Because Bodhisattva Aśvaghoṣa had unconditioned great compassion, he was distressed over those people whose minds, moved by the wind of ignorance and delusion, are easily tossed about. He was grieved that the true nature of original enlightenment, which sleeps in a long dream, is difficult to awaken. Since Bodhisattva Aśvaghoṣa had the power of wisdom by which one regards others as his own body, he patiently wrote this treatise that expounds the deep meaning of the Thus Come One's profound scriptures. He wished to cause scholars who open this small treatise even for a moment to completely extract the meaning of Tripiṭaka; he wished to cause practitioners to permanently stop myriad illusory phenomena and finally return to the source of one mind. Although what is discussed in the treatise is vast, it may be summarized as follows. By revealing two aspects in one mind,[25] it comprehensively includes the 108 jewels of the Mahāyāna teaching.[26]

Such being the intent of this treatise, when unfolded, there are immeasurable and limitless meanings to be found in its doctrine; when sealed, the principle of two aspects in one mind is found to be its essence. Within the two aspects are included myriad meanings without confusion. These limitless meanings are identical with one mind and are completely amalgamated with it.The meaning of this treatise is so profound, however, that interpreters hitherto have seldom presented its doctrine completely. Indeed, since all of them were attached to what they had learned, they distorted the meaning of the sentences. Not able to abandon their preconceptions, still they sought the meaning. Therefore, their interpretations do not come close to the author's intent.   SP

Ŭisang and the Flower Garland School

Ŭisang (625–702) won great acclaim as the founder of the Flower Garland school in Korea. Upon returning from his study under Chih-yen (602–668), Ŭisang expounded the school's philosophy and trained disciples. Unlike his colleague Fa-tsang (643–712), who systematized Flower Garland metaphysics, Ŭisang stressed practice and monastic life. His emphasis on practice is reflected not only in his diagram but also in the works of his disciples, who either summarized the essence of the scripture for the purpose of practice or elucidated the gate of contemplation and action to attain Buddhahood. Mount Nak, the school's holy place where Avalokiteśvara was believed to reside, and Mount Odae, where Mañjuśrī was said to reside, illustrate the contemporary cults of the two bodhisattvas. Ŭisang considered Mount Nak to be the holiest of places, and the Buddhist communities on Mount Odae had close connections with the ruling house during the unification and the political struggles that took place later in the capital. There were also religious societies on the mountain that, under state protection, lectured on scriptures, copied them, or repaired monasteries. The religious activities of these societies congregating around the Flower Garland school promoted its spread among the nobility.

The Flower Garland school teaches that principle or noumenon (*ri/i*) and phenomenon (*sa*), the two aspects of the dharma realm, are interfused without obstruction and that all phenomena are mutually identified with one another—the interpenetration and mutual identification of all the dharmas. Because every phenomenon is a manifestation of principle, one is the many and the many are the one. This all-inclusive system has everything leading to one point, the Buddha, and sees everything in the universe as a representation of the same supreme mind. This cosmology provides a spiritual background for both individual freedom and the harmony that must exist between the individual and the state and between the individual and the universe. At the time of unification, therefore, when Silla had to assimilate the aristocracy and loyalists of Koguryŏ and Paekche, Flower Garland metaphysics provided a unifying ideology that embraced subjugated states and peoples as well as a religious sanction for the centralized administration proceeding from the royal authority. *PL*

Diagram of the Dharmadhātu According to the One Vehicle

[From *Taishō Tripiṭaka* 45:711a]

Based on the doctrinal essentials of the *Flower Garland Scripture* and the *Treatise on the Scripture Concerning the Ten Stages (Daśabhūmika sūtra śāstra)*, this thirty-line heptasyllabic verse in two hundred and ten logographs begins with the logograph *pŏp* (dharma) at the center, goes through fifty-four meanderings, and ends at the logograph *pul* (Buddha).

First Ŭisang explains the meaning of the seal and analyzes its marks. The form of the seal expresses the idea that three worlds—the material world, the world of sentient beings, and the world of perfectly enlightened wisdom—contained in Śākyamuni's teaching are produced from the ocean-seal *samādhi*, and the three worlds contain and exhaust all dharmas. He then interprets the seal's marks in three sections: the marks of the sentences, the marks of the logographs, and the meaning of the text. The one path of the seal expresses the one sound of the Thus Come One, the wonderfully skillful expedient means. Many meanderings in his expedient means show the differences in the capacities and desires of sentient beings and stand for the teachings of the three vehicles [triyana]. The poem, however, has no beginning and end, because the Thus Come One's expedient means have no fixed method but correspond to the world of dharmas so that the ten worlds mutually correspond and are completely interfused. This is the round teaching of the one vehicle, the Flower Garland school. The four sides and four corners in the diagram manifest the four embracing virtues (almsgiving, kind words, conduct benefiting others, and adaptation to others) and the four immeasurables (benevolence, compassion, sympathetic joy, and impartiality). This shows the one vehicle by means of the three vehicles. The fact that the logographs at the center have a beginning and end shows that cause and effect are not equal from the standpoint of expedient means in practice. The unenlightened perceive a great distance between cause and effect; but from the standpoint of the dharma nature, cause and effect are simultaneous, and this is the essence of the Middle Path.

The dharma nature is perfectly interfused; it has no duality.
All dharmas are unmoving; by nature they are quiescent;
They have no names or characters; all distinctions are severed.
It is known through realization wisdom and not by any other means.
True nature is very profound and supremely fine.
It has no self-nature, but arises from causation.
It is the one in the all, the one in the many.
The one is the all, the many are the one.
A mote of dust contains the ten directions;
All the motes are thus.
The immeasurably distant cosmic age is the same as a single thought-moment,
A single thought-moment is the same as the immeasurably distant cosmic age.
Nine time periods and ten time periods are mutually identical;
They are not in confusion, but have been formed separately.
The first production of the thought of enlightenment is the same as true enlightenment.
Samsara and nirvana are always in harmony.
Noumenon and phenomenon are invisible and indistinct.
The ten Buddhas and Samantabhadra are the realm of great men.
Śākyamuni, in his ocean-seal meditation,
Constantly manifests inconceivable supernatural power —
A rain of jewels that benefits the living fills all space,

And all the living benefit according to their capacity.
Therefore the practitioner of conduct must return to the original source,
For he cannot attain it without ceasing from false thoughts.
By expedient, unconditional means, he attains complete freedom,
Returns home, and obtains food according to his capacity.
With the inexhaustible treasure of dhāraṇī,
He adorns the dharma realm—a true palace of jewels.
Finally, seated on the throne of the Middle Way of Ultimate Reality,
From times long past he has not moved—hence his name is Buddha.   PL

WŏNCH'ŭK AND THE CONSCIOUSNESS-ONLY SCHOOL

While the Flower Garland school of Ŭisang emphasized practice, the Consciousness-Only (Wei-shih) school, which also flourished in unified Silla, stressed doctrinal studies. Here the pioneer was Wŏnch'ŭk (613–696), who studied the *Compendium of Mahāyāna* under Fa-ch'ang and Seng-p'ien and later the Wei-shih doctrines under Hsüan-tsang. Because he lectured at Hsi-ming Monastery in Ch'ang-an, his disciples were known as the Hsi-ming school. When Wŏnch'ŭk gained public favor with his lectures on the *Treatise on the Completion of Consciousness-Only, Stages of Yoga Practice*, and *Explanation of Profound Mysteries Scripture*, K'uei-chi (632–682) stoutly opposed Wŏnch'ŭk's theory. This polemic may have given rise to "absurd" apocryphal stories attributed to both Wŏnch'ŭk and K'uei-chi.[27] Wŏnch'ŭk's philosophy was influenced by that of Paramārtha (499–569), while K'uei-chi upheld only that of Dharmapāla (c. 530–561), rejecting all others as heterodox.

With the doctrinal study of the Consciousness-Only philosophy was born the Pŏpsang (Fa-hsiang) school. Second in importance only to the Flower Garland school, it flourished until the end of Koryŏ. But because the school was too abstruse, did not accept the theory of dependent origination (*pratītyasamutpāda*) of the dharma realm, and denied that all sentient beings possess Buddhahood, it was not for the common people.   PL

Sung Fu: Memorial Inscription to Wŏnch'ŭk

[From *Ta-Chou Hsi-ming ssu ku ta-te Yüan-ts'e (Wŏnch'ŭk) fa-shih fo she-li t'a-ming ping hsü*, in *Chin-shih ts'ui-pien* 146:34b–37a]

The dharma master's taboo name was Muna [Wen-ya]; his sobriquet was Wŏnch'ŭk [613–696]. He was a descendant of a prince of the Silla kingdom. At the age of three he left home to be ordained as a novice; at fifteen he asked for his vocation and traveled to T'ang China, where initially he listened to the discourses of the two dharma masters Fa-ch'ang [567–646] and Seng-p'ien [568–642]. His natural astuteness was striking in the extreme. Although he might listen to several tens of millions of words, if his ears heard them only once his mind never forgot them. During the period of Chen-kuan[28] [627–649] of the Civil Emperor T'ai-tsung, [Wŏnch'ŭk] was ordained a monk and resided at Yüan-fa Monastery in Ch'ang-an. Just as the Tripiṭaka Master, the venerable Hsüan-tsang, was returning from India, Dharma Master Wŏnch'ŭk had a dream in which a Brahman gave him fruit until he was completely satisfied. The message conveyed by this dream was that his superior affinities would soon coalesce. The first time that the venerable Hsüan-tsang saw Wŏnch'ŭk, he was well disposed toward him without any ado, and he ordered that Wŏnch'ŭk be entrusted with such works as the *Treatise on the Stages of Yoga Practice* and the *Completion of Consciousness-Only Treatise,* as well as with the Mahāyāna and Hīnayāna scriptures and treatises Hsüan-tsang had translated. Wŏnch'ŭk's understanding of these texts was as clear as instinctual knowledge.

Later, Wŏnch'ŭk was summoned to become master of Hsi-ming Monastery. He protected the secret canon of Buddhism and opened the eyes and ears of his contemporaries. Thus, he was one of those who assisted the venerable Hsüan-tsang in bringing about the eastward flow of the Buddhadharma and promoting greatly the infinite teachings.

Wŏnch'ŭk: Commentary on the *Explanation of Profound Mysteries Scripture*

[From *Hsü Tsang-ching* 34:291a–298a]

The *Explanation of Profound Mysteries Scripture (Sandhinirmocana sūtra)* is considered a seminal text of the Yogācāra school, for its doctrine of the three turnings of the dharma wheel justifies that school's claim to be the consummation of Mahāyāna Buddhism. The introduction to Wŏnch'ŭk's commentary to the text, portions of which are translated here, epitomizes the East Asian commentarial style and shows the author's familiarity with a wide range of Indian exegetical materials. The central issue explored in this selection is fundamental to the Indian Buddhist schools and their East Asian counterparts: defining the essential character of the Buddhist teachings. There were two basic propositions: First, following the Sautrāntika and Yogācāra schools, the teachings could be characterized as sound—an element that was considered to be part of the aggregate of matter. Second, following the Vaibhāṣika school of Abhidharma, the teachings could be considered a unique type of force that was dissociated from both mentality and materiality *(viprayuktasañskāra)*—that is, they were "word" *(nāmakāya)*, the peculiar force that allows the meaning of a word to be comprehended. Through extensive citations of the various positions on this issue given in Indian philosophical treatises, Wŏnch'ŭk attempts to substantiate the position of his teacher, Hsüan-tsang, that both proposals are acceptable. Wŏnch'ŭk's treatment illustrates the communality of concerns important to the elites among Buddhist doctrinal exegetes, whether Korean, Chinese, or Indian in national origin, and it demonstrates that Korean Buddhism cannot be considered in isolation from pan-Asian developments.

The Promotion of the Various Teachings of Buddhism and the Meaning of the Title of This Scripture

I have reflected on the fact that the true nature is extremely profound: while it transcends the varieties of images, it is itself still an image. The complete sound of the Buddha's voice is secretly arcane: while it disseminates all varieties of words, it is not itself a word. This complete sound, then, is just a word, and yet words are left behind. The true nature is not an image, and yet it is bound up with images. Although the principle is quiescent, it can be discussed. "This complete sound, then, is just a word, and yet words are left behind": this is because, although words are disseminated, there is no speech. For this reason, even though Vimalakīrti was silent as an expression of nonduality in the discussion that took place in his bedroom, that nonduality could still be discussed. Similarly, when the three natures[29] were analyzed in the pure palace, the bodhisattva Maitreya explained the true and the mundane while actualizing both. The great being Nāgārjuna discussed emptiness and existence while refuting both. Nevertheless, actualization does not contradict refutation: thus the meaning of "consciousness-only" increases in clarity. Refutation does not contradict actualization: thus the purport of signlessness is thoroughly established. Being both empty and existent properly accomplishes the proposition of the two truths, mundane and absolute. Being neither existent nor empty correlates with the principle of the Middle Way. For this reason, we know that those who are deluded still cling to existence even while talking about emptiness. Those who are awakened understand emptiness thoroughly by analyzing existence. How could the ultimate fountainhead of the Buddhadharma be anything but this?

There are many ways to guide sentient beings to salvation; there is not just one entrance to the principle. For this reason, the King of Dharma, the Buddha, taught three turnings of the dharma wheel. First, for the benefit of those who aspire to the Disciple Vehicle, at the Deer Park in the kingdom of Banaras the

Buddha inaugurated the causes and effects that result in either birth-and-death or nirvana. This is the first dharma wheel, that of the Four Noble Truths. Next, for the benefit of those who undertake the Bodhisattva Vehicle, at the sixteen assemblies, such as Vulture Peak Mountain and so forth, the Buddha proclaimed all the *Perfection of Wisdom* texts. This is the second dharma wheel, that of signlessness. Finally, for the benefit of those who undertake the All-Encompassing Vehicle, in such pure and defiled realms as the Lotus-Womb World and elsewhere, the Buddha proclaimed the *Explanation of Profound Mysteries* and other scriptures. This is the third dharma wheel, that of the Mahāyāna of definitive meaning. This is the meaning of the promotion of the teaching by the Thus Come One.[30]   *RB*

The Life of Sungyŏng

[From *Sung kao-seng chuan* 4:728a]

Sungyŏng was another of the Korean disciples of Hsüan-tsang who drew the ire of K'uei-chi, the monk generally regarded as Hsüan-tsang's orthodox successor. The dispute that set K'uei-chi against Sungyŏng concerns the latter's charge that an inference used by Hsüan-tsang to establish a key thesis concerning the nature of visual objects was fallacious. Sungyŏng criticizes Hsüan-tsang's reasoning in this syllogism because it involves a fallacy in which two different, though equally acceptable, reasons lead to contradictory conclusions. Hsüan-tsang asserts that the three elements of form, the sense faculty of the eye, and visual consciousness are interrelated categories; therefore, visual objects are not distinct from visual consciousness. Sungyŏng employs a different reason, one that is not ruled out by the form of Hsüan-tsang's syllogism, to prove the opposite conclusion—that form must be distinct from visual consciousness because it is classified separately in the list of the eighteen elements. Since Tsan-ning's account of this dispute is hopelessly addled, I have reconstructed it from K'uei-chi's earlier account.[31]

The monk Sungyŏng was from Nangnang [Lo-lang].[32] His clan was Chinese, but his family's lineage was Korean; for this reason, it is difficult to ascertain many details about his life. His multiple translations and his studies on the philosophy of language came naturally to him; this was so even for his scholarship on logic. His comprehension of the seminal research entrusted to him by Master Hsüan-tsang was equaled by few Chinese monks. What else if not the power generated in past lives could have brought about Sungyŏng's competent understanding?

He received by transmission Master Hsüan-tsang's inference regarding the true doctrine of Consciousness-Only and ascertained that it was an inference that contained the fallacy of an inferential mark that is inconclusive in that it proves contradictory results.[33] During the period of Ch'ien-feng [666–667], he tried to apprise Hsüan-tsang of his position through an envoy on a tributary mission to T'ang, but by that time Master Hsüan-tsang had been dead for nearly two years.

Hsüan-tsang's syllogism ran as follows:

THESIS: As one type of reality, what are commonly accepted as visual forms are inseparable from visual consciousness.

REASON: Because they are not included within the category of vision among the first three of the eighteenfold classification of perception[34] accepted by us.

EXAMPLE: Visual consciousness.

It would seem here that the Tripiṭaka Master was constructing his syllogism with great subtlety; it is not that his great wisdom was unclear.

Sungyŏng constructed a contradictory thesis:

THESIS: As one type of reality, what are commonly accepted as visual forms are quite distinct from visual consciousness.

REASON: Because they are not included within the category of visual consciousness among the first three of the eighteenfold classification of perception accepted by us.

EXAMPLE: The faculty of vision.

In this wise, he skillfully proved the converse idea.

At that time, Ta-sheng K'uei-chi [632–682] studied this syllogism and saw then what Sungyŏng had not understood. In the end, however, he had to accept that this was the view held by the provincial monks regarding cognition. He sighed, saying: "The fame of the Silla Dharma Master Sungyŏng moves T'ang and Tibet, and his scholarship covers both great and small points. His actions honor Kāśyapa by being solely devoted to the cultivation of the ascetic practices. His mind emulates Bakkula by constantly seeking to be known for fewness of desires. Since he has mastered even Tangut (Hsi-hsia), his brilliance has spread among the Eastern Barbarians. His fame and virtue are daily renewed, and both ordained and lay bow to him respectfully. Although other ecclesiastical eminences are not few, these foreigners praise him as being extraordinary for showing that this inference of Hsüan-tsang's does result in the fallacy of allowing a contradictory thesis to be proved." What Master K'uei-chi meant was that these provincials, with their agitated and keen wit, impudently assail Master Hsüan-tsang. Amidst this delusion, an opportunity will arise to vindicate the meaning of the Tripiṭaka Master. Alas, this did not prove to be so.

In his native country, Sungyŏng wrote a number of works. The perspective of those works that have also circulated in China is that of the definitive teachings of Mahāyāna of the Fa-hsiang (Dharmalakṣaṇa) school. After seeing the passage in the *Flower Garland Scripture* that says "upon the initial activation of the thought of enlightenment Buddhahood is already achieved," he then ridiculed this scripture and would not have faith in it.

Others say that once he stretched out his arms and legs and ordered his disciples to support him and lower him to the ground. The ground then was rent asunder; Sungyŏng's body suddenly sank, and in that very body he fell into hell. Today there is still a pit over ten feet wide there, and the cavity is virtually bottomless. It is called Sungyŏng Naraka [*"The Interminable," the deepest of the hells*].   RB

The Life of T'aehyŏn

[From *Samguk yusa* 4:208–209]

The founder of the Yogācāra school, the venerable T'aehyŏn, resided in Yongjang Monastery on Mount South. There he would circumambulate the sixteen-foot stone image of Maitreya, whereupon the image would turn its face toward him. Wise, discriminate, and nimble, T'aehyŏn possessed clear decision. Generally, the doctrine of the Fa-hsiang school was mysterious and profound and difficult to analyze. Hence the Chinese poet Po Chü-i [772–846] could not fathom it and said, "The doctrine of Dharmalakṣaṇa (which holds that all is mind in its ultimate truth) is too profound to be mastered, and the science of logical reasoning defies analysis." It was indeed difficult for the learned to study. But being well versed in all teachings, T'aehyŏn alone was able to detect errors and elucidate the subtle and arcane. Therefore Korean students all followed his teachings, and Chinese scholars took him as their model.   PL

T'aehyŏn: Study Notes to the *Treatise on the Completion of Consciousness-Only*

[From *Hsü Tsang-ching* 80:1a–3a]

> In this passage from the introduction to his commentary on the *Treatise on the Completion of Consciousness-Only*, T'aehyŏn examines the controversy between the Indian philosophical schools of Vijñaptimātratā-Yogācāra, as represented by Dharmapāla, and Svātantrika-Mādhyamika, as represented by Bhāvaviveka. The two differ on a variety of fundamental issues concerning absolute and phenomenal realities. As far as their positions on the

phenomenal realm are concerned, Bhāvaviveka asserts that, from the standpoint of the absolute, all phenomena (the dharmas) are empty and illusory; Dharmapāla declares instead that all dharmas have an empty and nonempty aspect, both of which are equally valid from the standpoint of absolute truth. Concerning the absolute itself, Dharmapāla states that the absolute, suchness, is distinct from both existence and nonexistence; Bhāvaviveka argues that since the emptiness of phenomenal objects is itself suchness, the absolute is directly associated with the phenomenal world. Finally, Dharmapāla asserts the ultimate reality of consciousness, which is considered to exist in reality. By giving a positive description to ultimate reality, the Yogācārins thus accept the validity of positive descriptions of truth. Bhāvaviveka and the Mādhyamika school, however, assert that even positive concepts—such as the summum bonum of Buddhist spiritual culture, nirvana—can only be considered to exist from the standpoint of mundane truth; emptiness alone is ultimately real. Their ultimate position is therefore fundamentally negative. Finally, T'aehyŏn explores the different implications of this controversy as given by such Korean exegetes as Wŏnch'ŭk and Sungyŏng.

As far as the revelation of the doctrinal themes is concerned, there are two positions. First, discussing the *Perfection of Wisdom*, Bhāvaviveka [c. 500–570] and others mention the concepts of compounded things, uncompounded things, mundane existence, and true emptiness. Second, basing themselves on the *Explanation of Profound Mysteries Scripture*, Dharmapāla [c. 530–561] and others have said that the existence of all dharmas is both empty and nonempty.[35] As far as compounded things are concerned, the *Treatise on the Completion of Consciousness-Only* says: "Self and dharmas do not exist; emptiness and consciousness do not nonexist. Leaving behind existence and nonexistence, conform to the Middle Path." This refutes the imaginary nature of dharmas and maintains the remaining two natures of conditional dependency and perfection. The *Jewel in Hand Treatise* says: "Just as the eye faculty is explained as nonexistent in order to remove the defect of falling into the extreme of annihilationism, so also is it explained as existent in order to remove the defect of falling into the extreme of annihilationism. That is to say, the eye faculty and so forth, which arise through the power of cause and conditions, are included in the mundane truth and have an own-nature that is existent. They are not the same as sky flowers, which are completely devoid of any semblance of existence. It is merely from the standpoint of the true nature that they are substantiated as being empty." This maintains the validity of the mundane truth while ensuring that from the standpoint of the absolute truth all dharmas are empty.

Furthermore, with reference to uncompounded things, the explanations of the two are not the same. Dharmapāla Bodhisattva opposed Bhāvaviveka's position that the two emptinesses of self and dharmas are identical to truth. As the *Treatise on the Completion of Consciousness-Only* says: "The two emptinesses of self and dharmas revealed through the nature are not perfected reality. This is because the nature of true suchness is separate from existence and separate from nonexistence."

The Bodhisattva Bhāvaviveka countered the descriptions of the two emptinesses given according to the position of Dharmapāla. As the *Jewel in Hand Treatise* says: "That state which is merely devoid of all objectivity is proved to be true suchness." It is not merely in their disclosure of the essence that these two explanations are not the same; there is also considerable controversy as to whether the ultimate meaning is existent or nonexistent. Wŏnch'ŭk and others relate that this was no controversy over the nature of real existence. They say there was no controversy whatsoever between the two teachers, because Bhāvaviveka does not accept that the absolute truth is nonexistence. For Dharmapāla, absolute truth also does not allow existence. As his *Exegesis to the Mahāyāna's "Expanded Hundred Verses Treatise"* [Ta-sheng kuang po lun shih-lun] states: "In the present, it is also not correct to claim that the absolute truth exists. This is because it arises from conditions, because it is like a magical illusion and so forth." It also explains emptiness with the words: "It is a negative form of discourse, not a positive form. It is not merely the emptiness of existence; it is also the emptiness of emptiness." This is discussed extensively there. Master Sungyŏng [fl. 666–667] and others maintained that this was a controversy over nonexistence. They explained that these two descriptions might be conflicting in their expressions, but their meaning is identical. It is like disputing over the fact that the bottom of a stupa is broad while it narrows toward the top: it is only through accepting the one feature that the other feature is also possible. The position of Dharmapāla perforce brings up the imaginary nature of dharmas without indicating that it is separate from the four antinomical propositions.[36] This is because the natures of emptiness, existence, and so forth are all imaginary, and because these two natures have a sublime existence that is not completely nonexistent.

For this reason, this explanation is given: The two emptinesses of self and dharmas are not real. Emptiness, considered from one standpoint, is also nonexistent. This is because the elimination of the road of emptiness and existence is called true suchness. Bhāvaviveka Bodhisattva posited existence that was mundane, nonexistence that was separate from everything, and true nonexistence that distinguished everything. This is because the mundane is also nonexistent. The sublime nonexistence of the two natures of emptiness and existence cannot be apprehended. Hence if one only rejects existence, one can then gain nonexistence; but by also rejecting nonexistence, it is said that the state achieved cannot be apprehended.

"Unapprehensible" means that it is separate from the four antinomical propositions. This is because Asaṅga says in his *Po-jo lun:* "The four antinomical propositions are all associated with grasping at dharmas." According to this logic, the words of Master Wŏnhyo [617–686] and others might be in conflict, but their ideas are identical. These differences in the words were designed so that disciples of dull faculties in the latter dharma-ending age will skillfully give rise to understanding through examination of this controversy.   *RB*

Belief in the Pure Land

Early Buddhism in Silla, as noted earlier, was used by reigning monarchs as a political tool. The conversion effort by Wŏngwang and Chajang contributed to the establishment of unified Silla and a new moral system, but their audience was limited to the nobility in the capital. The sixteen-foot Śākyamunibuddha statue (574) and the nine-story stupa (645) in Hwangnyong Monastery (566–645) demonstrated the splendor of court Buddhism as a means of controlling society. The purpose of the Assembly of One Hundred Seats *(Paekkojwa hoe)* at Hwangnyong Monastery, where the *Scripture on Benevolent Kings* was recited and commented upon, was not so much to propagate the faith or convert the people as to pray for the Buddha's protection of the country and to enhance the ruler's prestige. Doctrinal development after the unification was too esoteric and abstract to serve the people as a guide to salvation. The form of Buddhism that fulfilled their needs was belief in the Pure Land and Avalokiteśvara ("He Who Observes the Sounds of the World").

Belief in the Pure Land of Maitreya was prevalent among the nobility during the Three Kingdoms period (some twenty images of Maitreya remain from this period), while belief in Amitāyus ("Infinite Life") was prevalent about the time of unification. The worship of Amitāyus was intended for the people, as only faith and devotion were deemed necessary to ensure that one would be reborn in the Sukhāvatī ("Happy Land"), where Amitābha ("Infinite Light"), or Amitāyus (Amit'a is a short form), dwells. Thus its appeal lay in its promise of salvation to all people regardless of class, wealth, sex, or age. Viewing this world as a sea of sorrow, it sought rebirth in the future.

Belief in the Sound-Observer stressed that the bodhisattva's mercy would save people from suffering and calamity. The spread of Amitāyus worship fostered the worship of the Sound-Observer, as believers sought not only rewards in this world but also deliverance and enlightenment in the future. Stories of miracles performed by the Sound-Observer were joyfully transmitted from mouth to mouth. Faith in Amitāyus and the Sound-Observer was preached by monks who went among the people to proselytize. Unaided by the court or the nobility, they preached on the roadside or in the market-place, making Buddhism a popular faith for the first time in Silla.

Monks active around the time of unification include Hyesuk, Hyegong, Taean, and Wŏnhyo. Hyesuk, who had formerly been a *hwarang* and lived in Chŏksŏn village in Angang, sliced the flesh from his thigh to admonish Lord Kudam for indulging in pleasures. He was summoned to court by King Chinp'yŏng (579–632), but he declined. Hyesuk built Amit'a Monastery for the people and taught them to utter Amita's name. The slave girl Ungmyŏn is said to have been transported to the Pure Land while invoking the name of Amit'a in the same monastery. Hyegong, the son of an old maid, is said to have carried a basket, the common people's tool for earning their livelihood. Drinking, dancing, and singing were the expedient means he adopted to teach and convert people of inferior capacity. Hyegong was sought out by Wŏnhyo for consultation on doctrinal matters. Taean, too, used unusual means to teach the people: he would beat on a copper bowl in the market-place shouting "Taean, taean!" ("Great peace!"). He also shunned the privileged, as shown in Wŏnhyo's biography. Wŏnhyo was both a great scholar-monk and a friend of the people, respected by court and populace alike. He showed how one can practice one's faith so as to overcome the contradiction between *saṃvṛti-satya* (secular, relative truth) and *parmārtha-satya* (absolute truth). Leading a life different from that of the regular clergy, Wŏnhyo frequented the taverns or meditated in the wilderness. Some failed to understand his true intention, which was to mingle with the masses and teach them the faith and encourage them to live it. Putting aside the distinction between absolute and relative truth, he would wander about striking a gourd inscribed with the word "unhindered." He also taught that rebirth in Amitāyus's Pure Land was easier than in Maitreya's Tuṣita Heaven—belief in the former, he claimed, was a faith for the common folk.   *PL*

Ungmyŏn

[From *Samguk yusa* 5:217–219]

During the reign of King Kyŏngdŏk [742–765], a group of male devotees in Kangju set their minds on the Western Paradise, erected Amitābha Monastery on the border of Kangju, and prayed for ten thousand days. At that time a female slave, called Ungmyŏn, in the house of *Agan* Kwijin would follow her master to the middle courtyard and stand there chanting the name of Amitābha. Taking offense at this practice of Ungmyŏn, which was too exalted for her station, her master bade her pound two piculs of grain a night. She would finish her work in the early evening, go to the monastery, and call upon the name of Amitābha diligently day and night. She planted two poles, one to the left of the courtyard and one to the right, gouged holes in her hands, and passed a straw rope through them. This Ungmyŏn tied to the poles, and then moved her joined palms to the left and to the right in order to spur herself on.

Then a voice called to her, "Ungmyŏn, enter the main hall and invoke Amitābha." The worshipers then urged her to enter and devote herself to prayer as usual. Soon the sound of heavenly music was heard from the west, and the slave girl soared high through the roof beam and headed west to the outskirts of the town. There her mortal body fell away, and she changed into a true Buddha. Seated on a lotus and emitting brilliant rays of light, she slowly disappeared to the sound of music. The hole in the hall remains.

According to the lives of monks, the monk P'alchin, a reincarnation of the Sound-Observer, formed a society of one thousand, which was divided into two groups—one called "Labor" and the other "Spiritual Cultivation." A supervisor among the first could not fulfill the commandments and was reborn as a cow at Pusŏk Monastery. While carrying the scriptures, the cow, through the power of these scriptures, was reincarnated as Ungmyŏn, a slave in the household of Kwijin. One day she went on an errand to Mount Haga, where in a dream she was stirred to aspire to enlightenment. The house of Kwijin was near Amitābha Monastery, which had been erected by Dharma Master Hyesuk. Whenever Kwijin went there to pray, Ungmyŏn followed him and invoked the name of Amitābha. After nine years of devotion, on the twenty-first day of the first month of the fourteenth year, *ŭlmi* [8 February 755], during her worship she soared through the roof and reached Mount Sobaek, where she let fall one of her sandals. There she built Bodhi Monastery. Because she had shed her earthly form at the foot of the mountain, there she built the second Bodhi Monastery, calling the hall "Ungmyŏn's Ascension Hall." The hole in the roof is about ten arms' lengths wide, but a storm or thick snow could not wet the inside. Later, one of her followers covered the hole with a gilt stupa and recorded her miraculous deeds on it. Even today the tablet and stupa still stand.   PL

Kwangdŏk

[From *Samguk yusa* 5:219–220]

During the reign of King Munmu [661–681], the monks Kwangdŏk and Ŏmjang formed a warm friendship, vowing day and night that the first of them to attain the Promised Land would inform the other. Kwangdŏk retired to West Punhwang-ri and made sandals out of rushes to support his wife and children; Ŏmjang built a hermitage on South Peak and followed the plow.

One day, as the sun cast a crimson shadow and stillness settled on the pine grove, a voice spoke to Ŏmjang from outside:"I'm going to the West. Fare you well, but follow me soon." Going out, Ŏmjang heard heavenly music in the clouds and saw a bright light gathering below them. When he went to visit his friend the following morning, he learned that Kwangdŏk had died. Together with the widow he buried his friend's remains and then asked the widow, "Now that your husband is dead, will you live with me?"

The widow agreed. When Ŏmjang was about to embrace her at night, she warned, "Your seeking of the Western Paradise is like looking for a fish in a tree."

Startled, Ŏmjang asked, "You and Kwangdŏk were husband and wife. Why can you not be mine?"

The widow replied, "My late husband and I lived together for more than ten years, but he never shared his bed with me. Each night we knelt erect, invoked the name of Amitābha, and mastered the sixteen meditations expounded in the *Meditation on the Buddha Amitāyus Scripture*. When the bright moon shone through the window, we sat cross-legged. Such was his devotion. Where else could he have gone but to the Pure Land? A journey of a thousand *ri* is determined by the first step. You are headed toward the east, not toward the west."

Overwhelmed with shame, Ŏmjang went to Dharma Master Wŏnhyo, begging to be taught the essentials of faith. Wŏnhyo taught him the method of contemplation. Ŏmjang then cleansed himself, repented and cultivated meditation, and went to the Western Paradise. Kwangdŏk's wife, the slave of Punhwang Monastery, was one of the nineteen bodies displayed by the Bodhisattva Sound-Observer. A poem by Kwangdŏk goes:

> O Moon,
> Go to the West, and

Pray to Amitāyus
And tell

That there is one who
Adores the judicial throne, and
Longs for the Pure Land,
Praying before him with folded hands.

Would he leave me out
When he fulfills the forty-eight vows?

PL

DIVINATION CEREMONIES

As we have seen, monks were active in the Silla capital and the nearby countryside, bridging the gap between the classes and leading many to salvation. Then, from the middle of the eighth century on, monks began to arrive from distant provinces to convert the people. The representative figure is Chinp'yo (fl. 742–780), who was born in Kimje in North Chŏlla and used divination as a means of conversion. He emphasized the rules of prohibition and confession by divining good and evil deeds in the past, present, and future—his way of adapting Buddhism to indigenous beliefs and practices. Chinp'yo's method, originating with Wŏngwang, entailed throwing 189 bamboo sticks in the air and divining the relative merit or demerit of one's actions by observing how the sticks fell. Chinp'yo also taught people to believe in Maitreya and Kṣitigarbha (Guardian of the Earth), who vowed to deliver everybody from the suffering world. In Chinp'yo's system, Kṣitigarbha was an attendant of Maitreya; in Koryŏ he was worshiped independently and, together with the Sound-Observer, became the bodhisattva closest to the people. Chinp'yo's teaching spread far and wide, extending to the Diamond Mountains; it was continued in the Koryŏ period by his disciples.

Chinp'yo

[From *Samguk yusa* 4:200–202]

The monk Chinp'yo was a native of Mangyŏng county in Wansan province [now Chŏnju]; his father was Chinnaemal; his mother was Kilbo, surnamed Chŏng. At the age of twelve Chinp'yo became a monk, studying under the Dharma Master Sungje[37] of Kŭmsan Monastery. Once the master said, "Early in my life I studied under the T'ang Tripiṭaka Master Shan-tao [618–681] and then went to Mount Wu-t'ai, where I received the five commandments from the bodhisattva Mañjuśrī, who appeared in response to my prayers."

Chinp'yo asked, "How long must one cultivate the Way before receiving the commandments?"

"If you are sincere, you can receive them within a year," answered the master.

Chinp'yo then made pilgrimages to famous mountains and settled at Pursaŭi Monastery on Mount Sŏngye, where he worshiped the Buddha with perfect sincerity of body, mouth, and mind and performed the repentance rite of abandoning the body [mangsinch'am]. [Three graphs are missing at this point.] He struck his forehead, the elbows, and the knees against a rock for seven nights, his knees and elbows broken and blood raining down on the rock, but there was no response. Resolved to cast off his body, he continued for seven more days. Then, at the time of the Dragon [7–9 A.M.], on the fifteenth day of the third month of the twenty-eighth year, kyŏngjin, of K'ai-yüan [15 April 740], the Guardian of the Earth Bodhisattva appeared to Chinp'yo and gave him the commandments. He was then twenty-three.

Wishing to behold Maitreya, Chinp'yo continued his practices and moved to Yŏngsan Monastery, where he was as diligent and courageous as before. At last Maitreya appeared to him, gave him a copy of the Scripture That Divines the Requital of Wholesome and Unwholesome Actions [Chan-ch'a shan-o ye-pao ching] in two rolls and 189 divination sticks as fruits of his vigorous efforts, and said: "The eighth stick represents the newly obtained wondrous commandments; the ninth, all the prohibitions. These two sticks are my finger bones, while the others are made of sandalwood, signifying all depravity. These are rafts to ferry the suffering across to nirvana. Use them to spread the dharma and save the masses!"

Following Maitreya's instruction, Chinp'yo proceeded to Kŭmsan Monastery and set up a platform and taught the Buddha's truth. In its refinement and dignity, his platform was unparalleled in the period of the degenerate dharma.

After transforming the people by religion, when he arrived in Asŭlla province on his tour, the fish and turtles of the sea formed a bridge between the islands and led him to the underwater world, where he expounded dharma and gave commandments to those who dwelt there. King Kyŏngdŏk invited Chinp'yo to his palace, received from him the bodhisattva ordination, and gave him seventy-seven thousand bags of tax grain. The courtiers and the queen's family also received the commandments, donating five hundred rolls of silk and fifty ounces of gold. Chinp'yo distributed these donations to various mountain monasteries for the support of Buddhist services. His bones are now enshrined at Paryŏn Monastery, near the place where he had given the commandments to the fish and turtles. *PL*

COPYING SCRIPTURES

Buddhists copied scriptures to accumulate merit and pray for salvation. This act of devotion was popular in Silla times, but until recently the oldest example of a scripture copied by hand was part of the *Ta pao-chi ching* (*Ratnakūṭa sūtra*; *T.* 11, no. 310), written in gold on purple paper, dating from 1006. It consists of one roll and is preserved in Japan. But in 1979, two scrolls of the *Flower Garland Scripture* copied on white paper in black ink were discovered and designated a national treasure. One scroll comprises chapters 1–10; the other, chapters 41–50. Thus the copied scripture originally consisted of eight scrolls, each containing ten chapters of the new translation (695–699) of the *Flower Garland Scripture* by Śikṣānanda (652–710). Each scroll, consisting of thirty white papers joined together, is fourteen meters long and twenty-nine centimeters wide. In order to fit ten chapters into one scroll, each line consists of thirty-four instead of the usual seventeen logographs. The copyists used a number of new logographs current in Empress Wu's times. Written in *idu* transcription, the following is the postscript in fourteen lines that provides the dates, tells who made the vows to copy the scripture, and offers related rules and rites.

Postface to the *Flower Garland Scripture*

[Copied in 754–755]

The copying began on the first day of the eighth month of the thirteenth year, *kabo,* of T'ien-pao [23 August 754], and was completed on the fourteenth day of the second month of the following year, *ŭlmi* [30 March 755].

One who made a vow to copy the scripture is Dharma Master Yŏngi of Hwang-nyong Monastery. His purposes were to repay the love of his parents and to pray for all living beings in the dharma realm to attain the path of the Buddha.

The scripture is made as follows: First scented water is sprinkled around the roots of a paperbark mulberry tree to quicken its growth; the bark is then peeled and pounded to make paper with a clean surface. The copyists, the artisans who make the centerpiece of the scroll, and the painters who draw the images of buddhas and bodhisattvas all receive the bodhisattva ordination and observe abstinence. After relieving themselves, sleeping, eating, or drinking, they take a bath in scented water before returning to the work. Copyists are adorned with new, pure garments, loose trousers, a coarse crown, and a deva crown. Two azure-clad boys sprinkle water on their heads and azure-clad boys and musicians perform music. The processions to the copying site are headed by one who sprinkles scented water on their path, another who scatters flowers, a dharma master who carries a censer, and another dharma master who chants Buddhist verses. Each of the copyists carries incense and flowers and invokes the name of the Buddha as he progresses.

Upon reaching the site, all take refuge in the Three Jewels [the Buddha, the Dharma, and the Order], make three bows, and offer the *Flower Garland Scripture* and others to buddhas and bodhisattvas. Then they sit down and copy the scripture, make the centerpiece of the scroll, and paint the buddhas and bodhisattvas. In this manner, azure-clad boys and musicians cleanse everything before a piece of relic is placed in the center.

Now I make a vow that the copied scripture will not break till the end of the future—even when a major chilicosm is destroyed by the three calamities, this scripture shall be as intact as the void. If all living beings rely on this scripture, they shall witness the Buddha, listen to his dharma, worship the relic, aspire to enlightenment without backsliding, cultivate the vows of the Universally Worthy Bodhisattva, and achieve Buddhahood. [*The names of nineteen persons follow: a papermaker, eleven copyists, two makers of the centerpiece, four painters, and the writer of the scripture's title.*]   PL

CHAPTER SIX

Poetry and Song

Even in ancient times, poetry and music played an important part in the daily lives of the Korean people. This love for song and dance impressed the ancient Chinese, as is attested by their early records. Little of the earliest flowering of Korean poetry has survived, however, owing to the unreliability of oral transmission and the lack of a unified writing system.

Broadly speaking, the word *hyangga* designates Korean songs as opposed to Chinese poetry *(si)*, but the term specifically covers twenty-five extant poems produced from the seventh to the tenth centuries. (A collection of *hyangga* compiled by the monk Taegu during the reign of Queen Chinsŏng [887–897] is now lost.) In the absence of a native system of writing, the Koreans devised the *idu* system to provide particles and inflections for Chinese texts. In the *hyangga*, however, the *hyangch'al* system is used to transcribe entire Korean sentences with Chinese logographs. Some graphs were used for their meaning (nouns); others transcribed verbs, particles, and inflections. While the *idu* is said to have been systematized by Sŏl Ch'ong, the creator of the *hyangch'al* system is not known.

The songs and music of the Three Kingdoms were closely allied to the religious life of people living in clan-tribal societies. Both songs and music were essential to such rites as the Puyŏ, Koguryŏ, and East Ye worship of Heaven or during the sowing and harvest festivals in the south. Earlier songs, originating in shamanist chants, were sung during festivals and rites; they were transmitted orally and had a magic function. Later songs were more lyrical.

Seventeen of the twenty-five *hyangga* are Buddhist in inspiration and content, reflecting certain trends in Silla and early Koryŏ Buddhism. Belief in the Pure Land of Maitreya and Amitāyus is reflected in "Prayer to Amitāyus," "Song of Tuṣita Heaven" (760), and "Requiem"; belief in the Sound-Observer is reflected in "Hymn to the Thousand-Eyed Sound-Observer."

The selections also include poems in praise of Silla's elite corps of knights, the *hwarang*; poems thought to have magical powers: and poems on the temporality of man. The "Song of Ch'ŏyong," of shamanist origin, is perhaps the most popular of all *hyangga*. That the dragon, and the tutelary spirits of South Mountain, North Mountain, and the earth danced means that actors wearing such masks performed a shamanist exorcism. When the ruler was the chief shaman and bore the title *ch'ach'aung*, he was himself the officiator in the exorcism. During his tour of inspection, King Hŏngang perhaps saw performances of a popular dance preserved at Kaeunp'o and revived it; his purpose was to beseech the gods to quell the popular uprisings besetting his kingdom. The evil spirit that transformed itself into a man is symbolic of the corruption that destroyed the fabric of Silla society. Although the last two lines seem to indicate that the song accompanied a dramatic dance with two actors representing good and evil, the Ch'ŏyong dance performed at the temporary capital on Kanghwa Island during the Mongol invasion (1236) appears to be a solo dance. During the Chosŏn dynasty, the Ch'ŏyong dance, combined with the crane dance, became an important court pageant.   PL

Master Ch'ungdam: "Statesmanship" and "Ode to the Knight Kip'a"

[From *Samguk yusa* 2:79–81]

In the twenty-fourth year [765] of King Kyŏngdŏk, the gods of the five sacred mountains and three other mountains appeared from time to time and attended the king.

On the third day of the third month [28 March 765], the king mounted the tower in Kwijŏng Gate and asked his subjects to bring him an imposing monk. Just then an eminent monk was loitering on the road and was brought before the king. "He is not the one," the king said, and let him go. Another monk, dressed in a cassock, then came from the south carrying a tube of cherry wood on his back. Pleased, the king received him in the tower and looked into his tube, which contained utensils for the brewing of tea.

"What is your name?" asked the king.

"I am called Ch'ungdam."

"Where have you come from?" asked the king.

"It is my practice to offer tea to the World-Honored Maitreya at Samhwa Peak on Mount South on the third day of the third month and the ninth day of the ninth month. I am on my way from there now."

"Will you brew a cup of tea for me?" asked the king. Ch'ungdam offered a cup, which the king found to have an uncommon flavor and a rich bouquet.

"I have heard that your eulogy of the knight Kip'a has a noble intent. Is this true?" asked the king.

"Yes," replied the monk.

"Then compose a song of statesmanship."

The king praised Ch'ungdam's song and made him a royal preceptor, but the monk bowed twice and declined firmly. The song of statesmanship goes:

> *The king is father,*
> *And his ministers are loving mothers.*
> *His subjects are foolish children;*
> *They only receive what love brings.*
>
> *Schooled in saving the masses,*
> *The king feeds and guides them.*
> *Then no one will desert this land—*
> *This is the way to govern a country.*
>
> *Peace and prosperity will prevail if each—*
> *King, minister, and subject—lives as he should.*

His "Ode to the Knight Kip'a" goes:

> *The moon that pushes her way*
> *Through the thickets of clouds,*
> *Is she not pursuing*
> *The white clouds?*

The knight Kip'a once stood by the water,
Reflecting his face in the blue.
Henceforth I shall seek and gather
Among pebbles the depth of his mind.

Knight, you are the towering pine
That scorns frost, ignores snow.   PL

Master Wŏlmyŏng: "Song of Tuṣita Heaven" and "Requiem"

[From *Samguk yusa* 5:222–223]

On the first day of the fourth month of the nineteenth year, *kyŏngja*, of King Kyŏngdŏk [20 April 760], two suns appeared in the sky and remained for ten days. The astrologer recommended, "Please invite a monk destined by karma to compose a song on the merit of scattering flowers." Thereupon an altar was erected at Chowŏn Hall, and the king went to Ch'ŏngyang Tower to await the coming of a monk. Just then Master Wŏlmyŏng came walking southward on the levee path. The king had a messenger bring the monk to him, and asked him to compose a song and prepare the platform. The master replied, "As a member of the *hwarang*, I know vernacular songs, but not Sanskrit verses." The king said, "Since you are the chosen one, compose the song in the vernacular."

Thereupon the master composed the "Song of Tuṣita Heaven":

O flowers strewn today
With a song. Since you attend
My honest mind's command,
You serve Maitreya!

The transcription reads, "On the Dragon Tower I sing a song of scattering flowers and send a petal to the blue cloud. In place of my sincere wish, go and welcome the Great Sage in the Tuṣita Heaven." People wrongly call it the "Song of Scattering Flowers" instead of the "Song of Tuṣita Heaven."

Earlier, Wŏlmyŏng had had an abstinence ceremony performed in memory of his sister. When a sudden gust of wind blew the paper money away to the south, he composed a song:

On the hard road of life and death
That is near our land,

You went, afraid,
Without words.

We know not where we go,
Leaves blown, scattered,
Though fallen from the same tree,
By the first winds of autumn.

Abide, Sister, perfect your ways,
Until we meet in the Pure Land.

　　　The master used to reside in Sach'ŏnwang Monastery and played the flute well. Once, when he was walking down the road past the gate in the moonlight playing his flute, the moon stopped in its path. The road was thereupon named Wŏl-myŏng-ni, and Wŏlmyŏng's fame spread far and wide.　　　　PL

Ch'ŏyong: "Song of Ch'ŏyong"

[From *Samguk yusa* 2:88–89]

During the reign of the forty-ninth ruler of Silla, Hŏngang [875–886], homes with tile roofs stood in rows from the capital to the seas, with not a single thatched roof in sight. Music and song flowed in the streets day and night, and wind and rain came in due time throughout the seasons.

　　　One day, the king went on a pleasure trip to Kaeunp'o (now Ulchu), and on his way back he stopped to rest on the beach. It was daytime, but black clouds arose suddenly, a dense fog closed in, and his men could not find the way. Inquiries were made, and an astrologer answered that this was due to the anger of the dragon of the Eastern Sea, which could be appeased only by prayers. As soon as the king ordered a monastery built nearby for the dragon, the fog lifted. The place was therefore named Kaeunp'o [Cloud Opening Cove]. The dragon, pleased by the offering, appeared before the king with his seven sons, praised the king's virtues, and gave a musical performance. When the dragon returned to the sea, one of his sons did not accompany him but instead followed the king to the capital and helped him in state affairs. He called himself Ch'ŏyong. In order to keep him in the capital, the king gave him a beautiful woman for his wife and the title of *kŭpkan*. Seeing that she was beautiful, a demon of plague transformed himself into a man and attacked her in her room while Ch'ŏyong was away. But Ch'ŏyong returned and witnessed the scene. With calm he sang the following song and danced:

> *Having caroused far into the night*
> *In the moonlit capital,*
> *I return home and in my bed,*
> *Behold, four legs.*

> *Two were mine;*
> *Whose are the other two?*
> *Formerly two were mine;*
> *What shall be done now they are taken?*

When Ch'öyong was about to leave the scene, the demon appeared in his true from, knelt before him, and said, "I admired your wife and now I have committed a grave crime. But you were not angry, and I am moved by your magnanimity. Henceforth, when I see even the picture of your face, I promise that I will not enter the house." Because of this, people pasted likenesses of Ch'öyong on their gates to protect themselves from evil spirits and to welcome happy events.   PL

Great Master Kyunyŏ: Eleven Poems on the Ten Vows of the Universally Worthy Bodhisattva

[From *Kyunyŏ chŏn 7*, in *Korean Tripiṭaka* 47:260c–261b]

Great Master Kyunyŏ (b. 20 September 923; d. 19 July 973) was a learned monk-poet who singlehandedly revived the Flower Garland school in the tenth century. A voluminous commentator and a popularizer of Buddhism, he composed poems in the vernacular, taught them orally, and encouraged the congregation to chant and memorize them. (Some of his commentaries on Buddhist texts were also written in the vernacular before being translated into Chinese.) In his Chinese preface to the eleven devotional poems written in the *hyangch'al* system, Kyunyŏ explains his intention in using the vernacular:

> While the *sanoe* is a medium of popular entertainment, the practice of the vows is essential to the cultivation of the bodhisattva's practice. One must proceed therefore from the easy to the profound, from the near at hand to the distant. If one does not proceed according to the way of the world, one cannot lead men of inferior faculties. If one does not express

oneself in common language, one cannot make known the path of universal causation. Thus I begin from the easily comprehensible and the near at hand and then lead people to the more difficult and profound teachings of Buddhism. I have written eleven poems on the model of the ten great vows. The poems may appear disgraceful in the eyes of the people; yet they may tally with the wishes of the many buddhas. My intent may be lost and my words awry, and my poems may not conform to the wonderful teachings of our saints, but I wish to convey these teachings through poetry to plant wholesome roots among the living. Thus even those who memorize these poems laughingly may lay a basis for their salvation, and those who chant them abusingly may benefit from them. I beg to make it known that it is a matter of indifference to me whether posterity denounces or praises my poems.

Ch'oe Haenggwi, the translator of Kyunyŏ's poems into Chinese in 967, praises the great master in these words:

As the teacher of three thousand disciples, Kyunyŏ has an influence second only to that of Varaprabha [Wonderful Light]. As the master of eighty chapters of the *Flower Garland Scripture,* he was the head of his school and taught the masses to take refuge in the Three Jewels. As a great tree moistened by the rain of dharma, he benefited all living beings.

Worshiping and Honoring the Buddhas

> I bow today before the Buddha,
> Whom I draw with my mind's brush.
> O this body and mind of mine,
> Strive to reach the end of the dharma realm.

> He who is in every mote of dust;
> He who pervades every Buddha field;
> He who fills the realm of dharma—
> Would that I could serve him in the nine time periods.

> Ah, idle body, mouth, and mind—
> Approach him and be with him, unimpeded.

Rejoicing in the Merit of Others

> The truth of dependent origination tells me
> That illusion and enlightenment are one.

From the buddhas down to mortal men,
The other and myself are one.

Were I able to practice his virtues,
Were I able to master his ways,
I would rejoice in the merit of others;
I would rejoice in the good of others.

Ah, were I to follow in his footsteps,
How could the jealous mind be aroused?

Constant Harmony with the Living

Śākyamuni takes the deluded as roots.
With his vows of great mercy,
He waters the fields of the mind,
That they might not wither.

I, who am one of the living,
Would live and die with him,
And serve and respect the living
Single-mindedly, without pause.

Ah, the day we attain his peace,
He, too, will rejoice in our progress.

Transfer of Merit

Would that all my merit
Might be passed on to others,
I would like to awaken them—
Those wandering in the sea of suffering.

When we attain the vast realm of dharma,
Removed karmas are jewels in dharmahood;
Since aeons ago
Bodhisattvas, too, have devoted their merit to others.

Ah, he whom I worship and I are one,
Of one body and one mind.   PL

C H A P T E R   S E V E N

Local Clans and the Rise of the Meditation School

During the final years of Silla (780–935), the administration was tailored not to the state but to the True Bone aristocracy to prevent its disintegration and internal strife. The king's role shrank to that of protector of his own clan's power. When the bone rank system ceased to be functional, the True Bone class became divided, and powerful clans in the provinces rose to replace it. They built their economic base on international maritime trade or on the peasantry. In time, the course of history was determined by the composition and political character of such clans.

Silla Buddhism after the unification made great strides in the doctrinal studies pursued by Wŏnhyo, Ŭisang, and Wŏnch'ŭk. Wŏnhyo popularized Buddhism and spread it among the people. The more cultured circles, however, gradually distanced themselves from such studies. The Meditation school, with its emphasis on individual attainment of truth, was able to overcome both the ideological tendency of doctrinal schools and the superstitious Buddhism that resulted from the combination with native shamanism. By allying themselves with Meditation school adherents, provincial clans were able to oppose the central aristocracy.

Silla in its middle period was ruled by the direct descendants of King Muyŏl (654–661). By the time of King Kyŏngdŏk (742–765), the aristocracy had risen in revolt. To deal with the crisis, the king attempted to initiate a political reform, but without success. Under King Hyegong (765–780), revolts again broke out. Indeed, the king was assassinated by nobles who were his collateral relatives and who began to occupy the throne from the time of Sŏndŏk (780–785). One of the changes brought about by the aristocracy's revolt against the king's authoritarian rule was that the monarch no longer represented the aristocracy as a whole but only the group that installed him. With wealth of their own and private armies, members of the aristocracy now indulged in the struggle for power. Amidst this warring among the aristocracy and provincial rebellions, members of the sixth head rank groped for a solution. But lacking local support and an economic base, they could not emerge as leaders. Such roles were reserved for powerful local clans. Denied participation in politics, some local chiefs had turned to international trade, weakening the economic position of the central nobility. The typical example is Chang Pogo, who built a naval garrison of ten thousand men on Wan Island in 828 and controlled the Yellow Sea. Silla settlements (Silla bang), administered by Silla nationals, emerged on the Shantung peninsula and in the Kiangsu area. Chang also built the famous Dharma Blossom Cloister in Chih-shang village in Shantung as described in Ennin's Diary.

Other strong leaders, originally village chiefs, allied themselves with the peasantry and had the power to collect taxes and mobilize soldiers. Heavy taxation and famine also drove many to banditry, and chiefs such as Yanggil were powerful enough to develop their own administrations. The power base of Kungye, a subordinate of Yanggil, was built by bandits. Exploiting the anti-Silla sentiments in an area that had once belonged to Koguryŏ, he founded Later Koguryŏ (T'aebong) but was unable to stop the plunder or to envision a better social structure. Indeed, he indulged in atrocities. By dealing a blow to Silla, however, Kungye helped to prepare Wang Kŏn's emergence as the founder of the Koryŏ dynasty. In the area of Paekche, Kyŏnhwŏn rose to found Later Paekche. Kyŏnhwŏn was a peasant-soldier who united the military, local clans, and pirates. Although he showed some skill in administration and diplomacy, he lacked any vision of a new society. By making a display of military might, he alienated the people and was destroyed. But by breaking down Silla's social iniquity, he too prepared the way for Wang Kŏn.   PL

The Rise of Local Chiefs

Chang Pogo (d. 846) was a Korean adventurer and merchant prince whose name was once synonymous with the Korean maritime dominance in East

Asia in the early ninth century. Son of a fisherman from Wan Island off the southwestern coast of the Korean peninsula, Chang Pogo migrated to T'ang China as a youth, and there he advanced to the position of captain in Hsü-chou in the lower Huai River valley. Returning to Korea in 828, he alerted the throne to the danger of Chinese piracy in the Yellow Sea, whereupon the king appointed him commissioner of Ch'ŏnghaejin, the military head-quarters of Wan Island. There Chang raised a private navy, at times number-ing ten thousand men, by which he controlled the ocean commerce be-tween China, Korea, and Japan.

The ships engaged in this international trade were owned and manned by Chang, and Korean trading communities flourished along the southern coast of the Shantung peninsula and the lower reaches of the Huai. Some of these colonies, such as the famous Mount Ch'ih community overlooking the sea route between China and Korea, enjoyed extraterritorial privileges. These colonies often served as intermediaries between Chinese authorities and Japanese visitors; indeed, the Japanese pilgrim Ennin once addressed a letter to Chang asking for his assistance and shelter.

In 836, Chang was involved in a royal succession struggle. From the end of the eighth century on, the Silla court had been beset by contention between the rising aristocracy and the authoritarian monarchy based on the bone rank system. Hence a claim to the throne, hitherto determined solely by bloodline, came to require political skill and military might. Often a contender, to bolster his claim, had to ally himself with local chiefs who were disillusioned nobles depending for their power on private soldiers recruited from serfs and vagrants. In 839 the son of the former king's rival ascended the throne as Sinmu.

History relates that Chang's downfall can be traced to his efforts to marry his daughter to the king. The marriage alliance had probably been promised by Sinmu during his protracted sojourn on Wan Island, but because of his untimely death Chang sought to force Sinmu's son to abide by the pledge. Chang's attempt in 845 to force the throne to adopt his daughter as royal consort irritated the central aristocracy, who frowned upon such an alliance as unsavory and potentially dangerous. Chang's death by assassi-nation is traditionally placed in 846. In 851 Ch'ŏnghaejin was abolished as a military base. Thus ended the maritime kingdom of Chang Pogo and with it Silla's brief maritime dominance in East Asia. What follows is a brief account concerning Chang Pogo in the *Historical Record of the Three Kingdoms*.

Chang Pogo

[From *Samguk sagi* 44:416–417]

Chang Pogo (or Kungbok or Kungp'a) was a man of Silla whose clan site and ancestors were unknown. He fought a good battle. He went to T'ang, where he became *Wu-ning-chün hsiao-chiang,* and he was peerless in horsemanship and wielding a spear.

Upon his return to Silla, Chang had an audience with King Hŭngdŏk. To the king he reported, "Everywhere in China they use our people as slaves. I beg Your Majesty to build headquarters at Ch'ŏnghae to prevent pirates from kidnapping our people and shipping them west."

Ch'ŏnghae, now Wan Island, was a strategic point on Silla's sea routes. The king gave Chang an army of ten thousand men and bade him pitch camp on the island [828]. Thereafter Silla people were no longer enslaved on the high seas.   PL

ESTABLISHMENT OF THE MEDITATION SCHOOL

The introduction of the Meditation school (Sŏn in Korean; Ch'an in Chinese; Zen in Japanese) to Silla is traced to Pŏmnang (c. 632–646), who returned to Silla in the latter half of the seventh century after studying with the Fourth Patriarch Tao-hsin (580–651). He transmitted the gradual teaching of the Northern school to his pupil Sinhaeng (d. 779). Robert Buswell suggests that Pŏmnang may have been the author of the *Adamantine Absorption Scripture.* Musang (680–762), a Silla monk, made seminal contributions to the school in China.

The Life of Musang

[From *Li-tai fa-pao chi; T.* 51:184c–185a]

Said to be the third son of King Sŏngdŏk of Silla, Musang went to T'ang China in 728. There he was received by Emperor Hsüan-tsung and played an active part in the development of the Meditation school. In the area of Ch'eng-tu he practiced the meditation of Ch'u-chi (648–734), a disciple of Chih-shen (609–702), and became an abbot of Ching-chung Monastery. Musang was known for meditating on the name of Buddha and for his ascetic practices. He built a number of meditation centers and supervised the construction of Ta-sheng-tzu Monastery in Ch'eng-tu by order of Emperor Hsüan-tsung. Musang became the monastery's abbot upon its completion. His disciples include Wu-chu (714–774) and Ma-tsu (709–788). The biographical account presented here comes from *Record of the Dharma Jewel in Successive Generations.*

The secular surname of Dhyāna Master Musang of Ching-ch'üan Monastery in Ch'eng-tu, Chien-nan, was Kim; he was of the royal family. For generations his family lived in Korea. While he was still in his native country, his young sister, upon hearing that she was about to be given in marriage, cut her own face and vowed to become a nun. Upon seeing this, Musang said, "A woman is gentle and weak, but she has such a lofty determination. How can a man who is robust and strong be without aspiration?" At last he had his hair shaved and bade his parents farewell.

He sailed west and reached T'ang China. There, in order to search for a teacher and seek the Path, he made a tour of the country. He arrived at Te-shun Monastery in Tzu-chou and sought to pay his respects to Master T'ang [Ch'u-chi]. The master was ill, however, and would not see Musang. Then Musang let his finger burn as a lamp and offered it to the master. Perceiving that Musang was an extraordinary person, the master allowed him to remain for two years. Then Musang lived on Mount T'ien-ku. Master T'ang sent one of his followers, Wang Huang, and secretly transmitted his cassock to Musang. "This robe was transmitted from the patriarch Bodhidharma; Empress Wu bestowed it on Master Chih-shen, who transmitted it to me. Today I entrust it to you." Thus Musang received the dharma succession and the robe. . . .

In the twelfth and first month of every year, Musang, together with millions of mendicant monks and nuns, lay brothers and sisters, set up the Platform of the Path and preached the dharma from the pulpit. "First, softly invoke the name of the Buddha. With all your breath meditate on the Buddha. Then stop the voice and stop thinking," he taught them. "The absence of memory, the absence of thought, and the absence of delusion: the first is *śīla* [morality]; the second, *samādhi* [concentration]; and the third, *prajñā* [wisdom]. These three phrases furnish absolute control over good and evil passions and influences." Musang said again: "With the absence of thought, the mind is like a bright mirror that reflects all phenomena. The rise of thought is like the back of a mirror that cannot reflect anything."

He also said, "To know clearly birth and death—and to know them without interruption—is to see the Buddha. It is like a story of two men who went together to another country. Their father sent them a letter with instructions. One son obtained the letter, finished it, and followed his father's teachings without breaking the discipline. Another did the same, but he went against his father's teachings and committed many evil deeds. All living beings are like this. One who relies on the absence of thought is like an obedient son. One who is set on words is like a disobedient son. To use another parable, when one man was drunk and lying about, his mother went and called him, 'Let's go home.' But the drunken son was bewildered and railed against his own mother. Likewise, all living beings, drunk with ignorance, do not believe that by looking into their own nature they can become buddhas."

PL

The Life of Toŭi

[From *Tsu-t'ang chi* 17:106b–c]

Toŭi (d. 825) played an important role in transmitting the Meditation school to Silla. The *Collection from the Hall of Patriarchs (Tsu-t'ang chi)* quotes the inscription on the monument erected in his honor at Chinjŏn Monastery, but the monument itself has been lost. Toŭi went to T'ang in 784 and received the doctrinal transmission from Chih-tsang (735–814) at K'ai-yüan Monastery in Hung-chou, Kiangsi. Then he sought Huai-hai (720–814) and returned home in 821. Thus Chih-tsang, one of the main disciples of Ma-tsu (709–788), played a role in the transmission of the Meditation school to Silla.

Toŭi's return marked a turning point in Silla Buddhism. Indeed, the Meditation school that Toŭi transmitted shook the foundations of the Doctrinal school. As contemporary Silla Buddhism either emphasized study of the scriptures or espoused a superstitious form of Buddhism mixed with native shamanism, the Meditation school, which questioned the true existence of man, could not be tolerated. Toŭi's teaching was denounced as devilish or fantastic, and he had to withdraw to Chinjŏn Monastery on Snow Mountain in Yangyang.

A stream of Meditation monks returning from China gradually helped establish the teaching. They then built monasteries in the deep mountains, and the so-called Nine Mountains came into being. The spread of the Meditation school was facilitated by the assistance it received from provincial chiefs. Most founders of the nine schools were provincially located. (Their ancestors may have been of the central aristocracy, but in their own generation, they were members of the local gentry.) They encouraged the establishment of Meditation centers, usually near their power bases. The Sŏngjusan school was set up with the help of Kim Hŭn, for example, who owned a large manor near Poryŏng, South Ch'ungch'ŏng. Thus the Meditation school became the faith of the powerful clans. Because Meditation stressed practice based on intuition, it appeared to some members to promote a warrior-like spirit: the possibility of sudden enlightenment was revolutionary and hopeful. Meditation monks in turn realized their need for the clan's financial aid and other forms of help during their confrontation with the Doctrinal schools.

According to the *Record of Seven Generations in Korea (Haedong ch'il-tae rok)* quoted in the *Sŏnmun pojang nok* (1293), compiled by Ch'ŏnch'aek, Toŭi attempted to teach the "absence of thought and the absence of cultivation" and encouraged questions and answers that would lead to sudden awakening. Thus he adopted the tactics of the Southern school of Hung-chou and challenged the Flower Garland school, which represented the scholastic Buddhism of the day. The *Record of Seven Generations in Korea* is no longer extant, but it appears to have been a work on the Meditation school in Silla. Although Toŭi's exchange with Chief of Clerics Chiwŏn is an apologia stressing the superiority of the Meditation school over its rivals, it sheds light on the relationship between the Flower Garland school and the Meditation school at its beginning in Silla.

Dharma Master Wŏnjŏk of Chinjŏn Monastery on Snow Mountain [Sŏrak] was a successor to Chih-tsang [735–814]. He resided in Myŏngju. His taboo name was Toŭi, his clan name was Wang, and he was from Pukhan prefecture.

In the fifth year, *chia-tzu,* of Chien-chung [784], Toŭi accompanied the Silla envoys Han Ch'anho and Kim Yanggong to T'ang China. Straightaway he went to Mount T'ien-t'ai and received miraculous responses from Mañjuśrī. In the void the sacred bell echoed, and in the woods wondrous birds flitted about. He received full ordination at Pao-t'an Monastery in Kuang-fu. When, at Ts'ao-ch'i, he was about to pay his respects to the patriarch, the gate opened of itself. When he left the gate after worship, the gate closed of itself. Then he went to K'ai-yüan Monastery in Hung-chou, Kiangsi, to visit Great Master Chih-tsang and study under him. His doubts were dispelled, and all hindrances were dissolved. The master felt as if he had found jade among stones, a pearl among oysters. He said to himself, "I will sincerely transmit the dharma to him. Who else is there but him?" He then had his disciple's name changed to Toǔi. Thereupon, as an ascetic practitioner, Toǔi went to visit Master Huai-hai [720–814] on Mount Pai-chang.

Master Chih-tsang used to say, "The meditation schools in Kiangsi are carried on by Silla monks." The rest is as the inscription records.   *PL*

Toǔi: Questions and Answers with Chief of Clerics Chiwŏn

[From *Sŏnmun pojang nok* 2, in *Hsü Tsang-ching* 113:499a–b]

Chief of Clerics Chiwŏn asked National Preceptor Toǔi, "What other dharma realm is there besides the four dharma realms of the Flower Garland school? What other approach to dharma is there besides this progressive approach taught by fifty-five good friends? Except for the doctrine of this school, is there a separate path of meditation preached by the patriarch?"

Toǔi answered, "The four dharma realms you mention are the essence of the principle the school of patriarchs has brought up straightaway, and they dissolve like melting ice. Inside the fist of the True Principle the signs of the dharma realm cannot be found. One cannot see the signs of Mañjuśrī and Samantabhadra in the meditation of the patriarch's mind where originally there are no practice and wisdom. And the dharma gates of the fifty-five good friends are like foam on water. Such paths as the four forms of wisdom and enlightenment are like ore containing gold. Since it is mixed in indiscriminately, one cannot find it in the scriptural teachings. Therefore, when asked what is elucidated in the *Great Scripture Store [Tripiṭaka]*, Master Kuei-tsung of T'ang merely raised his fist."

Chiwŏn asked again, "What is the purpose, then, of the principle and practice of the Doctrinal school, such as faith, understanding, practice, and realization? And what fruit of Buddhahood can one attain thereby?"

Toǔi answered, "Without thought and without cultivation, we understand the principle and nature by faith, understanding, practice, and realization. When the patriarch showed the dharma, he said, 'Buddhas and living beings cannot obtain it; the true nature of the Path can only be manifested straightaway.' Hence, in addition to the five doctrines, there is another transmission of the dharma, namely the patriarch's mind-seal transmission. The reason for the manifestation of the forms of the buddhas is for those who have difficulty in understanding the patriarch's True Principle. This is an expedient device of manifesting the body. Even if you desire to realize the transmission of the mind seal by reading scriptures for many years, you would not be able to do so even after many cosmic ages have passed."

Chiwŏn rose, bowed, and said, "Until now, I had only heard the Buddha's ornate teachings. The Buddha's mind-seal method cannot be obtained by a sideways glance." He then respectfully gave himself to Toŭi and had an audience with him.

PL

The Life of Sunji

[From *Tsu-t'ang chi* 20:124a]

The Meditation school has prided itself on being a "separate transmission outside the scriptural teachings" that rejects philosophical treatments of Buddhism in favor of direct personal experience. For this reason, verbal descriptions of Meditation teachings and techniques were generally considered inferior to nonverbal explanations. Sunji's sets of circle-symbols were one such attempt to describe various aspects of Meditation ideology and practice without having recourse to verbalization. The use of circles as a teaching tool in the Meditation school seems to have begun with Nan-yang Hui-chung (d. 775), who transmitted a set of ninety-seven forms that apparently survived until Sunji's time but are no longer extant. Yang-shan Hui-chi (803–887), cofounder of the Kuei-yang school of Chinese Meditation and the teacher of Sunji, is said to have used circles and Chinese logographs in order to teach his students. Sunji's circle symbolism is apparently a further elaboration of these expedients, used commonly in the Kuei-yang school. Perhaps the best-known use of such circles is in the five rankings of Sunji's contemporary, Tung-shan Liang-chieh (807–869), cofounder of the Ts'ao-tung school. The explicit parallels between Flower Garland teachings and Sunji's explanations of the meanings of his circles—as well as his descriptions of the different levels of attainment of Buddhahood and his account of the reality limit that follow—exemplify the close associations between the doctrinal outlooks of the two schools, which are quite characteristic of Korean Buddhism. The following account is a narrative summary of the extensive presentation of Sunji's teachings found in the *Tsu-t'ang chi*.

The taboo name of the master of Sŏun Monastery on Mount Ogwan was Sunji. He was a disciple of Yang-shan Hui-chi of Mount Yang in Kiangsi. Sunji's secular name was Pak, and he was from the area of the Taedong River. He entered Mount Ogwan to have his head shaved and received the full prohibitions on Mount Songji.

Then, in the twelfth year of Ta-chung [858], Sunji made a vow to go to China and boarded a ship that was to take the Korean envoy to T'ang. During his voyage over myriad layers of billows, he was absorbed in meditation and never entertained any fear. Upon reaching the abode of Master Hui-chi, Sunji paid his respects to the master and expressed a wish to be his disciple. Laughing indulgently, Hui-chi said, "I wish this meeting could have taken place earlier. I already have something in view. Remain here." Sunji never left the master's side, and, like Yen Hui under Confucius or Mahākāśyapa in the presence of Śākyamuni, he consulted him about the mysteries of the school. Thus he won the esteem of his colleagues in meditation.

In the beginning of Ch'ien-fu [874–880], Queen Wŏnch'ang, the donor of Songak prefecture, and her son, Great King Wimu, gave alms to Yongŏm Monastery on Mount Ogwan, and Sunji went there to stay. Hence the name of the monastery was changed to Sŏun [Auspicious Cloud].   PL

Summary of Sunji's Teachings

[From *Tsu-t'ang chi* 20:124a–125b]

Eight Symbols in Four Sets to Explain the Noumenon [abridged]

Master Sunji developed a series of eight symbols in four sets to guide his students in their realization of the noumenon.

I. EMPTY CIRCLE: ◯

This is the sign of the absolute, "the nirvana which serves as a resort"; it is also called "the noumenal Buddha nature." Whether ordinary men or saints, all beings depend on this sign. Although the sign itself can never be differentiated, that is not to imply that delusion and enlightenment are the same; that is why there are ordinary men and saints. One who knows this sign is called a saint; one who is deluded in regards to it is called an ordinary person.

Once when the Buddhist patriarch Nāgārjuna was in southern India preaching the dharma, his body became like the orb of the moon. While the sound of his preaching could be heard from above where he had been sitting, no one could see his body. His disciple Āryadeva explained to the nonplussed congregation that this miracle was a way for his teacher to reveal the Buddha nature and show that the form of the signless absorption—the gate to enlightenment—was like the full moon. Before Āryadeva could finish his explanation, however, Nāgārjuna reappeared and spoke the following verse:

My body appeared in the form of a full moon,
In order to represent the essence of all the buddhas.
Preaching the dharma does not involve this form,
It is done through erudition, it is not sound.

If someone were to ask me about this sign of the full moon, I would answer him by adding the logograph for "ox" inside the circle.

II. OX INSIDE THE CIRCLE: ⊕

This sign is known as "ox eating the grass of endurance." It is also called the sign of "seeing the nature and attaining Buddhahood." A scripture says, "In the Himalayan Mountains there is a kind of grass, called 'endurance,' which, if eaten by an ox, produces ghee." It also says: "If a sentient being can hear and accept the teaching concerning the great extinction, he will see the Buddha nature." In this figure, the grass refers to the dharma; the ox to a person who has the capacity to awaken suddenly; and the ghee to Buddha. Hence just as an ox who eats this grass will give ghee, so too will a person who comprehends this dharma achieve full enlightenment.

Three Levels of the Attainment of Buddhahood

I. ATTAINMENT OF BUDDHAHOOD THROUGH REALIZATION OF THE NOUMENON

Through the words of a meditation master, one traces the light of the mind back to its source and discovers that the fountainhead of one's mind is fundamentally devoid of everything. This type of attainment of Buddhahood is not a realization brought about through the gradual cultivation of the bodhisattvas' myriads of subsidiary practices; this is why it is called "attainment of Buddhahood through realization of the noumenon." For this reason, a scripture says: "The initial arousal of the thought of enlightenment is the attainment of perfect enlighten-ment." As an ancient master also said: "The path to Buddhahood is not far off—it is nothing other than returning to the mind."

At this level of attainment, if it is said that the essential nature is completely devoid of even a single thing, this would imply that all three bodies of the Buddha—that is, one Buddha and two bodhisattvas—would have to be inherent therein. Here the Buddha Vairocana represents the noumenon; the Bodhisattva Mañjuśrī symbolizes wisdom; and the Bodhisattva Samantabhadra portrays prac-tice. Because these three all have the same essence, each of them must be present.

II. ATTAINMENT OF BUDDHAHOOD THROUGH COMPLETION OF THE INCUMBENT PRACTICES

After one has penetrated to the noumenon, one must then continue to cultivate the bodhisattva path in accordance with the practices and vows of Samantabhadra and to perfect both compassion and wisdom. That is why this level of attainment is called "attainment of Buddhahood through completion of the incumbent practices." An ancient master said that the place where you finally arrive in your practice is the same place from which you departed. Therefore, you should know that when your spiritual quest is completed, you return to your original place. This original spot is the noumenon. The noumenon that is realized at this level of attainment is no different from that achieved at the preceding level. Even though the noumenon is not separate from the practice, this second level of attainment involves a progression from cause (the cultivation of the path) to fruition (the attainment of Buddhahood), so it is given this name. Since this level involves the perfection of all the meritorious qualities inherent in the fruition of Buddhahood, it is achieved only through the practices of Samantabhadra.

This level of the attainment of Buddhahood also involves all three bodies of the Buddha. Because this level is concerned with the practices that result in the attainment of Buddhahood, the effort involved in bringing about this attainment is symbolized by Samantabhadra. It is for this reason that all of the bodhisattvas' myriads of subsidiary practices are referred to as "Samantabhadra." And because all the buddhas realize enlightenment through these myriads of practices, the ancients have said that Samantabhadra is the father of all the buddhas.

III. ATTAINMENT OF BUDDHAHOOD THROUGH MANIFESTING ONESELF IN THE WORLD

After completing the prior two levels of the attainment of Buddhahood, then, for the benefit of all sentient beings, the adept displays the eight stages in the achievement of Buddhahood that take place during a bodhisattva's final life: descent from the Tuṣita Heaven; entering the womb; residing in the womb; birth; leaving the household life; attaining enlightenment; turning the wheel of the dharma; entering *parinirvāṇa*. These eight stages are actually illusory transformations; they do not really happen. That is why the scriptures say: "Incalculable aeons have elapsed since my attainment of Buddhahood." Hence we know that, innumerable aeons in the past, Śākyamuni the Thus Come One had already achieved the full enlightenment that is brought about through the completion of the bodhisattva practices; yet, for the benefit of all sentient beings, he displayed this event of his initial attainment of Buddhahood.

A perusal of the scriptural teachings or an examination of the records of ancient Meditation masters will show that any person's attainment of Buddhahood always involves all three of these levels. All buddhas, whether past or future, follow this same procedure, just as people traveling the same road all follow along in the same ruts.

Three Types of Attainment of the Reality Limit[1]

I. SUDDEN ATTAINMENT OF THE REALITY LIMIT

A sentient being who, since time immemorial, has yet to awaken to the land of his self-nature continues to wander on in the three realms, receiving retribution according to conditions. If he suddenly meets a wise man who explains for him the true teaching and he suddenly awakens to his nature, he then attains perfect enlightenment without needing to progress through gradual stages of practice. For this reason, this is called the "sudden attainment of the reality limit." Although anyone may hear the dharma, not everyone will attain enlightenment with equal speed. That is because people's faculties and characters vary in accordance with their different actions in previous lives. Hence although everyone may hear the same teaching, one's realization will not be identical to another's; it is not that there is any deficiency in the teachings that are preached by the wise.

This does not mean, however, that one should preach only to the wise and not to the dull. The wise are not originally enlightened; the dull are not internally deluded. Even though a sentient being whose faculties are dull hears the true teachings continuously, he will not come to understand his nature. But as soon as a sentient being whose faculties are keen hears those teachings, he will suddenly understand his nature and become wise. Hence there is no inherent difference between ordinary men and saints; there is merely a difference as to whether their faculties are sharp or dull. Whether one understands or not is entirely dependent upon one's faculties and character; it has nothing whatsoever to do with that dharma.

After a sentient being has heard this true teaching and has suddenly seen the land of the true nature, he must not remain complacent in that understanding. Rather, he must continue to practice both compassion and wisdom in order to bring benefit both to himself and to others. There are three aspects to this practice; each is correlated with the practices of Samantabhadra.

1. Bond-overcoming Samantabhadra: This is the practice after enlightenment. The adept must first free himself from the bonds of the habituations that continue to plague the person even after awakening to the mind. Thanks to his earlier enlightenment, however, the person is able to work on overcoming these habituations, while recognizing that they are ultimately illusory.

2. *Bond-entering Samantabhadra:* In this second stage of practice, the individual enters the world for the benefit of all sentient beings who have yet to be enlightened. Out of his great compassion, he attempts to save all beings from their suffering and bring them also to enlightenment. When both of these types of practice are consummated, it is called "equal enlightenment," the fifty-first stage of the path to Buddhahood, because both wisdom and compassion are completely perfected.

3. *After-fruition Samantabhadra:* This stage, in which all mental absorptions are cultivated, is the stage of "sublime enlightenment," the fifty-second and final stage of the bodhisattva path. Here a person clings neither to wisdom nor to compassion, and yet these appear spontaneously in all his actions. He does not remain fixed in any one status but appears at will in all situations in order to exhibit his great compassion for the benefit of all types of beings.

II. ATTAINMENT OF THE REALITY LIMIT THROUGH THE GRADUAL TEACHINGS

Since time immemorial, there might be a sentient being who has yet to awaken to the land of the nature and continues to wander on in samsara. He might hear the gradual teachings of the three vehicles and awaken to that dharma. Because of the calamities inherent in the three worlds, an adherent of one of these three vehicles might later come to hear the true teachings; his provisional understanding would then be transformed into sublime wisdom, and he would realize the reality limit. Hence this is called "attainment of the reality limit through the gradual teachings." For this reason, the ancients said that the three carts in front of the gate were the provisional vehicles, while the white ox in the open pasture was the reality limit.

Even though these two types of attainment are classified separately, they are not ultimately distinguishable. That is because, even though one may initially have fallen into the provisional understanding of the three vehicles, one need not remain forever bogged down in that understanding. Just as when hundreds of rivers return to the ocean they all lose their individual names, so it is when the three vehicles return to the one Buddha vehicle.

III. GRADUAL REALIZATION OF THE REALITY LIMIT

There might be a sentient being who, since time immemorial, has yet to awaken to the land of the nature and continues to wander on in samsara, receiving the incumbent karmic retribution. Suddenly, he may hear the gradual teachings of the three vehicles and gradually give rise to faith and understanding. Following all the stages of the bodhisattva path for three incalculable aeons, he endures that which is difficult to endure, practices that which is difficult to practice, and finally brings an end to his delusion and achieves merit. At that point he finally achieves the non-outflow wisdom and exposes the dharma body. Hence this is called "gradual realization of the reality limit."

Although this gradual attainment of the reality limit differs from the sudden approach discussed earlier, the two are ultimately identical—just as when rivers enter the sea, they all come to have the same taste of salt. As explained previously, after the sudden attainment of the reality limit one still performs all the incumbent practices of the bodhisattva—that is, the three types of Samantabhadra practice. One who follows the gradual attainment of the reality limit relies on the expedients of the gradual teachings and cultivates the bodhisattva practices over three incalculable aeons before he attains the non-outflow wisdom and displays the dharma body. After this gradual attainment, one's practice still is dependent upon the stages and levels of the path; hence it is not the same as the practices that follow the sudden attainment of the reality limit.   *RB*

GEOMANCY

The belief in geomancy was associated not only with Confucian and Taoist thought but also with Buddhism. In the period of transition from the end of Silla to the beginning of Koryŏ, geomancy became aligned with the revolutionary Meditation school; belief in prognostication lore and texts served as a force for change. Essentially, the divination of terrain was an effort to determine how local currents of the cosmic breath affected human fortunes. Based on the location of mountains, water, and direction, the awareness of terrestrial conformation prevalent in earlier times became the foundation for the rise of geomancy. As time passed, geomancy accepted the yin-yang and five elements theories and adopted the Buddhist notion that "wholesome root produces wholesome fruit"—it was thought that the erection of monasteries and stupas could alter the geomantic situation. At times, allied with prognostication texts, such ideas acquired a revolutionary character. Thus geomancy, already known in the Three Kingdoms period, gained force with the adoption of a Buddhism that embraced native beliefs.

At first, the application of geomancy was restricted to the ruling classes in the capital, who used it to enhance the ruler's authority or to choose sites for palaces and royal tombs. With the spread of the Meditation school to the provinces, however, it too was disseminated. Local clans who revolted against the central aristocracy used geomancy to rationalize the formation of their independent power. When the center of power moved from the aristocracy to provincial clan chiefs, these leaders singled out their power bases as centers of a new era. The area of Songak, for example, the base of Wang Kŏn, was known as an auspicious place worthy of being a capital. Although contenders for power did not leave records concerning their views on the subject, the phrase "an auspicious place of the Three Han," current among the Meditation centers, indicates that they too believed their bases to have been ideally chosen.   PL

Ch'oe Yuch'ŏng: Stele Inscription at Jade Dragon Monastery

[From *Tong munsŏn* 117:18b–22b; *Chōsen kinseki sōran* 1:560–561]

Tosŏn, the geomancer and Meditation master, systematized contemporary theories on the subject, helping to lead popular sentiment away from Kyŏngju to the provinces. The shift of influence from Kyŏngju in the southeast to the middle of the peninsula was advantageous to Wang Kŏn, who rose from the Songak area to unify the Later Three Kingdoms. Most historical materials on Tosŏn date from later times, but a comparatively reliable one is the inscription (1150) by Ch'oe Yuch'ŏng on a monument at Ongnyong (Jade Dragon) Monastery. The monument no longer stands, but the inscription is preserved in the *Tong munsŏn*. It consists of three parts: Tosŏn as a Meditation monk; the relationship between Tosŏn and geomantic thought; and the relations between Tosŏn and Wang Kŏn.

The master's taboo name was Tosŏn. His secular surname was Kim; he was a man of Yŏngam in Silla. The genealogy of his father and grandfather have faded from the record; some say that he was an illegitimate descendant of Great King T'aejong [654–661]. His mother, born Kang, dreamed that someone gave her a beautiful pearl and had her swallow it. Accordingly she became pregnant and for a full month abstained from strong-smelling vegetables and rank meats, devoting herself entirely to chanting the Buddha's name with scriptures in hand. When in due course she suckled and cared for the infant, he was incomparably superior to ordinary children. Even while laughing or crying as a babe in arms, his intention seemed to be to express his reverence and awe for the Buddha's vehicle. His mother and father, knowing that he was certain to become an instrument of the dharma, in their hearts assented to his leaving home. Versatile and precocious, he combined understanding with practice. Having had his hair shaved, he proceeded to Hwaŏm Monastery on Wŏryu Mountain where he read and practiced the scriptures of the Great Vehicle, penetrating the Great Meaning before a month had passed. The ineffable wisdom of Mañjuśrī and the mystic gate of Samantabhadra entered his mind [with nothing left over]. Students by the hundreds and thousands all submitted in astonishment, considering him divinely intelligent. In the eighth year of King Munsŏng [846], at the age of twenty, he bethought himself: "A real man should be able to achieve tranquillity by himself apart from the dharma. How can he do this while holding steadfastly to the letter of the dharma?" At that time Great Master Hyech'ŏl transmitted the secret seal to Sŏdang, Meditation Master Chijang, and opened a hall on Tongni Mountain. Many who were wandering in search of something better gravitated to him. And so Master Tosŏn lifted his robe at the dharma gate and asked to be accepted as a disciple. Great Preceptor Hyech'ŏl commended him for his intelligence and sagacity and welcomed him with utmost sincerity. All of what has been termed the unsaid saying and the dharmaless dharma was handed on to him as in the void, and in a vast serenity he achieved transcendent realization.

On White Chicken Mountain in Hŭiyang county there is an ancient monastery called Jade Dragon. Stopping here after having wandered all around, the master loved the secluded beauty of the place and proceeded to repair and refurbish the halls. Then, with a start, he made a resolve to spend the rest of his days there. And indeed he sat quietly, forgetting to speak, for thirty-five years. At that time, students from all the four quarters converged upon him like clouds and adhered to him like shadows. Holding their towels and basins and presenting their staffs and sandals, those who became his disciples numbered several hundreds. Just as a single rain enriches all things however varied their motive power, so he with a piercing look made divine bestowals of enlightenment, and they who had gone to him empty went back filled up. King Hŏngang [875–885], out of respect for his lofty virtue, sent an emissary to extend welcome to him. At one meeting with him the king greatly rejoiced and kept him within the forbidden precincts, where he frequently opened and roused the king's heart with his mystic words and subtle discourse. But before long he took no delight in the royal amenities of the capital and earnestly requested that he might return to his home monastery.

Suddenly one day he summoned his disciples and said, "I am about to go. It was riding upon my conditioning that I came, and now that the condition has exhausted itself I shall depart. Why should you afflict yourselves with sorrow?" Having finished speaking, he lapsed into quiescence while seated in the lotus position. It was the tenth day of the third month of the first year of Kuang-hua of Great T'ang [898], the years of his life numbering seventy-two.

Earlier, before the master had divined for the site of Ongnyong Monastery, he had set up a hut and stopped for rest on Bowl Hill of Chiri Mountain. One day a strange man paid a visit to his meditation seat and reported to the master, saying, "For several hundred years I the disciple have lodged in obscurity beyond the phenomenal world. I am in predestined possession of a minor art, which I can proffer to you. If the venerable master will not look down upon my humble technique, I shall one day on the sandy seashore have something to confer upon him. This too is a method whereby the great bodhisattvas rescue the world and save all men." Then suddenly he disappeared. The master marveled at this. Later he went to the place agreed upon and indeed he met that very man. Bringing sand together to form configurations of harmony and antagonism, the man showed this; and when Tosŏn turned his head around to look, the man was no longer there. That place was in what is now Kurye county, which the local people call Sand Chart village. Thereafter the master, with a breakthrough of understanding, polished more than ever this knowledge of yin and yang and the five-phases techniques: occult secrets, however recondite, of golden tabernacle or jade cask were all as if imprinted in his heart.

Later on, the doctrine of Silla's rule gradually declined and there would soon be a sage who would receive the mandate and rise to preeminence. Accordingly, he made several trips to Songak prefecture. At that time our epochal progenitor Wang Yung was in the commandery building his residential villa. The master, passing his gate, said: "This place is fated to produce a king. But I'm not yet acquainted with the one who will initiate the process." It happened that an azure-clad servant boy heard this and went in to inform the epochal progenitor; the latter immediately ordered him to go out and welcome the master, who entered and conferred about the epochal progenitor's plans, making some changes in them. The master then said, "After two years you are certain to beget a noble son." Thereupon he wrote one roll of text and sealed it securely. Presenting it to the epochal progenitor, he said: "This writing is to be proffered to the yet unborn lord. But you should present it to him only after the years have brought him to stalwart manhood." In this year Silla's king Hŏngang ascended the throne; it was the second year of Ch'ien-fu of the T'ang [874]. In the fourth year [877] our grand progenitor T'aejo was born in the earlier villa. Upon reaching manhood he obtained the writing and perused it, whereupon he knew that Heaven's mandate had found in him its lodgement. He proceeded to exterminate the bandit rabble and undertook the creation of his realm. Respectfully mindful as he was of the spirits and the sages, how could it be that he ever had his mind set on conquering the world? As for the means whereby he eliminated chaos and turned the world back to rectitude, uplifting the people and prospering the region—granted that he restored the situation in which Heaven supported the virtuous and the people were embraced in humaneness—nonetheless, it was in the Source of Transformation that he inaugurated the holy era, and it was in Fate's hidden numbers that he fixed the fulfillment of his destiny. All these achievements have their origin in our master's instigation. One may indeed say that the preeminence and glory of his accomplishments were indeed as fully attested as this. It is only right that he be praised and posthumously exalted.

Many of the yin-yang theories the master transmitted in his writings are current in the world, and those who have later spoken about the principles of earth consider him to be their exemplar.   *MR*

PART TWO

Koryŏ

INTRODUCTION

The Koryŏ kingdom (918–1392) developed out of the ruins of Silla. The process was slow, taking more than a decade and a half and ending in 936, when Koryŏ destroyed Later Paekche. Having accepted the formal surrender of the last Silla king the previous year, the dynastic founder, Wang Kŏn, established a state that lasted for nearly five hundred years before being succeeded by the Chosŏn kingdom (1392–1910). As the vital link between Silla and Chosŏn, Koryŏ inherited Silla's legitimacy and traditions and enriched this heritage before yielding the mandate of rule to Chosŏn.

Koryŏ history commonly is divided into three periods: aristocratic rule (918–1170), military rule (1170–1270), and Mongol domination (1270–1392). This division appropriately shows the changes in leadership and power. In this volume, however, Koryŏ is divided in half at the year 1170, the start of the military period. Certain themes appearing in the first half of the dynasty set the stage for subsequent development in the latter half. This periodization shows the inner coherence of Koryŏ while still making clear the differences that arose from the dramatic change in leadership and power structure that occurred in 1170.

During its first century, Koryŏ went through an intense period of development into a state. When Silla collapsed under mounting internal pressures, disintegration and chaos quickly set in, affording upstart regional figures opportunities to split Korea into rebel strongholds. Wang Kŏn emerged as a powerful general under Kim Kungye in T'aebong in central Korea. In 918, he founded Koryŏ, overthrowing Kungye. Seventeen years later, the last Silla king formally acknowledged Wang Kŏn's hegemony by recognizing the new dynasty and peacefully transferring power to it. In 936, after militarily destroying the internally torn Later Paekche, Wang Kŏn became the unchallenged authority in the Korean peninsula.

Yet Koryŏ owed much to Silla. In Silla, birth determined one's social and political functions. Koryŏ was never able to escape totally from this rigid order, as the architects of Koryŏ were themselves mostly men from Silla aristocratic clans and some of the great clans would continue to dictate Koryŏ politics until the kingdom's collapse in the fourteenth century. Silla's religious beliefs also influenced Koryŏ thought. Buddhism, which had matured during the Silla period, continued to dominate Koryŏ society. The Buddhist hierarchy grew rich through its links with the court and great clans and influenced the life and thought of the kingdom. Indigenous shamanism merged with Buddhist beliefs as well as Taoism and folk cults, leaving indelible marks, particularly in the popular culture.

Chinese culture also contributed to Koryŏ's development. As Koryŏ's early kings searched for an effective system of government, they naturally turned to China's rich and varied experience and borrowed liberally from Chinese political thought and institutions, eventually affording Koryŏ a sophisticated system of administration. Koreans also adopted the Chinese system of official recruitment, which relied in good part on a state examination on skill in literary Chinese and the Confucian classics. The state examination became an important means to select civil officials of varied backgrounds, who in the latter half of the dynasty became an active check on the entrenched power of the aristocratic establishment.

Early Koryŏ, compared to Silla, was a much more mobile society and had a greater resemblance to China both intellectually and politically. Koryŏ kings were generally well versed in Confucian thought while also devoted to Buddhism. Through its international contacts and internal maturity, Koryŏ achieved a level of sophistication that put it on a par with China, setting high standards in literature and art that became the envy of its world. Literary and artistic works of eleventh-century Koryŏ won the admiration of Chinese intellectuals for their refined style and erudition, for example, and the celadon produced in Koryŏ kilns has never been equaled to this day. Early Koryŏ was a prosperous society that offered a degree of stability for both the rulers and the ruled.

Koryŏ was not, however, immune to foreign attack. Khitan and Jürchen tribes living to the north harassed Koryŏ from the start. The Khitan invaded Koryŏ on three separate occasions between 993 and 1018, forcing one Koryŏ king to flee his capital. When later challenged by the Jürchen, Koryŏ responded by building a long wall across its northern territory. But even with such fortifications, relations with the northern tribes remained tense and perilous. Through preemptive attacks and diplomatic appeasement, Koryŏ was able to keep frequently belligerent neighbors in the north in check until the massive onslaught of the Mongols in the thirteenth century.

The mid-twelfth century, which brought Koryŏ to the peak of its prosperity, also saw the dynasty in crisis. First, members of one of the kingdom's great clans, the Yi of Kyŏngwŏn, tried unsuccessfully to take control of the government. Less than a decade later, in 1135, a monk named Myoch'ŏng dared to challenge the power of the aristocratic establishment and even tried to establish a new dynasty with its capital at the site of modern P'yŏngyang. On both occasions the aristocratic elite establishment, calling on military officers, defeated these attempts, but the rebellions indicated growing political and societal unrest and tensions. In 1170 a group of disgruntled military officers who had been ostracized by members of the civilian elite revolted, enthroned a new king, and purged a large number of civilian aristocrats. The revolt commenced a century of military rule, as generals became the key figures in determining state policy.

In the middle of the military period a new danger threatened the dynasty: the Mongol invasions. By 1258, after nearly thirty years of resistance, the military ruler fell and a new civilian leadership ready to sue for peace emerged. The Mongols answered by imposing a number of mechanisms of control upon Koryŏ. But with the eventual defeat of Yüan in China by the new Ming dynasty in 1368, Mongol domination over Koryŏ weakened. The end of the Mongols and the end of Koryŏ came nearly at the same time, as Neo-Confucian reformers, under the leadership of General Yi Sŏnggye, took control, instituting reforms and finally establishing the Chosŏn kingdom in 1392.

Despite the changes in its leadership, first with military rule and then with Mongol domination, Koryŏ remained a fairly stable, well-organized society. Although the literati officials had a more limited role in determining state policy in the latter half of the dynasty, the esteem for scholarship was undiminished. Much of Koryŏ's extant literature comes from the twelfth, thirteenth, and fourteenth centuries. The state examination, which had always been important, was maintained and even invigorated in the early fourteenth century. There is also evidence to suggest increased social mobility in late Koryŏ times. Nevertheless, great clans continued to dominate late Koryŏ life much as they had earlier.

Although Buddhism remained the spiritual anchor of the kingdom, its thrust changed significantly. The Meditation school, which had spread in the closing days of the Silla kingdom, predominated in late Koryŏ society. With lavish donations and patronage from Koryŏ's leading families, meditation monasteries dotted the countryside. But this school was not the property of the elite alone. Because of its simple message, calling for meditation and relying on sudden enlightenment, the poor peasant and struggling merchant also found it a source of inspiration.

Koryŏ, lodged between Silla and Chosŏn, is often overlooked in Korea's historical development. This is unfortunate because Koryŏ's legacy to contemporary Korea is impressive. Through the introduction of the civil service examination, it established merit as a criterion for government service. With its elaborate state apparatus, Koryŏ institutionalized government and made decisions in a rational manner. In Koryŏ, Buddhism expanded to become not only a religion of the aristocrats but a spiritual foundation for the entire society. In Koryŏ, as Koreans defended their land against invading troops, first from the north and then from Japanese pirates in the south, a sense and spirit of a people with a common heritage grew, heightening national consciousness. Koryŏ also produced priceless artistic and literary masterpieces. It was during the Koryŏ kingdom that the Western world first learned of Korea and began using the name Koryŏ for the country.

C H A P T E R   E I G H T

Early Koryŏ Political Structure

This chapter focuses on Koryŏ's political development through the early twelfth century, especially on the political foundations of the dynasty. King T'aejo (918–943) relied on both indigenous institutions and borrowed systems from China as he cautiously formed his new government. This structure was further strengthened by reforms launched by his successors, Kwangjong (949–975) and Sŏngjong (981–997) in particular. It was in the latter reign that Koryŏ's state organization clearly emerged through the efforts of Confucianized officials such as Ch'oe Sŭngno (927–989). Reform-minded officials like Ch'oe urged the implementation of Confucian practices that stressed proper moral conduct while trying to curtail Buddhist practices considered corrupting influences. Throughout the eleventh century, the political institutions were further refined as Koryŏ modified the dynastic structure through the successful transplantation of major Sung organizational forms.

While working on internal political stability, the dynasty also endeavored to normalize ties with the continental powers in the north. In response to shifting power, as first the Sung and then the Liao and Chin states emerged in succession, Koryŏ pursued a realistic foreign policy that sought a peaceful settlement of disputes through diplomacy while not shirking from military confrontation when necessary. The northern orientation thus set remained the basic direction of foreign relations for the rest of the Koryŏ period.

Founding of the Later Three Kingdoms

Before Wang Kŏn (877–943) founded the Koryŏ dynasty in 918, two leading rebel contenders, Yi Kyŏnhwŏn (d. 936) and Kim Kungye (d. 918) vied with one another for hegemony while at the same time posing a serious threat to Silla's sovereign power in the peninsula. Yi Kyŏnhwŏn's social background, judging from his surname as well as his father's rise to general (changgun), indicates that he was probably of Head Rank Six lineage in the Silla aristocracy. He himself rose to be a valiant warrior while assigned to Silla's southwestern coastal defense, at a time when its offshore waters served as important sea lanes for the thriving triangular maritime trade in East Asia.

Taking advantage of Silla's enfeebled state, Kyŏnhwŏn rebelled in 892, and, evoking memories of Paekche's glorious past, proclaimed himself king of Later Paekche in 900. His power rapidly expanded to the rich farmlands and lucrative coastal lanes of old Paekche and beyond. Engaging Kim Kungye and subsequently Wang Kŏn in numerous battles, he proved himself a formidable foe. Furthermore, alone among the rebel leaders of the Later Three Kingdoms he dared to raid the Silla capital itself and return triumphantly after having installed a new king on the Silla throne. As a result, however, of internal family strife over the selection of his own successor, he had to flee to Wang Kŏn's camp and tragically, in the last battle against Later Paekche, found himself assisting Wang Kŏn in the destruction of his own once-mighty army.

Kim Kungye was a rejected scion of the Silla royal family, whose belated discovery of his abandonment at birth led him to seek a monastic life in a Buddhist temple. But being a restless youth, he later broke his vows and joined a rebel band when Silla's power disintegrated, rising quickly to become a prominent rebel leader in former Koguryŏ's southernmost frontier. Wang Kŏn's father, then a local chieftain in the area of present Kaesŏng, close to Silla's northwestern defense command, joined Kungye's camp, opening a door for Wang Kŏn's subsequent career under Kungye.

Harboring a bitter hatred against the Silla court that had so cruelly rejected him, Kungye openly vowed to destroy Silla. His relentless anti-Silla policy, while alienating many Silla aristocrats in his camp, set in motion the forces that would end Silla's bone rank order. The passage below is noteworthy not only for its vivid description of Kungye's moral bankruptcy but also for its justification of the coup against Kungye by his lieutenant, not (so he said) out of a desire for power but out of his professed commitment to a higher principle, namely the carrying out of a needed change according to the Mandate of Heaven.

All three rebel leaders of the Later Three Kingdoms period hoisted the banners of their independence in former Paekche and Koguryŏ territories. To rally support behind them, they exploited, with apparent success, the residual anti-Silla sentiment in these areas by invoking memories of long-vanquished kingdoms. That such sentiments could be exploited some two and a half centuries after the first attempt at unified rule in the peninsula is suggestive of a less than complete success in that original endeavor. Perhaps even more revealing is the fact that those who exploited it were persons with no known Paekche or Koguryŏ lineage in their background.

Yi Kyŏnhwŏn

[*Samguk sagi* 50:454–461]

The following passage dealing with the last days of Kyŏnhwŏn and the triumph of Wang Kŏn (T'aejo in this account), is illustrative of the pseudo-Confucian rhetoric by which claimants to power justified their actions.

Kyŏnhwŏn married many women who bore him more than ten sons. As his fourth son, Kŭmgang, was tall and quite intelligent, Kyŏnhwŏn treated him with special fondness and wanted to have him succeed as king. His older brothers, Singŏm, Yanggŏm, and Yonggŏm, knew of this and were greatly distressed over this prospect. At that time Yanggŏm was governor-general [*todok*] of Kangju, Yonggŏm was the governor-general of Muju, and Singŏm alone was at Kyŏnhwŏn's side. *Ich'an* Nŭnghwan sent men to Kangju and Muju to plot with Yanggŏm and others. In spring, the third month of the second year of Ch'ing-t'ai [935], *P'ajinch'an* Sindŏk, Yŏngsun, and others urged Singŏm to imprison Kyŏnhwŏn at Kŭmsan temple and also sent a man to kill Kŭmgang. Singŏm proclaimed himself great king and granted a general amnesty in Later Paekche. He also issued a royal message that said

> As no one can change the Mandate of Heaven, the throne always belongs to its destined occupant. I humbly think no one has surpassed the great king [Kyŏnhwŏn] in terms of his extraordinary martial skill and his excellence in strategy. Born in an age of decline, he took as his responsibility the management of the state. Going around the land of the Three Hans, he has revived Paekche. The people gathered to him, living in peace as he

eliminated their miseries. Stirred up as if by a storm or lightning, people came to him from places near and far, competing to submit. [Yet] With his regal efforts nearly complete, his prudence suddenly got misdirected as he gave way to love for a small boy [Kŭmgang]. It is fortunate that the Heavenly Ruler looked down with compassion and had the king correct his mistake and command me, the crown prince, to govern the state. Since I consider myself unfit to be crown prince, how should I have the wisdom to be king?[1] I feel as if I am treading cautiously and fearfully on thin ice over a deep pond. To repay this blessing of my being jumped over the proper order, I must now demonstrate a revitalization of the government by proclaiming a general amnesty throughout the country. From before dawn on the seventeenth day of the tenth month of the second year of Ch'ing-t'ai [935], those who have committed crimes deemed lesser than those calling for the death penalty, whether they have been disclosed or not, and whether they have been judged or not, pardon them all. Let the officials in charge carry out the pardon.

Kyŏnhwŏn was at Kŭmsan temple for three months. On the sixth month, with his youngest son Nŭngye, his daughter Aebok, and his concubine Kobi and others, Kyŏnhwŏn fled to Kŭmsŏng [Naju] and sent a man to request to see T'aejo. When they arrived, [T'aejo] treated them in lavish style and because Kyŏnhwŏn was ten years older, he honored Kyŏnhwŏn by calling him esteemed father [sangbu], and gave him the South Palace as an official residence. His position was made superior to those of the other officials and he had Yangju bestowed upon him as a fief [sigŭp] along with gold, silk, folding screens, bedding, forty male and female slaves each, and ten horses from the court stables

In summer, the sixth month, Kyŏnhwŏn said to T'aejo, "When I submitted to Your Majesty, I only wanted to rely on Your Majesty's authority to punish my traitorous son. It is my hope that you will enlist your divine troops to destroy the traitorous rebels and then I can die with no regrets." T'aejo assented to this and first dispatched Crown Prince Mu and General [Pak] Surhŭi leading ten thousand foot and mounted soldiers to Ch'ŏnan-bu. In autumn, the ninth month, T'aejo led the Three Armies to Ch'ŏnan, and the combined forces then advanced to Ilsŏn-gun. Singŏm resisted with his troops. On the eighth day, kabo, they faced each other at Illi stream [east of Sŏnsan] poised for battle.

Lieutenant General Konghwŏn and General Wang Hamyun with fifteen thousand soldiers became the vanguard, and sounding the drums, they advanced. The Later Paekche generals, Hyobong, Tŏksul, Myŏnggil and others, seeing that the [Koryŏ] forces were mighty and orderly, abandoned their armor and surrendered to the Koryŏ camp. T'aejo, consoling them in their surrender, asked the location of the commanding general of Later Paekche. Hyŏngong and others replied, "Marshall Singŏm was with the central army." T'aejo commanded General Konghwŏn to launch a frontal attack against the central army while ordering other troops to advance by attacking the flanks. The Later Paekche army fled in defeat as Singŏm, his two brothers, Generals Pudal, Sodal, and Nŭnghwan, and more than forty others surrendered. T'aejo, on accepting their surrender, comforted everyone except Nŭnghwan, and permitted them to come to the [Koryŏ] capital with their wives. Addressing Nŭnghwan, he said "From the start secretly plotting with Yanggŏm, imprisoning the great king [Kyŏnhwŏn], and enthroning his son was all your scheme. Is this the integrity of a subject?" Nŭnghwan bowed his head and was unable to speak. T'aejo ordered him to be executed. [T'aejo also said], "As Singŏm's usurpation was due to coercion by someone else and not something he bore in his heart, and furthermore since he submitted himself begging for punishment, I especially remit his death penalty." (One source says all three brothers were executed.) Kyŏnhwŏn, under severe depression, developed a tumor on his back, and several days later died in a temple on Mount Hwang.

As T'aejo had ordered his armies to maintain strict discipline, the soldiers did not harm anyone even in the slightest. All the localities [of Later Paekche] became peaceful and everyone cried out, "Long live the King!" Thereupon T'aejo soothed the officers and soldiers, appointing them according to their talents, and all the people found peace in their occupations.

Kyŏnhwŏn had held power from the first year of T'ang's Ching-fu [892] to the first year of Chin's T'ien-fu [935], altogether forty-five years until his demise.

HK AND ES

Kim Kungye

[*Samgnk sagi* 50:451–454]

Kungye, surnamed Kim, was from Silla. His father, Ŭijŏng, King Hŏnan [857–861], was Silla's forty-seventh ruler, and his mother, whose name has been lost, was a concubine to King Hŏnan. Some say Kungye was the son of Ŭngnyŏm, Silla's forty-eighth king, Kyŏngmun [861–875]. When he was born on the fifth day of the fifth month at his maternal residence, there was a white ray like a long rainbow above his house stretching up to heaven. An official in the astrology office reported, "Because this child was born on double five [the fifth day of the fifth month] with all his teeth, and moreover there was a strange glow from a ray of light, I fear he will be of no benefit to the kingdom in the future. Accordingly it is better not to raise him."

The king ordered one of his courtiers to go to the house and kill [the child]. Upon arriving, the courtier took away the child wrapped in a cloth and threw him down some stairs. A wet nurse secretly scooped him up but in the process accidently damaged one of his eyes with her hand. She carried him off and hid him, raising him despite much hardship. When he was over ten years old yet very naughty, the wet nurse said to him, "Because I could not bear to see you abandoned at birth by the king, I have secretly raised you until now. But if you continually act without restraint like this, people will certainly come to know it, and then you and I will not be able to escape death. Do you realize this or not?" Kungye weeping said, "If this is so, I will leave home and not cause you any more worries."

He then left for Sedal Monastery, which is today's Hŭnggyo Monastery [in Kaep'ung] and shaved his head, becoming a monk and calling himself Sŏnjong.

These were the declining days of Silla, when the government was in disorder and people went adrift; moreover outside the capital half the country was in rebellion, and everywhere in the provinces near and far bandits rose up like hornets. Sŏnjong thought if he took advantage of the chaos and assembled people, he could realize his political ambitions.

In the fifth year of Queen Chinsŏng, the second year, *sinhae,* of Tai-shun [891], he joined Kihwŏn, the bandit chief from Chukchu. But as Kihwŏn was arrogant and discourteous, Sŏnjong was grieved and ill at ease. So he secretly conspired with Kihwŏn's subordinates Wŏnhui and Sinhwŏn to be comrades.

In the first year, *imja,* of Ching-fu [892], he went over to the Pugwŏn [Wŏnju] bandit Yanggil, who received him warmly and entrusted him with important matters. Later Yanggil, assigning bandit troops, had him attack territory to the east. Thereupon Sŏnjong went out and stayed at Sŏngnam Monastery on Ch'iak Mountain [in Kangwŏn] and attacked Chuch'ŏn [Wŏnsŏng], Naesŏng [Yŏngwŏl], Uro [P'yŏngch'ang] and Ŏjin [Ulchin], and other districts and subjugated all. As his military reputation grew, many rebels in the P'aesŏ region (north of the Yesŏng river) came and surrendered to him.[2] Sŏnjong, believing that the multitude [under his control] was large enough to found a kingdom, began to call himself king, and set up central and local offices [for governing].[3]

Our T'aejo [Wang Kŏn] submitted from Songak [Kaesŏng] and then received the position of prefect *[t'aesu]* of Ch'ŏrwŏn-gun. In the third year, *pyŏngjin,* of Ch'ien-ning (896), Sŏnjong attacked and took the two districts of Sŭngnyŏng [Yŏnch'ŏn] and Imgang [Changdan]. In the fourth year, *chŏngsa* [897], Inmŭl-hyŏn [Kaep'ung] surrendered. Sŏnjong said that Songak-kun, a well-known town north of the Han River, had an unusually pretty landscape, and made it his capital.

In spring, the second month of the first year, *muo,* of Kuang-hua [898]our T'aejo then became a commander of the picked cavalry *[chŏnggi taegam]* and subdued Yangju [Seoul] and Kyŏnju [Yangju]. In the third year, *kyŏngsin* [900],[4] [Kungye] ordered T'aejo to subdue Kwangju, Ch'ungju, Tangsŏng [Hwasŏng], Ch'ŏngju (or Ch'ŏngch'ŏn [modern Ch'ŏngwŏn]), and Koeyang [Koesan], and he pacified all of them. Because of this merit T'aejo was given the post of *ach'an.*[5]

In the first year, *sinyu,* of T'ien-fu [901],[6] Sŏnjong called himself king *[wang]* and said to the people, "Formerly Silla requested troops from T'ang to defeat Koguryŏ. Therefore P'yŏngyang the capital was reduced to a vast wasteland, becoming a tangle of weeds. I must revenge this." Because he resented the fact that he was abandoned [by the Silla court] at his birth, he spoke [ill of Silla] like this. Once when he was patrolling the south he arrived at Pusŏk Monastery in Hŭngju [Yŏngju, North Kyŏngsang], where he saw a painting of Silla kings. He drew his sword and slashed it. The marks left by his blade are still there.

In the first year, *kapcha,* of T'ien-yu [904], Sŏnjong founded a kingdom, calling it Majin, with the reign year Mut'ae.

Sŏnjong because of his growing strength became boastful and wanted to absorb Silla. He ordered his countrymen to call the Silla [capital] the "fallen capital," and generally executed anyone who came from Silla. In Ch'ien-hua's first year [911], *sinmi,* of Later Liang,[7] the reign year of "Hallowed Investiture" [Sŏngch'aek] was changed to "Long Live the Power of Water" [Sudŏk manse], making it the first year, and the name of the country was changed to T'aebong. He sent T'aejo [Wang Kŏn] to lead troops to attack Kŭmsŏng and other towns and changed Kŭmsŏng to Naju. Because of his success in this attack, Sŏnjong promoted T'aejo to general with the rank of *taeach'an.*[8]

Sŏnjong proclaimed himself to be a Maitreya Buddha, wearing like a monk a peaked gold hood on his head and a square robe on his body. He made his oldest son to be Ch'ŏnggwang Bodhisattva and his last son to be Singwang Bodhisattva. When he went out he always rode a white horse, its mane and tail decorated with silk. He had young boys and girls lead the way, carrying banners and umbrellas with incense and flowers. He also commanded more than two hundred monks to follow chanting Buddhist hymns. Once he wrote more than twenty chapters of Buddhist canons, but their language was frivolous and incorrect. Sometimes, sitting upright, he expounded on them, but the monk Sŏkch'ong deplored this and said, "All these explanations are heresy, deviant and unreliable for instruction." Sŏnjong on hearing this was angry and taking an iron mallet, bludgeoned him to death.

In the third year, *kyeyu* [913], T'aejo became chancellor with the rank of *p'ajinch'an,* and in the fourth year, *kapsul,* the reign title was changed from "Long

Live the Power of Water" to the first year of "Beginning of Rule" [Chŏnggae], and T'aejo became Admiral of the Hundred Fleet *[paeksŏn changgun]*.

In the first year of Chen-ming [918], Sŏnjong's wife Lady Kang seriously reprimanded him because of his many improper activities. He resented this, however, and retorted, "Why have you had illicit relations with other men?" Lady Kang said, "How could anything like this be possible?" He replied, "Because of my supernatural powers I have seen this." Taking a burning iron rod, he thrust it into her womb and killed her, and he also killed their two sons. From this time on he became easily suspicious and so angry at others that his various advisers, military officers, and clerks down to commoners were from time to time massacred without being guilty. People from Puyang [P'yŏnggang] and Ch'ŏrwŏn were not able to endure this treachery.

As the king's evil and tyranny were without restraint, the officials became terrified and did not know what to do. In summer, the sixth month, Generals Hongsul, Paegok, Samnŭngsan, and Pok Sagwi together made a plot. At night they went to T'aejo's [Wang Kŏn's] house and said, "Now the punishments the lord [Kungye] meets out are outrageous, and he has killed his wife, executed his sons, punished his officials, and driven the peasants into dire distress, making it difficult for them to live. From the ancient past overthrowing the dark [bad] and putting the bright [good] on the throne have been the great principle of rightness in the world. We request that you carry out what King T'ang [of Shang] and King Wu [of Chou] did [in this respect]."

T'aejo [Wong Kŏn], the color of his face changing, resisted them, saying, "I have allowed myself only to be loyal, and now even though the lord is extremely cruel, I dare not carry two minds. Replacing a ruler with his subject is changing the Mandate of Heaven. As I am in fact a man without virtue, how could I imitate the founders of Shang and Chou?" The generals replied, "This opportunity will not come again. What is not easy to come across is easy to lose. If you don't take advantage of the opportunities provided by Heaven, you may find yourself accepting its consequences. Now the government is in chaos, the kingdom in crisis, and the people all hate the lord [Kungye] like an enemy. Now in terms of virtue and vision there is no one who equals you."

His wife Lady Yu heard this discussion with the generals and said to T'aejo, "To use humaneness to vanquish inhumaneness has been the norm from the past. Now listening to the discussions, I too have become indignant. How couldn't you also be indignant? The people have swiftly withdrawn their support, and the change in the Mandate of Heaven is due." With her hands she took his armor and offered it to T'aejo. The generals guarded T'aejo as he passed through the gate and had those in front yell loudly, "Lord Wang has taken up the banner of rightness." Thereupon people all rushed out, following him in numbers too numerous to count. There were also those who had already reached the palace gate, waiting for Lord Wang's arrival, and clamoring noisily. They numbered over ten thousand. When the king [Kungye] heard this he did not know what to do, and in disguise escaped to the mountain forests. Later he was killed by the people of Puyang. From the second year of T'ang's Tai-shun [891] to the fourth year of Later Liang's Chen-ming [918], Kungye ruled for twenty-eight years until his demise.   *HK AND ES*

FOUNDING OF KORYŎ

Wang Kŏn, Koryŏ's dynastic founder, came from a locally prominent family in central Korea that joined the new leader of the region, Kim Kungye, in rebelling against Silla's supremacy in the final days of the ninth century. Wang Kŏn rose quickly in Kungye's state of T'aebong, but as Kungye became more and more despotic in his rule, Wang Kŏn led disgruntled followers in a revolt, and they founded Koryŏ in 918.

It was not until 936, however, that Wang Kŏn was able to gain full control of the peninsula, and until this was done, legitimacy was the foremost issue confronting him. When Silla's last king, Kim Pu (927–935), transferred his mandate to rule in 935, Wang Kŏn achieved the status and respectability necessary for his kingdom to gain dynastic legitimacy.

Wang Kŏn, also known by his posthumous title, T'aejo, spent the rest of his life consolidating political power in his reunified kingdom. The examples of his proclamations presented here attempt to justify his usurpation of the throne. They are cautious, reassuring statements promising that as the new ruler he will look for honest and able officials. He also declares that he will seek consensus by using the best traditions of both Silla and T'aebong (which first appeared as Later Koguryŏ).

Besides gaining acceptance for his leadership, Wang Kŏn wanted to assure his subjects of a well-managed government. In the edict he issued while visiting Yesan-jin in western central Korea, he poignantly displayed his concern about the capricious and unscrupulous way local leaders exercised power in his new kingdom and urged them to be disciplined and compassionate. The edict also reveals how hard he had labored to secure fair and just authority.

In the "Ten Injunctions," Wang Kŏn left his descendants clear instructions at the end of his reign to assure the success and continuation of the dynasty. This important document exerted a powerful influence throughout the remainder of the Koryŏ period. It was significant not only as Wang Kŏn's final statement, but also because of its wide-ranging advice covering Buddhism, geomancy, potential threats to dynastic security, and royal succession. The "Ten Injunctions" provide another view of early Koryŏ's intellectual climate.

Wang Kŏn's genealogy, which glorifies both his family inheritance and the forces that were to secure the dynasty, reaffirms the dynastic legitimacy. The earliest known publication of this genealogy dates from the twelfth century, and there is no reason to take literally his family's alleged aristocratic origins, links with T'ang China's imperial family, and sociopolitical prominence in central Koryŏ. The genealogy, rich in Buddhist, shamanistic, and geomantic references, is also revealing of certain mythological ideas prevailing in early Koryŏ.

Wang Kŏn: Enthronement Proclamation

[From *Koryŏ sa* 1:8b–9a]

On the fifteenth day, *pyŏngjin*, of the sixth month of T'aejo's first year [918],[9] Wang Kŏn was enthroned in the Hall of Statesmanship, calling the kingdom Koryŏ and taking the reign title Heaven's Bestowal [Ch'ŏnsu]. The king published a proclamation:

> The former lord Kungye gradually expanded the boundaries and eliminated bandits as Silla was collapsing like a pile of dirt. Even before the country was unified, however, his rule had suddenly become tyrannical and cruel. He considered treacherous means to be the best, and intimidation and insults necessary devices. Frequent corvée labor and heavy taxes exhausted the people, forcing them to abandon the land. Yet the palace was grand and imposing, and he ignored the established conventions. Endless public construction gave rise to popular resentment and criticism. He stole august titles to confer upon himself and killed his wife and children. Heaven and earth could not tolerate this. The deities and men all resented it. As his rule was collapsing, who would not take this to be a warning?
>
> Owing to your hearty support, I became king. By joining together to correct laws, we can rejuvenate the country. Learning from past mistakes, we should look for solutions to problems in our immediate surroundings and recognize the mutual dependence of ruler and subject, realizing that our relations are like those of fish and water. The country will join in a celebration of the peace. I hope that people all over will know of my cherished intentions.

The ranking officials bowed in thanks and said: "At the time of the former ruler, we witnessed the gentle and good being harmed and the innocent being cruelly treated. The old and young wailed, harboring only resentment. Now, fortunately, under your enlightened rule, we can continue our lives. Why should we not exhaust ourselves to repay our indebtedness?" *HK AND ES*

Formation of Government

[From *Koryŏ sa* 1:9b–11a]

On the twentieth day of the sixth month of T'aejo's first year [918], the king issued a proclamation that stated:

> In establishing government offices and assigning functions, it is most important to appoint men of ability. In making conventions beneficial and the people peaceful, the most urgent task is choosing the wise. Truly if there is no negligence, how could the government be out of control? I recall that, having undeservedly received the Heavenly Mandate and being about to manage the affairs of government, I was not at ease in accepting the responsibilities of the throne. I remember my fear of appointing the mediocre and pretentious. My greatest fear still is that I might not know clearly who the right people are, and therefore there may be many oversights in appointing them to appropriate offices. This leads me to worry that I may omit the wise, profoundly violating the process of selecting the right scholars. I worry about this all the time. If all officials of the central and local governments perform their duties properly, it will not only help in governing today but will be commended by later ages. Everyone in the country should know that I intend to be fair and just in giving fitting employment to the local gentry and in continuously testing and carefully selecting all officials. *HK AND ES*

Wang Kŏn: Edict at Yesan-jin

[From *Koryŏ sa* 2:6a–7b]

On the sixth day of the fifth month, summer, of T'aejo's seventeenth year [934], the king visited Yesan-jin and issued a proclamation:

> Recently, as Silla deteriorated politically, many bandits suddenly appeared, and people scattered in all directions, leaving skeletons exposed on the ground. Although the former lord Kungye had pacified contending factions and laid the foundation for the country, in his later years he brought harm

to the people and endangered the kingdom. Succeeding at this perilous time, I founded this new state.   *HK AND ES*

Wang Kŏn: Ten Injunctions

[From *Koryŏ sa* 2:14b–17a]

In the fourth month, summer, of T'aejo's twenty-sixth year [943], the king went to the inner court, summoned *Taegwang* Pak Surhŭi, and personally gave him the injunctions, saying:

I have heard that when great Shun was cultivating at Li-shan he inherited the throne from Yao.[10] Emperor Kao-tsu of China rose from humble origins and founded the Han. I too have risen from humble origins and received undeserved support for the throne. In summer I did not shun the heat and in winter did not avoid the cold. After toiling, body and mind, for nineteen years, I united the Three Han [Later Three Kingdoms] and have held the throne for twenty-five years. Now I am old. I only fear that my successors will give way to their passions and greed and destroy the principle of government. That would be truly worrisome. I therefore wrote these injunctions to be passed on to later ages. They should be read morning and night and forever used as a mirror for reflection.

His injunctions were as follows:[11]

1. The success of every great undertaking of our state depends upon the favor and protection of Buddha. Therefore, the temples of both the Meditation and Doctrinal schools should be built and monks should be sent out to those temples to minister to Buddha. Later on, if villainous courtiers attain power and come to be influenced by the entreaties of bonzes, the temples of various schools will quarrel and struggle among themselves for gain. This ought to be prevented.

2. Temples and monasteries were newly opened and built upon the sites chosen by the monk Tosŏn according to the principles of geomancy. He said: "If temples and monasteries are indiscriminately built at locations not chosen by me, the terrestrial force and energy will be sapped and damaged, hastening the decline of the dynasty." I am greatly concerned that the royal family, the aristocracy, and the courtiers all may build many temples and monasteries in the future in order to seek Buddha's blessings. In the last days of Silla many temples were capriciously built. As a result, the terrestrial force and energy were wasted and diminished, causing its demise. Vigilantly guard against this.

3. In matters of royal succession, succession by the eldest legitimate royal issue should be the rule. But Yao of ancient China let Shun succeed

him because his own son was unworthy. That was indeed putting the interests of the state ahead of one's personal feelings. Therefore, if the eldest son is not worthy of the crown, let the second eldest succeed to the throne. If the second eldest, too, is unworthy, choose the brother the people consider the best qualified for the throne.

4. In the past we have always had a deep attachment for the ways of China and all of our institutions have been modeled upon those of T'ang. But our country occupies a different geographical location and our people's character is different from that of the Chinese. Hence, there is no reason to strain ourselves unreasonably to copy the Chinese way. Khitan is a nation of savage beasts, and its language and customs are also different. Its dress and institutions should never be copied.

5. I achieved the great task of founding the dynasty with the help of the elements of mountain and river of our country. The Western Capital, P'yŏngyang, has the elements of water in its favor and is the source of the terrestrial force of our country. It is thus the veritable center of dynastic enterprises for ten thousand generations. Therefore, make a royal visit to the Western Capital four times a year—in the second, fifth, eighth, and eleventh months—and reside there a total of more than one hundred days. By this means secure peace and prosperity.

6. I deem the two festivals of Yŏndŭng and P'algwan of great spiritual value and importance. The first is to worship Buddha. The second is to worship the spirit of Heaven, the spirits of the five sacred and other major mountains and rivers, and the dragon god. At some future time, villainous courtiers may propose the abandonment or modification of these festivals. No change should be allowed.

7. It is very difficult for the king to win over the people. For this reason, give heed to sincere criticism and banish those with slanderous tongues. If sincere criticisms are accepted, there will be virtuous and sagacious kings. Though sweet as honey, slanderous words should not be believed; then they will cease of their own accord. Make use of the people's labor with their convenience in mind; lighten the burden of corvée and taxation; learn the difficulties of agricultural production. Then it will be possible to win the hearts of the people and to bring peace and prosperity to the land. Men of yore said that under a tempting bait a fish hangs; under a generous reward an able general wins victory; under a drawn bow a bird dare not fly; and under a virtuous and benevolent rule a loyal people serves faithfully. If you administer rewards and punishments moderately, the interplay of yin and yang will be harmonious.

8. The topographic features of the territory south of Kongju and beyond the Kongju River are all treacherous and disharmonious; its inhabitants are treacherous and disharmonious as well. For that reason, if they are allowed to participate in the affairs of state, to intermarry with the royal family,

aristocracy, and royal relatives, and to take the power of the state, they might imperil the state or injure the royal safety—grudging the loss of their own state [which used to be the kingdom of Paekche] and being resentful of the unification.

Those who have been slaves or engaged in dishonorable trades will surrender to the powerful in order to evade prescribed services. And some of them will surely seek to offer their services to the noble families, to the palaces, or to the temples. They then will cause confusion and disorder in government and engage in treason through crafty words and treacherous machinations. They should never be allowed into government service, though they may no longer be slaves and outcasts.

9. The salaries and allowances for the aristocracy and the bureaucracy have been set according to the needs of the state. They should not be increased or diminished. The classics say that salaries and allowances should be determined by the merits of those who receive them and should not be wasted for private gain. If the public treasury is wasted upon those without merit or upon one's relatives or friends, not only will the people come to resent and criticize such abuses, but those who enjoy salaries undeservedly will also not be able to enjoy them for long. Since our country shares borders with savage nations, always beware of the danger of their invasions. Treat the soldiers kindly and take good care of them; lighten their burden of forced labor; inspect them every autumn; give honors and promotions to the brave.

10. In preserving a household or a state, one should always be on guard to avert mistakes. Read widely in the classics and in history; take the past as a warning for the present. The Duke of Chou was a great sage, yet he sought to admonish his nephew, King Ch'eng, with *Against Luxurious Ease (Wu-i)*. Post the contents of *Against Luxurious Ease* on the wall and reflect upon them when entering and leaving the room.   HP

Development of Confucian Polity I

Ch'oe Sŭngno (927–989), the son of a Silla aristocrat, met King T'aejo at the age of twelve and so impressed the king that the latter gave Ch'oe an academic appointment. Ch'oe Sŭngno remained aligned with the court, and by the time Sŏngjong (981–997) became king, Ch'oe was one of the kingdom's leading statesmen.

Alert to potential dangers confronting the dynasty and anxious to consolidate dynastic authority throughout the kingdom, Ch'oe presented an ambitious twenty-eight–point memorial on contemporary affairs. In the opening section, the first passage presented here, Ch'oe recounts how Wang Kŏn, with his confederation of great families, established Koryŏ. In reviewing the events of the dynasty's first five reigns, he emphasizes T'aejo's merit in founding and securing the dynasty. Through Ch'oe's numerous descriptions, T'aejo takes on the image of a superhero, a reputation worthy of a dynastic founder.

The subsequent reigns did not match the first. Hyejong, Koryŏ's second king, was racked by suspicions. His successor, Chŏngjong, while diligent, mistakenly tried to move the capital to P'yŏngyang. Ch'oe Sŭngno roundly condemns Koryŏ's fourth king, Kwangjong. Although Kwangjong started well, he quickly attracted mediocre followers. Ultimately, his reign gave way to ostentation and collapsed into purges that threatened the life of his own son as well as the dynasty. Kwangjong's son, Kyŏngjong, succeeded to the throne and brought a measure of stability, but he too relied on powerful figures who undermined the kingdom. To Ch'oe Sŭngno, the events of the first five reigns were powerful lessons that the new king, Sŏngjong, should study in order to avoid the mistakes of the past.

Having presented a chronology of the first five reigns, Ch'oe then offers a specific reform package. The original memorial, containing twenty-eight points, six of which have been lost, is here divided into two parts to facilitate comprehension. "On Current Affairs" is a broad discussion of contemporary abuses that demanded urgent attention. Ch'oe treats border relations and ties with China as well as the need for tighter internal governance. To Ch'oe, adherence to Confucian norms of frugality and social responsibility would resolve most dynastic woes. Ch'oe also wanted to see a new order imposed on Koryŏ, one that would place centrally appointed officials in the twelve regional provinces *(mok)*.

"On Buddhism" presents Ch'oe's critique of contemporary Buddhism. Although he acknowledged the functions of Buddhism, Ch'oe, a committed Confucian, felt that too much reliance on Buddhist practices would undermine the good of society. Ch'oe was especially critical of past Buddhist extravagances and clearly warned that unless reform was pursued, the future of the dynasty was in peril. Ch'oe believed that Buddhism should be fostered to meet the spiritual needs of the people and Confucian ideology should hold sway in affairs of state.

Ch'oe Sŭngno: On the First Five Reigns

[From *Koryŏ sa* 93:2b—12a]

I grew up in the countryside and am by nature simple and unscholarly, but I have been fortunate to live at a propitious time and have long attended all the Koryŏ kings, often receiving special honors. Although I have no brilliant plans to correct the problems of the age, still, having some concerns, I have pledged to work for the country. I humbly think of the historian Wu Ching [670–749] of the K'ai-yüan period [713–742], who compiled and presented his work, *Essentials of Government of the Chen-kuan Period [Chen-kuan cheng-yao],* to encourage Emperor Hsüan-tsung to emulate the policies of Emperor T'ai-tsung. Because of the similarities of the two periods, though in different countries, the successful policies of Emperor T'ai-tsung can be a model for us.

In my humble view, King T'aejo's founding of the dynasty and its passing on to posterity is the so-called ancestral merit. The successive kings' guarding of the throne can be called the successors' virtue. Although by establishing a dynasty a founder extends blessings to his descendants, not all the descendants succeed and prosper. They could not escape the vicissitudes of their age because in governing one has to distinguish between right and wrong, just as in affairs there is good and bad. Usually one is not as careful at the end as at the beginning; so one is led to difficulties as well as to crises, truly regrettable though this is.

Since King T'aejo's founding of the dynasty, all that I have come to know I still know by heart. I therefore wish to record all the policies of the last five reigns, tracing the marks left, good and bad, all of which can guide Your Majesty's conduct of government through this presentation.

I reckon that when our T'aejo, Great Divine Holy King, ascended the throne, it was a time of chaos, manifesting the destiny that occurs once in a thousand years. That he could first suppress the unruly and destroy the evil was due to the hand lent by Kim Kungye, which heaven produced. Afterwards, as T'aejo received Heaven's Mandate, people recognized his sagely virtue and turned to him. Thereupon Silla destroyed itself and Koguryŏ rode the destiny of restoration.

From late Silla to the beginning of our dynasty, the people of the northeast frontier frequently suffered from the Jürchen horsemen who came to invade and rob. T'aejo himself decided to send a capable officer to guard the area—guarding it so effectively, in fact, that without a single weapon's actually being used, the Jürchen came to surrender. After this, the area beyond the border became quiet, and the frontier was free of troubles. Such was his ability to recognize and employ capable men and to induce people in distant lands to come into close association.

Even after unifying the country, he worked diligently on government affairs for eight years, treating China with respect and neighboring countries with propriety. Even in times of peace he was not lax. In meeting with people of inferior status, he was courteous, demonstrating his lofty virtue. He esteemed frugality, building his palace with no excess but only enough to withstand storms. He dressed in simple clothes adequate only to protect him from heat and cold. He held dear the wise and loved the good, giving up his own on behalf of others. A feeling of respect and politeness sprang from his natural disposition. Moreover, growing up among the peasants, he had experienced hardship and danger. Of the people's feelings there was nothing he could not discern. In everything, he could foretell peace and foresee danger. Because of this, his rewards and punishments were timely, and rights and wrongs could be distinguished. Such was his way of moral purpose, which gave him the dignity of an emperor.

When T'aejo knew a person, moreover, he did not overlook that person's talent, and through his management of people below him, he used their strength. In appointing the wise, T'aejo manifested trust; in eliminating evil, he had no doubt. Through his respect for Buddhism and his emphasis on Confucianism, T'aejo attained the excellent virtue of a ruler. His wise dynastic policies are thus worthy of being emulated.

As crown prince, King Hyejong resided in the Eastern Palace for a long time and often conducted state military affairs, respecting his teachers and receiving his advisers with propriety. Accordingly, he had a good reputation in the country, and when he first came to the throne, many people happily accepted him. At that time, some people slandered Chŏngjong and his brother, saying they planned treason. Hearing this, Hyejong did not respond and raised no questions. He became even kinder toward Chŏngjong and his brother, treating them as before. People admired his great magnanimity. In a little while, however, his virtuous rule was tarnished as he became unduly fearful for his personal safety, always surrounding himself with armed soldiers. In general, as his suspicions of people grew more severe, he lost much of the dignity of a king. Increasingly he became inclined to reward military officers, extending favors unequally so that all over the country resentment grew, and people began to harbor disaffection. Within a year of his enthronement, he suddenly fell ill and passed his remaining time in bed. Thereupon ranking officials and the erudite lost access to the king, and petty people from his local village always lingered in the royal sleeping quarters. As his sickness became more serious, Hyejong's anger and resentment daily grew worse. For three years the people did not see virtuous rule, and only the day of his death removed potential calamity. Is this not truly lamentable?

For the last thirty-eight years, since Chŏngjong ascended the throne, the royal succession has not been broken. This is due to the actions taken by Chŏngjong. Having received the throne from his half-brother Hyejong, Chŏngjong unselfishly worked hard at governing day and night. He would give audiences to court officials, even lighting a candle [after dark] to do so; he would make decisions on government affairs, even forgoing his meals to do so. Accordingly, in the early days of his reign, people all rejoiced in his success at governing. Because of his misplaced belief in geomantic prophecies, however, he decided to move the capital. As he was by nature resolute and unbending, he recklessly mobilized people for corvée, initiating public works and overworking laborers. Although it was the king's wish, popular sentiment did not accede, and resentment rose among the populace. Calamity quickly followed. He passed away before he could move the capital to P'yŏngyang. This is truly regrettable.

King Kwangjong, even in his childhood, had a remarkable appearance and an outstanding disposition. He received special care and love from his father King T'aejo. At King Chŏngjong's command on his deathbed, he inherited the throne, which was thus affectionately passed from older brother to younger brother. He treated those under him with much propriety, and he never lost his eye for judging people. He did not hold his royal relatives and high nobles too close, always restraining the mighty and powerful. He never neglected the humble, and accorded favors to widows and orphans. For eight years after he ascended the throne, the government was clean and equitable, meting out no excessive rewards or punishments. From the time he employed Shuang Chi, he leaned heavily toward the literati, dispensing excessive favors and courtesy to them. Thereupon, even the untalented came forward, upsetting the order of seniority, and advanced quickly, becoming high ministers in less than two years.Thereupon, mediocre people from north and south all competed to join in. Regardless of whether a person had knowledge or talent, the king treated all with special kindness and favor, so that even junior persons competed to advance, and the initial virtue of the king gradually disappeared.

Moreover, the king became excessive in his devotion to Buddhism and unduly valued Buddhists. Although regular observances of Buddhist fasting services were already numerous, many additional incense-burning prayers for special wishes were held. Prayers were merely offered to obtain blessings and longevity. Even though our financial means were limited, he tried to produce unlimited acts of merit. Taking his position as sovereign lightly, he sought to elevate the petty. His outings and banquets were all done with extreme extravagance. Not taking immediate hardship around him to be indicative of the future—which he assumed would be peaceful, thanks to the Buddha's power—he did not seek to correct wrongs in performing his deeds.

In his later years, many innocent people were put to death. Had Kwangjong had always been as respectful and frugal in his expenditures and as diligent in governing as he was early in his reign, could he not have lived longer rather than having passed away at the age of fifty years? I, perhaps foolishly, believe so.

Earlier, when kings Hyejong, Chŏngjong, and Kwangjong succeeded each other, not everything in the new dynasty had been settled. As a result, half of the military and civil officials of the two capitals [Kaesŏng and P'yŏngyang] were killed or injured in succession disputes.

I humbly believe that, owing to the virtue of the ancient sages, Your Majesty has a new opportunity for restoration, as the glorious royal mandate has been passed on to Your Majesty because of the previous king's unselfish considerations. If Your Majesty truly follows King T'aejo's precedents, how would you be different from Hsüan-tsung's cherishing T'ai-tsung's old ways? Your Majesty, be selective, if you can, from the events of the last four reigns. It can be said that Hyejong upheld the principle of brotherly love, as his merit rests in having protected his close relatives. It can also be said that Chŏngjong exemplified the brilliance of strategy, as his early detection of a germinating rebellion allowed him to suppress disturbances in the palace, safeguard the dynasty, and preserve the crown to this day. Kwangjong's initial eight-year rule can be compared to the Three Ages of Hsia, Shang, and Chou; particularly noteworthy was his systemization of court ceremonies, but it might be said that the balance sheet of his achievement was evenly divided between the good and the bad. Kyŏngjong's freeing of thousands of unjustified prisoners of the preceding reign and his burning of the slanderous documents of many years may be considered the apex of generous leniency.

In general, this is the record of the four reigns. Your Majesty should selectively put into practice the good points and caution yourself on the bad by eliminating nonessential tasks and halting unbeneficial endeavors. Only by so doing will the ruler presiding above be at ease and the people below be joyful. If you do so, how could Your Majesty's life not last for a long time and the dynasty cease only after one hundred generations?

HK AND ES

Ch'oe Sŭngno: On Current Affairs

[From *Koryŏ sa* 93:12a–b, 19b–22a]

Although I am not bright, I unworthily hold an important position in the government. I therefore desire to memorialize the throne with no thought of avoiding my duty, humbly record my thoughts on current affairs in not more than twenty-eight points, and present them under separate cover in accordance with prescribed form.

It has been forty-seven years since our country united the Later Three Kingdoms. Our soldiers have yet to see peace, however, and military provisions are still in excessive demand. This is all because to the northwest there are many places to defend, as we border on barbarians. I hope Your Majesty will keep this fact in mind. Generally it was King T'aejo's intention to make Mahŏl Rapids a border, whereas it was the Chinese decision to make the stone wall on the banks of the Yalu River a border. I beg that between these two places Your Majesty in the future choose a more strategic location and establish a border for our territory. Then choose from among the local people those who are good at archery and riding and assign them to defend the area. Select from among them two or three as adjutant officers and put them in command so that the central army will be free from the task of defending the area in rotation and the cost of transporting military provisions will decline.

Because soldiers in our dynasty's royal regiments during T'aejo's reign were charged with protecting the palace, their number was not large. King Kwangjong, believing slander, executed generals and ministers, creating suspicions himself, and then increased the number of soldiers. Selecting men of talent from the rural districts, he put them in the royal regiments and had them all quartered in the palace. Contemporaries considered this burdensome and useless. Although the number decreased slightly in Kyŏngjong's reign, there are still too many to this day. If Your Majesty will follow the precedents of T'aejo and retain only the strong and brave and dismiss the rest, the people will have nothing to lament and the country will have much to save.

Our T'aejo was sincere in his devotion to China, but he sent officials to affirm ties only once in several years. Nowadays envoys are sent frequently, not only for tributary visits but also because of trade. I fear that the Chinese may look upon this with disdain. Moreover, ships traveling back and forth frequently are shipwrecked, and many lives are lost. I ask that from now on we combine tribute missions with trade and strictly forbid all other contacts.

The king, in governing the people, cannot visit them at home daily, and so he sends out magistrates to look into their welfare. After our T'aejo unified the country, he wished to set up provincial governments, but as it was still the formative age, many conditions were too unsettled for this. As I observe it now, the powerful local strongmen, under the pretext of public works, extort the people to the point that they can no longer endure it. I request that you establish provincial governments. And even if you cannot fill every office at once, first establish one provincial government for about ten *chu* and *hyŏn* and place two or three officials in each government to nourish and attend to the people.

In Silla the clothing, shoes, and stockings of nobles, officials, and commoners each had its designated color. Nobles and officials in court wore formal clothing and shoes and held tablets, and when they were out of court, they wore what they wished. To differentiate the noble and humble and distinguish the high and low, commoners could not wear patterned clothing. In this way, even though official robes were not locally produced, the supply was adequate for the use of officials. Since King T'aejo's time, we have worn clothes as we please regardless of social status. Even if one's rank is high, if his house is poor, he cannot afford an official robe. And if one is unemployed but has money, he can use silk gauze and elegant brocade. As for products in our country, there are few good items but many coarse goods. Even though none of the materials with designed patterns is locally produced, everybody wears them. I fear that the formal wear of the officials will not follow set regulations and will cause us embarrassment when we welcome officials from other countries. I ask that you command all officials to wear formal robes and shoes and to hold tablets at court meetings in accordance with Chinese and Silla conventions. In court presentations, have them wear socks and silk or leather shoes. Commoners should not be allowed to wear patterned silk but only plain silk fabrics.

Although Chinese systems are good to follow, as the customs of each area have their own characteristics, it would be difficult to change every custom. As for the teachings of the classics on rites, music, poetry, and documents, as well as the ways of the ruler and subject and the father and son, we must fittingly follow China and reform our vulgar ways. In the rest of the systems, however, such as transport and clothing, we should follow our native traditions so that the ostentatious and frugal will be balanced. We need not be like China in everything.

The people who live on the various islands grew up in the middle of the sea because of crimes committed by their forefathers. But as their land produces little food, their livelihood is very difficult. And yet as the government agent presses demands for levies from time to time, he daily impoverishes them. I request that we adhere to the levies set for the mainland districts and equalize their tax burdens and corvée levies.

According to the *Book of Changes,* "The sage influences the heart of the people, and consequently the world enjoys peace and harmony."[12] It is also stated in the *Analects,* "May not Shun be instanced as having governed efficiently without exertion? What did he do? He did nothing but gravely and reverently occupy his royal seat."[13] The sage can move Heaven and man because he has the purest virtue and an unselfish mind. If Your Majesty maintains a humble spirit and is always respectful and courteous to your subjects, then who while in government would not exhaust mind and strength in exposing evil plots and who while in retirement would not think only of serving you? This is referred to as the ruler treating the subject with respect and the subject serving the ruler with loyalty. I hope that Your Majesty will always be singularly prudent and never arrogant and will be gentle in dealing with your subjects. Even though there are criminals, if you deliberate on their crimes in accordance with the law, you can expect great peace imminently.

Except for the court slaves doing labor in the palace, King T'aejo sent the rest to live outside to till land and pay taxes. In Kwangjong's reign, because his many Buddhist activities daily increased public construction works, he enlisted the slaves living outside to carry out the public works. As the funds appropriated for the palace were not sufficient to pay for all the expenses, the rice stored in the government warehouses was also diverted. Your Majesty has not yet been able to correct this abuse. Moreover, since the number of horses raised in the palace stable is considerable, the expense is extravagant, causing people to suffer. Should disturbances occur on the frontier, provisions will not be adequate. I ask Your Majesty, strictly following the systems established by T'aejo, to limit the number of horses and slaves in the palace and resettle the remainder outside the palace.

According to the *Record of Rites*, "The hall of the Son of Heaven was ascended by nine steps; that of a prince by seven."[14] This has been the established practice. Recently, however, there has been no social distinction between the high and the low, and if a person has financial means, the first thing he does is build a house. Accordingly the powerful in all local administrative districts compete to build large houses exceeding the earlier standards. They not only exhaust the resources of their families but also cause harm to the people, and the result is excessive abuse. I humbly urge you to order officials of the Board of Rites to regulate house construction according to social status and to command all in the country to comply with this. Those who have already built in excess of these standards should be ordered to demolish the houses as a warning for the future.

In earlier times, as China's virtue declined, its eight great families, Lüan, Hsi, Hsü, Yüan, Hu, Hsu, Ch'ing, and Pai, ended up as slaves. Although the descendants of the meritorious subjects[15] of our dynastic founding should have received emoluments as stipulated each time royal commands have been issued, there are still some who have never received any rank and remain mixed among the slaves. As newly rising groups frequently insult them at will, discontent festers.

Ever since numerous court officials were purged in Kwangjong's last years, many descendants of the great families have been unable to continue their family lineages. I urge you to adhere to the often-issued royal commands and employ descendants of the meritorious subjects according to their rank. If you weigh the recipients of meritorious land grants in the year *kyŏngja* [940] and the officials who entered government service after the unification of the Later Three Kingdoms and confer upon them appropriate ranks and positions, this will mitigate past errors in regrettable charges and slights and avoid misfortune that could arise in the future.

In winter and summer, the dynasty's prayer meetings and memorial services for former kings and queens have been practiced for a long time and are not something to be set aside. I urge you, however, to reduce other services that can be done away with. If they cannot be reduced, then observe them in accordance with the *yüeh-ling* of the *Record of Rites*.[16] This states that since the spirit of the fifth month connotes the struggle between yin and yang, resulting in distinction between life and death, the gentleman must purify his body and soul, confining himself to his living quarters, certainly moving about without haste, abstaining from music and women, and eating moderately. By so controlling desires, he puts his mind in order. All officials also cleanse their bodies and submit to the king no litigation to be heard, thus assisting the completion of yin.

Since the spirit of the eleventh month connotes the struggle between yin and yang, resulting in the destruction of all living things, the gentleman should purify his body and soul, confining himself to his living quarters, moving about without haste, dismissing music and women, forbidding addiction to lust, and putting the mind and body at peace. By so conducting everything in quiet, he waits for the stabilization of yin and yang. This then is a time to desist. Why? When it is very cold, people on corvée labor will suffer and food may be unclean. When it is extremely hot, one perspires profusely. Or one may kill many insects by mistake, and so make sacrificial offerings impure. What kind of virtuous merit can this bring? Moreover, even if today produces good things, tomorrow will not necessarily bring good rewards. This being the case, nothing is as good as improving government policies.

I request that you divide the twelve months of the year into two halves and, from the second to the fourth month and from the eighth to the tenth, devote half the time to government affairs and half to acts of religious piety. From the fifth to the seventh month, and from the eleventh to the first, exclude pious acts and concentrate only on government affairs. Every day listen to government matters, and day and night assiduously deliberate on government policies. Every afternoon, in compliance with the four daily rituals of the gentleman,[17] refine government orders and look after health. In this way the seasonal conduct of the government will be orderly and Your Majesty will dwell in peace. This will also reduce the people's toils. How could all this not bring great religious merit?

The *Analects* states: "For a man to sacrifice to a spirit that does not belong to him is flattery."[18] The *Tso Commentary* states: "If a spirit is not your clan's, it will not receive sacrifices."[19] This is to say that offering sacrifices where one has no right to offer them brings no blessings. The services at our dynasty's ancestral temples and national altars still have many deviations that do not adhere to established rules. The services to the mountain peaks and the sacrifices to the constellations are vexing and excessive. It is said that sacrifices should not be done too frequently. If they are too frequent, they become burdensome. If they are burdensome, they become unrespectable. Although Your Majesty cleanses your heart in a most respectful way and certainly has no trace of laziness, if the sacrificial officials regard this as a routine affair, it becomes wearisome and is done without respect. How then will the spirits happily receive the service?

In ancient times, Emperor Wen of Han China had officials conduct the sacrificial service with respect, but he did not lead them in prayer. This detached view of the service can be called a great moral sense. If the spirits are unaware of the supplicant's needs, how can they extend blessings to him? If they are aware that these services are for self-gain and favors, as even a gentleman would have difficulty in responding to this, would the spirits not have even more difficulty? Furthermore, the expense of these services all comes from the toil and blood of the people. It is my belief that if you ease the people's labor, you will win their hearts, and the blessings from this will certainly exceed those blessings gained from prayers. I hope Your Majesty will eliminate extraneous prayers and services and always preserve an attitude of humility and self-reproach toward Heaven. In this way, calamity will of itself vanish and blessings appear.

The laws governing the free and the lowborn in our country have existed for a long time. When King T'aejo first founded the country, except for those officials who had originally had slaves, all other officials who became slave owners had acquired them while in the army, either by obtaining prisoners of war or through purchase. T'aejo once wanted to free the slaves to be commoners, but being concerned about agitating the feelings of the meritorious subjects, he followed a course of expediency. Since then, for the last sixty years, no one has ever made an appeal. In Kwangjong's reign, the king began to direct an investigation of slaves to determine their true status. All the meritorious subjects resented the investigation, but none dared to remonstrate. Even when Queen Taemok urgently remonstrated, the king did not heed. The lowborn and slaves gained their wishes and slighted the nobles, and those who competed to lie and scheme against their masters were numerous. Kwangjong himself created the causes for calamity and was unable to stop it. By the end of his reign, many innocent people had been killed, and the result was his great loss of virtue.

In early China when Hou Ching[20] encircled the palace in Liang, the house slave of the high official Chu I[21] crossed over the palace wall and surrendered to Hou Ching, who conferred on him the high title of *i-t'ung san-ssu.*[22] The slave, riding a horse and wearing a silk robe, faced the palace and shouted, "After serving for fifty years, Chu I just got the command of the central army, but I merely began to serve King Hou and immediately received the highest title of *i-t'ung.*" It is said that the household slaves in the palace thereupon competed to escape and surrender to Hou Ching and that the palace accordingly fell. I hope that Your Majesty will carefully reflect on this earlier incident and not allow the lowborn to put the noble to shame, but will follow the Golden Mean by separating slaves and masters. Generally people who hold high office are reasonable and few commit illegalities. How can people of low status, when they have insufficient wisdom and gloss over their wrongdoings, be made commoners? Although some royalty and nobles may have committed illegal acts because of their influence, at present the government is as clean as a mirror, with no pursuit of personal interest. [How can anyone transgress?] The misconduct of King Yu and King Li of Chou could not conceal the virtue of King Hsüan and King P'ing, and although Queen Lü of Han was unvirtuous, it did not tarnish the worthiness of Emperors Wen and Ching. Try to make important judgments with clarity so as to have no future regret. There is no need to rekindle disputes by reopening investigations of decisions that were made in earlier times.

HK AND ES

Ch'oe Sŭngno: On Buddhism

[From Koryŏ sa 93:15b–19b]

I have heard that Your Majesty, in order to hold Buddhist rites to accumulate merit, at times personally grinds tea and barley. Your Majesty's diligent labor troubles me deeply. Such practices started from Kwangjong's reign. Believing slanderous defamations, he had many innocent people killed. Misled by the Buddhist theory of just retribution and wishing to remove the consequences of past sins, he exacted provisions from the peasants to hold Buddhist services. He established Vairocana confessional rituals, held Buddhist maigre feasts on the polo fields, and set up Buddhist Festivals of Equal Bestowal of Wealth and Law on Land and Sea in Kwibŏp Monastery.

The offerings at the Buddhist services were invariably provisions exacted from the people. At that time, children turned against their parents and slaves against their masters, and all sorts of criminals disguised as monks, many actually mingling with real monks, wandered about begging and came together to hold Buddhist services. What good would this do? Although Your Majesty's actions since ascending the throne are not like this, the matters you have troubled yourself with are without any benefit. I hope Your Majesty will rectify the regal policy and do nothing that is not of benefit.

I have heard that monks, when traveling to the countryside, stay at government hostels and postal stations, chastising the local clerks and people for carelessness in their reception and provision of food. The clerks and people, fearing that the monks might be under royal orders, do not dare to speak out, which results in great abuses. From now on, please forbid monks to stop and stay at public facilities, in order to end these abuses.

As everyone following his own wishes builds temples in the name of sowing good to reap future reward, the number of temples has become excessive. In order to use monasteries as their own private residences, monks all over the country compete in building them. They urge the heads of the local districts to enlist people in corvée work, making their need for the labor more urgent than that for public projects, thereby troubling the people deeply. I request that you strictly forbid this practice, so as to exempt the people from toil.

Although the worship of Buddhism is not bad, the merits of pious acts performed by kings, officials, and commoners are in fact not the same. Since what the commoner toils on comes from his own labor and what he spends comes from his own wealth, harm comes to no others. In the case of a king, however, it comes from the toil of the peasants and it spends the wealth of the people.

Moreover, the Three Teachings [Buddhism, Confucianism, and Taoism] all have their own special qualities, and those who follow them should not get confused but keep them separate. Practitioners of Buddhism take spiritual cultivation as the basic principle. Practitioners of Confucianism take governing the state as the basic principle. Spiritual cultivation is valuable for the afterlife, but governing the country is the task of the present. The present is here and the afterlife is extremely distant. How could it not be wrong to sacrifice the present for the distant?

A king should single-mindedly be unselfish so as to give relief to all universally. Why should he make unwilling people work and waste the savings in the warehouse in order to seek no benefits?   HK AND ES

DEVELOPMENT OF CONFUCIAN POLITY II

Sŏngjong's reign witnessed a rapid expansion of the authority of the central government throughout the kingdom. Confucian reforms were accompanied by much more subtle developments in Koryŏ society. Court procedures were refined as ceremony became a set part of official life. The first passage presented here, written in the fourteenth century by Yi Chehyŏn (1287–1367), describes the formal procedures used in meetings of the highest state council early in the dynasty and then goes on to deplore their subsequent decay. The Privy Council, composed of officials of the highest ranks of the Secretariat Chancellery and Security Council, met as needed and deliberated on important matters of state. The king made final decisions but only after carefully considering the Privy Council's recommendations, which were arrived at on the basis of unanimous consent. Precedent and regularized behavior were important in this Confucian order, as was consensual decision making. In this passage, Yi Chehyŏn shows how a formal atmosphere was created to allow adequate discussion and the rendering of a decision on which all members had pondered.

Good government was important not only in the highest echelons of authority but throughout the realm. King Hyŏnjong (1009–1031), who ascended the throne in the wake of the forced abdication of King Mokchong (997–1009) and under increasing military pressure from the Khitans, built on the earlier reforms by reorganizing the local government system. As part of his reorganization of local government, in 1018, on the eve of the third and most massive Khitan invasion, which Koryŏ resolutely repulsed, he directed local officials to be more responsible in assuring good government and preventing possible corruption.

Yi Chehyŏn: The Etiquette of Privy Council Meetings

[From *Yŏgong p'aesŏl* 1:10a–11b]

In Sinjong's reign [1197–1204] Ki Hongsu [1148–1210] and Ch'a Yaksong [d. 1204] became executives in the Royal Secretariat and sat in the joint meetings [of the Privy Council],[23] where Ch'a asked Ki how the peacocks were doing and Ki too queried Ch'a about the method of raising peonies. [Because of their lack of seriousness] they were ridiculed by their contemporaries.

[Earlier] Koryŏ set up the Privy Council and made the chancellor, executives of the Secretariat Chancellery, assistant executives in political affairs and letters, and administrator of the Chancellery its superintendents, whereas officials in the Security Council below the superintendent became state councilors. When the state had a serious decision to make, they all met, calling the meeting *hapchwa* [joint meeting]. The joint meeting, however, sometimes met only once a year, and at other times it did not meet for several years. Later, the Privy Council changed its name. It was not until Koryŏ was placed under the suzerainty of the Mongols and began to have a great increase in urgent affairs of state that the state councilors of the Chancellery and the Security Council met all the time.

[*There follows a detailed account of the protocol and etiquette that should prevail at Privy Council meetings. (See SKC 1:294.)*]

When the chief registrar announces the items on the agenda before them, everyone should express a yes or no based on his opinion on the issues. The registrar moves back and forth among them and tries to bring the discussion to a consensus, and after consensus is reached, it should then be implemented. This is called *ŭihap* [deliberating for a consensus]. Aside from this, those present sit properly and say nothing. Looking solemn, they are to be truly respectful and stately.

Nowadays the state councillors of both the Chancellery and the Security Council have needlessly increased in number, and each has an official consultant to promote his interests. The superintendent of the Finance Commission improperly sits above the deputy prime minister, while the junior and senior commissioners sit above and below the minister of punishment. They come and go in a group, frequently making loud conversation and laughing. They show no restraint in talking about the personal matters of others and even about profiting from the gains and losses in rice and salt market prices. This may be compared to the dialogue on peacocks and peonies by Ki Hongsu and Ch'a Yaksong. Likewise this will pass.   *HK AND ES*

King Hyŏnjong: Six Instructions to Magistrates

[From *Koryŏ sa* 75:13a–b]

In the second month of Hyŏnjong's ninth year [1018], six points to be observed by the staffs of all provincial governments were newly issued:

One, inquire into the hardships of the people.
Two, examine the abilities of the local head clerks.
Three, detect thieves and the crafty.
Four, investigate the breaking of laws by the people.
Five, encourage filial and fraternal conduct as well as modesty and honesty among
    the people.
Six, investigate local clerks' loss of public funds.   *HK AND ES*

KORYŎ'S FOREIGN RELATIONS

Foreign affairs remained a major concern for Koryŏ. Wang Kŏn had warned in his "Ten Injunctions" of potential problems with the Khitans to the north. This warning proved to be prophetic, for by the end of the tenth century, Khitan raids were creating a crisis in Koryŏ. The northern state of Parhae, overwhelmed by the Khitans, fell in the early tenth century (926). From their new base in Manchuria, the Khitans attacked northern China, took control of the area around modern Peking, and founded the Liao kingdom. At the same time Koryŏ was consolidating its control over the peninsula and pushing north. It was only a matter of time before the two would collide. The Khitans were just one of several powers to test Koryŏ's resolve. Later,

Koryŏ also had clashes with the Jürchens and their Chin dynasty while trying to maintain ties with Sung China and casual links with the Japanese.

Koreans were pragmatic, yet resolutely defended their national interests. Sŏ Hŭi (940–998), one of the dynasty's great statesmen, helped structure a foreign policy that did not compromise Korean interests. When confronted with exorbitant Khitan demands backed by armed force, Sŏ Hŭi negotiated boldly. In asserting Koryŏ's right to territory once occupied by the earlier Koguryŏ kingdom, he won a temporary respite from Khitan attacks.

Nearly one hundred years after Sŏ Hŭi, another Koryŏ statesman, Yun Kwan (d. 1111), faced a similar crisis, this one caused by the Jürchens. Khitan power had waned after the middle of the eleventh century and then collapsed before the Jürchens. The Jürchens followed the Khitan pattern and consolidated their power in Manchuria, attacked Sung China, and established the Chin dynasty, which controlled all of northern China by 1126. In contrast to Sŏ Hŭi, however, Yun Kwan proposed a much bolder policy of resistance. He led several expeditions to attack the Jürchens and established "Nine Forts" on Koryŏ's northeastern frontier to control the region.

Yet, throughout this period, Koryŏ's foreign relations still remained precarious. Kim Puŭi (d. 1136), a contemporary of Yun Kwan, for example, proposed a policy marked by caution. Anxious to avoid unnecessary conflict, Kim pragmatically suggested that tributary ties be established with Chin. The court wavered but ultimately normalized its contacts with Chin. Wary of his realm's northern neighbors, the Koryŏ king Munjong (1046–1083) had earlier wanted to reestablish relations with Sung, but his counselors, concerned to avoid complications with the Khitans, had advised against such a policy. Ultimately Munjong did set up formal relations with China, but even in the absence of diplomatic exchanges, Koreans and Chinese had frequent commercial and cultural contacts throughout this period. Koreans openly embraced Sung China, if for no other reason than for its cultural benefits. That Koreans were comfortable with Chinese ideas and norms is readily apparent in many Koryŏ documents.

Sŏ Hŭi: Arguments on War

[From *Koryŏ sa chŏryo* 2:49b–52b]

In the winter, the tenth month of Sŏngjong's twelfth year [993], Chancellor Pak Yangyu was appointed commander of the Upper Army; the executive of the Royal Secretariat, Sŏ Hŭi, became commander of the Middle Army, and the executive of the Chancellery, Ch'oe Yang, became commander of the Lower Army. They were stationed in the Northern Frontier Provinces to defend against the Khitans. In the intercalary month, the king visited the Western Capital and then proceeded to Anbuk-pu, where he heard that armies led by Hsiao Sun-ning of the Khitans had attacked Pongsan-gun and captured the commander of our advance guard army, Reviewing Policy Adviser Yun Sŏan, and others. The king, unable to proceed any further, returned.

As Sŏ Hŭi led the army hoping to rescue Pongsan, Hsiao Sun-ning made an announcement that said: "Our great country has already taken the former territory of Koguryŏ. Now we have sent an expedition against you because your country invaded across the border." Moreover, he sent a letter that said: "As our great country is about to unify land in all four directions, we will exterminate those who have not submitted to us. You should promptly surrender to us without delay."

After seeing the letter, Sŏ Hŭi returned and drafted a memorial declaring that there might be a possibility for peace. The king sent the investigating censor, Yi Mongjin, with a temporary appointment as deputy director of protocol, to the Khitan camp to seek peace. Hsiao Sun-ning again sent a letter, saying: "The army of eight hundred thousand has just arrived. If you do not come out from [beyond] the Taedong River and surrender, we will destroy you. The ruler and officials must all surrender swiftly before our army." Yi Mongjin went to the Khitan camp and asked the reason behind their invasion. Hsiao Sun-ning said: "Since your country does not take care of the people's needs, we solemnly execute Heaven's punishment on its behalf. If you want to seek peace, you must come swiftly and surrender."

After Yi Mongjin's return, the king met with the ranking officials and discussed the matter. Some said that the king should return to the capital and order the highest officials to lead the soldiers and seek a surrender. Others advised giving the land north of the Western Capital [P'yŏngyang] to the Khitans and drawing a line from Hwangju to P'aryŏng as the border.

King Sŏngjong decided to follow the proposal to cede the territory. He opened the granaries in the Western Capital and let the people help themselves to the rice. As there was still a lot of rice left over, the king, fearing that it would be used as provisions by the enemy, ordered that it be thrown into the Taedong River.

Sŏ Hŭi memorialized the king: "If provisions are sufficient, then a fortress can be defended and a war can be won. Whether troops win or lose does not depend on their strength, but only on whether they can take advantage of rifts and move quickly. How can the rice be suddenly abandoned? Moreover, provisions are the sustenance of the people. Even if they may become the enemy's provisions, how could we wastefully throw them into the river? I fear this would not agree with Heaven's wishes." The king, agreeing with Sŏ Hŭi, then retracted his order.

Sŏ Hŭi also sent a memorial that said: "From the Khitans' Eastern Capital to our Anbuk-pu there are several hundred *ri* of land that were all occupied by the Jürchens. King Kwangjong took this land and constructed fortresses at Kaju, Songsŏng, and other places. Now the Khitans have come with the clear intention of taking these two northern fortresses. Their vow to take the former Koguryŏ territory stems from their fear of us. It is not a good strategy therefore to cut off the land north of the Western Capital and give it to them, for as we see, their military strength is already too great. Moreover, the land north of Mount Samgak was former Koguryŏ territory. Should their insatiable greed demand it relentlessly, would we give it all to them? To relinquish our territory to the enemy would be an ultimate shame to us. It is my hope that Your Majesty will return to the capital and let us, your officers, wage one more battle. Even then, it will not be too late to discuss our peace offer."[24]

Having received no reply long after Yi Mongjin had returned, Hsiao Sun-ning finally attacked Anyung-jin. Senior Colonel Tae Tosu and Junior Colonel Yu Pang together fought back and won the battle. After this battle Hsiao Sun-ning dared not advance his troops again but sent messengers urging surrender. King Sŏng-jong sent the presenting official of the Royal Archives, Chang Yŏng, to the Khitan camp as the emissary of peace. But Hsiao Sun-ning said, "You ought to send a minister to the front to see me face to face." The king met with ranking officials and asked, "Who could go to the Khitan camp to repel the enemy through words and make a lasting contribution?" No one among the officials responded except Sŏ Hŭi, who said: "Although I am not bright, how dare I not follow your orders?" The king personally went out to the riverbank and, clasping Sŏ Hŭi's hands, consoled him as he sent him off.

Sŏ Hŭi, taking the state letter with him, went to Hsiao Sun-ning's camp and insisted on the protocol for equals, refusing to bow to Hsiao Sun-ning. Hsiao Sun-ning thought Sŏ Hŭi was extraordinary. Hsiao Sun-ning said to Sŏ Hŭi, "Your country rose in Silla territory. Koguryŏ territory is in our possession. But you have encroached on it. Your country is connected to us by land, and yet you cross the sea to serve China. Because of this, our great country came to attack you. If you relinquish land to us and establish a tributary relationship, everything will be all right."

Sŏ Hŭi replied, "That is not so. Our country is in fact former Koguryŏ, and that is why it is named Koryŏ and has a capital at P'yŏngyang. If you want to discuss territorial boundaries, the Eastern Capital of your country is within our borders.

How can you call our move an encroachment? Moreover, the land on both sides of the Yalu River is also within our borders, but the Jürchens have now stolen it. Being obstinate and crafty, they shift and deceive, and they have obstructed the roads, making them more difficult to travel than the sea. That we cannot have a tributary relationship is because of the Jürchens. If you tell us to drive out the Jürchens, recover our former territory, construct fortresses, and open the roads, then how could we dare not to have relations? If you take my words to your emperor, how could he not accept them out of sympathy?" Sŏ Hŭi's words and complexion were so patriotically indignant that Hsiao Sun-ning knew he could not be forced. Accordingly, he reported this to the Khitan emperor, saying, "Koryŏ has already requested peace, so we ought to withdraw our troops."

Sŏ Hŭi remained in the Khitan camp for seven days and then returned with ten camels, one hundred horses, one thousand sheep, and five hundred rolls of brocaded silk. King Sŏngjong was very pleased and went out to meet him on the bank of the river. The king at once was going to send Chancellor Pak Yangyu as an ambassador of goodwill to see the Khitan emperor. But Sŏ Hŭi again memorialized him: "I made an agreement with Hsiao Sun-ning that we would exterminate the Jürchens and recover the former territory, and then we would open tributary relations. We now have only the territory south of the Yalu River. I suggest that it will not be too late to set up relations after we have acquired the land north of the river." The king said, "If we delay in sending a tributary mission for a long time, I fear there may be undesirable repercussions later." Finally Pak Yangyu was dispatched.   *HK AND ES*

Kim Puŭi: Relations with Chin

[From *Koryŏ sa* 97:3a–b]

The Jürchens, having recently defeated the Khitans, have sent emissaries to Koryŏ asking to establish fraternal ties. High officials have, however, vigorously objected to doing this to the point of wanting to behead the Chin envoy. Kim Puŭi alone submitted a memorial, stating:

> In my humble view, Han China, in its relations with the Hsiung-nu, and T'ang China, in its relations with the Turks, sometimes called themselves subjects and sometimes sent princesses in marriage. Generally they did everything possible to establish friendly relations. Now Sung China and the Khitans have established relations accepting inferior and superior status respectively and have maintained harmony for a long time. The veneration

of the Chinese emperor has made no enemies in the world; instead, barbarian countries submit and serve. This is called "the sage using circumstances to facilitate the Way" and is an excellent policy to protect the nation completely. Earlier, during Sŏngjong's reign, we committed an error in guarding our frontier, hastening the intrusion of the Liao people. Truly this should be a lesson. I humbly hope that your august court will consider a long-range policy to preserve the state so there will be no regrets later.

The members of the State Council all sneered and rejected Kim's suggestions, and thus no reply was made to the Chin envoy. *HK AND ES*

Memorial on Relations with Sung

[From *Koryŏ sa* 8:11a–b]

The king wished to cut timber on Cheju and in Yŏngam and build large ships to be used to establish contacts with Sung China. The Royal Secretariat Chancellery memorialized the king:

The country has established friendly ties with the Khitans, and as a result the northern frontier has experienced no urgent alarms. The people are enjoying their lives. This is a good strategy to protect the country. Earlier, in 1010, the Khitans asked in an accusatory letter, "To the east you have ties with the Jürchens, and to the west you have contacts with Sung China. What are you scheming to do?" And when Minister Yu Ch'am went as an envoy, the resident governor of the Eastern Capital of Liao inquired about Koryŏ's exchanging envoys with Sung, indicating the displeasure and suspicion of the Khitans. If this affair leaked out, certainly it would cause a split. Moreover, Cheju Island is barren, and the people are poor. They are able to make a living only through sea products and sailing. Last autumn, the government required them to cut timber, carry it across the ocean, and use it to build a new Buddhist temple. They overworked themselves to extremes. Now if we again cause a heavy burden, we fear it will provoke other incidents. Moreover, our country has for a long time enjoyed civilized ways, including rites and music. Merchant ships come and go continually, bringing precious goods daily. We do not rely on the Chinese government for trade. If we do not intend to break our ties with the Khitans forever, it is not wise to send envoys to Sung. *HK AND ES*

C H A P T E R   N I N E

Koryŏ Society

This chapter presents a glimpse of the people and society of the first half of
the Koryŏ dynasty, as revealed in the surviving historical sources. The men
of letters who were at the helm of Koryŏ's social order led lives centered on
statecraft, scholarship, and literature. Their task was to apply learning to the
benefit of society by becoming involved in governing. In theory, honest
officials would run the government in a humane and judicious manner,
assuring efficient rule. But Koryŏ, like every other society, had officials who
abused their power and used their influence to intimidate the weak. Despite
the infectious evils of their corruption, however, there were others who, on
reaching the summit of success, chose a path that rejected power and
influence in favor of tireless private efforts to improve the self and society.
Some took the extreme route of rejecting all secular values and led reclusive
lives devoted to spiritual salvation. For such men, Buddhism held an im-
mense appeal.

Confucianism, which stressed adherence to proper human relations based
on status, age, and sex, remained important to Koryŏ life. Loyalty and filial
piety were especially singled out as essential to a strong state and stable
family. Observance of Confucian principles was emphasized throughout the
society, and women as well as men were lauded for their contributions to
the observance. The Confucian emphasis on merit also blunted Koryŏ's

indigenous preference for lineage. In contrast to conditions in Silla, social mobility was possible in Koryŏ; indeed, the selections on social change in this chapter provide examples of people who advanced their social status in different periods of the dynasty. Nevertheless, slaves and other lowborn people were carefully watched and restricted in the roles they could play.

THE CONFUCIAN SCHOLAR

By the start of the eleventh century, the state-building process had been completed and Koryŏ entered a new phase of maturity. The success of Koryŏ's earlier kings made possible the emergence of a strong Confucian state that provided a high level of social stability and prosperity. Koryŏ was clearly one of the most sophisticated states of the age.

At the top of the Koryŏ social order were the civil aristocrats. As a class, the civil aristocrats monopolized the highest offices in the government, controlled extensive wealth, and dominated the educational institutions. The aristocrats led comfortable lives that increasingly centered on educational and literary pursuits.

Ch'oe Ch'ung (984–1068), living during this age, advanced the ideals of Confucian education by establishing an academy that became the model for all Korean centers of learning. To advance into the highest ranks of the civil government, a man often had to pass the state examination. The academies that Ch'oe Ch'ung and his disciples founded flourished, producing many successful civil examination candidates. As the initial passage tells, scholars balanced the time spent in rigorous preparation with relaxed occasions such as poetry contests and elaborate banquets. The relationship between a teacher and his students had increasingly gained a Confucian overtone.

Ch'oe Cha (1188–1260), writing a century later, discussed several men who were in charge of the state examination and passed a number of their candidates. These successful candidates remained forever faithful to their examiners. The state examination played an important political and social role in Koryŏ.

Scholar-officials had numerous functions. These men frequently held political office and determined policy for both central and local areas. They also engaged in diverse cultural pursuits, many expressing themselves as accomplished poets and artists. The scholar often had a studio in which he could read, write, and practice calligraphy.

Ch'oe Ch'ung's Academy

[From *Koryŏ sa* 74:34a–35a]

In Munjong's reign, Ch'oe Ch'ung, the grand preceptor and secretary-general of the Royal Secretariat, gathered the young and instructed them diligently. His classes overflowed with students and others, and so he divided them into nine academies. The students were called Lord Chancellor Ch'oe's Disciples. All children of high-ranking officials intending to sit for the state examination first joined his academies and studied under him. Every year in the hot summer months they rented monastic quarters and continued lessons. He selected instructors from among those who had passed the examination and were superior in scholarship and talent but did not hold government office. Their course of study included the nine Confucian classics and three Chinese histories.[1]

Occasionally scholars would visit, and, burning a candle to measure the time, they would compose rhyme-prose and poetry. Listed in the order in which their poems ranked, they would enter as their names were called. Then, setting up a banquet, the young and the old would line up to the right and left and would be presented with wine and food. Acting with propriety and orderly in their relations, they sang and exchanged verses throughout the day. Everybody who watched thought it beautiful and admired it. From this time on, all those who sat for the examination had their names registered on the roster of the nine academies and were called Lord Chancellor Ch'oe's Disciples.

There also were eleven other Confucian scholars who brought their disciples together. These, together with Lord Chancellor Ch'oe's Disciples, were referred to as the twelve student assemblies, but Ch'oe Ch'ung's school was the most successful.   HK AND ES

Ch'oe Cha: Teachers and Disciples

[From *Pohan chip* 1:7a–b]

Examinees respect examiners of the state examination as sons would respect fathers. P'ei Hao[2] three times oversaw the T'ang state examination. His disciple Ma Yin-sun[3] supervised the examination once and took those who passed to greet P'ei. P'ei then composed a verse:

> *Three times I supervised the examination,*
> *And I have reached the age of eighty.*
> *Now I meet my disciple's disciples.*

In our own Koryŏ dynasty, when Academician Han Ŏnguk led his students to greet Lord Munsuk Ch'oe Yuch'ŏng [1095–1174], the latter composed a poem:

> *How great an honor to have you all come and visit.*
> *Happy indeed am I to see my disciple's disciples.*

Lord Yangsuk [Im Yu, 1150–1213] was the maternal uncle of three kings [Ŭijong, 1146–1170; Myŏngjong, 1170–1197; and Sinjong, 1197–1204)] and held the position of first minister. His disciple Lord Munjŏng Cho [Ch'ung, 1171–1220], supervisor of sacrificial wines, supervised the state examination and took his successful examinees to the Office of Royal Edicts to greet Im Yu. Yi Illo [1152–1220] composed a poem of congratulations:

> *For ten years at the Secretariat Chancellery you have assisted the promotion of peace.*
> *Four times you have single-handedly managed the state examination.*
> *The nation's new scholar has repaid his indebtedness to its former leading scholar.*
> *Now the former disciple has himself obtained new disciples.* HK AND ES

LIFE OF THE ARISTOCRAT

Aristocratic power in Koryŏ peaked in the early twelfth century. Two clans in particular, the Kims of Ansan and the Yis of Kyŏngwŏn, dominated court life. Through intermarriage with the royal family and extensive political and economic power, these lineages placed many of their clansmen in important dynastic offices. The Kyŏngwŏn Yi lineage makes an especially good study, for some of their clansmen controlled the kingdom for nearly three generations and ultimately tried twice to usurp the throne. Despite their later arrogance and occasional abuse of power, Kyŏngwŏn Yi clansmen were highly literate scholars schooled in the Confucian classics, as seen in the first selection presented here.

Yi Chagyŏm (d. 1126), one of the most powerful and despised civil officials in early Koryŏ, at the peak of his power had his grandson Injong on the throne, and two of his daughters were married to the monarch.[4] Indicating the arrogance of power, the second selection portrays the decadence of Yi Chagyŏm's age. Symptomatic of the times, such arrogance was not limited to the leading Kyŏngwŏn Yi lineage, as other civil aristocrats increasingly abused their privileges too. Kim Tonjung (d. 1170), the son of Kim Pusik (1075–1151), of the prestigious Kim clan of Kyŏngju, epitomized the pursuit of ostentation and luxury as he expended great sums to build gardens and temples.

The Splendors of the Yi Clan of Kyŏngwŏn

[From *Pohan chip* 1:6a]

From early in the dynasty, the Yi clan of Kyŏngwŏn has produced great officials generation after generation. At the time of the Duke of Changhwa Yi Chayŏn [d. 1086], his son Ho became Count of Kyŏngwŏn, and three other sons, Chŏng, Ŭi, and An, all became state councillors. Yi Chayŏn's grandchildren all intermarried with the royal family and prospered as royal relatives. From ancient times to today, this may be unprecedented.

Earlier, when Ŭi was an official of the Policy Critics, there were some yin-yang practitioners who, insisting on geomancy, talked about each others' deficiencies. When the king asked about this, Ŭi responded: "Yin and yang principles are rooted in the *Book of Changes,* but the *Book of Changes* does not discuss the deficiencies of geomancy. Later irrational practitioners, incorrectly asserting this, wrote things that have confused the people. Besides, since geomancy is false and foolish, there is nothing in it worthy of acceptance." The king in his heart agreed with this. *HK AND ES*

THE SCHOLAR AND BUDDHISM

The Koryŏ literati generally were of the Buddhist faith and saw no apparent contradiction in pursuing Buddhist beliefs along with Confucian practices. Confucianism addressed their societal concerns while Buddhism met their spiritual needs. The first selection, written by Kim Puch'ŏl (d. 1136) of the renowned Kyŏngju Kim lineage, discusses the scholar-official Yi Chahyŏn, who gave up his government posts to practice his faith more devoutly. Yi Chahyŏn was from the same clan as Yi Chagyŏm, and his life reveals that the aristocratic Kyŏngwŏn Yi clan also produced refined, disciplined individuals. Clearly there was an aesthetic side to the life of the Koryŏ official that was not always satisfied by active political involvement.

Kim Puch'ŏl: The Disciplined Life of Yi Chahyŏn

[From *Tong munsŏn* 64:27a–30b]

Lord Yi Ŭi, former senior policy adviser and commissioner of the Security Council, became the inspector of warehouses for the Ch'unju circuit. Cherishing the beautiful scenery of Mount Kyŏngun, he built a temple on the former site of Paegam Meditation Cloister and called it Pohyŏn Hall. This was the first year of Hsi-ning [1068]. Later Master Hŭii [Yi Chahyŏn, 1061–1125] gave up his government positions and secluded himself here, and from then on robbers disappeared and tigers vanished from the area. And the name of the mountain was changed to Ch'ŏngp'yŏng. After having seen the Bodhisattva Mañjuśrī twice, he thought he should study the fundamentals of Buddhadharma, and therefore he changed the name of the hall to Mañjuśrī and renovated it.

Master Hŭii was Lord Yi Ŭi's oldest son. His name was Chahyŏn, and his courtesy name was Chinjŏng. His appearance was exceptional; his disposition was calm and dispassionate. In the sixth year of Yüan-feng [1083] he passed the state examination [*chinsa* degree], and in the fourth year of Yüan-yu [1089], when he was executive assistant in the Bureau of Music, he resigned his government post and withdrew from an active official life. While traveling about, he reached the Imjin River. Crossing it, he vowed to himself, "With this crossing I will never return to the capital." Although there was generally nothing he did not study, he researched deeply into Buddhist principles and especially liked Meditation teachings. He said to himself, "Once I read in the *Recorded Sayings of Hsüeh-feng I-ts'un* [822–908] the statement, 'When the truth is everywhere, why do you look for it in only one place?' Looking at these words, I suddenly realized their truth. From that time on, I understood and carried no doubts about the teachings of Buddha." After this, he traveled to all the famous mountains of Korea and visited the sites of the ancient sages.

Yejong [1105–1122] several times instructed his palace attendants to grant Master Hŭii royal gifts of tea, incense, and Buddhist paintings in large amounts and ordered him to come to the palace. But not wishing to abandon the vow made when he crossed the river, to the end Hŭii did not comply with this royal request.

If we try to evaluate Master Hŭii's life, we must note that from ancient times there have been many gentlemen of high principle who have lived as recluses. Generally, lonely officials or unlucky people with no hope of advancing in life choose secluded lives. In the beginning they contentedly live in the wilderness, but in the end they fail to maintain their intentions, becoming troubled. Moreover, I have never before heard of a person from a powerful house related to the royal family who has been able to live his life in the wilderness. Master Hŭii, born to wealth and power, passed top in the state examination through his literary skill and entered government service with many advantages. Thus to him advancing to a ministerial position or becoming a general was as easy as picking up straw off the ground. He rejected wealth and power as one might discard a worn shoe. Thinking life was like a drifting cloud, he went into the mountains forever, never returning to the capital. Is this not strange indeed?

Moreover, Master Hŭii's family had for successive generations intermarried with the royal family, becoming one of the first families of Korea. Yet Master Hŭii alone, indifferent to worldly concerns, remained unaffected by worldly ambition. And yet with his virtue and personality so respected, how could men of wisdom help admiring him and at the same time not regret his withdrawal from government?

HK AND ES

The Family

Lineage was at the very core of Koryŏ's political order. Not only did the clan lineage enable great families to rise in society, but as the following passages demonstrate, it determined one's status, whether aristocrat or slave. Accordingly, relations within the family were extremely important for the smooth functioning of this society, an attitude that was reinforced by Confucian ideology.

Of all the values Confucianism emphasizes, filial piety receives special attention. King Sŏngjong (981–997), Koryŏ's sixth monarch, in his rescript on filial piety, asked that filial subjects be recognized and rewarded. As the king indicated, to be filial at home meant to be loyal to the state. In short, filial behavior would help to secure the state and bring harmony to society.

Sound family relations are evident too in Ch'oe Nubaek's twelfth-century tomb inscription for his wife, Yŏm Kyŏngae. In this beautiful tribute, Ch'oe describes his deceased wife's humility and untiring devotion to him and his family. The woman's role in Koryŏ society is revealed to a limited degree through this eulogy. The description also provides a rewarding glimpse of social history, convincingly demonstrating that not all court officials lived lives of splendor.

King Sŏngjong: Rescript on Filial Piety

[From *Koryŏ sa* 3:17a–18b]

Generally in governing the country, one must first attend to what is fundamental. In doing so, nothing surpasses filial piety. This was exemplified by the Three August Sovereigns and the Five Emperors.[5] Filial piety is the order of myriad affairs and the core of all virtues. Accordingly, a Chinese emperor congratulated Yang Yin[6] for honoring his parents and built a gate to commemorate this in his home town. The emperor of Chin China commended the extreme filial piety of Wang Hsiang [185–269][7] by ordering his name recorded in histories.

As a child, I lost my father, and I may have grown up foolish and ignorant. Entrusted with the succession, I inherited the responsibility to protect the dynasty. Recalling my deceased grandfather, I grieve over the brevity of human life. Whenever I think of past times with my brothers, I feel even more fraternal affection. Accordingly, if we take the precepts from the six Confucian classics and rely for a ritual norm on the three ritual texts,[8] this will make the customs of a country return to the five filial virtues expected of rulers, feudal lords, officials, scholars, and peasants.

Recently I have dispatched officials to the six provinces to spread instructions to help the old and the weak who are starving and wandering, to rescue destitute widowers and orphans, and to look for and visit filial sons, obedient grandchildren, righteous husbands, and chaste women.

There was in Kurye-hyŏn, Chŏnju, a person named Son Sunhŭng. When his mother died of an illness, he painted a portrait of her and placed it on an altar. Once every three days he attended her grave, serving her as if she were living.

In Chibul station, Unje-hyŏn, a person named Ch'adal had three brothers, and together they supported their old mother. Ch'adal told his wife to attend his mother, but she was not diligent, and so he immediately divorced her. His two younger brothers also single-heartedly served their mother without even a thought of marrying.

The mother of Pak Kwangyŏm of Moran-ri in the Western Capital [P'yŏngyang] had been dead for seven days. Suddenly he saw some dried wood that seemed to be shaped like his mother. He carried it to his home and revered it with all propriety.

The ruler is the sovereign of all the people, and the people are the subjects of the ruler. If there are good deeds, it is my blessing. If there are evil deeds, it is my worry. Illuminate action that respects parents so as to display the spirit of good customs. If humble, rural peasants diligently think about filial piety, how can government officials neglect serving their parents? Truly if one is filial at home, he will certainly be a loyal official for the state. All scholars and commoners, please take my words to heart.   *HK AND ES*

Ch'oe Nubaek: Tomb Inscription of Yŏm Kyŏngae

[From *Chōsen kinseki sōran* 1:357–359]

On the twenty-eighth day, *musul,* of the first month of the sixth year of Huang-t'ung [12 March 1146], the wife of Hannam Ch'oe Nubaek, Lady Yŏm, Duchess of

Pongsŏng-hyŏn, died in her country house. Ch'oe Nubaek composed the following tomb inscription.

As a person, my wife was pure and modest. She was very literate and well understood moral obligations. In speech, appearance, skill, and conduct, she was superior to others. Before marriage she ably served her parents; after marriage she was extremely diligent in wifely ways. She was the first to perceive and carry out the wishes of elders, and with filial piety she nourished my now deceased mother. In good and bad fortune, in congratulations and condolences, she could share the feelings of immediate family members and in-laws. There was no one who did not praise her.

Earlier, I was sent out as a magistrate to P'aeju [in Chŏlla] and Chungwŏn [in Ch'ungch'ŏng]. Without hesitation, crossing mountains and streams, she accompanied me all the way. And when I was involved in military matters, she endured hardship in our poor home and often made and sent military uniforms. And when I was a palace attendant, she used every means possible to supply delicacies to present to the king. How she followed me through all of these difficulties for twenty-three years I cannot entirely record.

One day she said to me, "You are a man of letters. Mundane matters should not be important to you. I consider providing clothes and food for the family to be my task. Even though I repeatedly put forth effort to do this, it does not always come up to my expectations. Later on, even if I unfortunately die first and you attain more income, enabling you to do everything you wish, please remember me for trying to ward off poverty, not for my lack of talent." As she finished speaking, she released a vast sigh.

In the spring of [1145], ŭlch'uk, I advanced from supervising attendant in the Office of Heir Apparent to junior monitor, drafter of royal edicts and proclamations. My wife, showing her happiness in her face, said, "It seems we have almost seen the end of our poverty." I responded to her, "Being a policy critic is not a position to earn a rich stipend." My wife said, "If suddenly one day you are standing in the palace court with the king arguing over an issue, even if I am forced to wear a thorny wooden barrette and poor cotton skirts and carry heavy burdens in making our life, I will accept it willingly." These were not the words of an ordinary woman.

I continued to be promoted many times and successively received higher stipends. In looking at my family's present situation, however, it is not as good as in the days when my wife struggled to make ends meet. How could anyone say my wife did not have talent? When my wife was about to die, in leaving her last instructions to me and our children, all her words were reasonable and many were worth listening to.

When she died, her age was forty-seven. Her epitaph reads: "I, your husband, pledge not to forget you. That I am not yet buried together with you gives me great pain. The children will live in harmony and expect to be prosperous forever."

HK AND ES

SOCIAL STATUS

Only a small minority in Koryŏ enjoyed lives of luxury and wealth. Although most people lived lean, austere lives, Koryŏ society permitted a limited degree of mobility. For the intellectually able, there were always opportunities to advance, for example, through the state examination. Marriage presented a potential means of moving up the social ladder.

An Hyang (1243–1306), who lived in the later period of the dynasty, came from the middle level of Koryŏ society. The short description offered here reveals the personal interaction between a hereditary local clerk and a centrally appointed official. Both had their own bases of power that could conflict but assured orderly dynastic rule when used effectively. Chŏng Kasin (d. 1298), the subject of the next selection, was another official who lacked an esteemed lineage. This anecdote clearly reveals the importance of one's lineage in establishing marriage ties even for those who were not members of the elite.

An excellent source for understanding twelfth-century Koryŏ is the *Illustrated Account of Koryŏ (Kao-li t'u-ching)* by Hsü Ching (1091–1153) of Sung. Hsü visited Koryŏ on a mission from China in 1123 and compiled this work describing Korea and the Koreans. In this particular passage, he briefly identifies the major social classes of Koryŏ for his Chinese readers and then gives a frank account of what he interprets to be Korean behavioral norms. Although Hsü's ethnocentrism is readily apparent in this and other passages, his work sheds precious and otherwise unavailable light on aspects of Koryŏ life.

The Career of An Hyang

[From *Koryŏ sa* 105:28a–b]

An Hyang's original name was Yu, and he was from Hŭngju. His father, Pu, was a local clerk with a degree in medicine who advanced to the post of deputy commissioner of the Security Council by the time he retired. As a boy, An Hyang enjoyed studying, and early in King Wŏnjong's reign he passed the state examination. Once he went to Andong and ordered a local clerk to wash his feet. The clerk responded, "I am a local official. How can you disgrace me?" The clerk then plotted with a number of other local clerks to reproach An Hyang. An old clerk who had observed An's appearance came out and said, "I have seen many people. He will certainly become prominent. Do not take him lightly."

HK AND ES

The Career of Chŏng Kasin

[From *Koryŏ sa* 105:23b–24a]

Chŏng Kasin's courtesy name was Honji. His name originally was Hŭng. He was from Naju. His father, Songsu, passed the examination as a locally recommended candidate.[9] From birth, Chŏng Kasin was precocious. Contemporaries especially commended his reading and writing. He went to the capital with the monk Ch'ŏngi. As he was poor and had no one else to rely on, he depended on Ch'ŏngi for food. Ch'ŏngi pitied him and sought to marry him into a rich family, but there were no interested parties except Deputy Director An Hongu, who consented. Even after the engagement was settled, Hongu still lamented, "Although I am of a poor scholarly family, how can I have as a son-in-law the son of a locally recommended candidate?" Not long afterward, Hongu died. As the family daily grew poorer, it permitted the marriage. Ch'ŏngi, taking Kasin's hand, went to Hongu's house. An old woman met them at the gate. With lighted kindling, they could see that it was just a small thatched house. Ch'ŏngi returned and said, crying, "Oh, how has the student Chŏng come to be like this!" *HK AND ES*

Hsü Ching: The Life of the People

[From *Kao-li t'u-ching* 19:99]

Although the Koryŏ territory is not expansive, there are many people living there. Among the four classes of people, Confucian scholars are considered the highest. In that country it is considered shameful not to be able to read. There are many mountains and forests, but because there is not much flat land, their skill at farming has not developed as much as their craftsmanship. As the products of the countryside are all committed to the state, merchants do not travel widely. Only in the daytime do they go to city markets and exchange what they have for what they do not have. Although the people are prosperous, the favors they extend, however, are few. As they are lascivious, they love freely and value wealth. Men and women take marriage lightly and divorce easily. They do not follow proper ritual, which is deplorable.   HK AND ES

PEASANTS AND SLAVES

Koryŏ accepted the Confucian social differentiation into four classes: scholars, farmers, artisans, and merchants. At a still lower level were slaves and other menials. For them, upward mobility was difficult, if not impossible. They were the exploited underdogs of society whose labor helped pay for the extravagances of the elites.

Farmers, ranking second on the social ladder, produced the crops and paid the taxes in the kingdom, but impoverished peasants, as "The Burden of Corvée Labor" tells, were especially hard pressed. In fact, desperate social conditions like these ultimately contributed to the military coup of 1170 and to the accompanying social unrest.

Koryŏ enacted strict codes to limit the upward mobility of slaves. The rationale for this policy, undoubtedly influenced by Silla norms, is presented in the second selection. Although this memorial was written in 1300 in protest against the Mongol attempt to reform the slavery system in the Koryŏ kingdom, it describes events common to the entire dynastic period.

On occasion, slaves caused problems. In "Social Mobility of Slaves," the final passage presented here, the slave P'yŏngnyang, through his own hard work, became rich and bought his freedom. He then overstepped social boundaries, committed hideous crimes, and was punished. To the man of Koryŏ, the message was clear. Slaves, aside from being an indispensable source of labor, were inherently corrupt and must be suppressed. To the modern reader, this episode provides yet another insight into Koryŏ's social order.

The Burden of Corvée Labor

[From *Koryŏ sa* 18:31b]

Earlier, when building pavilions, each corvée worker brought his own food. One worker was too poor even to do that, so the other workers shared with him a spoonful of their own food. One day his wife came with food and said, "Please ask your friends to come and share it with you." The worker said, "Our family is poor. How did you prepare food? Did you have intimate relations with another man to get it, or did you steal it?" His wife replied, "My face is too ugly for me to be intimate with anyone, and I am too stupid to know how to steal. I simply cut my hair and sold it." Then she showed her head. The worker sobbed and could not eat. Those who heard this story were all deeply moved.   *HK AND ES*

Inheritance of Slave Status

[From *Koryŏ sa* 85:43b–44a]

In the past, our founding ancestor, setting down instructions to posterity on the question of inheritance, stated: "In general, the offspring of the lowest class [ch'ŏnnyu] are of a different stock. Be sure not to allow the people of the lowest class to become emancipated. If they are permitted to become free, later they will certainly get government positions and gradually work [their way] into important offices, where they will plot rebellions against the state. If this admonition is ignored, the dynasty will be endangered."

Accordingly, the law of our country provides that only if there is no evidence of lowborn status for eight generations in one's official household registration may one receive a position in the government. As a rule, in the lowborn class, if either the father or mother is low, then the offspring is low. Even if the original owner of a lowborn person frees him, allowing him to achieve commoner status, the descendants of that freed individual must return to low status. If the owner has no heirs, the descendants of his freed lowborn belong to his clan. This is because they do not want to allow lowborns to achieve permanent commoner status.

Still there is fear that some may flee and escape their status, becoming commoners. Accordingly, even though we take preventive measures, many take advantage of the situation and become crafty. There is also fear that some, relying on power or merit, will dare to take the law into their own hands and plot rebellion against the state, but eventually they are destroyed. Although we know it is not easy to heed the founder's admonition, we still fear there is no way to check all disloyal feelings.   *HK AND ES*

Social Mobility of Slaves

[From *Koryŏ sa* 20:24b–25a]

P'yŏngnyang was exiled to a distant island. The house slave of Executive Kim Yŏnggwan,[10] he once lived in Kyŏnju. Through hard work at farming, he became rich. By sending bribes to rich and powerful people, he was manumitted from his low status, became a commoner *[yangmin]*, and achieved the position of executive captain.[11] His wife was Deputy Director Wang Wŏnji's house slave. Wŏnji's house was poor, so he took his family and became dependent upon P'yŏngnyang. P'yŏngnyang treated him generously, urging him to return to the capital. Secretly with his wife's brothers, Inmu, Inbi, and others, they killed Wŏnji, his wife, and children on the road. He then felt happy that he had no master and would forever be able to be a commoner. P'yŏngnyang's son Yegyu was appointed lieutenant and was married to the daughter of Pak Yujin, superintendent of the P'algwan endowment. Inmu married the daughter of Instructor of Classics Pak Usŏk. People were highly indignant over this. Thereupon, the censorate arrested and interrogated them and banished P'yŏngnyang. It dismissed Yujin and Usŏk. Inmu, Inbi, and Yegyu all fled.   *HK AND ES*

CHAPTER TEN

Military Rule and Late Koryŏ Reform

The military coup of 1170 brought important political and social changes to Koryŏ. After rebellious officers seized power, military rule remained unstable until the rise of General Ch'oe Ch'unghŏn (1149–1219) in 1196. Under General Ch'oe and his immediate successor, there was a concerted effort to resolve the major social and political issues then confronting Koryŏ society. To strengthen control over the kingdom, the military leaders devised new institutional mechanisms to administer authority and recruit personnel as well as to support military force. They also continued to rely on civilian scholars to manage the government bureaucracy. Nevertheless, the start of the military period was accompanied by considerable domestic unrest as monks, peasants, and slaves rebelled, hoping to use the political instability triggered by the military revolt to redress their own grievances and to further their own interests. The power of the Ch'oe house rose as it demonstrated its mastery by quickly suppressing these uprisings.

By the middle of the thirteenth century, with the invasion of the Mongols, Koryŏ's military leaders faced a new challenge to their power. Although the military regime first met defeat by the Mongols in 1231, they continued resistance until 1259, when the Koryŏ court finally sued for peace, following the fall of the Ch'oe house. Despite the peace, relations with the Mongols frequently remained adversarial as Koryŏ officials and monarchs sought to sustain Koryŏ's independent identity. As Mongol power waned, Koryŏ leaders pursued anti-Mongol policies with greater vigor, and in the last decades of the dynasty, Neo-Confucian reformers came forward with sweeping reform proposals. Buddhism, which had closely associated itself with the old order, now came under attack as the reformers sought in their ideology a new framework for governance.

ESTABLISHMENT OF MILITARY RULE

The 1170 military coup d'état brought a distinct change to the Koryŏ kingdom as military officers vaulted into positions of power, crushing the traditional civilian leadership. Chŏng Chungbu (d. 1178), the mastermind of the coup, was a member of an old military family that had produced generals in preceding reigns. Unable any longer to stomach the insulting injustices being heaped upon military officials, he led a revolt. Joined by his subordinates, Yi Ŭibang and Yi Ko, in overthrowing the king, he attacked in particular those powerful officials and eunuchs who had belittled the military and discriminated against it. In the purge that followed, Chŏng and his men did not kill all high-ranking civilians, as has often been claimed—indeed, they executed some military officials unsupportive of their cause, as well. Employing both civil and military officials who were not antagonistic toward the new leadership, Chŏng and his associates attempted to build a new order.

With the military takeover, however, political and social conditions rapidly deteriorated as generals contended among themselves for power. This situation did not begin to improve until 1196, when another general, Ch'oe Ch'unghŏn, successfully revolted and established a new order through which he dominated the kingdom until his death. Then his son U (also known as I; d. 1249), grandson Hang, and great-grandson Ŭi (d. 1258) in succession perpetuated the Ch'oe leadership until 1258.

But the Ch'oe house was not without its own internal power struggles, as Ch'unghŏn's brother Ch'ungsu vied with him for control. But Ch'oe realized that even though he possessed supreme military authority, it was unwise for his family to penetrate the highest lineages through a marriage tie with the royal family. He fought his brother Ch'ungsu over this issue, marking the first major power struggle after the establishment of his control.

Ch'oe Ch'unghŏn endeavored to build a strong and effective government. Shortly after seizing power, he presented a memorial (the second selection) delineating the fundamental faults of the previous rule and proposing ways to rectify the wrongs of the past. The memorial is a Confucian document chastising the king for allowing treacherous men to rule and for not being diligent in searching for honest officials. In it, Ch'oe also points out that abuses perpetrated by the Buddhist establishment and great families were the causes of the dynasty's woes. Through this call for reform and subsequent actions, he sought to revitalize the dynasty and its institutions with the goal of building a new, lasting order centered on Ch'oe authority.

The Ch'oe house inaugurated the privatization of government power through the construction of its own political and military machines. It never denied the court's nominal authority; it simply overshadowed the court. The two principal organizations through which the Ch'oes handled government affairs were the Directorate General of Policy Formation (Kyojŏng togam) and the Personnel Authority (Chŏngbang). The Directorate General coordinated the enactment of decrees for the Ch'oe house. The Personnel Authority, described in the third selection, specifically concerned itself with civil personnel matters in the government under Ch'oe control. The men who held positions in the Personnel Authority formed a high-caliber group including a number of the learned scholars of the day, many of whom had passed the examination. These officials, while holding positions in the personnel administration of the Ch'oe, frequently held concurrent offices in the dynastic government structure, thereby enjoying stipends and land grants in addition to benefiting from Ch'oe largess.

A similar pattern emerged in the military sector. Ch'oe's private forces were already influential during the early years of Ch'oe rule, and this trend became all the more dramatic with the passage of time. At the core of Ch'oe's private forces was his Personal Security Force (Tobang), but this unit did not originate with Ch'oe. Rather, another strongman, Kyŏng Taesŭng (1154–1183), fearing for his life after seizing power, had institutionalized this special military detachment in 1181, and Ch'oe twenty years later further strengthened it. In addition to the Personal Security Force, which served as his personal bodyguard, Ch'oe and then his son U nurtured a large private army that eventually replaced the regular dynastic troops.

The Ch'oe house also perpetuated its power by building a strong financial base. From the start of his rule, Ch'oe sought to use the traditional land system as a means to pay the military and civilian personnel he used to strengthen his authority. He was also quick to abuse the traditional order for his personal gain. Throughout the period of military rule, the Ch'oe house remained the greatest landowner in the kingdom, with especially large estates in the southern provinces.

This trend continued even after the Ch'oe house was toppled by Kim Injun (d. 1268). Kim, a personal slave of the Ch'oes, tried to build a system following the pattern of his earlier masters. Although Kim's rule lasted only a few years, he too aggressively seized land wherever possible to build an economic base for his power. With the help of his sons and retainers, as shown in the final selection, he terrorized the countryside, amassing wealth and property, especially in the fertile southern regions of the kingdom.

The 1170 Military Coup

[From *Koryŏ sa* 128:2a–3b]

In Ŭijong's twenty-fourth year [1170] the king was attending a memorial service, and again he partied with his favorite civilian officials, exchanging poems and forgetting the time. The military escorts became especially hungry. When Chŏng Chungbu went out to relieve himself, Executive Captains Yi Ŭibang and Yi Ko of the Kyŏnyŏng Royal Regiment followed and talked to him in secret, saying, "Now the civilian officials are haughty, drunk, and full, but the military officials are hungry and troubled. How long can we endure this?" Chŏng Chungbu, who still resented having had his beard burned by Kim Tonjung, replied, "You are right," and thus they began to plot a coup.

Later, when the king went from Yŏnbok Pavilion to Hŭngwang Monastery, Chungbu said to Ŭibang and Ko, "Now is the time to act. If the king returns directly to the palace from the monastery, we will wait and endure; if he goes to Pohyŏn Hall, however, we cannot lose this opportunity."

On the next day, the king was going to Pohyŏn Hall, and in front of Five Gates, he called his attending officials to prepare wine. Feeling drunk, he said to the officials around him, "What a splendid spot! Maybe it would be a good place for military training." He ordered his officers to hold boxing matches for the five armies.

Knowing that the military officers were disgruntled, the king wanted to soothe them with generous rewards. Han Noe, fearful that the officers were getting special favor, became very jealous. General Yi Soŭng, although an officer, was thin and weak in appearance. He was boxing with another man but lost and fled. Han Noe slapped him and pushed him down below the royal platform. The king and his officials applauded and laughed heartily. Im Chŏngsik and Yi Pokki cursed Yi Soŭng. Thereupon Chŏng Chungbu, Kim Kwangmi, Yang Suk, Chin Chun, and others looked at each other, blanching with rage. Chungbu rebuked Noe in a loud voice, exclaiming, "Even though Soŭng is a military officer, he is an official of third-grade rank. How can you heap so much disgrace on him?" The king took Chungbu's hand and soothed him. Yi Ko pulled out a knife and looked at Chungbu, whereupon Chungbu stopped him.

As the day was getting dark, the king and his entourage approached Pohyŏn Hall. Yi Ko and Yi Ŭibang went ahead with a false royal command to mobilize the Sungŭm troops. As soon as the king entered the gate and his high officials were about to retire, Yi Ko and others killed Im Chŏngsik and Yi Pokki at the gate with their own hands. Han Noe, relying on his close relationship to the eunuchs, hid inside the royal quarters under the king's bed. The king, greatly alarmed, sent his eunuch Wang Kwangch'wi to stop him. Chŏng Chungbu remarked, "The cause of this trouble is Han Noe, and he is still at the king's side. Please send him out to be executed." Palace attendant Pae Yunjae went before the king to report this. Noe, seizing the king's clothing, would not leave. Yi Ko threatened him with a knife, so Noe went outside, where he was immediately killed. Instruction Officer Kim Sokchae told Yi Ŭibang, "Ko dared to draw his knife in front of the king." With an angry look, Ŭibang scolded Sokchae, who did not reply.

Shortly afterward, Transmitter Yi Set'ong, Palace Attendant Yi Tangju, Censor of Miscellaneous Affairs Kim Kisin, Warden Yu Ikkyŏm, Director of Astrology Kim Chagi, Director of Astronomy Hŏ Chadan, and others, along with the accompanying civil officials, functionaries, and eunuchs, all met tragedy. Their corpses were piled as high as a mountain. Earlier, Chŏng Chungbu, Yi Ŭibang, and others had vowed, "Our group will bare our right shoulders and take off our caps; those who refuse will all be killed." Therefore the many military personnel who refused to take off their headgear were also killed. The king, in terror, wanting to soothe them, gave the various generals double-edged swords, whereupon the military officers became even more arrogant. *HK AND ES*

Ch'oe Ch'unghŏn: The Ten Injunctions

[From *Koryŏ sa* 129:4b–6b]

Ch'oe Ch'unghŏn and Ch'oe Ch'ungsu submitted a sealed memorial to the throne saying:

> We humbly submit that the treacherous outlaw Yi Ŭimin's character was treasonous. He slighted his superiors, belittled those below him, and plotted against the throne. As a result, disaster prevailed, causing calamity for the people. Relying on Your Majesty's august power, we took to arms to exterminate him. We wish Your Majesty to reform the failures of the past

and plan the future, emulating the just rules of King T'aejo [Wang Kŏn] so as to brighten and restore the state. We solemnly present ten articles point by point.

Formerly King T'aejo united the Later Three Kingdoms and divined a location for a capital, which he established in Songak. At a propitious site, he built a great palace so his descendants could live there as rulers for myriad generations. Some time ago, the palace was burned and then rebuilt in a grand style. But because he believed in taboos, it was unoccupied for a long time. How does one know that one can rely simply on yin and yang? Your Majesty should, on an auspicious day, move into the palace and follow the eternal heavenly commands.

The number of government offices is based on a fixed number of stipends available. Lately there have been excesses in the number of positions of the Chancellery, the Security Council, and other agencies. Since the fixed number of stipends is insufficient, this has caused great difficulties. Your Majesty should take the old system as a standard, reduce the number of positions, and make appointments accordingly.

Under the system set up by the former king, all land except "public" land was granted to officials and people according to rank. Those in office, however, have become very greedy and have snatched both "public" and "private" land and held them indiscriminately. A single family's holdings of fertile land may extend across districts, and that causes the state's taxes to decline and the military to wither. Your Majesty should instruct the agencies concerned to check official records and see that all illegally seized property is returned to its original owners.

Rents from "public" and "private" land all come from the people. If the people are destitute, how can sufficient rent be collected? The local officials are sometimes dishonest and corrupt; they only seek profits, thereby injuring the people. The slaves of powerful houses fight to collect land rents, making the people groan in anxiety and pain. Your Majesty should select good and able officials and appoint them to the provinces to prevent the powerful families from destroying the people's property.

The state dispatches officials to govern the two frontier districts and examine the five circuits, wishing merely to control local officials' treachery and alleviate the people's suffering. Now, although the various circuit commissioners ought to investigate conditions in the provinces, they do not. Rather they demand exactions, and on the pretense of presenting them to the king, they burden public facilities with transporting them. Sometimes they even appropriate them for personal expenses. Your Majesty should forbid the various circuit officials to present tributes, and make inspections their only duty.

Now few monks are mountain dwellers. Most loiter around the royal palace and even enter the royal sleeping quarters. Your Majesty, being enticed by Buddhism, has on each occasion willingly allowed them to do this. The monks already abuse Your Majesty's good graces and through their activities often tarnish Your Majesty's virtue. But Your Majesty has aided them by commanding the palace attendants to take charge of the Three Jewels—Buddha, Dharma, and Saṅgha—and to use grain as loans to collect interest from the people. The evils of this policy are not trivial. Your Majesty should expel the monks and keep them away from the palace and refuse interest on grain lent to the people.

Recently we have heard that many functionaries in the provinces are avaricious and that their behavior is shameless. The various circuit commissioners who are sent out do not question this. Sometimes even when people are honest, the commissioners do not recognize them. As they allow evil to continue and honesty to be of no benefit, how can one reprove vice and promote goodness? Your Majesty should order the two frontier district commissioners and the five circuit royal inspectors to examine the performance of local officials and then have them report their findings. Promote those who are able; reprimand those who are not.

Today court officials are neither frugal nor thrifty. They repair their homes and decorate their clothes and playthings with precious materials, thereby worshiping the exotic. Their customs have degenerated, and they soon will be in disarray. Your Majesty should admonish the bureaucracy by forbidding ostentation and luxury, and promoting frugality.

In King T'aejo's day, temples were sited in accord with favorable and unfavorable features of geomancy, and this accordingly made the country peaceful. In later times, generals, ranking officials, and unreliable monks, without examining the topographical conditions, built Buddhist temples, calling them their prayer halls. Thus, injuring the earth's vital system, they often produced calamity. Your Majesty should make the officials in charge of yin and yang investigate and destroy immediately any additional temples besides those built by the dynasty, and prevent yourself from becoming the target of ridicule for later generations.

The officials of the Chancellery and the censorate have the duty to remonstrate. If Your Majesty has any shortcomings, they should admonish regardless of the danger to themselves. Now everybody only thinks of flattering even with self-abasement and blindly agrees without discretion. Your Majesty should select the right men and have them speak out in court even to the point of subjecting Your Majesty to severe admonishment.

HK AND ES

Establishment of the Personnel Authority

[From *Yŏgong p'aesŏl* 1A:8b–9a]

The Ministry of Civil Personnel handled the appointment of civilian officials, while the Ministry of Military Personnel was in charge of selecting military officials. They prepared the personnel files, recording personal information like the date of entrance into the government service and degree of hardship of positions held, merits and demerits, and appraising ability. The Royal Secretariat drew up a list of who was to be promoted and demoted, and reported it to the king for approval. The Chancellery received royal decisions and implemented them. This was the law of the country, and it generally coincided with Chinese practices.

When Ch'oe Ch'unghŏn arbitrarily exercised power, deposing and installing kings at will, he resided in the government compounds and with his subordinates controlled the personnel files, deciding on appointment. Through his partisan royal transmitters, he presented the list of his choices to the king for approval. *HK AND ES*

Private Armies

[From *Koryŏ sa* 129:23a–b]

At this time they were about to send troops to defend against the Khitans. The bravest soldiers were all Ch'oe Ch'unghŏn's and U's retainers. Those in the government army were all thin and weak and useless.

Ch'oe Ch'unghŏn reviewed his private troops: From Chwagyŏng-ri to Ugyŏng-ri they formed several lines stretching two or three *ri*. Their lances held three or four silver vases to display to the people of the kingdom in order to recruit more soldiers. His son U's troops, stretching from Sŏni Bridge to Sungin Gate, hoisted banners and beat drums as they trained for battle. Anyone among his retainers who asked to join the government army to defend against the Khitans was at once banished to a distant island. *HK AND ES*

The Estates of Kim Injun

[From *Koryŏ sa* 130:17a]

Kim Injun set up numerous estates and had his retainer Mun Sŏngju control those in Chŏlla and retainer Chi Chun (d. 1268) control those in Ch'ungch'ŏng. They competed in extorting wealth by giving the peasants one peck *[tu]*[1] of rice seed for planting, for which they collected one bushel of rice at harvest. All his sons, imitating this, competed in assembling hoodlums and relied on their power to seize other people's property without restraint. The grievances against them were rampant.   *HK AND ES*

CIVILIANS UNDER MILITARY RULE

The Ch'oe house, while upholding its own military supremacy, took an interest in scholarship. The bounty of literature appearing during the military period revealed that there still was intellectual vitality in this age. Some of this literature is still extant today.

The piece presented here explains the changes that had occurred during the military period as seen by Yi Chehyŏn (1287–1367), who lived nearly a century later. Yi Chehyŏn's description presents a rather bleak picture of the life of literati during the century of military control, reflecting an outlook that favored Confucian values over Buddhist practices.

Yi Chehyŏn: Education Under Military Rule

[From *Koryŏ sa* 110:22b–23a]

King Ch'ungsŏn [1308–1313]asked: "It was said that in the past our country was the equal of China in literary pursuits, but now the scholars all study under Buddhist monks to become skilled in composition. Why is that?"

Yi Chehyŏn replied: "In the early period of the dynasty, King T'aejo wasted no time in building schools to foster talent. As soon as he went to the Western Capital, he ordered the talented Chŏng Ak to become a professor to teach the students of the six ministries. He granted silk to encourage learning and provided a government stipend to nourish them. One can see the earnestness of his commitment. From King Kwangjong's reign on, we fostered education even more, looking up to the Royal Confucian Academy in the capital and promoting rural schools in the countryside so that in all schools one could hear the recitation of poems and plucking of stringed instruments. This is why it was no exaggeration to say that literary pursuits in Korea equaled those in China.

"Unfortunately, a military revolt occurred in the last year of King Ŭijong's reign, and there was indiscriminate destruction of the good and the bad alike. Those escaping death fled deep into the mountains, where, shedding their rank and putting on Buddhist garments, they spent their remaining years. They were like the divine horse being freed of obligation and going off to a mountain to gain freedom.

"Since then, the state has gradually restored civilian rule, but those who desire to study have had no place to go. Therefore, they have all followed Buddhists to study. That is why I said that the idea of students' learning from monks started from this period. Now if Your Majesty is attentive to this expansion of the schools, valuing the six arts[2] and making known the teaching of the five cardinal relations to explain the Way of the former kings, who will turn his back on the true Confucian scholars and follow Buddhist monks?"   *HK AND ES*

PEASANT AND SLAVE UNREST

The military coup of 1170 and the subsequent turmoil in Koryŏ society unleashed political and social tensions and incited the impoverished peasantry and slaves. Indeed, two slaves, Mangi and Manjŏk, tried to take advantage of the turmoil to win their own freedom. Mangi's uprising started shortly after the 1170 coup amid the unsettled conditions sparked by the murder of King Ŭijong and the struggle for power among the generals. Manjŏk, several decades later in 1198, sought to foment a slave rebellion, believing the Ch'oe military leaders would be unable to suppress it. Manjŏk's capture and execution, however, and the quick defeat of the plot, revealed the ability of Ch'oe Ch'unghŏn to assert his authority and maintain his control over the kingdom. Thus even in the politically uncertain military period, many Koryŏ social norms remained intact.

The Slave Leader Mangi's Protest

[From *Koryŏ sa* 19:32a]

Mangi and others burned Honggyŏng Monastery, killed more than ten resident monks, and then forced the head monk to take a letter to the capital. The letter, in short, said: "After having already elevated our locality to a *hyŏn* [county] and appointed a magistrate to win over the people of the area, you have now turned around and again dispatched troops to subjugate us. You arrested my mother and wife. What is the meaning of this? Even if I have to meet death under the knife's blade, I will never surrender and be a prisoner. Make no mistake, I will continue our struggle until I reach the capital."   *HK AND ES*

Manjŏk's Slave Rebellion

[From *Koryŏ sa* 129:12a–13a]

In King Sinjong's first year [1198], the private slave Manjŏk and six others, while collecting firewood on a northern mountain, gathered public and private slaves and plotted, saying, "Since the coup in the year *kyŏngin* [1170] and the countercoup in the year *kyesa* [1173], the country has witnessed many high officials rising from slave status. How could these generals and ministers be different from us in origin? If one has an opportunity, anybody can make it. Why should we still toil and suffer under the whip?"

The slaves all agreed with this. They cut several thousand pieces of yellow paper and on each put the graph *chŏng* [adult man] as their symbol. They pledged: "We will start from the hallways of Hŭngguk Monastery and go to the polo grounds. Once all are assembled and start to beat drums and yell, the eunuchs in the palace will certainly respond. The public slaves will take control of the palace by force, and we will stage an uprising inside the capital, first killing Ch'oe Ch'unghŏn and others. If each slave will kill his master and burn the slave registers, there will be no people of humble status in the country, and we can all become nobles, generals, and ministers."

On the date set to meet, their numbers did not exceed several hundred, so they feared they would not succeed and changed their plans, promising to meet at Poje Temple this time. All were ordered: "If the affair is not kept secret, then we will not succeed. Be careful not to reveal it." Sunjŏng, the slave of Doctor of Legal Studies Han Ch'ungyu, reported this incident to his master. Ch'ungyu told Ch'oe Ch'unghŏn, who seized Manjŏk and more than one hundred others and threw them into the river. Ch'ungyu was promoted to warder in the Royal Archives, and Sunjŏng was granted eighty *yang*[3] of white gold and manumitted to commoner status. Since the remaining gang could not all be executed, the king decreed that the matter be dropped.

HK AND ES

RELATIONS WITH THE MONGOLS

Koryŏ first encountered Mongol troops in the middle of Ch'oe Ch'unghŏn's rule. Wary from the beginning, Koryŏ soon learned of the terrifying power of this new enemy. After almost forty years of resistance, and with the kingdom in ruins, Koryŏ negotiated peace. The Mongols, taking the Chinese dynastic name of Yüan, dominated both Korea and China for nearly one hundred years and forced Koryŏ into a subordinate position.

Koryŏ experienced a gradual Mongolization of its aristocratic culture. The royal house, although still descendants of Wang Kŏn, was forced to intermarry with the Yüan imperial household, and Koryŏ princes spent much of their youth in the Yüan capital. The Eastern Expedition Field Headquarters *(Chŏngdong haengsŏng)*, which the Mongols established in 1280 to subjugate Japan, became their major instrument for dominating Koryŏ.

When the Mongols first attacked Koryŏ in 1231, the Ch'oe leadership quickly met the challenge and stymied Mongol advances. Soon, however, Mongol attacks became much more threatening, throwing Koryŏ's leadership into crisis. The question was whether to surrender or to resist by fleeing to offshore islands. Yu Sŭngdan (1168–1232), realizing that it was the peasantry who paid the price of resistance, advised a negotiated peace. The Ch'oe leadership, in the hands of Ch'oe I (d. 1249), rejected this appeal and called for the evacuation of the Koryŏ capital, Kaesŏng, to Kanghwa Island.

Resistance to the Mongol invasion was energetic. Peasants across the country retreated to forts and fought. One of the greatest battles took place at Kuju in northern Korea, where a beleaguered town withstood months of Mongol attempts to destroy it. Under the leadership of Pak Sŏ, every Mongol siege tactic was effectively checked. Indeed, the people of Koryŏ resisted the Mongol war machine for as long and as effectively as any power in the world could. Slaves also helped in the struggle, but tensions existed within Koryŏ towns and malcontents used the Mongol attacks to redress domestic grievances.

The Mongol invasions finally ended with the Koryŏ court's capitulation. The dispute over the question of surrender ultimately brought about the fall of the Ch'oe house in 1258, leading to a restoration of the court's political authority. Mindful of the destruction inflicted by the Mongols, the civil leaders sued for peace in 1259, but they could not return to the capital until 1270, because of disaffected military leaders who resisted this move. The diehard Sam Pyŏlch'o troops carried their resistance from Kanghwa Island south to the islands of Chin and Cheju. The Sam Pyŏlch'o were destroyed in 1273, but their legacy of resistance to the Mongols has conferred on them a mantle of honor in the minds of Koreans.

Under Mongol domination, Koryŏ leaders were forced to spend years at the Yüan court and to explain every Koryŏ move. They endured Mongol rule but were anxious to avoid entangling their dynasty with Yüan ploys. The Mongols' grand design was the conquest of Japan, and they expected Korea to pay the bulk of the costs, both in manpower and provisions. Yi Changyong

(1201–1272), the Koryŏ envoy to the Yüan court, repeatedly tried to blunt Mongol demands, placing Koryŏ interests above all other concerns.

By the middle of the fourteenth century, Mongol power was eroding, and in 1368 the Ming dynasty rose in China. Korea responded to these events by increasing resistance to Mongol demands. Yi Chehyŏn (1287–1367), one of the period's major writers, used many means to circumvent Mongol policy, while King Kongmin (1351–1374) led the struggle to eliminate Yüan interference.

Resistance to the Mongol Invasion

[From *Koryŏ sa* 103:23a–26a]

Pak Sŏ was from Chukchu, and in 1231 he became military commissioner of the Northwestern Frontier District. The Mongol commander Sartaq swept over Ch'ŏlchu and reached Kuju. Pak Sŏ, as well as the general of Sakchu subcircuit, Kim Chungon; the general of Chŏngju subcircuit, Kim Kyŏngson; and the magistrates of Chŏngju, Sakchu, Wiju, and T'aeju, all leading troops, met at Kuju. Pak Sŏ had General Kim Chungon's troops defend the town on the east and west; Kyŏngson's army defended the south; the special patrol troops of the regional military command and the special patrol troops of Wiju and T'aeju, numbering more than two hundred and fifty men, defended three sides.

The Mongols encircled the town in several layers and attacked the west, south, and north gates day and night. The troops in the city went out at once and attacked them. The Mongol troops captured Wiju Deputy Commissioner Pak Munch'ang and ordered him to enter the town to persuade the defenders to surrender. Pak Sŏ beheaded him. The Mongols selected three hundred crack cavalrymen and attacked the north gate. Pak Sŏ counterattacked and checked them.

The Mongols constructed wheeled observation towers as well as a great platform wrapped with cowhide in which they hid soldiers, using it to approach the base of the town walls to excavate a tunnel. Pak Sŏ bored through the city walls and poured molten iron to burn the wheeled observation towers. The ground also collapsed, crushing more than thirty Mongols to death. Pak Sŏ then burned rotten thatch to ignite the wooden platform, alarming the Mongols and causing them to scatter.

The Mongols suddenly attacked the south of the town with fifteen large catapults. Pak Sŏ constructed platforms on the town walls, and mounting catapults on them, he hurled stones and drove the attackers off. The Mongols also piled up faggots soaked with human fat and used them to attack the town with fire. When Pak Sŏ tried to put them out by pouring water on them, the fire burned even more fiercely. Pak Sŏ then had his men throw mud mixed with water to stop the fire. The Mongols also ignited a cart loaded with grass to attack the gate tower. As Pak Sŏ had prepared water reserves in the tower and poured these from the top of the tower onto the flames, the fire subsequently went out. The Mongols encircled the town for thirty days and attacked it in every conceivable way. Pak Sŏ, quickly responding to the changing situation, steadfastly defended the town. Unable to win, the Mongols retreated, and then, deploying troops regrouped from assaults on various northern frontier district towns, they attacked Kuju again. Lining up thirty catapults for the attack, they destroyed a fifty-*kan*-long corridor in the town wall.[4] As quickly as the walls were smashed, Pak Sŏ chained iron links across the holes and repaired them. The Mongols did not dare attack again.

Then when Pak Sŏ went out fighting and won a great victory, the Mongols attacked Kuju again with a great catapult. But as Pak Sŏ, too, set catapults flinging rocks and killing the enemy in endless numbers, the Mongol troops retreated and camped in a wooded palisade in order to protect themselves.

The next year, the king sent the administrator of the Military Commission of the Rear Army and Junior Policy Critic Ch'oe Imsu, as well as Investigating Censor Min Hŭi. They led the Mongols to a point outside the Kuju wall to order the town's surrender, saying: "We have already sent Chŏng, the Lord of Hŭian, to discuss peace with the Mongol troops, and our three armies have already surrendered. You may cease fighting and come out to surrender." They tried to persuade them four times, but Pak Sŏ would not surrender. Min Hŭi was exasperated by the firm refusal and wanted to draw his sword and stab himself. Ch'oe Imsu again ordered Pak Sŏ to surrender, stressing that he was seriously violating the king's orders. Only then did he surrender.

When the Mongols encircled Kuju, there was a Mongol general whose age was about seventy, and he went below the city wall and looked around at the fortress's ramparts and military weapons and sighed, saying: "Since my youth I have followed the army, and I am accustomed to seeing the cities of the world fought over and defended, but I have never seen anyone being attacked like this and to the end not surrendering. Certainly those military leaders in the city will later become distinguished generals and ministers of the state." Later Pak Sŏ in fact became executive of the Chancellery. *HK AND ES*

Yi Chehyŏn: Opposition to Yüan Policies

[From *Koryŏ sa* 110:23b–25b]

I humbly submit that my country, from its founding by the Wang clan, has lasted more than four hundred years. We have submitted to Yüan, sending tribute every year. Since this has continued for more than one hundred years, our people have benefited profoundly, just as our contributions to Yüan have been plentiful.

In the year *muin* [1218] the surviving bastard Liao prince Chin-shan attacked, plundering the Chinese people and entering the islands in the east. As he continued to act recklessly, Genghis Khan sent marshals Qaji and Jalatai to suppress his plundering, but they encountered heavy snow, which made it difficult to get provisions through. Our King Kojong, however, ordered Cho Ch'ung [1170–1220] and Kim Ch'wiryŏ [d. 1234] to supply provisions and assist with weapons. They captured and killed the bandits with the speed of wedging up bamboo. Thereupon the two marshals and Cho Ch'ung vowed to be brothers and to remember this occasion forever.

When Emperor Shih-tsu [Kublai Khan, 1260–1294] returned from his conquest of South China, our King Wŏnjong, realizing that the Mongols had the Mandate of Heaven and popular support, traveled more than five thousand *ri* to have an audience with the emperor in the distant land of Liangch'u. Moreover, King Ch'ungnyŏl had personally never neglected having audiences with the emperor. At the time of the Mongol conquest of Japan, he not only did everything to supply weapons but was in the vanguard of the army. And at the time of the punitive expedition against the rebellious Yüan prince Qadan [d. 1292], the king assisted the Mongol government troops, killing rebel leaders and thereby assisting the emperor immeasurably. As a result, the emperor gave his princess in marriage to the king, thus strengthening our ties through marital relations. It is also due to Emperor Shih-tsu's rescript that the Koryŏ dynastic tombs and state shrines have been preserved in accordance with ancient customs.

Now I have heard that the imperial court intends to make Korea into a Yüan province by establishing a provincial government there. If this is true, even if we disregard Koryŏ's earlier contributions, what has become of Emperor Shih-tsu's rescript? In reading the provisions of the new imperial decree issued in the eleventh month of last year, I humbly find that by distinguishing right and wrong and establishing peace throughout the world, it purports to restore the wise policies of Emperor Shih-tsu's reign. What His Majesty has said in this decree is truly a blessing for the whole world, but how is it possible that only in the affairs of Koryŏ it has not upheld Emperor Shih-tsu's rescript? The Confucian instructions for posterity in the *Doctrine of the Mean* are no empty statement. According to this book: "The successors I will govern. Those destroyed I will raise. Those in chaos I will control. Those in danger I will pacify."[5] Now for no reason, Korea, a small country that has existed for more than four hundred years, will be extinguished one morning. Its state shrines will have no spirits to enshrine; its royal tombs will no longer have sacrifices. This certainly is not reasonable.

Furthermore, Koryŏ's land does not exceed one thousand *ri*. Its mountains, forests, streams, and marshes, which compose seven-tenths of its area, are useless land. The rent on the land is not sufficient to cover the cost of transporting it. The tax from the people does not meet the cost of official salaries. In terms of Yüan's court expenditures, it is a drop in the bucket. Moreover, Koryŏ is far away and the people are simple. Its language is not the same as China's, and its problems are very different from China's. I fear that if people hear about this decree, it will certainly cause apprehension, and it is not possible to go to every household to explain and put them at ease. Besides, we face the Japanese across the narrow strait of Korea, and when they hear what has been done to us, would they not take this to be a warning and use it to their advantage?

I humbly wish your excellency, keeping in mind how Emperor Shih-tsu remembered our merit and what the instructions in the *Doctrine of the Mean* said, will allow the state to be as a state should be and allow the people to be as they should be. By fostering their government and tax system, you will make Koryŏ your defender. This will sustain boundless happiness for us, and accordingly not only will the people of Koryŏ congratulate each other and praise your virtue, but the spirits of the dynastic ancestral tombs and the state shrines will cry in gratitude, though invisibly.   *HK AND ES*

Late Koryŏ Reforms

Koryŏ leaders were divided among themselves on policy toward China in the waning days of the Yüan dynasty. Those who advocated a sharp break with Yüan eventually grew more vocal in their criticism of the Koryŏ order itself and ultimately moved to found a new dynasty, Chosŏn. Although these leaders were themselves products of the Koryŏ social order, their desire to reform society led them to the eventual overthrow of the dynasty. Ironically, King Kongmin (1351–1374), one of the first to understand his society's need for reform, was also instrumental in inaugurating the liberation from Mongol influence. As shown in the excerpt from the biography of Sin Ton (d. 1371), the king, with the help of his monk-adviser, launched a series of reforms that ultimately broke the control of the Mongol-backed elite. Although the reforms may have been necessary, they evoked harsh criticism from contemporaries and later Confucian historians, as seen in this biography (which, at least in parts, need not be taken literally), written by later Chosŏn court historians.

In the next two selections, Yi Chehyŏn and Yi Saek (1328–1396), leading intellectuals of the period, present their strong arguments for urgent reforms.

Both men entered the central bureaucracy through the civil service examination and distinguished themselves as able officials and scholars active not only in Koryŏ but also in Yüan. As forerunners of the Neo-Confucian reformers of late Koryŏ, they addressed themselves to the most serious economic and military issues facing the government.

Pak Ch'o (1367–1454) was a classics licentiate at the Royal Confucian Academy at the time of King Kongyang (1389–1392). His anti-Buddhist memorial was the most vehement of the various memorials attacking Buddhism at that time. The selection given here is considered the principal section of his memorial. Chŏng Tojŏn (d. 1398) wrote the twenty-chapter *Discourses on Buddha (Pulssi chappyŏn)* as a Neo-Confucian critique of various Buddhist doctrines such as the transmigration of souls, causation, human personality, and mercy. Two chapters considered among the book's most important—those on the transmigration of the soul and on the similarities and differences between Confucianism and Buddhism—are presented here.

The Reforms of King Kongmin and Sin Ton

[From *Koryŏ sa* 132:3a–7a]

Although King Kongmin [1351–1374] had been on the throne for a long time, he did not regard many of the state councillors as satisfactory. He thought that the aristocratic officials and great families were linked in personal cliques, mutually protecting each other. When newcomers first entered the government, they took on affectations and embellished their actions to gain fame. As they became noble and famous, ashamed that their origins were humble, they married into powerful families, entirely casting off their earlier intentions. As for Confucianists, they lacked backbone. But relating to each other as disciples, state examiners, or peers, they formed factions and engaged in favoritism. Since these three groups were all unsuitable for employment, the king had to obtain a man of independence who had abandoned the secular world and use him extensively to correct the abuses of the past.

When the king met Sin Ton [d. 1371], he saw that Sin Ton followed the Way and had few wants. Because Sin Ton was of humble origins and had no close associates, the king believed that if Sin Ton were appointed to handle important affairs of state, he would resolutely pursue them. Accordingly, the king finally decided to choose one among the monks and entrust him with state affairs.

The king asked Sin Ton to save the world by temporarily forgoing his priestly pursuits. Sin Ton pretended to be unwilling, which only strengthened the king's wishes. When the king strongly insisted, Sin Ton replied, "I once heard that the king and his ministers often give in to slander and act against each other. For the benefit of all concerned, I do not wish this to be the case." The king then wrote a pledge in his own hand stating, "May you help me and I help you by letting it be like this in life and death. I will not be misled by the words of others. May Buddha and heaven bear witness."

Thereafter they deliberated state affairs together. Within a month, however, vilifying the ministers, they dismissed Grand Chancellor Yi Kongsu [1308—1366], Chancellor Kyŏng Ch'ŏnhŭng, Superintendent of the Finance Commission Yi Susan, Executive of the Grand Chancellery Song Kyŏng, Deputy Commissioner of the Security Council Han Kongŭi, Assistant Executive in Letters Wŏn Songsu [1323–1366], Co-administrator of the Security Council Wang Chunggwi, and others. The state councillors, censors, and policy critics were all chosen by him, and the position of grand chancellor was for a long time left vacant until he himself filled it. Thereafter, he at last moved out of the palace and lived in a house owned by illustrious people. All the officials went to the house to discuss the affairs of state with him.

Sin Ton asked the king to establish the Directorate-General of the Regularization of Land and Slaves and made himself its superintendent. Throughout the country, placards bearing a proclamation announced:

Recently law and order have greatly deteriorated and graft has become common. The lands of the dynastic ancestral shrines, schools, granaries, temples, and salary stipends, as well as land for military appropriations and patrimonial land and people, have nearly all been taken by powerful families. Some lands that it had been determined were to be returned to the original owners are still held up, and the people who have already been recognized to be commoners are still held as slaves. Among the clerks of the administrative districts [*chu, hyŏn,* and *yŏk*], the government slaves, and commoners who have escaped from the corvée, all have avoided detection and are hidden, greatly contributing to the establishment of great estates. All of this, harming the people and impoverishing the state, causes heaven to send down floods and droughts, as well as unending pestilence. Now we have established a directorate-general to investigate all of this. There should be no interrogation of those who admit their transgressions and reform themselves within a fifteen-day limit in the capital or forty days in the countryside, but those who have passed the deadline and are found guilty will be subject to disciplinary action. Those who make false charges will also be tried.

When this proclamation came out, powerful households that had seized much land and many people returned them to their owners, which caused joy throughout the country. Sin Ton appeared every other day at the directorate-general, where Yi Inim [d. 1388], Yi Ch'unbu [d. 1371], and all others made decisions as Sin Ton dictated. Outwardly feigning concern for public justice and wishing to win over the people through displays of kindness, Sin Ton manumitted all lowborns and slaves who claimed to be commoners. Thereupon slaves rose against their masters and declared, "A sage has appeared."

When beautiful women came to make claims, Sin Ton would outwardly show sympathy and entice them to his house, where he would seduce them. Their appeals would then certainly be redressed. Thereupon petitions from women increased, while officials ground their teeth in disgust.

Superintendent Chang Hae's house slave became a junior colonel. Upon meeting Hae, he offered a bow without dismounting from his horse. When Hae whipped him in anger, the slave made charges to Sin Ton, who then had Hae and his daughter imprisoned by the Patrol Army. Desiring to win people over with these small favors, Sin Ton assisted the wicked this way. As the officials met at Sin Ton's home, carriages and horses filled the streets, while the palace gates remained deserted. Those who understood the implications of this were chilled to their core.

HK AND ES

Yi Chehyŏn: Reform Proposals

[From *Koryŏ sa* 110:34a—37b]

Now Your Majesty, complying with the Yüan emperor's clear commands, has inherited the dynastic accomplishments of your ancestors at an age at which a crown prince customarily would enter school. Ascending in the wake of the former king's failures, how could you not be very careful, if only out of reverence and prudence?[6] As for the substance of reverence and prudence, there is nothing like cultivating virtue.

The important point in cultivating virtue is desiring to approach learning. Now as Master of Sacrifice Chŏn Sungmong has already been named royal tutor, select two wise Confucian scholars to lecture, together with Chŏn Sungmong, on the *Book of Filial Piety*, the *Analects*, *Mencius*, the *Great Learning*, and the *Doctrine of the Mean*. Learn the way of attaining knowledge through the investigation of affairs and things and rectifying the heart through a sincere mind. From among the children of officials, select ten who are honest, genuinely attentive, and fond of learning and propriety to assist Your Majesty as scholars-in-waiting. After mastering the Four Books, study in sequence the Six Classics so that arrogance, extravagance, lewdness, indolence, music, women, and venal officials will not reach your eyes and ears. When you achieve this and it becomes second nature, you will effortlessly realize virtue. That should be the most urgent priority at this time.

Since the correct relationship between ruler and subject is that they be as one, how could they not be closely bound to each other? At present the state councillors only get together when they have banquets, and without a special summons they do not have an audience. What kind of principle is that? Fittingly I request that when Your Majesty sits in your rest hall daily, you discuss state affairs with the state councillors. Even if you have to divide your days to meet them, and even when there are no urgent matters, do not forgo this practice. Otherwise, I fear the great ministers will daily become distant, the eunuchs will daily get closer to you, and you will not be informed on the conditions of the people and the security of the dynasty.

If you get the right people in the posts of prefect and magistrate, then the people will reap benefits. If you do not get the right men, then the people will be harmed. When a high-ranking official is demoted to a lower position, he becomes arrogant and inattentive to laws in his office. When those advanced in age get appointments, they are too feeble to perform their duties. Needless to say, one cannot say enough about those rustic rural gentry who begged for audience and obtained high posts. I request that, as in the ancient system, those officials who have yet to reach the court ranks [third to sixth grade] first be appointed as district magistrates. On reaching fourth grade, as in the regulation, they should be appointed provincial governors and have the royal inspectors evaluate their records before according them rewards and punishments. If unavoidable, give the so-called high officials, the aged, and those rural gentry who were recruited through a requested audience capital appointments but do not give them responsibilities close to the people in the provinces. If Your Majesty carries out this policy for twenty years, those who abandoned the land will all return and tax revenues will not be insufficient.

Gold, silver, and brocaded silks are not produced in our country. In the past, court officials used only plain satin, silks, and cotton for clothing, and for utensils they only used brass and earthenware. One can see that the country has been able to last more than four hundred years and preserve its dynastic state shrines only because we respected the virtue of frugality. Recently, extremely extravagant customs have brought hardship to the peasants' life and exhausted the state treasury. I request that the state councillors from now on use no brocaded silk for clothing or gold and jade for utensils. And those who ride horses in fine clothes should have no escort follow. If each task is done frugally, remonstrating those above and inspiring those below, the customs will return to their former state of decency.

It has been nearly fifty years since the land in the capital province, except *choŏp* and *kubun*,[7] was all reallocated as land for official salaries. Recently, as most of the land has been seized and occupied by powerful families, the government in the meantime has often discussed radical reform. But because of frightening words deceptively used in reporting to Your Majesty, in the end this was never carried out. That is also why the ministers did not insist on the reform. If we carry out the reform, many people will rejoice, while in the end only a few dozen powerful families will not share this joy. Hence why do you hesitate and not boldly enact this?   *HK AND ES*

Yi Saek: Memorial on Current Affairs

[From *Koryŏ sa* 115:1a–4b]

Your Majesty's subject Saek [1328–1396], on mourning leave, here offers some ideas.

I have learned that the demarcation of boundaries and the equalization of landholdings are the first tasks of governing people. Broadly speaking, the systems created and the regulations maintained by our dynastic ancestors left nothing uncovered, but after more than four hundred years have elapsed, how could there be no problems? This is especially so in the land system. The demarcation of boundaries is unjust, as powerful families compete to amalgamate small landholdings, much like eagles nesting in pigeon coops. Even if the authorities, having considered all the conditions, determine ownership of a given tract of land on the basis of official land documents, if one claimant is powerful, the second finds himself helpless.

The one thing that is indispensable to the people is land. Although the peasants diligently work several *mu*[8] of land throughout the year to feed their families, it is still insufficient. When rent collectors arrive, however, if there is only one claimant to the land, it is not so bad. But sometimes there are three or four claimants, or even seven or eight. If their strength and influence are about the same, who will willingly yield? Thereupon if the rent paid is insufficient, the collectors call the unpaid portion a loan, making even more profit. How can one support parents and rear a family? The impoverishment of the peasant arises especially from this.

I humbly implore you to use the principles established in the land and tax laws of the year *kabin* [1314] as your basis. By referring to the corrected official documents, rectify those lands forcibly seized and survey newly reclaimed land. If you tax newly reclaimed land and reduce excessive land grants, state revenues will increase. If you adjudicate land that has been forcibly seized and pacify people who cultivate the land, then the people will obey with happiness. The happy obedience of the people and increases in tax collections are aims greatly sought by rulers. Your Majesty, why would you hesitate to pursue these goals? Some say, "It is difficult to seize a rich man's land abruptly, and after succeeding years of abuse, it is difficult to reform suddenly." That is true of an incapable ruler, but not what we would hope for from Your Majesty. The questions of how to implement the reform and how to refine it are things that advising ministers must certainly deliberate on, and a newcomer like me dare not discuss this. But whether to carry it out or not depends only on Your Majesty's will. Recently Japanese pirates have invaded our borders, causing Your Majesty to worry day and night. The venerable and virtuous officials must have together planned a course of action aimed essentially at handling this problem. As I am in mourning for my deceased father and living by the seashore, however, I have on my own given a lot of thought to the problem.

I consider that if you defend on land, then enlist the people from the land, sharpen their weapons, place them at strategic locations, raise the morale of the troops, and sparingly use beacons to confuse the Japanese. This is something that the royal inspector and magistrates can adequately carry out. There is no need to use the inspecting high commissioner, who would humiliate the magistrate and drain expenses. As for the strategy of fighting on sea, our country is surrounded on three sides by water, and no fewer than one million people live on offshore islands. I believe handling boats and swimming are their special skills. These people do not farm but make their living from fishing and gathering salt. Recently, because of pirates, they have left their homes and lost their livelihood. Compared to the people living on the land, they hate the pirates ten times more. If you speedily send a detailed plan and summon those living by the water, offering them rewards, then you can get several thousand people in no time. If you use their great skills and have them fight against those whom they hate, how can they not be victorious? Moreover, if they kill the enemy and are rewarded, how can it not be more profitable than fishing and gathering salt? If you put them under the command of the police commissioner and have them always in boats at the ready, the local areas will benefit and the pirates can be defeated. These are the two main strategies to resist the invaders. If we simply guard the land and do not fight at sea, they will consider us cowards, and we will have no way to anticipate their raids. If we fight at sea but fail to guard the land, the enemy may come ashore at an unanticipated spot, causing considerable harm. Therefore, we defend the land to protect ourselves and fight at sea to overpower the enemy. If we follow this strategy, will we not accomplish both aims?

HK AND ES

Pak Ch'o: Anti-Buddhist Memorial

[From *Koryŏ sa* 120:34b–39a]

I, His Majesty's subject, have heard that it was after heaven and earth existed that the myriad things came into being; that it was after the myriad things existed that man and woman came into being; that it was after man and woman existed that husband and wife came into being; that it was after husband and wife existed that father and son came into being; that it was after father and son existed that king and minister came into being; that it was after king and minister existed that senior and junior came into being; and that it was after senior and junior existed that ritual and rightness were established. This is the universal way of the world and the normal law of all times that cannot be disregarded even briefly. If it is abolished, heaven and earth will not tolerate its abandonment, the sun and moon will not shine, the ghosts and spirits will carry out executions jointly, and all the generations under heaven will concur in the joint beheading.

What kind of man is this Buddha, who makes a son that should carry on the family line betray his father and sever the affection between father and son; who makes men resist the Son of Heaven and destroy the rightness between lord and minister; who says that for men and women to live together is not the Way; who says that for men to plow and women to weave is not right, thus severing the way of generating life and blocking off the source of food and clothing; and who thinks that through his way he can transform all under heaven? If his way were really carried out, humanity would be finished in a hundred years. Heaven would carry on above and earth would bear below, but the only things to grow would be grasses and trees, birds and beasts, fishes and turtles, and dragons and snakes. How, finally, could the Way of the Three Bonds and the Five Relations endure?

Generally speaking, since the late Silla our country has upheld the Buddhist way, and stupas and shrines can be found throughout our villages. The doctrines of Buddha have spread widely, permeating our people's skins and penetrating their bones so that the doctrines can neither be dispelled by rightness nor differentiated by discourse. When Koryŏ King T'aejo [918–943] reunited the country, he took severe measures against accumulated abuses and prohibited subsequent kings and ministers from privately establishing temples. Thereupon, Ch'oe Ŭng [898–932] urged him to abolish Buddhism, but T'aejo replied: "In late Silla, the doctrines of Buddhism penetrated the bones of the people. Everyone thinks that life and death, disaster and fortune, are all due to the Buddha. Now we have just reunited the country, and the people's minds are still unsettled. If we suddenly abolish Buddha, the people will be shocked."

Thereupon T'aejo drew up an admonition saying, "You must take a lesson from Silla, which carried out many Buddhist affairs yet perished." Thus was T'aejo's admonition to later generations profound and earnest. But kings and ministers over the ages were not able to realize the founder's testament and followed shabby precedent to build without cease so that now the abuses are even worse.

These Buddhists eat without plowing and dress without tending silkworms. There is no way of knowing how many millions of them live and nourish themselves in comfort, and there is no way of knowing how many people have frozen and starved because of them. Even if they drink wind, imbibe dew, and live in birds' nests out in the fields, one who is concerned about the state must drive them out. Furthermore, will there ever come a day when heaven and earth will accept these Buddhists who sit in fancy houses, eat fine food, and play idly while making obeisance to kings and parents? This is something we truly cannot live with.

I, His Majesty's subject, respectfully think that His Majesty should follow the ways that flourished in the time of Yao and Shun and draw a lesson from the reasons why Ch'en, Ch'i, Liang, and Hsiao perished; that His Majesty should succeed to the intentions of the dynastic founder above and meet the simple hopes of us Confucianists below and return these Buddhists to their villages and use them to strengthen the military, levy corvée on their houses and increase the number of households, burn their books and cut off their roots forever, have the Military Supply Agency take charge of the lands given to them and meet military provisions, have the Directorate take charge of their slaves and divide them among the various agencies, have the Military Armament Agency receive the Buddhists' bronze statues and bronze implements and rearm the soldiers, have the Dignitary Reception Agency receive the Buddhists' dishes and implements and divide them among the various agencies. After this, if His Majesty teaches the people with ritual and rightness and trains them with virtue, within a few years the people's minds will be settled and moral suasion will be carried out, granaries and warehouses will be full, and the dynasty's finances will be sound.   JD

Chŏng Tojŏn: Discourse on Buddhism and Confucianism

[From *Sambong chip* 9:18a–21a]

Confucianists of old said: "In the ways of the Confucianists and the Buddhists, the terms are the same but the things they represent are different."

Now, expanding on this, we say void [*hŏ*] and they say void, and we say tranquillity [*chŏk*] and they say tranquillity. Yet our void, even though empty, exists, while their void is empty and does not exist, and our tranquillity, even though quiet, is felt, while their tranquillity is quiet and ceases to exist.

We speak of knowledge and action while they speak of enlightenment and self-cultivation. Our knowledge is being aware that the principle of the myriad things is embodied in our mind, and their enlightenment is realizing that the mind is originally empty and without anything; our action is behaving according to the principle of the myriad things without mistake or omission, and their self-cultivation is cutting off the myriad things so they will not accumulate in the mind.

Regarding us, it is said that we interact with the myriad changes; regarding them, it is said that they submit in all things. The words seem similar. But the expression "interact with the myriad changes" means that the mind responds to things that present themselves and deals with them in the appropriate way, employing them without losing propriety. Sons must be employed to become filial, not undutiful, and high officials employed to be loyal, not traitorous. Regarding things, oxen are employed to plow and not to butt, horses to carry burdens and not to bite, and tigers and wolves to be caught in traps and not to harm people. Generally, each is dealt with according to its innate principles.

The Buddhists' so-called "submission in all things" means that in the case of sons, the filial is filial of himself and the undutiful is undutiful of himself; in the case of high officials, the loyal is loyal of himself and the traitorous is traitorous of himself; and in the case of oxen and horses, they plow and carry of themselves and butt and bite of themselves so that all we hear is that things become of themselves and that there is no place for our minds.

The Buddhists' learning is like this: even while themselves employing things, they say things are not being employed. Wouldn't it be strange, however, if when given a coin one did not know what to do with it? And why, then, did Heaven make humans to be the essential spirit of the myriad things and give humans responsibility for their well-being?

If I may repeat Master Chu Hsi's argument, even though the mind is master of the body, the spirit of its essence can manage the principle of all under heaven;

even though principle is dispersed among the myriad things, the subtlety of its function in fact is not beyond the single mind of a man, so that fundamentally there is no distinction between [principle] within and without [self and other] or what is subtle and what is gross. If, however, one does not know and does not keep the spirituality of his mind, things will be obscure and confused, and he will not be able to study the subtlety of all the principles. If one does not know and does not study the subtlety of all principles, he will be narrow and obstinate and unable to exhaust the fullness of his mind. Whether in theory or in reality, this is inescapable.

Thus the sage teaches to make people quietly know for themselves the spirituality of this mind, to dwell in propriety, dignity, and tranquillity, and to know the fundamentals of study; to make people know the subtlety of all the principles and to study them when learning, asking, and reflecting so as to achieve the merit of the full employed mind and so that the huge and the minute take in each other and the active and the quiet foster each other; to make people not differentiate from the very beginning between the innner and the outer [self and others], between the perceptive and the imperceptive, to make people truly accumulate effort over a long time so that they widely understand the Way, whereupon they know that all is perfectly one and can say that there is no inner and outer [self and other], no perceptive and imperceptive.

Now, however, people persist in seeing this as shallow and incoherent and try to cover the form and hide the shadow while separately making an arcane, rapturous, tangled, and closed-off doctrine, striving to have the learner place his mind outside of writing and speech and saying that "one can only obtain the Way like this." This only aggravates the imbalance, lewdness, deceitfulness, and escapism of Buddhism, and it is also wrong to try to use this to obfuscate the ancients' practical learning of illustrious virtue and renewing of the people. The words of Master Chu reiterate, discuss, and kindly illuminate this; the learner should immerse his mind there and gain this for himself.   JD

C H A P T E R E L E V E N

Buddhism: The Ch'ŏnt'ae and Chogye Schools

Buddhism, which first entered Korea in the Three Kingdoms period, remained a major religious and intellectual force in Koryŏ. It flourished at the
start of the dynasty and then underwent several stages of reform in the
middle period of the kingdom. Throughout the dynasty, Buddhism had close
ties with the court as monarchs frequently allowed a son to enter the
priesthood and sought advice on both political and religious problems from
learned monks. Two major schools, Kyo (Doctrinal) and Sŏn (Meditation),
dominated Buddhist thought, although in the late eleventh century the royal
monk Ŭich'ŏn (1055–1101) tried to fuse the practices of the two schools into
the Ch'ŏnt'ae (T'ien-t'ai) school. Apart from its intellectual vigor, Buddhism
thrived economically through its monasteries, some of which, like T'ongdo,
held vast tracts of land. Like many other powerful institutions, Buddhism
became inevitably tainted by corruption and misuse of power, abuses that
sometimes led to criticism of the monastic establishment.

Shortly after the rise of the military, Buddhism underwent a significant
reform with the growth of the meditation-inspired Chogye school. The
monk Chinul (1128–1210)—one of Koryŏ's most prolific Buddhist writers and
profound thinkers—played an especially important role in this effort, calling
for a new emphasis on the practice of meditation along with the study of
texts. Ŭich'ŏn, writing a century earlier, had sought to compile the com-

ments and interpretations of other Buddhist thinkers into a comprehensive compendium. This tradition of respect for printed scriptures was again dramatically demonstrated at the height of the Mongol invasions, when the Koryŏ court, in its search for the Buddha's divine protection, supervised the recarving of more than eighty thousand woodblocks that were needed to publish the complete Buddhist canon, the *Tripiṭaka*.

BUDDHISM IN EARLY KORYŎ

Buddhism first came to Korea during the Three Kingdoms period. Initially, foreign monks propagated the faith on the peninsula, but as the indigenous states matured, Koreans traveled first to China and then to India in search of scriptures and greater understanding of the tenets of the faith. By the time of late Silla, Buddhism was an established, integral part of Korean culture. The religion was intellectually vital with two major schools—Kyo (Doctrinal) and Sŏn (Meditation)—providing different paths to Buddhist enlightenment.

The leading figures of late Silla and early Koryŏ allied themselves with Buddhist masters, often masters of the Meditation school. Through links with Buddhism, regional leaders could gain spiritual sustenance as well as potential economic ties to well-endowed monasteries and both practical and tactical knowledge useful in maintaining their autonomous power. While giving protection to the Buddhist clergy, each of the potential unifiers had monks to whom he turned for assistance. Wang Kŏn's family had close ties with several Meditation monasteries, and Wang Kŏn himself sought out Meditation monks coming from China for practical and political advice as well as for new religious learning. One such confidant was Yiŏm (870–936), who acted as his close adviser, frequently counseling him on pressing problems facing the infant dynasty. Nevertheless, Wang Kŏn valued the teachings of both the Doctrinal and Meditation schools and sought their unified support, as is evident in his "Ten Injunctions" (see ch. 8), which discuss the importance of assistance from both schools.

Kyunyŏ (923–973), an erudite monk of the Flower Garland school, was an adviser to King Kwangjong. Through liberal borrowing from the teachings of the Pŏpsang (Dharma Characteristics) school, Kyunyŏ furnished a religious ideology that helped Kwangjong to solidify his monarchical authority and to justify many of his high-handed political reforms. Kyunyŏ was also a poet, the author of a major portion of the *hyangga* surviving from early Koryŏ, and he used his literary skill to spread early Koryŏ Buddhist thought through the fusion of the Doctrinal tenets expressed in the Flower Garland with those expressed in the Dharma Characteristics schools.

Ŭich'ŏn (1055–1101), a son of King Munjong (1046–1083), also sought to bridge the gulf between the Doctrinal and Meditation schools. Although, like Kyunyŏ, he belonged essentially to the Flower Garland school, Ŭich'ŏn was very critical of the former and tried to bring about the fusion of the Flower Garland and Dharma Characteristics schools. Trained in China first in the Flower Garland and then in the T'ien-t'ai schools, he eventually promoted the latter after his return to Koryŏ. In his exposition of the unity of the original nature (*sŏng*) and the phenomenal characteristic (*sang*), Ŭich'ŏn found the teaching of the Silla monk Wŏnhyo (617–686) especially important. Wŏnhyo, one of the seminal figures in the evolution of a uniquely Korean tradition of Buddhism, had expounded the unity of *sŏng* and *sang* earlier in his works. In stressing Wŏnhyo's theory, Ŭich'ŏn tries to restore his forerunner to what Ŭich'ŏn considered his rightful place as the "primate" of Korean Buddhism. In the eulogy presented here, Ŭich'ŏn notes the prominent syncretic tendencies in Wŏnhyo's thought, which inspired Ŭich'ŏn's own attempts to synthesize doctrinal study with meditation practice.

The principal thrust of Ŭich'ŏn's approach to Buddhism was the development of a system in which scholarship and meditation flourished in a symbiotic relationship. In his instructions to the disciple Ch'isu, Ŭich'ŏn laments the degenerate state of Buddhism in his country, which had failed to preserve a comprehensive program of spiritual training and engaged only in arguing over "opinionated theories." Ŭich'ŏn argues that such futile controversies should be abandoned and that scriptural study and meditation practice should be merged together into a comprehensive regimen of training. Only such a system would encourage students to use their doctrinal training not as a tool of disputation but "as a bright mirror to reflect their own minds."

The Monk Yiŏm and King T'aejo

[From *Chōsen kinseki sōran* 1:127–128]

His Majesty Wang Kŏn had heard that the way of Great Master Chinch'ŏl was among the best in the world and that his reputation was spreading throughout Korea. Hoping to see him, His Majesty frequently sent out royal invitations asking the master to come to the court. The master, addressing the laity, said: "Living in this land, who would dare disobey the king's commands? One has no choice but to comply with a royal summons to become an adviser. I am about to go to the capital in compliance with the royal request to bring imperial dignity to the royal land." His Majesty, wishing to greatly increase the splendor of the dynasty, looked to the master for assistance. Consequently, he repaired T'aehŭng Temple and requested that the master stay there.

At another time, the king, taking advantage of free time in the evening, quietly visited the Meditation cottage and said: "I, the disciple, would respectfully like to tell you my old wish directly. Now the enemies of the nation are increasingly behaving rather haughtily, and unfriendly neighboring countries invade one after another. This is just as when Ch'u and Han in China, opposing each other, could not decide who would be master. Now for nearly three years we have had two cruel enemies nearby who, despite our earnest desire to be friendly, have increasingly intensified their belligerence. I once took vows pledging to observe the teachings of Buddha and secretly developed a compassionate heart. But I fear I may bring destruction upon myself because of my leniency toward aggressors. Master, despite the great distance between us, you have come to transform the country, thus saving our inflamed land. Please make people see the light through your words of wisdom."

The master replied: "Generally, the Way rests in the heart and not in events. Buddha's law comes from the self and not from others. Moreover, the cultivation of an imperial ruler is different from that of an ordinary man. Even though a ruler may wage war, should he not have greater consideration for the people? A king makes the world his home, all the people his children. He does not kill innocent people but punishes the guilty, thus manifesting good conduct. This is called great assistance *[hongje]*."

The king, greatly moved, put his hands on his desk and said: "I have feared that the lay person may fall to hell because he has no way to know profound truth. As I listen to you, the master, however, it is like speaking with a heavenly being I have encountered."

Thereafter, the king saved criminals whose crimes deserved death and saved the people from suffering by not randomly waging war. This was the result of the master's teaching. *HK AND ES*

Teachings of Great Master Kyunyŏ

[From *Kyunyŏ chŏn 4*, in *Korean Tripiṭaka* 47:260a]

Kyunyŏ was a follower of the Northern school. Toward the end of Silla at Haein Monastery on Mount Kaya, the Flower Garland school was divided into two branches under the leadership of Lords Kwanhye and Hŭirang. Kwanhye's branch was called the Southern school, while Hŭirang's was known as the Northern school. Kwanhye was the teacher of the chief rebel, Kyŏnhwŏn [d. 936], of Later Paekche, while Hŭirang was the teacher of the founder of Koryŏ, Wang Kŏn [918–943]. Both masters were trusted by their patrons and vowed to serve them. But since their convictions differed, how could their minds be one? This division even affected their followers, who opposed one another like fire and water. They even began to distinguish salty and sour tastes in the flavor of the dharma. It was difficult to eradicate these long-standing disputes. Kyunyŏ, deploring this deep schism, tried to heal it and unite the two branches of thought. To this end he went with the abbot Inyu on a tour of famous mountains and monasteries, beat the drum of the dharma, raised the standard of the Buddha truth, and made all young believers follow him.

Master Hŭirang's commentary on some thirty topics in the Flower Garland school included the following: the same substance of the three teachings; emptiness and existence; the exhaustible and the inexhaustible; the provisional and the real; theories on the Lotus Treasury World *[the padmagarbha lokadhātu of Vairocana]*; the creation of the world system; explication of the profound; sigh and nonsigh; absorbing the essence throughout the three births that constitute a past life of seeing and hearing Buddha truth; liberation in the present life and realization of life in Buddhahood; the transmission of office; the six characteristics of all dharmas;[1] following and settling in the real; the complete removal of the abstruse and small; the Tuṣita prince *[Maitreya]*; the five types of attainment of Buddhahood; the characteristics of the division of buddhas according to their understanding and cultivation; efflux and property; turning one's mind away from the Lesser Vehicle; the six levels of the bodhisattva path; the eight assemblies;[2] the hundred and six cities; Sukhāvati *[Pure Land]*; the bodhi tree; nature origination; the five results; the four modes of reality;[3] wide cultivation and making offerings; and host and guest. PL

Ŭich'ŏn: Instruction to the Disciple Ch'isu

[From *Hanguk pulgyo chŏnsŏ* 4:556a–c]

In order to indicate the primary and secondary aspects of both doctrine and meditation, I used to point out to my disciples that the attainment and elucidation of the ultimate characteristic were the ten mysteries,[4] while its transformation became the five teachings.[5] These words are not deceitful.

For superior doctrinal students who are equally intent upon the one Buddha vehicle; who practice together the manifold practices of the bodhisattvas; whose great minds intent upon Buddhahood are unswayed; who have made vast vows for themselves; who hold in their hands Samantabhadra's vehicle of expedient means; and who roam leisurely in the realm of Vairocana there is nothing better than initially to investigate phenomena exhaustively by means of the three contemplations[6] and the five teachings, and use this as the eye for entering the path. In fact, apart from this universal dharma, there is no other road by which to attain Buddhahood.

Furthermore, Kuei-shan [780–841] said: "One seeking the path must nurture the dharma eye. The dharma eye cannot open by itself; one must seek a master in order to scratch open its lid." Whenever I reached this passage, I would shut the volume and breathe a long sigh, thinking to myself: "The doctrine established by the saints valued development in practice. That doctrine is not something that should merely be proclaimed by the mouth but ought, in fact, to be practiced by the body. How can practice be considered something as useless as a bitter gourd that is hung to one side and never eaten?"[7]

Finally, I received some cursory information about doctrine and meditation during the lectures of the great Dharma Master Chin-shui. During that master's spare time from lectures and lessons, he used to admonish his disciples: "Although one who does not cultivate meditation and only imparts the scriptures might hear of the five pervasive causes and effects,[8] he does not, however, penetrate to the three levels of the qualities of the nature. Although one who does not transmit the scriptures and only cultivates meditation might awaken to the three major qualities of the nature, he cannot distinguish among the five pervasive causes and effects. This being the case, meditation cannot but be cultivated, and scriptures cannot but be transmitted."   *RB*

BUDDHISM AND KORYŎ SOCIETY

Buddhism, the state religion in Koryŏ, was closely intertwined with secular affairs. Individuals turning to Buddhism for religious inspiration gave generously to temples and shrines. Thus the Buddhist establishment became rich through large landholdings and accumulated wealth.

When individuals chose to endow a temple, they often were concerned about its operation. The first selection is from the will of Ch'oe Chean (d. 1046), grandson of the reform-minded Koryŏ Confucian official and historian Ch'oe Sŭngno, who was trying to reestablish a monastery in the Kyŏngju area, the place of origin of his clan. Especially noteworthy is his concern that, despite his high position in the government and his family's influence, the monks should select their own abbot rather than have an outsider imposed on them.

Through such generous donations, monasteries came to control vast holdings. T'ongdo Monastery, in southeastern Korea, became one of Koryŏ's richest. The second entry, taken from a memorial stone inscription, provides just a glimpse into the large holdings that were under the control of this monastery.

Some monks used Buddhist devotion for their own ends. The final selection is about charlatans who readily misled the simple with promises and threats. Using techniques and ideas that are not unfamiliar to us today, they asked only that the faithful believe. One even claimed that he was an incarnation of the Bodhisattva Maitreya and implied he would rescue the faithful, leading them to the Buddhist paradise. The monk Irŏm lived during the troubled years shortly after the military coup of 1170.

Ch'oe Chean: On Endowing a Buddhist Monastery

[From *Samguk yusa* 3:173–174]

I, Executive of the Royal Secretariat and Chancellery, Ch'oe Chean [d. 1046], benefactor of this temple, offer the following will.

Recently Ch'ŏllyong Monastery at Mount Kowi in the Eastern Capital [Kyŏngju] has fallen into disrepair. Especially desiring long life for the king and peace and prosperity for the people and state, I, a lay follower of Buddha, having built a prayer hall with connecting hallways and living quarters with a kitchen and storage areas and having provided several stone and ceramic Buddhist images, will hold a ten-thousand-day Śākyamuni prayer meeting *[toryang]*.

As these things have been donated for the benefit of the state, it is also correct for the state to appoint an abbot. The monks of the services, however, are likely to be concerned with an abbot's changes. When we look at other examples of land donations to monasteries, we find the lands donated for adequate support are two hundred *kyŏl*[9] to Chijang Temple at Mount Kong, twenty *kyŏl* to Tosan Temple at Mount Pibi, and ten *kyŏl* to each temple on the mountains surrounding the Western Capital. At each of these monasteries, candidates were selected on the basis of their observance of Buddhist commandments and their talent, not on the basis of where they were employed. Furthermore, it was made a rule to select them in a sequence determined on the basis of popular support by the monks of the temple.

I, a lay follower, was delighted when I learned of these customs and wish to have selected from among the monks of Ch'ŏllyong Temple a person who is of the most virtuous *[taedŏk]* [10] rank and possesses great virtue and talent, making him a pillar of the temple. Make such a person the abbot and have him hold services and maintain conduct for a long time.

HK AND ES

Landholdings of T'ongdo Monastery

[From *T'ongdosa chi*, pp. 24–30]

The mountains and streams providing the land base supporting T'ongdo Monastery are in an area of seventeen thousand *pu* [11] with stone posts totaling twelve in all. [12]

The land allotted to the caretakers of the posts in the four directions spread to the environs of Pukt'a [North Tea] village in the southeastern ward, and it also was on the boundary line of Kŏhwa-gun. Divided always into eastern and western groups, the three thousand monks of the *taedŏk* rank in the halls of east and west piled stones along large streams.

Stupas are divided in a row on the four boundaries, and each has ten caretakers who are supplied with land allocated to their position and land allocated to their households. These are all lands from within the area of the *changsaeng* posts in the four directions. There has never been any public or private landholding except that belonging to the monastery, which extends to the Ŭich'un district boundary. The rest of the information will not be recorded here, as it is actually all found in the original documents of the history of the monastery.

HK AND ES

The Monk Irŏm

[From *Koryŏ sa* 99:23b–24b]

A monk named Irŏm, who lived in Chŏnju, claimed he could make the blind see again and the dead live. King Myŏngjong [1170–1197] sent Palace Attendant Kŭm Kŭgŭi to receive him at the court. On the way, the monk wore a colorful scarf and rode a piebald horse, hiding his face with a silk fan. His escorts warded people off and protected him so they could not see him directly. When he stayed at Pohyŏn Hall, the people of the capital, high and low, young and old, competed to have an audience, emptying the village. All the sick, blind, deaf, crippled, dumb, and incurably diseased scattered about before him. The monk directed them with his fan.

Received at Ch'ŏnsu Monastery, he lived on the top floor of the south gate pavilion. State councillors and great ministers hastened to see him, while scholars and their wives competed to put their hair before him to have him walk on it. When the monk ordered them to chant to Amitābha, the chant was heard for ten *ri*. If they received even the smallest drop of the water with which he had washed and bathed, it was like giving them one thousand pieces of gold. They all drank it and called it holy water, claiming it could cure all kinds of illnesses. Day and night, men and women mingled together, and illicit words spread. Although countless people shaved their heads to become followers, no one at that time admonished them to cease.

As King Myŏngjong gradually came to know of the monk's falseness, the monk was compelled to return home. Earlier, the monk had deceived the people, saying: "All laws stem from only one mind; if you diligently pray to Buddha and say, 'My illness is already cured,' then your illness will be cured. Never say, 'My illness has not yet been cured.' " From this, the blind said they already saw and the deaf said they already heard. This is why the people were so easily deceived.

HK AND ES

RESURGENCE OF BUDDHISM

The military coup of 1170 signaled the beginning of a new order. The great aristocratic lineages lost their preeminence and ability to dictate all state matters, a sign of a decline in their political and social power. The coup led to equally significant changes in Koryŏ's religious order as the Chogye sect of the Meditation school gradually emerged as the dominant spiritual voice in the kingdom.

During early Koryŏ, Kyo (Doctrinal) beliefs rather than Sŏn (Meditation) prescripts captured the imagination of the elite. By the start of the twelfth century, however, government officials and scholars alike, unhappy with the Doctrinal school's approach, had reinvigorated the Meditation school. And by the end of the twelfth century, the highest military and civil authorities were patronizing Meditation monks and monasteries.

Yi Kyubo (1168–1241) described Ch'oe Ch'unghŏn's active support of Meditation in his "On a Trip to Ch'angbok Monastery." The military leader Ch'oe Ch'unghŏn not only rebuilt many Meditation monasteries but also sought out Meditation monks and sponsored religious meetings to propagate the faith. The Meditation school's simple spiritual message of finding truth and spirituality within the self undoubtedly appealed to Ch'oe Ch'unghŏn and other military leaders, but the Ch'oe house's patronage of Meditation practices was also a reaction to the earlier opposition to Ch'oe rule by monks of the Doctrinal school. Since the Doctrinal monasteries had been closely aligned with the former aristocratic forces before the military rose to power, they felt threatened by the new military leadership. And as the passage describing the clash between the monks and military rulers shows, the monasteries were dealt a crippling blow by Ch'oe Ch'unghŏn's well-organized and well-equipped forces.

Chinul (1158–1210), one of the leading masters of Meditation of this period, was mostly responsible for the Meditation school's phenomenal rise under military rule. A devotee of Meditation practices from his youth, Chinul, also known as the National Preceptor Pojo, called for the individual to empty the mind and free the self from the world of the senses. The final passage offered here was issued in 1190 upon the formal establishment of Chinul's Samādhi and Prajñā Community. The community sought to achieve enlightenment through worship, scriptural recitation, common work, and meditation. In this composition, Chinul explains the development of the Meditation community at Kŏjo Monastery and then its move to the Chogye region in southwestern Korea. The work served as both the compact of the community members and a call to others to develop the practices Chinul considered crucial to a successful Buddhist vocation.

Yi Kyubo: On a Trip to Ch'angbok Monastery

[From *Tongguk Yi sangguk chip* 25:8b–10a]

In 1211, Lord Chingang [Ch'oe Ch'unghŏn] obtained the old Ch'angbok Monastery southeast of the capital and renovated it. King Hŭijong [1204–1211] had ascended to the throne just two years earlier and wanted to hold a large Meditation meeting to explain the mind dharma. Before this, Lord Chingang heard that Pyŏngong,[13] the patriarch of the Meditation school, had secluded himself deep in the mountains to cultivate the divine within. The lord had earlier summoned the monk several times, but he did not come. Lord Chingang laughingly said: "All buddhas and bodhisattvas carry the same intention of saving all sentient beings. How can one be so sparing of the dharma and not spread it? It is like a man accumulating vast wealth and not being able to dispose of it. Surely he would not be the one."

Later the king heard this and sent a man to persuade Pyŏngong cordially, and in the end he responded to the king's command and came, as Lord Chingang had predicted.

When Pyŏngong came, other high monks followed him. As they all organized themselves into a religious society and earnestly cultivated themselves in right practice, those who had cultivated themselves as highly as the monk Chingong[14] all came, responding to the summons. Without exception, the virtuous followers of the remaining schools, too, gathered like clouds. The popularity of Meditation assemblies had never been like this. In this assembly Pyŏngong became the patriarch and Chingong the deputy. They explained the *Platform Scripture of the Sixth Patriarch [Liu-tsu t'an-ching]* and the *Recorded Sayings of Ta-hui [Ching-shan yü-lu]*,[15] and every night they discussed the meaning of emptiness, making it a regular event.

Thereupon, from those who followed the five Doctrinal schools to literati poets, all came to the assembly—which made it necessary to hold separate daily meetings—and together discussed the principles of its teaching. In the beginning, they all insisted on their own ideas, contradicting each other. Although they listened to the Meditation tenets, they did not take them to heart and seemed disappointed. Slowly they comprehended the Meditation tenets, gradually realizing their true meaning and attaining ultimate understanding.

Didn't Bodhidharma say: "The one thousand scriptures and ten thousand treatises clarify only the mind"? In the sudden enlightenment that comes through these words, what use will there be for doctrinal explanations? Great indeed is the way of meditation. It cannot be reached through knowledge and cannot be investigated by words. The essence of meditation is awakening to the mind. If one wants to awaken to the mind, it is through no-mind that one can awaken. The awakening that is no awakening is the true awakening. Awakening, then, is this very mind, and apart from this mind there is no Buddha. If one does not realize that there is a shining spiritual treasure that is commensurate with one's own province but seeks enlightenment from others, even though one searches for it the whole day long, one will only be wasting one's time in vain.   HK AND ES

Chinul: The Compact of the Samādhi and Prajñā Community

[From *Hanguk pulgyo chŏnsŏ* 4:698a–b, 707a–c]

Reverently, I have heard:

> A person who falls to the ground gets back up by using that
> very same ground. To try to get up without relying on that
> ground would be impossible.[16]

Sentient beings are those who are deluded in regard to the one mind and give rise to boundless defilements. Buddhas are those who have awakened to the one mind and have given rise to boundless sublime functions. Although there is a difference between delusion and awakening, essentially these both derive from the one mind. Hence to seek Buddhahood apart from the mind is impossible.

Since my youth, I have cast myself into the domain of the patriarchs of the Meditation school and have visited meditation halls everywhere. After investigating the teachings the Buddha and the patriarchs so compassionately bestowed on beings, I have found that they are primarily designed to make us bring to rest all conditioning, empty the mind, and then remain centered there quietly, without looking for anything outside. As it is stated in the *Flower Garland Scripture,* "If a person wants to comprehend the state of Buddhahood, he should purify his mind until it is just like empty space." Whatever we see, hear, recite, or cultivate, we should recognize how difficult it is to come into contact with such things; examining these things using our own wisdom, we should practice according to what has been expounded. Then it can be said that we are cultivating the Buddha mind ourselves, are destined to complete the path to Buddhahood ourselves, and are sure to requite personally the Buddha's kindness.

Nevertheless, when we examine the inclination of our conduct from dawn to dusk, we see that we rely on the Buddhadharma while adorning ourselves with the signs of self and person. Infatuated with the way of material welfare and submerged in the secular realm of wind and dust, we are not cultivating virtue but are only wasting food and clothing. Although we have left home, what merit does it have? How sad! We want to leave the triple world, but we do not practice freeing ourselves from sense objects. Our male body is used in vain, for we have not a man's will. From one standpoint we fail in the dharma's propagation; from another we are negligent in benefitting sentient beings; and between these two we turn our backs on our four benefactors.[17] This is certainly shameful! For a long time I have lamented these problems.

In the first month of *imin* [1182], I traveled to Poje Monastery in the capital for a convocation called to discuss meditation. One day I made a pact with more than ten fellow cultivators saying: "After the close of this convocation we will renounce fame and profit and stay in seclusion in the mountain forests. There we will form a community designed to foster the constant training in *samādhi* [concentration] and *prajñā* [wisdom]. Through worship of the Buddha, recitation of scriptures, and even through common work, we will each discharge the duties to which we are assigned and nourish the self-nature in all situations. We vow to pass our whole lives free of entanglements and to follow the higher pursuits of accomplished and true men. Wouldn't this be wonderful?"

All of those present who heard these words agreed with what was said and swore, "On another day we will consummate this agreement, live in seclusion in the forest, and be bound together as a community that should be named for *samādhi* and *prajñā*." In this manner the pledge was put in writing and everyone's intentions were decided. Later, becuase of unforeseen problems with the selection of an appropriate site, everyone was scattered in all four directions. It has been almost ten years now, and we still have not been able to fulfill our promise. In the early spring of last year, *musin* [1188], the revered Meditation monk, venerable Tŭkchae, who had also made the pledge, happened to be staying at Kŏjo Monastery on Mount Kong. He had not forgotten the earlier vow concerning the formation of the Samādhi and Prajñā Community, and he sent a letter to Pomun Monastery on Mount Haga inviting me to join him. As he earnestly requested me a second and a third time also, even though I had been dwelling in the forest ravines keeping my stupidity and my utterly useless mind to myself, nevertheless, remembering our earlier agreement and moved by his honest sincerity, I chose this year's spring season to move my abode to that monastery and left together with the Meditation practitioner Hang. We invited those who had previously made the same vow to gather there with us. Some of them had died, others were sick, and still others were pursuing fame and profit and so were not able to join us. Finally, with the remaining group of three or four monks, we started this dharma assembly in fulfillment of our previous vow.

I humbly hope that men of high moral standards who have grown tired of world affairs—regardless of whether they are adherents of Meditation, the Doctrinal school, Confucianism, or Taoism—will abandon the dusty domain of this world, roam high above all things, and devote themselves earnestly to the path of inner cultivation, which is commensurate with this aim.   *RB*

CHINUL AND THE CHOGYE SCHOOL

Chinul spent much of his life explaining and discussing both Meditation and Flower Garland beliefs. His extensive writings show him to be one of Korea's greatest Buddhist thinkers. The first selection in this section is Chinul's abridgement of an important commentary to the *Flower Garland Scripture* by the Chinese exegete Li T'ung-hsüan (635–730). Chinul's own success in developing a synthesis between scholarship and meditation in Buddhism was to a large extent inspired by Li's innovative, practice-oriented interpretations of Buddhist doctrinal teachings. In his preface to these excerpts, Chinul provides an extensive autobiographical account of his own quandary concerning the connection between doctrine and practice. Scholars of the *Flower Garland Scripture* whom Chinul consulted claimed that the Meditation school focus on "seeing the nature of the mind" produced only introspective awareness, not the consummate, holistic knowledge of the "unimpeded interfusion of all phenomena" that they presumed to be the quintessence of Buddhism. This claim prompted Chinul to undertake a three-year study of the Buddhist canon to discover scriptural passages that would vindicate Meditation. He believed that he found such vindication in the *Flower Garland Scripture* and Li's commentary on that text. His reading suggested to him that the words of the Buddha were what matured into the doctrinal teachings of Buddhism, while the mind of the Buddha was what evolved into Meditation. Just as the words of the Buddha reflected what was in his mind, so too the doctrinal teachings of Buddhism reflected the mystical knowledge engendered through meditation. Hence Chinul discovered a basis for synthesizing the Flower Garland and Meditation schools into a comprehensive system of Buddhist thought and practice, one that would inspire all future generations of Korean Buddhists.

Fundamental to Chinul's syncretic vision was the basic unity he perceived between the descriptions of truth presented in Buddhist doctrine and the experience of that truth that occurs through meditation. Through a series of questions and answers in the selection from "Straight Talk on the True Mind," Chinul sought to prove that the variant accounts of the absolute in both Doctrinal and Meditation records can all be traced to a single concept: the true mind. The true mind for Chinul meant Buddhahood itself; but it also referred to that quality of sentience that is basic to all ordinary "sentient" beings as well. The true mind, therefore, serves as the matrix between the conventional reality of the ordinary world and the absolute truth of the dharma realm. In order to gain access to absolute truth, and thus enlightenment, Buddhist practitioners need only recognize the enlightenment inherent in their own minds. Faith—the wholehearted acceptance of the fact of their innate enlightenment—is the soteriological attribute that will allow students to relinquish their delusion that they are unenlightened. It is this peculiar kind of faith in Meditation—what Chinul termed "right faith in the patriarchal school"—that will reveal to all persons that they are originally buddhas.

In "Secrets on Cultivating the Mind," the most accessible of his accounts of the process of Meditation training, Chinul offers a summation of his key ideas and reiterates his lament that people "do not recognize that their own natures are the true buddhas." Chinul demands that practice begin with a sudden awakening, which reveals to the student that he is innately enlightened. This initial awakening occurs through tracing the light emanating from the fountainhead of his mind back to its enlightened source. But simply because the student understands that he is a buddha does not mean that he will be able to act like one, any more than a clever infant will be able to act like an intelligent adult. Even after awakening, the student must continue to control the full range of old habits, to which he will still be subject, as well as to cultivate the host of wholesome qualities that will enable him to express his understanding to others. Finally, when the student's understanding and conduct work in perfect unison, he will become a buddha in fact as well as principle. Chinul's soteriological program of sudden awakening–gradual cultivation was unique among the mature Buddhist schools of East Asia and helped to define the indigenous Korean tradition of Meditation.

Chinul's most influential disciple was the monk Hyesim (1178–1234). *Sŏnmun yŏmsong chip* is Hyesim's indigenous collection of *kongan* (public cases)—exchanges between enlightened Meditation masters and their disciples. Such exchanges were used as pedagogical material and eventually came to be used as themes for meditative contemplation. Anthologies of these exchanges began to be compiled in China during the tenth century and typically included the case itself, along with interlinear annotation, variant explanations of other masters, and verse exegeses. Hyesim's collection covers some 1,125 *kongan* (expanded posthumously by a disciple to 1,472 *kongan*) in thirty fascicles, making it one of the largest such anthologies compiled in East Asia.

The arrangement of *Sŏnmun yŏmsong chip* is unusual, however, in that the *kongan* are listed so as to follow the traditional Meditation lineage from the Buddha Śākyamuni through the twenty-eight Indian and six Chinese patriarchs down to the many masters of the mature Meditation school. It therefore functions as both a *kongan* anthology and a lineage record. Establishing this lineality of the Meditation transmission was important, given Meditation's putative antipathy toward the scriptural teachings of Buddhism. This elaborate pseudohistory sought to prove that contemporary Meditation masters derived their authority not from scripture but from a direct line of spiritual experience going back to the Buddha himself. Hence Meditation had no need for the scriptural teachings of Buddhism, but merely transmitted the mind of the Buddha down through the generations: whatever "words and letters" may be recorded in such anthologies as this were intended only as expedient means of passing on the "profound intent" of Meditation to posterity.

Touching on an idea broached in an earlier section, Hyesim also asserts, in "Letter in Reply to Ch'oe Hongyun," the similarity between Confucian and Buddhist beliefs. In this letter, Hyesim attempts to show the fundamental unity of Buddhism and Confucianism by distinguishing the variant functions of the two religions from their identical essence. While the terminology used in Buddhism and Confucianism may differ, the essence of the minds of Buddhists and Confucians is nonconceptual, unconditioned, and all-pervasive. Hence, by ignoring the outward trappings of these religions and penetrating to their fundamental core, the adept will realize his true self, which transcends all religious expression. Hyesim's essay even leads to a discussion of Taoism, pointing to the intellectual expansiveness of this age, which allowed scholars and monks to discourse actively across a broad range of ideas. *RB*

Chinul: Excerpts from the *Exposition of the* Flower Garland Scripture: *Preface*

[From *Hanguk pulgyo chŏnsŏ* 4:767a–768b]

In the autumn months of Ta-ting, *ŭlsa* [1185], as I began living in retreat on Mount Haga, I reflected constantly on the Meditation adage "Mind is Buddha."[18] I felt that if a person were not fortunate enough to meet with this approach, he would end up wasting many aeons in vain and would never reach the domain of sanctity.

I had always had doubts about the approach to entering into awakening of the Flower Garland teachings: what, finally, did it involve? Accordingly, I decided to question a lecturer on the *Flower Garland Scripture.* He replied: "You must contemplate the unimpeded interpenetration of all phenomena." He entreated me further: "If you merely contemplate your own mind and do not contemplate the unimpeded interfusion of all phenomena, you will never gain the perfect qualities of the fruition of Buddhahood."

I did not answer, but thought silently to myself: "If you use the mind to contemplate phenomena, those phenomena will become impediments, and you will have needlessly disturbed your own mind; when then would there be a resolution of this situation? But if the mind is brightened and your wisdom purified, then one hair and all the universe will be interfused, for there is, perforce, nothing that is outside the mind." I then retired into the mountains and sat reading through the *Tripiṭaka* in search of a passage that would confirm the mind doctrine of the Meditation school.

Three winters and summers passed before I came upon the figure about "one dust mote containing thousands of volumes of scriptures" in the "Appearance of the Thus Come Ones" [*Ju-lai ch'u-hsien p'in* chapter] of the *Flower Garland Scripture*. Later in the same passage the summation said: "The wisdom of the Thus Come Ones is just like this: it is complete in the bodies of all sentient beings. It is merely all these ordinary, foolish people who are not aware of it and do not recognize it." I put the scripture volume on my head in reverence and, unwittingly, began to weep.

As I was still unclear about the initial access to faith that was appropriate for ordinary people of today, however, I reread the explanation of the Elder Li T'ung-hsüan [635–730] of the first level of the ten faiths in his *Exposition of the "Flower Garland Scripture" [Hsin Hua-yen ching lun]*. It said: "Chief of Enlightenment Bodhisattva has three realizations. First, he realizes that his own body and mind are originally the dharma realm because they are immaculate, pure, and untainted. Second, he realizes that the discriminative nature of his own body and mind is originally free from the subject-object dichotomy and is originally the Buddha of Unmoving Wisdom. Third, he realizes that his own mind's sublime wisdom, which can distinguish the genuine from the distorted, is Mañjuśrī. He realizes these three things at the first level of faith and comes to be known as Chief of Enlightenment."

It says elsewhere: "The difficulties a person encounters in entering into the ten faiths from the ordinary state are due to the fact that he completely accepts that he is an ordinary man; he is unwilling to accept that his own mind is the Buddha of Unmoving Wisdom."

It also says: "The body is the reflection of wisdom. This world is the same. When wisdom is pure and its reflection clear, large and small merge with one another as in the realm of Indra's net."

Thereupon, I set aside the volume and, breathing a long sigh, said: "What the World-Honored One said with his mouth are the teachings. What the patriarchs transmitted with their minds is Meditation. The mouth of the Buddha and the minds of the patriarchs can certainly not be contradictory. How can students of both Meditation and Doctrinal schools not plumb the fundamental source but instead, complacent in their own training, wrongly foment disputes and waste their time?" From that time on, I have continued to build my mind of faith and have cultivated diligently without indolence; a number of years have already passed.

I say to men who are cultivating the mind that first, through the path of the patriarchs, they should know the original sublimity of their own minds and should not be bound by words and letters. Next, through the text of Li T'ung-hsüan's *Exposition,* they should ascertain that the essence and function of the mind are identical to the nature and characteristics of the dharma realm. Then the quality of the unimpeded interpenetration among all phenomena and the merit of the wisdom and compassion that have the same essence as that of all the buddhas will not be beyond their capacity.   *RB*

Chinul: "Straight Talk on the True Mind"

[From *Hanguk pulgyo chŏnsŏ* 4:715c–716b]

Chinul's Preface

QUESTION: Can the sublime path of the patriarchs be known?

CHINUL: Hasn't this already been explained by the ancients? "The path is not related to knowing or not knowing. Knowing is a false thought; not knowing is blankness. If you have truly penetrated to the realm that is free of doubt and as vast and spacious as the immensity of space, then how could you go to so much trouble to make such discriminations?"[19]

QUESTION: But does this mean that sentient beings do not benefit from the patriarchs' appearance in the world?

CHINUL: When the buddhas and patriarchs "showed their heads," they had no teachings to offer men. They only wanted sentient beings to see their original nature for themselves. The *Flower Garland Scripture* says: "You should know that all dharmas are the own-nature of the mind. The perfection of the wisdom body does not come from any other awakening." For this reason, the buddhas and patriarchs didn't let people get snared in words and letters; they only wanted them to put deluded thought to rest and see the original mind. That is why when people entered Te-shan's room he struck them with his staff,[20] or when people entered Lin-chi's room he shouted.[21] We have all groped too long already for our heads;[22] why should we set up more words and language?

Right Faith in the True Mind

CHINUL: In the *Flower Garland Scripture* we can read:

Faith is the fountainhead of the path and the mother of all meritorious qualities.
It nourishes all wholesome faculties.

Also the Consciousness-Only texts say: "Faith is like a crystal that can purify cloudy water." It is clear that faith is the vanguard in the development of the myriads of wholesome qualities. For this reason the Buddhist scriptures always begin with "Thus I heard," which is an expression intended to arouse faith.

QUESTION: What difference is there between faith in the Meditation and Doctrinal schools?

CHINUL: There are many kinds of differences. The Doctrinal schools encourage men and gods to have faith in the law of karmic cause and effect. Those who desire the pleasures that come from merit must have faith that the ten wholesome actions are the sublime cause and that human or deva rebirth is the pleasurable result. Those who feel drawn to the void-calmness of nirvana must have faith that its primary cause is the understanding of the cause and conditions of arising and ceasing and that its holy fruition is the understanding of the Four Noble Truths: suffering, its origin, its extinction, and the path leading to its extinction. Those who would delight in the fruition of Buddhahood should have faith that the practice of the six perfections over three infinite aeons is its major cause and that *bodhi* and nirvana are its right fruition.

Right faith in the patriarchal school of Meditation is different. It does not believe in any conditioned causes or effects. Rather, it stresses faith that oneself is originally a buddha; that all people possess the impeccable self-nature; and that the sublime essence of nirvana is complete in everyone. There is no need to search elsewhere, for since time immemorial these have been innate in everyone.   *RB*

Chinul: "Secrets on Cultivating the Mind"

[From *Hanguk pulgyo chŏnsŏ* 4:708b–c, 709c–710a]

The triple world is blazing in defilement as if it were a house on fire.[23] How can you bear to tarry here and complacently undergo such long suffering? If you wish to avoid wandering on in samsara, there is no better way than to seek Buddhahood. If you want to become a buddha, you should understand that buddha is the mind; how can you search for the mind in the far distance? It is not outside the body. The physical body is a phantom, for it is subject to birth and death; the true mind is like space, for it neither ends nor changes.

QUESTION: You have said that this twofold approach of sudden awakening–gradual cultivation is the track followed by the thousands of saints. But if awakening is really sudden awakening, then what need is there for gradual cultivation? And if cultivation means gradual cultivation, then how can you talk about sudden awakening? We hope that you will expound on these two ideas of sudden and gradual some more and resolve our remaining doubts.

CHINUL: First, sudden awakening. When the ordinary man is deluded, he assumes that the four great elements are his body and the false thoughts are his mind. He does not know that his own nature is the true dharma body; he does not know that his own numinous awareness is the true Buddha. He looks for the Buddha outside of his mind. While he is thus wandering around aimlessly, the entrance to the road might by chance be pointed out by a wise adviser. If in one thought he traces back the light of his mind to its source and sees his own original nature, he would discover that the ground of this nature is innately free of defilement and that he himself is originally endowed with the non-outflow wisdom nature, which is not a hair's breadth different from that of all the buddhas. Hence it is called sudden awakening.

Next, gradual cultivation. Although he has awakened to the fact that his original nature is no different from that of the buddhas, as the beginningless habit energies are extremely difficult to remove suddenly, he must continue to cultivate while relying on this awakening. Through this gradual permeation, his endeavors reach completion. He constantly nurtures the sacred embryo and, after a long time, becomes a saint. Hence it is called gradual cultivation.

This process can be compared to the maturation of a child. From the day of his birth, a baby is endowed with all the sense organs just like everyone else, but his strength is not yet fully developed. It is only after the passing of many months and years that he will finally become an adult.   *RB*

Hyesim: Preface to *Collection of the Meditation School's Explanatory Verses*

[From *Hanguk pulgyo chŏnsŏ* 5:1a–b]

Now, since the time of Kāśyapa, the World-Honored One,[24] and continuing generation after generation, the light of the patriarchs' lamp has never been extinguished, and the secret entrustment of the Meditation school has been passed on consecutively; this is considered to be the orthodox transmission of Meditation. While this orthodox transmission and secret entrustment are not deficient in words and meanings, words and meanings are insufficient to reach them. Therefore, although the Meditation teachings are expounded, the patriarchs of Meditation do not establish words and letters: the mind is transmitted with the mind, and that is all.

Those who appreciate this matter of Meditation have contrived to record its traces. Entering it into records and documents, Meditation has been transmitted up to the present, but these coarse traces are certainly not worthy of honor. Nevertheless, such writings do not hinder one from following the flow to reach the fountainhead or relying on the branches to know the roots. Even though one who reaches the original fountainhead discusses the myriads of distinctions, he never misses the mark; but even if one who has not reached it excises all language and guards that fountainhead in silence, he is never unconfused. For this reason, venerable masters in all regions do not abandon words and letters and are not niggardly with their loving-kindness and compassion. Whether through verification or maintenance, whether in succession or separately, whether in verse or in song, they disseminate the profound intent of Meditation in order to bequeath it to posterity.

Receiving the compelling request of adherents, I reflected upon the original intent of the patriarchs and saints so as to offer merit to the kingdom and benefit to the Buddha's teachings. I then commanded my disciple Chinhun and others to compile a total of 1,125 cases of ancient exchanges, together with the "fingering verses" [yŏmsong]²⁵ and other spoken essentials of all the masters. This has been recorded in thirty rolls in order to sustain the transmission of the lamp.   RB

Hyesim: "Letter in Reply to Ch'oe Hongyun"

[From *Hanguk pulgyo chŏnsŏ* 6:46c–47b]

In the past, I worked in the magistrature, but the magistrates have now entered my religious society.²⁶ The magistrates are the Buddhist Confucians, but I am a Confucian Buddhist. We have become the guests and hosts of one another and call ourselves masters or disciples. This has been the case since of old: it is not something that has only now begun. If one acknowledges just their names, Buddhism and Confucianism are dramatically different. If one knows their core, Confucianism and Buddhism are without distinction.

Don't you see? Confucius said: "I have no idea [foregone conclusions]; I have no 'I' [egotism]; I have no stability [obstinacy]; I have no decisiveness [arbitrary predeterminations]."²⁷ The layman Wu-chin,²⁸ commenting upon this, said: "Now, if there is no idea, then there must be a true idea preserving it. If there is no 'I', then there must be a true 'I' overseeing it. If there is no stability, then there must be a true stability regulating it. If there is no decisiveness, then there must be a true decisiveness maintaining it. The true idea requites the myriads of transformations, but remains undisturbed. The true 'I' controls the varieties of actions, but remains unagitated. The true stability appears within birth and death, but remains unaffected. The true decisiveness decides all types of intent, but remains unconfused. The saints and sages live by this and die by this; they become poor and ignominious by this."

Confucius said: "Shen! My Way has one thread that runs right through it."[29] He also said: "In the morning, hear the Way; in the evening, die content."[30] This so-called Way thus strings together the myriads of phenomena; it is that which is neither destroyed nor extinguished. Since he knew that the Way was neither destroyed nor extinguished, he confided: "In the evening, die content." I do not know what the prime minister thinks about this. If your faith is sufficient, then you will accord with the adage of the Great Master Ma-tsu: "Mind is Buddha, but it is neither mind nor Buddha." Reflect carefully upon this all the time: this is the method leading to penetrating realization and penetrating awakening.   RB

PUBLICATION OF THE *TRIPIṬAKA*

The first orally redacted Buddhist canons are presumed to have been compiled in India shortly after the Buddha's death. The Chinese compiled their own manuscript canons early in the history of their own Buddhist tradition, and such canons were soon introduced into Korea. With the invention of xylographic printing techniques, a complete woodblock canon was carved in China during the tenth century, and the first Koryŏ canon, a similar project, was begun in 1011.

The Buddhist canons of East Asia were open collections, which permitted dramatic expansions in coverage when compared to their Indian counterparts. The monk Ŭich'ŏn (1055–1101) had the most liberal outlook toward the canon. Earlier Chinese Buddhist bibliographic cataloguers considered canonical chiefly translations of Indian materials. But Ŭich'ŏn believed that East Asian exegetes and authors also had made seminal contributions to Buddhist thought that warranted inclusion in the canon. Ŭich'ŏn feared that unless the canon were opened to such indigenous works, they would be doomed to drop from circulation and would be lost to posterity.

To prevent such a fate, Ŭich'ŏn sent agents throughout East Asia to procure Buddhist texts by native authors. In 1090, he published his catalog of this collection, which listed some 1,010 titles in 4,740 rolls. Woodblocks for each of these texts were carved, and the collection was termed a *Supplement to the Canon (Sokchanggyŏng)*. Unfortunately, the woodblocks of the first Koryŏ canon and its supplement were burned during the Mongol invasion in 1231. While the main canon was recarved between 1236 and 1251, the *Supplement* was not. As Ŭich'ŏn had feared, most of the texts collected in his *Supplement* were lost to history; only his catalog of that collection has survived, the preface to which is translated in the first selection.

The Koryŏ government actively supported Buddhism, and the most dramatic expression of state-sponsored Buddhist activities was the printing of the *Tripiṭaka*, the Buddhist canon. Centuries earlier, Buddhist devotion and advances in printing had already been linked. With the recent discovery of a copy of a *dhāraṇī* scripture dating from before 751, Silla claims the oldest extant example of woodblock printing in the world.

A printing of the *Tripiṭaka* in woodblocks was undertaken on two separate occasions. The first blocks were started in 1011 in the midst of Khitan attacks. Koreans believed that the publication of the *Tripiṭaka* would invoke the divine protection of the Buddha, sparing Koryŏ from further attacks. This project lasted nearly seventy years. When the Mongols invaded in the thirteenth century, Koryŏ once again turned to aid from the Buddha with the second manufacture of the *Tripiṭaka* in woodblocks. The eighty-one thousand separate blocks completed at this time can still be seen at Haein Monastery in south central Korea.

This last production of the *Tripiṭaka*, in the middle of the Mongol invasions, attracted considerable attention. In the second selection presented here, Yi Kyubo, reflecting on the significance of this project, believes that publishing the *Tripiṭaka* will guarantee the safety of the nation. The publication of the *Tripiṭaka* demonstrated the faith of the Koreans and their belief in the power of the Buddha to afford them divine protection. It is also another clear example of the technological sophistication of a people who could carry out such a mammoth project while fighting a terrible war.

RB AND HK

Ŭich'ŏn: Preface to a *New Catalog of the Teachings of All the Schools*

[From *Taegak kuksa munjip* 1:3a–4b]

During the K'ai-yüan era [713–741], a great dharma master, whose cognomen was Chih-sheng [669–740], finally corrected the mistakes and errors of previous catalogers, condensed the repetitions, and compiled all his material into one book, entitled *K'ai-yüan Catalog of the Buddhist Scriptures [K'ai-yüan Shih-chiao lu]*, in a total of twenty rolls. This was the most seminal of all the catalogs, and critics have considered it to have established the pedigree of the scriptural teachings. None was the equal of Chih-sheng's catalog, and none surpassed its achievement in preserving the bequeathed teachings of the Buddha.

Since the *K'ai-yüan Catalog*, though it includes scriptures and treatises translated from Indian languages, omits some of the tracts and commentaries [of East Asian authors], I was concerned lest these latter have no chance of being disseminated. Hence, while highly esteeming the venerable Chih-sheng's determination to protect the dharma, I have considered it my own duty to track down the traces of the teachings. For almost twenty years now, I have been diligent about this quest and have never abandoned it. I have put in order these new and old compositions, these illustrious treatises of all the schools, which I have recovered; unwilling to keep them private, today I publish them.   *RB*

Yi Kyubo: Royal Prayer on the Occasion of the Production of the *Tripiṭaka*

[From *Tongguk Yi sangguk chip* 25:18b–20a]

I, King Kojong [1213–1259], together with the crown prince, dukes, lords, counts, state councillors, and civil and military officials, have respectfully cleansed our bodies and souls and pray to all the buddhas and bodhisattvas and the Sakradevanam Indra everywhere in the infinite void as well as to all the spirit-officials who protect the dharma in the thirty-three heavens.

Severe indeed is the calamity caused by the Tartars. The nature of their cruelty and vindictiveness is beyond description. With foolishness and stupidity greater than that of beasts, how could they know what is respected in this world and what is called the Buddhadharma? Because of this ignorance there was not a Buddhist image or Buddhist writing that they did not entirely destroy. Moreover, as a state that worships the Buddhadharma when we do not have this great treasure we certainly cannot be content with its loss. How can we hesitate over its reproduction on account of the magnitude of such an undertaking.

As we are truly sincere in our prayer, we have nothing to be ashamed of before our ancestors. Therefore, we humbly pray that the various buddhas and sages in the thirty-three heavens receive our earnest prayers, extend to us divine power, cause the stubborn and vile barbarians to flee far away, and never again let them enter our territory. When the fighting ceases and peace prevails all over, may the queen dowager and crown prince enjoy long life forever and may Korea's good fortune last ten thousand years.   *HK AND ES*

CHAPTER TWELVE

Popular Beliefs and Confucianists

Koryŏ was eclectic in its religious beliefs. Apart from Buddhism, native beliefs, geomancy, shamanism, Taoism, and Neo-Confucianism provided spiritual and intellectual sustenance. The native beliefs involved respect for the deities and guardians of the land. Throughout Koryŏ, people called upon these spirits to defend them against foreign invaders as well as against internal forces of destruction. Geomancy (Chinese *feng-shui*, Korean *p'ung-su*), a practice of divination based on the belief that topography can dictate one's fortunes, was also widely accepted, giving rise to the notion that undesirable disturbances to the natural environment could cause unrest. Many of these ideas blended with Buddhism and became an integral part of the Koryŏ religious world.

Taoism, originally a Chinese philosophy advocating freedom from man-made constraints and attunement with nature, became popular among various segments of society. To the government official, it offered an escape from the restrictions of public life; to the peasant, it offered closer links with the natural order. Shamanism, the belief that spirits inhabit every object in the world and accordingly influence individual destiny, was yet another form of Koryŏ spiritual experience. Taken together, all of these concepts influenced the lives of Koryŏ people, providing them with spiritual strength to confront the vicissitudes of life.

The growth of Neo-Confucianism in Sung and Yüan China eventually influenced Koryŏ's Confucian heritage. With the growing distaste for Buddhism and a desire for a more rigorous philosophical base for needed reform, scholars of late Koryŏ studied Neo-Confucian treatises on human nature and applied their new learning to societal reform, laying the philosophical foundation for the rise of the Chosŏn kingdom (1392–1910).

NATIVE BELIEFS

Aside from the state-sanctioned Confucianism and Buddhism, indigenous religious practices also functioned in an environment influenced by shamanism and geomancy. These native traditions had been expressed since Korea's earliest times through religion, art, music, and dance, and later many of these native impulses gradually found their way into Buddhism and divination theory. One test of a culture is its ability to blend outside influences with indigenous ways, and the people of Koryŏ successfully adapted Confucianism, Buddhism, Taoism, and the concepts underlying geomancy—all originally external philosophies—to their indigenous beliefs.

Shamanistic beliefs held that spirits dwelled in natural objects such as old trees, rivers, rocks, and mountains, and that these spirits controlled everyone's destiny. If these spirits were properly treated and worshiped, they would bring peace and benefits to everyone. In the first selection in this section, Yi Chibaek urges a spiritual defense against the Khitan attacks at the end of the tenth century by appealing to the major native deities of the land. We find in his statement a clear sense of the need to preserve the Korean native traditions.

King Ŭijong, mid-Koryŏ's controversial monarch who was condemned by later historians for contributing inexcusably to the causes of the military coup of 1170, called for the restitution of such ceremonies as the Assembly of the Eight Prohibitions (*p'algwan hoe*) in the second passage. The *p'algwan*, originally a Buddhist celebration, was later transformed into an annual national festival to commemorate vows made to local spirits and was held in the two capitals, Kaesŏng and P'yŏngyang, in the eleventh and tenth lunar months, respectively. There was a pervasive belief that such celebrations would help ensure dynastic security and nationwide prosperity. Especially handsome young men were selected to oversee the observance of native traditions, reminiscent of the *hwarang* movement of Silla.

Yi Chibaek: Memorial on Territorial Integrity

[From *Koryŏ sa* 94:3a–b]

Since our august ancestor's inception of the dynasty, we have preserved our sovereignty to this day. Now, without a single loyal official voicing objection, we rashly want to surrender land to the enemy. Is this not lamentable indeed? The ancients had a poem:

> *A vast territory is disposed of in a casual manner.*
> *The civil and military officials of the two courts reproached Ch'iao Chou.*

Ch'iao Chou was a great minister of Shu in China who urged his young ruler to give up land to Wei, thus becoming the joke of eternity.

I propose that we bribe Hsiao Sun-ning with gold, silver, and other treasures to discover his real intentions. And rather than rashly cutting off land and handing it over to appease an enemy, is it not better to renew the practices of the Lantern Festival, the Assembly of the Eight Prohibitions, and the Immortal Lad to elicit spiritual protection,[1] as was done under our former kings? Is this not a better way to preserve the state and achieve peace than to resort to the strange practices of others? If we are to do this, we ought first to report to our deities. As to whether there be war or peace, Your Majesty alone should decide.

HK AND ES

King Ŭijong: Rescript on Native Traditions

[From *Koryŏ sa* 18:36b–37a]

Uphold the way of the immortals. In Silla times, the way of the immortals was widely practiced so that the dragon and heavenly protectors of the Buddhadharma were pleased and the people were at peace. Therefore, from the time of the dynastic progenitor on, we have upheld these traditions. Recently, the Assembly of the Eight Prohibitions in the two capitals has daily deteriorated from its former scale and quality, resulting in the gradual decline of the inherited traditions. From now on, in holding the Assembly of the Eight Prohibitions, first select from the civil and military services those of means and designate them preservers of native traditions. By practicing old native traditions, keep the people and Heaven both happy.

HK AND ES

GEOMANCY

Geomantic theories were popularized in Koryŏ by the works of the Buddhist monk Tosŏn (827–898), who enhanced their appeal through an infusion of Buddhist ideas. Tosŏn's application of the Buddhist theory of causation to geomancy led Wang Kŏn to state in his "Ten Injunctions" that the topography of his power base, Songak (Kaesŏng), had unequivocally determined his dynastic success. Following Wong Kŏn's political unification of the Later Three Kingdoms in 936, he built the Kaet'ae Monastery ("Exalted Beginning") to demonstrate his gratitude and gain further spiritual protection. He personally wrote the first selection presented here in appreciation of the divine protective powers of Buddha and the local mountain spirits, to which he attributed his success. Some of his political confidants, such as Ch'oe Ŭng (898–932), citing Confucian texts, criticized Wang Kŏn for his continuing reliance on Buddhist and native religious practices. But the king defended his stance on the grounds that the hard reality of the unsettled conditions of the time demanded these practices, which were close to the people of the land.

Believing that the strength of the dynasty was tied to the topographical powers of the land, Koryŏ formally set up four capitals: the central capital at Kaesŏng, the western capital at P'yŏngyang, the southern capital at Seoul, and the eastern capital at Kyŏngju. Kaesŏng was chosen because of its geomantic centrality in the kingdom, as well as because it was Wang Kŏn's political and economic power base. Subsequent attempts to move the capital, often rooted in the desire for political gain, were always foiled on the basis of geomancy. At the end of the eleventh century, Kim Wije urged that the southern capital (modern Seoul) be built and enhanced in stature to assure the continued success of the dynasty. In making this plea, Kim cited several sources, including the work of the monk Tosŏn, which had gained even greater respect by then than it had enjoyed in the monk's own time.

The most dramatic and ultimately for the dynasty the most dangerous attempt to move the capital occurred in the 1130s, when a nationalistic firebrand, the monk Myoch'ŏng (d. 1135), led a rebellion to establish the primacy of the western capital, P'yŏngyang. Myoch'ŏng was a charismatic monk who captured the attention of the troubled King Injong (1122–1146) and quickly gained the monarch's confidence. Taking advantage of an unsettled political scene that had led to the burning of the royal palace by Yi Chagyŏm (d. 1126) in 1126, the persuasive monk convinced many that the central capital, Kaesŏng, had lost its geomantic vigor. To resuscitate the dynasty it was imperative, according to Myoch'ŏng, to move the capital north. When blocked by the central aristocrats, Myoch'ŏng revolted, calling not only for a new capital but also for a new direction in foreign policy that would challenge the domination of China proper, then in the hands of the Chin dynasty.

In the end, the central aristocrats would rally to defeat the rebellious forces under Myoch'ŏng in P'yŏngyang, but as the monk first gathered strength, scholars fought him with ink and brush. The final passage, by Im Wan (Lin Wan in Chinese), a Chinese who had passed the examination in Koryŏ and served as an official at King Injong's court, cites natural calamities as a warning to the king not to listen to Myoch'ŏng. Calling on ideas first drafted by such prominent Confucian scholars as Han China's Tung Chung-shu (179–104? B.C.), Im appealed to logic to counter Myoch'ŏng's emotional demands. Im Wan also recalled Wang Kŏn's "Ten Injunctions" and the events of Munjong's reign (1046–1083) to support his request for King Injong's reform and the removal of Myoch'ŏng from the court.

King T'aejo's Reliance on Buddhism

[From *Pohan chip* 1:1b–2a]

In my lifetime, I have encountered many worrisome difficulties and was unable to overcome many of them. Soldiers encircled Hyŏndo Commandery;[2] disaster racked Chinhan.[3] People had nothing to rely on for their livelihood, and houses lacked protection. I pledged before Heaven to suppress great evil forces, to rescue the people from their misery so they could be free to farm and make handicrafts in their own villages. Relying first on the power of Buddha and then on the authority of Taoism, I have engaged through more than two decades in sea attacks and fiery battles, personally risking bombardment by arrows and stones. Advancing a thousand *ri* to the south or to the east, I used my weapons as pillows. In the autumn of 936, around Sungsŏn fortress, I faced the troops of Later Paekche. On hearing one battle cry, the cruel enemy collapsed. With the second beat of the war drum, the rebels melted like ice. Triumphant songs floated to heaven, joyful sounds shook the land. Thieves in the rushes and outlaws in the countryside repented and, wishing to make a new start, thought of surrendering to me. My intentions being to seize the bad and eliminate evil, aid the weak and help the dependent, I have not committed the smallest transgression or injured even a blade of grass. In order to respond to the sustenance accorded by the Holy

Buddha, to repay the support of the mountain spirits, I especially commanded the government offices concerned to construct a lotus palace [Buddhist monastery] and to name the mountain on which it sits Ch'ŏnho ["Heavenly Protection"] and the monastery Kaet'ae. May Buddha's authority provide protection and Heaven's power sustain me.   HK AND ES

King T'aejo and Confucian Advice

[From *Pohan chip* 1:1a—b]

When King T'aejo was still fighting to consolidate his newly founded kingdom, he resorted to the ideas of yin-yang and Buddhism.

Counselor Ch'oe Ŭng [898–932] remonstrated, saying: "The *Tso Commentary* says, 'At the time of disorder, cultivate letters to gain the hearts of man.'⁴ Even during warfare, the ruler must cultivate civil virtues. I have yet to hear of anyone relying on Buddhism or yin-yang ideas to win the world."

The king said: "How could I not know it? Yet the mountains and streams of our country are divine and extraordinary. Set in an out-of-the-way place, far removed from China, Koreans by nature love Buddha and spirits and expect blessings and prosperity. These days, war never ceases, and peace is never certain. Day and night, the peasants are troubled and are at a loss as to what to do. I only think of the hidden help of Buddha and the spirits as well as the divine response of the mountains and streams in the hope that they may yield results through my indulgences. How could this not be the great principle of ruling the country to win the people? After we settle these conflicts and live in peace and justice, then we can change our ways and enlighten the people."   HK AND ES

Kim Wije: On the Selection of a Site for the Capital

[From *Koryŏ sa* 122:1a–3b]

In 1096, Kim Wije became the executive assistant of royal insignia [*wiwisŭng tongjŏng*]. At the end of Silla, there was a monk called Tosŏn who went to T'ang to learn from I-hsing⁵ the methods of geomancy and then returned. He wrote a secret book to pass on his knowledge of the methods. Wije studied these methods and presented a memorial to the king that requested that the capital be moved to the southern capital, saying:

"The *Record of Tosŏn [Tosŏn ki]* said: 'In Koryŏ there are three capitals. Songak [Kaesŏng] is to be the central capital, Mongmyŏngyang [Seoul] the southern capital, and P'yŏngyang the western capital. If in the eleventh, twelfth, first, and second months the king resides in the central capital, in the third, fourth, fifth, and sixth months the king resides in the southern capital, and in the seventh, eighth, ninth, and tenth months the king resides in the western capital, then the thirty-six states of the world will offer tribute.' The book also said: 'One hundred and sixty years after the establishment of the kingdom, it will have the capital at Mongmyŏngyang.' I suggest that now is the right time to move and build a new capital."

In King Yejong's time [1105—1122], Ŭn Wŏnjung, using Tosŏn's explanations, also presented a memorial discussing this.   *HK AND ES*

The Monk Myoch'ŏng's Use of Geomancy

[From *Koryŏ sa* 127:26b–29b]

Myoch'ŏng [d. 1135] was a monk in the Western Capital who later changed his name to Chŏngsin. In the sixth year of Injong [1128], the diviner Paek Suhan [d. 1135], as honorary deputy director in the Office of Royal Lectures in the Western Capital, asked Myoch'ŏng to be his teacher. The two men used the secret art of yin-yang to delude the people. Chŏng Chisang [d. 1135] was also a person of the Western Capital who deeply believed their practices. He felt that the foundation of the main dynastic capital was already weakened, as the palace had burned completely, leaving nothing; that the Western Capital had the royal essence; and that the king ought to move to P'yŏngyang, making it his main capital.

The king finally made a trip to the Western Capital and ordered the accompanying state councillors, together with Myoch'ŏng and Paek Suhan, to divine the power of the topography at Imwŏn station. He commanded Kim An [chief of the palace attendants] to build a palace, pressing the construction with great haste. At that time the weather was freezing cold, and the people were resentful and complained bitterly.

The next year, when a stupa at Chunghŭng Monastery in the Western Capital burned, some asked Myoch'ŏng: "You asked the king to go to the Western Capital to ward off calamity. Why has there now been this great disaster?" Myoch'ŏng blushed in shame and could not answer. He bowed his head for a long time and then, raising his head, hit the desk with his fists and said: "If the king had remained in the main capital, this disaster would have been even greater. Because he came here, the disaster was confined outside, and His Majesty personally remains safe and well." Those who believed Myoch'ŏng said: "That explains it. How can one not believe him?"

Myoch'ŏng also persuaded the king to construct a wall around Imwŏn Palace and set up eight shrines in the palace. The eight shrines were for the following:

first, the truly virtuous Bodhisattva Mañjuśrī, the T'aebaek immortal of the nation-protecting Paektu peak; second, the truly virtuous Buddha Śākyamuni, the venerable Buddha of six supernatural powers of the dragon-encircled peak; third, ... And he had portraits of the eight sages drawn. Kim An, Yi Chungbu, Chŏng Chisang, and others thought this in accord with the laws of the sages, as well as with the art of benefitting the state and prolonging the dynastic foundation. Kim An and others also petitioned to make offerings to the eight sages, while Chŏng Chisang composed a statement for the offerings that said: "Not to go fast and yet to be quick, not to act and yet to arrive, this is called the spirit of obtaining the absolute way. Even nothing is something; and real is nonreal. In general, this is the original form of Buddhism. Only the Heavenly Mandate can control all things; only earthly virtue can enable the king to rule over all. Having divined the power of great splendor, we have constructed a new palace in the middle of P'yŏngyang. May we respect yin and yang and enshrine the eight immortals in the area, making the Paektu immortals and the immortals of Mount T'aebaek the first to be enshrined. May we consider divine virtue to be here with us; may we desire magical utilization to appear before our eyes; and may we see dazzling ultimate truth to be delivered.   *HK AND ES*

Im Wan: Memorial on Calamities

[From *Koryŏ sa* 98:33b–37b]

Once I have said it is not difficult to offer advice, but difficult to listen to it. But then it is more difficult to carry out the advice than to listen to it. Accordingly, it is said: "If a loyal official serves his ruler, his earnest and direct words will not enhance his employment but only endanger him. If his words are not earnest and direct, then they are insufficient to clarify the Way."

The *Book of Documents* says: "Great Heaven has no partial affections; it helps only the virtuous." It also says: "It is not millet that has the piercing fragrance; it is bright virtue."[6] As for what virtue is, where else can it be found but in the ruler's use of his mind and his conduct of affairs? Those who put their minds to good use and conducted affairs appropriately were Yao, Shun, Yü, T'ang; and the first four rulers of the Chou dynasty, Wen, Wu, Ch'eng, and K'ang.[7] Accordingly, since everything they said and did met Heaven's wishes, they were able to enjoy unlimited blessings.

In the last few years, calamity has frequently appeared, and famine has come again and again. Lately white rainbows have pierced the sun, and in the first month there was rolling thunder that was especially strange. Such occurrences have never been heard of before. Don't they mean that Your Majesty is responding to Heaven with words, not substance? Why are there so many strange happenings even though you continue to make sacrifices? As Heaven always admonishes like this, it must be an expression of Heaven's merciful love for Your Majesty. For the sake of Your Majesty's plan, I propose that by taking responsibility and reflecting on yourself, you respond to Heaven's warnings. This can be done by carrying out good government and the good laws of the illustrious dynastic ancestors.

Recently, grotesque theories of supernatural explanations have been extensively put forth by Myoch'ŏng. I believe Myoch'ŏng only deceives the king through his craftiness, and in this he is no different from Lin Ling-su of Sung China.[8] Ling-su, bearing heresy, bewildered the emperor. Gentry who sought quick advancement as officials bent over to flatter him to gain honor and fame. Thereupon calamities frequently arose, yet the emperor did not apprehend their significance. The original purpose in constructing this palace was to seek blessings. Now seven or eight years have passed, and there has not been one good omen; only calamities continue to arise. Why? Heaven's will is like the statement, "Treacherous people will bedevil the king. Even though they can cheat people, how can they cheat Heaven?" The incidents of the past days are perhaps Heaven's warnings to alert Your Majesty. Your Majesty, how can you cling to crafty officials and disregard Heaven's will? I urge Your Majesty to wield your authority strongly, to behead Myoch'ŏng, to respond to Heaven's warnings from above, and to console the hearts of the people below. This is the open expression of public opinion, not just the personal feelings of a foolish official. May Your Majesty look into this.

HK AND ES

Taoism and Shamanism

Religious Taoism developed in China, came to Korea, and spread gradually throughout the centuries of contact with China. Unlike Confucianism, Taoism put less emphasis on one's commitment to society, stressing instead bodily cultivation and spiritual refinement. The Taoist attempt to transcend life led some practitioners to delve into quasi-scientific searches for elixirs and potions. Taoists eventually became associated with the free-spirited activities found in Korean native traditions as well as in Buddhism.

The first selection was written by Hsü Ching (1091–1153) of Sung China during his official trip to Koryŏ in the early twelfth century. He visited the kingdom at the end of the reign of King Yejong (1105–1122), a period of intellectual vigor. In describing Taoism's new popularity at that time, Hsü Ching provides a brief history of its growth in Korea, where it was given new impetus by the rising influence of religious Taoism in late T'ang and Sung China.

"Shamanism" is a term often applied to native religious traditions practiced widely throughout Korea and northeastern Asia. Developed in close association with other native beliefs, including those underlying geomancy, shamanism maintains that natural objects are infused with a vital force and that shamans have the power to contact these spirits in nature and invoke them to bring blessings to the home, community, or country. To the uneducated peasant, the shaman was an important force in maintaining well-being; to the Confucian literati, however, the shaman was frequently an object of contempt, suspicion, and criticism.

King Injong (1122–1146), who listened for a time to Myoch'ŏng, was willing to allow the practice of shamanism. And some of his advisers, once their pockets were properly lined with bribes, petitioned to permit shamans to hold ritual sacrifices. Practitioners of shamanism, like certain Buddhist monks, claimed that their prayers had spared the country disaster. "Enfeoffment of the Kŭmsŏng Mountain Deity" (*SKC* 1:446) provides an example and also shows the close connection between mountain spirits and shamanism.

Superstition permeated the lives of ordinary people in Koryŏ. Fortune-tellers, geomancers, and shamans were everyday fare, especially for the commoner. When Yi Chagyŏm (d. 1126) exiled Yi Yŏng (d. 1123), who subsequently died in anguish upon learning of the enslavement of his mother and children, Yi Yŏng became something of a folk hero, as the third selection reveals. One's burial site was significant according to geomancy, and this, of course, caused his son to rebury Yi Yŏng.

The interpretation of dreams was thought to be an important means of understanding what the future had in store. Dreams were believed to contain hidden messages that could predict significant events when interpreted by a skilled fortune-teller. Although commoners often wholeheartedly accepted irrational beliefs and superstitions, the Confucian literati, placing more faith in rational explanations, generally manifested skepticism—though there were always exceptions.

Hsü Ching: History of Koryŏ Taoism

[From *Kao-li t'u-ching* 18:93]

Koryŏ is on the shores of the Eastern Sea, which must be situated not far from the Taoist mountains and the Islands of the Immortals. Its people would not have been unaware of the praise the Taoist teachings of longevity and immortality commanded. Earlier in China we had been too often engaged in military expeditions, and few tried to teach Taoism through the method of cleansing and nonaction. When T'ang rose, they honored the progenitor of the universe. Therefore, in the Wu-te period [618–626], Koguryŏ sent an envoy pleading that Taoist priests be sent to lecture on the five-thousand-word classic, the *Tao Te Ching,* and explain its profound and subtle meanings. T'ang Emperor Kao-tsu, since he was a sage ruler, was impressed and granted their petition. From then on, they started following Taoism even more than Buddhism.

In the *keng-yin* year of Ta-kuan [1110], the Emperor Hui-tsung of Sung China, caring for the distant land of Koryŏ, which wanted to hear about Taoism, sent envoys accompanied by two Taoist priests and had them instruct and guide selected Koreans well versed in the ways of religious teachings. King Yejong [1105–1122], a devout believer in religion, in the Cheng-ho era [1110–1117] started to construct Pogwŏn Taoist temple to receive more than ten eminently accomplished Taoist priests. The Taoist priests passed the day in the palace ancestral temple, however, and at night returned to their private chambers. Later, when the censors pointed this out, laws to restrict it were added. Some said that when King Yejong reigned over the country, he was constantly bent on supplying Taoists with books, wishing to replace Buddhism with Taoism. Although he never realized that goal, he seemed to have expected it to happen. HK AND ES

The Popularity of Shaman Customs

[From *Koryŏ sa* 16:16a–b]

The official astrologer memorialized [the king]: "Recently as shamanism has been widely practiced, its indecent sacrifices have increased daily. I request the king to instruct the offices concerned to expel all the shamans." The request was granted. Many shamans were grieved by this. They collected their valuables and exchanged them for more than one hundred silver vessels, using them to bribe powerful officials. The powerful officials thereupon memorialized [the king]: "Spirits being formless, we cannot know whether they are fake or real. To ban them completely is never advantageous." The king, agreeing with this argument, rescinded the earlier prohibition. HK AND ES

Yi Yŏng's Corpse

[From *Koryŏ sa* 97:17a–b]

When Yi Chagyŏm killed Han Anin [d. 1122], Yi Yŏng, being Han Anin's brother-in-law, was implicated and banished to Chin Island. Someone said to Yi Yŏng,

"Your mother and sons are going to be made slaves." Yi Yŏng said, "Reflecting on myself, as I have no cause for remorse, I have had no reason to bring death upon myself. So I have waited to this day. If because of me my old mother is made a slave, however, what am I living for?" Therefore he drank one *mal* of wine and died in anguish.[9] Contemporaries regretted his death. Yi Chagyŏm sent a conjurer to bury him on the side of the road. Cows and horses did not dare walk over the grave. When people who were gravely ill prayed there, they were cured. When Yi Chagyŏm was ousted, Yi Yŏng's son asked to change the burial site. When they dug it out, the corpse had not decomposed. *HK AND ES*

NEO-CONFUCIANISM

Confucianism remained an important ideology of the state throughout the Koryŏ dynasty, but in the closing years of Koryŏ new interest grew in Neo-Confucianism, which had developed earlier in Sung and Yüan China.

An Hyang (1243–1306) is traditionally credited with introducing Neo-Confucianism to Korea. An's first exposure to the ideas of Neo-Confucianism came in 1286 when he read the *Complete Works of Chu Hsi (Chu Tzu ch'üan-shu)* while staying in the Yüan capital as a member of a Koryŏ embassy to the Mongol court. Impressed by the ideas of Chu Hsi (1130–1200), An made a copy of the *Complete Works* and brought it back to Koryŏ. He subsequently devoted himself to reviving Confucian studies in Korea. As the first selection, taken from his biography in the *History of Koryŏ*, suggests, An's major contribution to the development of Neo-Confucianism in Korea came not from the originality of his thought but rather from his efforts to promote Confucian education and propagate the ideas of Chu Hsi. Nonetheless, it is important to note that when he cites social ethics in his discussion of Confucius's legacy, An introduces one of the major recurring themes of fourteenth-century Korean Neo-Confucianism. Within a century after its introduction by An Hyang, Neo-Confucianism spread rapidly among the ranks of the officialdom and became the major focus of the curriculum in the highest academic institution. This is illustrated in the second selection, from the biography of Yi Saek (1328–1396), one of the most prominent Neo-Confucianists of the fourteenth century.

Another prominent literatus, Chŏng Mongju (1337–1392), who was lionized by Chosŏn dynasty Neo-Confucianists as the first great Korean Neo-Confucian metaphysician, also epitomized this new interest. Unfortunately, there is virtually nothing in his surviving writings to allow us to gauge the breadth and quality of his understanding of Neo-Confucian metaphysics. We can, however, see in Chŏng the emergence of some of the salient characteristics of late Koryŏ and early Chosŏn Neo-Confucianism. The selection drawn from Chŏng's biography in the *History of Koryŏ* reveals two aspects of Neo-Confucianism that, while not unique to Korea, were much more emphasized there than in China, Japan, or Vietnam. One is anti-Buddhism, a central feature of Korean Neo-Confucianism from the late fourteenth century on. The other is the strong sense of moralistic rightness, which was firmly fixed in the Korean Neo-Confucian mind by Chŏng Mongju's 1392 martyrdom in defense of the doomed Koryŏ dynasty.

Chŏng Tojŏn (d. 1398) was a central political figure in the change of dynasties between Koryŏ and Chosŏn; he was a major scholar of statecraft who did much to shape the institutions of the new dynasty, and at the same time also a seminal thinker of the Nature and Principle philosophy who began to develop a new philosophical dimension in Korean Neo-Confucianism through his rebuttals of Buddhism and Taoism. One of Chŏng's most significant writings was the three-part work *Mind, Material Force, and Principle (Simgi ip'yŏn)*. In the first two parts of this work, mind (for Buddhism) and material force (for Taoism) criticize each other, leading to the crucial third part, where principle, representing Nature and Principle Neo-Confucianism, exposes (in Chŏng's view) the falseness in the underlying assumptions of both Buddhism and Taoism and presents Neo-Confucian principle as the only way that comprehends both mind and material force. It is this third part, entitled "Principle Admonishes Mind and Material Force," that is reproduced in part in the fourth selection, along with annotations by Kwŏn Kŭn (1352–1409), Chŏng Tojŏn's contemporary.

An Hyang: The Introduction of Neo-Confucianism

[From *Koryŏ sa* 105:29b–31a]

An Hyang, concerned about the daily decline of schools, raised the issue in the Two Directorates,[10] where he said: "There is nothing in the duties of the state councillors that takes precedence over educating talent. The Fund for Nurturing Worthies is now exhausted,[11] and there is nothing to use to foster scholars. I request that all persons of the sixth grade and higher give one *kŭn* of silver and all persons of the seventh grade and lower give cloth according to their rank. These resources will go to the fund to be left as principal whose interest will be used as educational assistance money." The Two Directorates concurred. When the king heard of this, he gave money and grain from palace funds to help.

Commissioner of the Security Council Ko Se, referring to himself as a military man, did not want to pay. Addressing the various state councillors, An said: "The way of Confucius has bequeathed to eternity the standards whereby the official is loyal to his lord, the son filial to his father, and the younger brother respectful to his elder brother. Whose teachings are these? If one says, 'I am a military man; why should I be pressed to pay money for the fostering of your students?' he is disregarding Confucius. How can this be?" Upon hearing this, Ko was deeply embarrassed and paid immediately.

An Hyang also gave surplus funds to the erudite Kim Munjŏng and others and sent them to China to paint portraits of the ancient sages and the seventy masters as well as to bring back sacrificial implements, musical instruments, the Six Classics, the works of the various masters, and the Chinese histories.

An Hyang was solemn and composed, and everyone held him in awe. When he was in the Chancellery, he was skilled at planning and exercised good judgment so that his colleagues followed quietly and industriously without daring to argue. He always held the promotion of learning and the nurturing of worthies to be his duty. Even when he declined to serve and stayed at home, he never lost his concern for affairs.

In his later years, An always hung up a portrait of Chu Hsi, whom he admired greatly. Eventually he himself took the pen name of Hoehŏn [after that of Chu Hsi]. Whenever he met potentially successful scholars, he encouraged them.

JD

The Spread of Neo-Confucianism

[From *Koryŏ sa* 115:10b–11a]

In the sixteenth year [1367] of King Kongmin, the Royal Confucian Academy [*Sŏnggyungwan*] was rebuilt, and Yi Saek [1328–1396] was appointed concurrently to be superintendent of the Capital District and supervisor of sacrificial rites in the Royal Academy. The number of classics licentiates [*saengwŏn*] was increased. Kim Kuyong [1338–1384], Chŏng Mongju [1337–1392], Pak Sangch'ung [1332–1375], Pak Ŭijung, and Yi Sungin [1349–1392], all scholars skilled in the classics, were given concurrent appointments as instructors in addition to the offices they held. Prior to this time, the number of students at the academy had been no more than a few dozen. But Yi Saek revised academic procedures and sat daily in Myŏngnyun Hall, where he divided the students [into sections] on different Confucian classics and taught them. When the lecture was over, the students debated among themselves, forgetting their fatigue. Scholars gathered to share their perceptions and feelings. Thus began the rise of the Ch'eng-Chu school of Neo-Confucianism in Korea.   *JD AND HK*

Chŏng Mongju and the Development of Neo-Confucianism

[From *Koryŏ sa* 117:1b–12a]

Chŏng Mongju [1337–1392] was given concurrent appointments as an office chief in the Ministry of Rites and as a professor in the Royal Academy in the sixteenth year [1367] of King Kongmin. At the time, the only commentary on the classics to have reached Korea was the *Collected Commentaries of Chu Hsi*. Chŏng Mongju's discourses were superior and so far exceeded people's expectations that those who heard him were very suspicious. Later, when a copy of Hu Ping-wen's [1250–1333] *Encyclopedia of Four Classics [Ssu-shu t'ung]* was obtained, it was found that there were no discrepancies between Hu's work and Chŏng's discourses. All the Confucianists were astonished. Yi Saek praised Chŏng highly, saying, "Even when speaking at random, Mongju says nothing that does not conform to principle," and exalted Chŏng as the founder of Neo-Confucianism in Korea.   *JD*

Chŏng Tojŏn: Philosophical Rebuttal of Buddhism and Taoism

[From *Sambong chip* 10:5b–9a]

The principle of Heaven resides in humankind to become human nature while the material force of earth resides in humankind to become physical form. The mind combines principle and material force to become master of the body. Thus principle exists prior to heaven and earth, and material force comes into being from principle, which is also received by the mind and becomes virtue. A human being is different from beasts because he has a sense of right. If a human being has no rightness, then his consciousness is no more than emotion, desire, and the selfishness of worldly gain, while his activity is like a mass of squirming insects. Even though he may be called human, how far removed can he be from the birds and beasts? That is why when examining his mind and cultivating his material force, the Confucianist necessarily emphasizes rightness.

The learning of Buddha and Lao Tzu worships purity and annihilation. Thus they necessarily strive to close off and eradicate even the greatness of moral duty and the beauty of ritual and music. The person who has no desire in his heart may be different from people who pursue worldly gain, but he does not know how to emphasize the impartiality of the principle of Heaven so as to control the selfishness of desire. Therefore, in his daily speech and conduct, he always becomes trapped in worldly gain but does not himself know it.

Furthermore, there is nothing a human being desires more than life and nothing he hates more than death. Chŏng looks at this through the arguments of both Buddhists and Taoists. Buddha strove to escape death and birth, which means that he feared death. Lao Tzu strove for longevity, which means that he craved life. If this is not worldly gain, what is it? Furthermore, because they have no emphasis on rightness, vacantly they acquire nothing, ignorantly they know nothing, and though their bodies may exist, they are nothing more than blood and flesh.

Mencius said: "Now when people suddenly see a young child about to fall in a well, they all have feelings of fear and pity."[12] He continued to say: "The feeling of commiseration is the beginning of humaneness." This means that the feeling of compassion is inherent in our minds and reveals the error of the Buddhist elimination of thought and forgetting of emotion. As for humans being born with the life-creating mind of heaven and earth, this is what is called humaneness. This principle is truly embodied in our minds. Therefore, that feeling of pity when we see a young child crawling into a well arises of itself and cannot be blocked. If one pursues this mind and expands it, his humaneness will be inexhaustible, and he will be able to join and succor the whole world. Thus the Confucianist does not fear the rise of concern but only follows the natural manifestation of the principle of Heaven. How could he be like the Buddhist, who fears the rise of feeling and concern and strives forcibly to eliminate them in order to return to annihilation?

The Analects says: "The determined scholar and the humane man will not seek life at the expense of their humaneness; they will sacrifice their bodies to achieve humaneness."[13] This means that rightness is important and life is unimportant, and it reveals the error of the Taoists' lusting after life by nurturing material [vital] force. Generally the superior man, having seen and acquired the genuine principle, cannot bear to save his life for even one day once it is rightly the time to die. Is his life or death important, or is his rightness important? Therefore, when the Confucian must come to the aid of his lord or his father, he will sacrifice his body and his life racing to them. This is not like the Taoists, who devote themselves to self-cultivation in their lust after life.

The Taoists do not know that material force is based in principle, and they use material force as their Way. The Buddhists do not know that principle is embodied in the mind, and they use mind as their religion. Both the Taoists and the Buddhists think of themselves as the ultimate in abstraction, but they do not

know what incorporeality is and speak only in reference to that which is corpo-
real. They ensnare themselves in the shallow and common, the crooked and the
skewed, but they do not know it.

Mencius said: "The self cultivates well my strong, moving power."[14] This tells
of the merit of the learning of the sages in cultivating alternately both the
internal and the external. If one keeps rightness in his heart and nourishes it, he
will eliminate the shroud of material desires, all will become lucid, and there will
be no deviations in his great purposes. If one concentrates his rightness while
nourishing and expanding his material force, it will become the greatest and
stoutest power, strong and moving, and coming into being by itself, filling up all
between heaven and earth. The beginning and the end will join together and the
internal and external will be cultivated alternately. This is why the learning of the
Confucians is correct and is not like the biased learning of the Buddhists and the
Taoists.

JD

History

Korea's oldest extant history is the *Historical Record of the Three Kingdoms*
(*Samguk sagi*), which was compiled by Kim Pusik (1075–1151) and others
during Injong's reign (1122–1146). The *Historical Record of the Three Kingdoms* is an official court-sponsored history that reflects the Confucian values
of its compilers. It was assembled to provide Koreans with a greater understanding of their own history and heritage; yet it is obvious that its compilers
did not include all the facts and legends then known, particularly those that
went against their own view of history. For this omission they have often
been criticized by modern historians.

Koryŏ's other great historical work is the *Memorabilia of the Three Kingdoms* (*Samguk yusa*). Written by the monk Iryŏn (1206–1289) during the
devastating Mongol invasions, it presents many traditions and tales that were
not included in the *Historical Record of the Three Kingdoms*. Reflecting its
author's religious beliefs, the *Memorabilia* is replete with Buddhist themes.
It is also interesting to note that Korea's mythical founder, Tangun, is
described for the first time in this work.

The second selection in this section was written by Paek Munbo (d. 1374).
Paek, a Confucian scholar writing in the last decades of the Koryŏ dynasty,
presented a cyclical view of Korean history. Like Iryŏn, he dated the founding of Korea from Tangun's birth and attributed the chaos in late Koryŏ
politics to the end of a long cycle. Regardless of their interpretations, each

of these passages tells of the Koryŏ people's concern for their past and the importance of history to their lives.

Kim Pusik: On Presenting the *Historical Record of the Three Kingdoms* to the King

[From *Tong munsŏn* 44:12b–13b]

Your subject, Kim Pusik, wishes to report. All the states of the past established official historians to record events. Accordingly, Mencius said: "Such were *Sheng,* the annals of Chin; *T'ao-wu,* the annals of Chu; and the *Spring and Autumn Annals* of Lu."[15] The histories of Korea's Three Kingdoms are long, and their events should be set forth in an official record. Therefore, Your Majesty has ordered your subject to compile this book.

In your leisure Your Majesty has read widely in histories of earlier ages and said: "Of today's scholars and high-ranking officials, there are those who are well versed and can discuss in detail the Five Classics and other philosophical treatises as well as the histories of Ch'in and Han, but as to the events of our country, they are utterly ignorant from beginning to end. This is truly lamentable. Moreover, because Silla, Koguryŏ, and Paekche were able to have formal relations with China from their beginnings to the unification wars [660–668], they were discussed in the biographical sections of Fan Yeh's *History of the Later Han* and Sung Ch'i's *History of the T'ang,* but these books are detailed on internal Chinese affairs and terse about foreign matters and did not record everything of historical significance. As for the ancient records of the Three Kingdoms, the writing is unrefined, and the recording of historical events is deficient. Accordingly, they do not always expose whether the ruler is good or evil, the subjects are loyal or treasonous, the country is at peace or in crisis, the people are orderly or rebellious. To create a history that can serve as a guide, I ought to have a person who has three talents—intelligence, scholarship, and wisdom. This will lead to a work of outstanding quality to be handed down for eternity, shining like the sun and stars."

Your subject basically lacks these talents as well as profound knowledge. Although his scholarship is shallow and the history of the earlier ages is vague, by exhausting his spirit and energy, your subject has barely been able to complete this volume. Although it may not be good enough to be stored on a sacred mountain, may it not be set aside as merely a useless thing. Your subject's foolish thought is to have Heaven's light shine down on it.   *HK AND ES*

Paek Munbo: Explanation of Tangun's Significance

[From *Koryŏ sa* 112:14b–15a]

The Koryŏ dynasty has protected the nation for generations. In customs, cere-mony, and music there are ancient ways that have been passed on. Heaven works in a cyclical way, continuously going around and starting again. Seven hundred years is a minor cycle, and accumulating these to thirty-six hundred years makes a major cycle. Within these cycles, emperors and kings have periods of order and chaos and rise and fall. In Korea, it has already been thirty-six hundred years since the time of Tangun, the fruition of a major cycle. May Your Majesty fittingly follow the teachings of the sage rulers Yao and Shun and the Six Classics and not practice shortsighted measures. If you do this, Heaven's pure protection will prevail, yin and yang will follow in orderly progression, and the dynasty's prosper-ity will extend for a long time. *HK AND ES*

PART THREE

Early Chosŏn

INTRODUCTION

Founded in 1392 by General Yi Sŏnggye (1335–1408; r. 1392–1398), the Chosŏn dynasty ruled Korea for more than five hundred years, until 1910. Rising from an obscure military family that became prominent only during the last decades of the Koryŏ dynasty, Yi Sŏnggye became one of the most powerful and preeminent military figures following a series of successful exploits against the Red Turbans and the Japanese marauders that had harassed Korea. When ordered to invade China's northeastern region (Manchuria) to take advantage of the Yüan-Ming dynastic transition in China, Yi Sŏnggye instead turned his army against the Koryŏ court and staged a successful coup in 1388. Four years later, in 1392, supported by the Neo-Confucian scholar-officials, Yi Sŏnggye proclaimed himself king, thus formally inaugurating a new dynasty of his own.

The founding of the Chosŏn dynasty was the work of a symbiotic alliance between a military strongman and a group of reform-minded Confucian intellectuals, such as Cho Chun (1346–1405) and Chŏng Tojŏn (d. 1398). The dynastic change from Koryŏ to the new dynasty was justified in the name of the Mencian concept of Heavenly Mandate as rationalized by the Neo-Confucian scholar-officials, who then went on to dominate the bureaucracy and set up the entire structure of government and society in the hope of realizing their Confucian ideals. This alliance in the end enabled the Confucian reformers to put their ideas into practice so that one of the architects of the new order, Chŏng Tojŏn, is said to have claimed that it was he, Chŏng, who used Yi Sŏnggye to realize his political goal.

In order to make a clean break from Koryŏ, the new dynasty, with the approval of the Ming emperor of China, adopted the official dynastic name of Chosŏn ("Morning Serenity") and moved its capital city from Kaesŏng to Hanyang (present Seoul) after carefully examining political, economic, military, and topographic as well as geomantic considerations. With its royal palaces and government office buildings, the new capital city was based on a well-laid-out plan and included main thoroughfares, living and shopping quarters, and drainage canals as well as fortified walls surrounding the city.

After a shaky start caused by fratricidal succession struggles, the Chosŏn dynasty laid its firm foundation during the rule of its third king, T'aejong (1400–1418). By reorganizing various military groups into one single command under the king and restructuring the central government under the State Council (Ŭijŏngbu), King T'aejong eliminated potential threats to the court and placed the dynasty on a solid footing, thus preparing the way for the rule of his third son Sejong (1418–1450).

King Sejong was undoubtedly one of the great rulers in Korean history. A remarkable scholar and versatile in many fields—classics, literature, linguistics, and science, among others—King Sejong ushered in the golden age of creativity in Korea. Using the Hall of Worthies (Chiphyŏnjŏn) as a royal research institute, where he assembled the best minds and talents of the country, King Sejong introduced truly remarkable achievements in many fields. To give only a few notable examples, the new Korean alphabet, now known as hangŭl, was invented after many years of research; a number of books were published with improved printing techniques, including Songs of Flying Dragons (Yongbi ŏch'ŏn ka) written in hangŭl; many scientific instruments, such as rain gauges, automatic-striking clepsydras, and devices for astronomical observation were invented or improved upon; a comprehensive inventory of music and musical instruments was made, with notation made for all the existing music; and more scientific farming methods were introduced, such as improved seeds and fertilizer, more efficient use of irrigation, and a more equitable land tax system. Moreover, it was during Sejong's rule that Korea's northern boundary along the Yalu and Tumen rivers was secured firmly through his successful military campaigns and his policy of settling people in the border regions.

In 1455, the Chosŏn court once again went through a succession crisis as the ambitious Prince Suyang forcibly deposed his fifteen-year-old nephew,

King Tanjong (1452–1455), and set himself up as King Sejo (1455–1468). The historical significance of Sejo's usurpation lies not so much in the bloodshed it produced as in the legacy it bequeathed to future generations of scholar-officials, raising the moral question whether usurpation might be justified and legitimated according to Confucian principles. This issue became an important contributing factor to the later split within the Confucian bureaucracy.

By the mid-fifteenth century, after long experimentation, the restructuring of the government was finalized with the publication of the *State Code* *(Kyŏngguk taejŏn)* in 1485, which prescribed the duties and functions of various offices. In assisting the king's rule, the State Council staffed by three high state councillors was the highest deliberative organ. Execution and administration of state laws and policies were carried out by the Six Ministries (Personnel, Taxation, Rites, Military Affairs, Punishments, and Public Works). For local administration, the country was divided into eight provinces—Kyŏnggi, Ch'ungch'ŏng, Kyŏngsang, Chŏlla, Hwanghae, Kangwŏn, Yŏngan (Hamgyŏng), and P'yŏngan—which in turn were subdivided into counties of various sizes *(pu, mok, kun,* and *hyŏn)*. Chosŏn Korea was a highly centralized state, with all the officials of local administration appointed by the central government.

The creation of various mechanisms to check arbitrary exercise of power was a unique feature of the Chosŏn government. Although according to the *State Code* (1485) each of the three censorate offices—Office of the Inspector-General *(Sahŏnbu)*, Office of the Censor-General *(Saganwŏn)*, and Office of Special Advisers *(Hongmungwan)*—had different duties, they often worked together, and through their criticism and surveillance they represented a powerful check against arbitrary decision-making or exercise of authority by a king or any other official. Moreover, a constant and persistent reminder to adhere strictly to rigid Confucian principles inhibited inappropriate behavior. And the ubiquitous presence of historians around the throne, taking notes of all the official transactions of the king and the officials so as to include them in the history being compiled for posterity, had the effect of obliging government officials to conform to Confucian norms.

One of the most firmly held beliefs under the Chosŏn dynasty was that the government must be staffed and run by men of virtue and talent. To recruit such men as government officials, the Chosŏn state depended largely on an examination system, which included civil, military, and technical examinations. Of these three, the civil service examinations carried far greater honor and prestige than the other two, as the civil officials exercised preponderant influence within the government. There were two tiers in the civil service examinations—the lower examination (sokwa) that offered saengwŏn or chinsa degrees and the higher examination (taekwa) that awarded the munkwa degree. Only the munkwa degree automatically qualified the recipient to serve in the civil bureaucracy, and thus it became the most coveted degree, sought by men of ambition and talent.

In addition, one could obtain a position within the bureaucracy through a protection appointment (ŭm), whereby family members of certain senior officials were allowed to become officials, or through a recommendation appointment (ch'ŏngŏ), whereby men of exceptional merit could be appointed through recommendation. But appointments through these routes carried far less honor and prestige during the Chosŏn dynasty.

The civil service examinations, conducted strictly on a competitive basis, tested candidates' knowledge of the Confucian classics as well as of history and literature. From time to time, the system was criticized on the ground that a competitive examination might not be the best way to select truly virtuous men. The system encountered its most serious challenge in 1519, when the idealistic Cho Kwangjo (1482–1519) attempted to replace it with the recommendation examination. For want of a better substitute, however, the examination system remained the government's main channel of recruitment until 1894. Until recently, scholars believed that only men of yangban birth could take part in the civil service examinations; this view, however, is now being challenged by new evidence that men of commoner origins were also allowed to take the examinations.

In the Neo-Confucian state of Chosŏn, education was considered vitally important for promoting the ideals of the Confucian sages and preparing qualified students for the civil service examinations. Therefore, the Chosŏn dynasty maintained a well-structured educational system. In the capital city, the Royal Confucian Academy (Sŏnggyungwan) was organized and maintained; saengwŏn and chinsa degree holders as well as other selected students enrolled there. In addition to the Four Schools in the districts of Seoul, a county school called hyanggyo was established in every county to offer Confucian education to qualified students. All these schools were maintained by funds provided by the state and local governments; their students received stipends and other privileges, such as exemption from military and other duties.

As many students in these schools began to lose their devotion to Confucian studies, concerned scholars in the countryside began to organize private academies called sŏwŏn to serve two objectives—to enshrine a favorite Confucian master of their choice and to pursue more serious Confucian scholarship. Founded by Chu Sebung (1495–1554) in 1543 while he served as the magistrate of P'unggi county in Kyŏngsang province, Paegundong (later changed to Sosu) Academy was the first private academy to receive a royal charter. Thereafter, private academies proliferated throughout the country and overtook county schools as centers of local education and scholarship. Organized at the initiative of local scholars, the private academies were usually well endowed financially through private contributions of land and slaves. When factional politics intensified during the seventeenth and eighteenth centuries, private academies often became involved as their scholars took sides in the disputes between the factions.

From its inception, the Chosŏn dynasty was governed by the ideals of Chu Hsi's Neo-Confucianism, the official ideology of the state. With a firm conviction that the fundamental principles of Neo-Confucianism are absolute and valid at all times and in all places, Chosŏn Neo-Confucianists zealously pursued policies promising the realization of the ideals of Confucian sages by remodeling the Chosŏn state and society to conform to Confucian norms. All other beliefs, customs, and traditions that did not comply with Confucian teachings were rejected as heterodox.

Buddhism—the source of consolation and inspiration in Korea for many centuries—now came under severe restrictions as the Neo-Confucian state of Chosŏn rejected Buddhism as a heterodox teaching and vigorously pursued a policy of persecution against Buddhist institutions. Although there were a few exceptions, such as kings Sejong and Sejo, who privately maintained their faith in Buddhism, the followers of Buddhist belief had to practice their religion under extremely restricted conditions throughout the duration of the Chosŏn dynasty. Placed constantly in a defensive position, the Buddhist leaders thus spent much of their intellectual energy rationalizing and reconciling their teaching with the Neo-Confucian order.

Many of the indigenous traditions and customs suffered curtailment as well. As the Neo-Confucianists tried to establish all state and family rituals in strict conformity with Confucian rules, many traditional practices, such as wedding and funeral ceremonies, which had been rooted deeply in Buddhistic, shamanistic, and other native beliefs, were discouraged or prohibited. Nevertheless, despite the zeal exhibited by the Neo-Confucianists, the transformation of social mores and practices came only at a slow pace over a long period of time.

The Chosŏn dynasty maintained a relatively rigid social structure. *Yangban* were a privileged class whose status was determined largely by birth and

Confucian education. The large majority of the people, however, were commoners (yangin), such as farmers and merchants, who bore most of the tax burden for the state. In between the yangban and the commoners was a small group, known as "the middle people" (chungin), who occupied mostly the technical and functionary positions within the government. At the bottom of the society were the lowborn, such as public and private slaves, whose status was determined by birth. Private slaves owned by individual families were sold and purchased as chattels.

The economy of the Chosŏn dynasty was predominantly agrarian, and land was the main source of revenue for the state and individuals. Determined not to repeat the chaotic land situation that plagued the last years of Koryŏ rule, the Chosŏn dynastic founders paid special attention to the equitable distribution of land and at the outset instituted a redistribution. Regarded as the fundamental source of life, agriculture was actively promoted by the state. With the introduction of the advanced Kiangnan technology from South China, wet-farming and rice transplanting methods were gradually adopted in the southern provinces during the fifteenth and sixteenth centuries. These new technologies, along with improved seeds and fertilizer, eliminated fallow land and ultimately enabled farmers to reap two crops in one year from the same soil.

Commerce, on the other hand, was regarded by the Confucianists as a nonproductive occupation and thus was discouraged by the state. Merchants were viewed as parasitic—living on the sweat and labor of the farmers—and hence the government permitted only licensed merchants to set up shops in Seoul to cater to the needs of the government and the people. Despite the government's position, commercial activities gradually grew: in the countryside, certain localities began holding markets at periodic intervals, such as every five days, and bands of itinerant merchants began traveling from town to town to attend these markets. In general, however, the Neo-Confucian government of Chosŏn scorned extravagance and stressed frugality and thrift in its approach to daily life.

In the traditional period, Korea had maintained a special relationship with China that was largely characterized by sadae (respect for the senior state). As part of the East Asian Confucian world order in which China occupied the central position, the Chosŏn dynasty accepted a status junior to China and scrupulously observed the ritual practices of a tributary state. Ever since Korea had accepted Confucian norms as the way of conducting state affairs, it had no qualms about accepting China as the senior state. In terms of strategy, Korea was vitally important to China's own security and thus had never been permitted to fall into hostile hands. The configuration of power so favored China that Korea had no choice but to remain friendly. Moreover, the two East Asian countries had historically shared a mutual interest in security as both had faced the same threat, namely, the tribal groups in the north. Only a strong China could keep them in check and maintain peace in the region. Under these conditions, Korea simply could not afford to lose China's friendship, even if it meant accepting the status of a junior state. In the final analysis, Korea's *sadae* policy enabled it to maintain its independent nationhood free from interference—political, military, or otherwise—from China. Furthermore, Korea's practice of *sadae* diplomacy ensured almost limitless access to Chinese culture and civilization.

In addition, Korea also maintained a careful diplomacy toward Japan. Initially, the Chosŏn government's foremost concern had been the problem of Japanese marauders. Although their pillaging had been drastically reduced by the beginning of the dynasty, there were still occasional harassments from Japan. To eliminate these marauders once and for all, King Sejong launched a military expedition in 1419 against their base, the islands of Tsushima. Once Tsushima was subdued, the Japanese were allowed to engage in trade with Korea at three ports at and near present-day Pusan under strict supervision of the Korean government. Following the Hideyoshi invasion in 1592–1598, Korea maintained basically friendly relations with Tokugawa Japan in the name of *kyorin* (neighborly relations).

As the Chosŏn dynasty passed the first century mark, tensions within the Neo-Confucian bureaucracy flared up in the form of literati purges known as *sahwa*. These purges took place four times within the span of less than fifty years—in 1498, 1504, 1519, and 1545—and a number of officials were either executed or banished. As a result, the whole bureaucracy was paralyzed. The literati purges have been explained largely in terms of political, ideological, and economic conflicts between the so-called meritorious elites (*hungu*) and the Neo-Confucian literati (*sarim*). The meritorious elites were those officials who had gained power and wealth over a period of time largely on the basis of their proximity to the throne and their lineage, whereas the Neo-Confucian literati constituted a new breed of scholar-officials who rose through the government ranks inspired by the ideals of Neo-Confucianism as practiced by some of the Koryŏ loyalists who refused to bend their principles even when faced with death. Ideologically more firmly committed than the meritorious elites and unencumbered by vested interests, the Neo-Confucian literati criticized and remonstrated without hesitation whenever they felt the conduct of the kings and high officials did not meet the high standards of Neo-Confucian principles. Although the Neo-Confucian literati became the victims of these purges, their moralistic causes, such as the sagely rule championed by Cho Kwangjo (1482–1519), were upheld as just by later generations, and in the end their Neo-Confucian worldview prevailed among the scholar-officials of Chosŏn as the Neo-Confucian orthodoxy.

While the Neo-Confucian orthodoxy was widely accepted as the sole foundation of the state and society, the officialdom split into factions in the last decades of the sixteenth century. Divided initially into Easterners and Westerners over the appointment of an official to a key middle-ranking post within the Ministry of Personnel, the two factions were later subdivided further into Northerners and Southerners, and Old Doctrine and Young Doctrine, respectively. (The directional references are merely formal designations and have nothing to do with regional ties.) The politics of the Chosŏn court thereafter followed largely the competition for power among these factions, and frequently involved important state policies, such as diplomatic relations with neighboring countries, the land tax and other revenue measures, and the rules governing various rites. The factional alignments may have followed the philosophical debate regarding the role of *i* (*li*, principle) versus *ki* (*ch'i*, material force)—argued by the two greatest philosophers of Chosŏn, Yi Hwang (T'oegye, 1501–1570) and Yi I (Yulgok, 1536–1584)—in which the scholar-officials favored one side or the other.

The *i–ki* debate was easily the most important philosophical issue occupying the minds of Korean scholars during the Chosŏn dynasty. The debate started when Ki Taesŭng (1527–1572) questioned Yi Hwang's position that "the Four Beginnings are the issuance of principle [*i*], and the Seven Feelings are the issuance of material force [*ki*]." The Four Beginnings are the Mencian concepts of humaneness, rightness, ritual decorum, and wisdom, which are inherently good, whereas the Seven Feelings—joy, anger, sorrow, fear, love, hatred, and desire—are sometimes good and sometimes evil. The two philosophers then exchanged a series of letters debating the role of principle and material force in the functions of the Four Beginnings and the Seven Feelings. This celebrated debate between the two, also known as the Four-Seven Debate, ended with Ki Taesŭng agreeing basically with Yi Hwang after Yi had modified his position somewhat.

Although the issue may have been settled between Yi Hwang and Ki Taesŭng, the controversy persisted among other scholars and was taken up anew by Yi I when he debated with his friend Sŏng Hon (1535–1598) and challenged Yi Hwang's position. In analyzing the functions of *i* and *ki*, Yi

Hwang, as explained by the modern Korean scholar Ki-baik Lee, "stressed particularly the role of the formative or normative element, *i*, as the basis of the activity of *ki*; thus *i* comes to be seen as an existential force that masters or controls *ki*." Thus, Yi Hwang emphasized the supremacy of *i* in the *i–ki* duality. Yi I, however, placed equal importance on both *i* and *ki* in the activation of the Four Beginnings and the Seven Feelings, but he came to be identified as emphasizing the supremacy of *ki*. The Four-Seven Debate thus became the most important philosophical issue of the Chosŏn dynasty.

The peace enjoyed by the Chosŏn dynasty for two centuries was abruptly shattered when Japan under Toyotomi Hideyoshi (1536–1598) launched an invasion against Korea in 1592. Long dominated by a civil bureaucracy that relied on Confucian civility in dealing with foreigners, the Chosŏn government was utterly unprepared for the crisis. Despite the gallant resistance offered by the Korean military, the capital city, Seoul, fell to the Japanese within three weeks, forcing King Sŏnjo (1567–1608) and his entourage to flee north toward the Chinese border. As the situation grew desperate, the Chosŏn government appealed to China for military assistance. To help Korea and to protect its own security, the Ming government sent a large number of troops to Korea and forced the Japanese to retreat southward. In the meantime, recovering from the shock of initial defeat, the Korean people organized militia units in various parts of the country to fight the invaders and inflicted significant damage upon the Japanese. At sea Korea maintained complete supremacy, as the Korean navy, under the able command of Admiral Yi Sunsin (1545–1598), vanquished the Japanese navy, using the iron-clad vessels known as "Turtle Ships." Though there was a short interlude, the war lasted six years, until the death of Hideyoshi in 1598. It decimated the population and destroyed innumerable cultural and historic treasures.

Before Korea was able to recover from the devastation of the Japanese invasion, the Manchu invaded Korea twice, in 1627 and 1636. The 1636 invasion was particularly painful for Korea; as the Manchu troops stormed into Korea, King Injo (1623–1649) and his court sought refuge in the mountain fortress of Namhansan, located in the present southeastern suburb of Seoul, only to suffer ignominious defeat in the end. Consequently, the Korean king was obliged to perform the kowtow to the Manchu conqueror and sue for peace. According to the terms of peace, Korea was to terminate its ties with Ming China and to accept the Manchu as the senior state. The Manchu then moved on to defeat Ming and established itself as the Ch'ing dynasty in China. Korea never forgot this humiliation at the hands of the Manchu, traditionally regarded as barbarians, and secretly harbored rancor in its dealings with Ch'ing for a long period of time—at one time even scheming to undertake a military retaliation against the Manchu.

Although the first half of the Chosŏn dynasty's rule witnessed a number of domestic conflicts and external threats, the Chosŏn state overcame them and maintained a remarkably stable political and social system. During this period, the Chosŏn dynasty attained a number of achievements. Particularly noteworthy is the spectacular success of King Sejong's rule; his successors, however, were unable to match the standard of rulership Sejong had set. With respect to intellectual pursuits, although a greater emphasis was placed on conformity than on heterogeneity, the early Chosŏn dynasty nevertheless made significant advances in the scholarly pursuit of philosophical and metaphysical issues. In the arts and literature, a number of creative men and women have bequeathed us an array of impressive works. In the social and economic sectors, though the Chosŏn dynasty never enjoyed spectacular wealth, its people in general lived in reasonable security and comfort, with adequate supplies of daily necessities. These are no small achievements for any preindustrialized state. *YC*

CHAPTER THIRTEEN

Founding the Chosŏn Dynasty

Founding the new dynasty of Chosŏn—replacing the Koryŏ dynasty that had ruled Korea for nearly five hundred years—was not an easy task for General Yi Sŏnggye. First he had to overcome the forces of opposition that had a vested interest in the Koryŏ court. This he accomplished with little bloodshed by means of a coup d'état. Imposing a new rule on the disaffected people, however, was an entirely different matter. Therefore, Yi Sŏnggye had to rely upon the Neo-Confucian literati to organize a new government and set up a new code of regulations for his fledgling state. Fortunately for him, he was able to attract a number of capable and reform-minded scholar-officials who were willing to work with him. With their help, Yi Sŏnggye justified the inauguration of the new dynasty in the name of the Mandate of Heaven.

Thus, the Chosŏn state embarked on its course toward realizing a Neo-Confucian society while rejecting or suppressing deeply rooted Buddhist beliefs and native traditions. To start anew, the dynastic founder decided to shift the capital from Songdo (now Kaesŏng). After careful considerations of several alternative sites, Hanyang (present-day Seoul) was chosen as the new capital, which then was developed in accord with careful city planning.

Upon his ascension to the throne on the seventeenth of the seventh month in 1392, King T'aejo issued decrees covering a variety of administrative issues, making appointments throughout the top bureaucracy, and reporting the founding of the new dynasty to the Ming emperor. On the twenty-eighth, he issued what may be called his "founding edict," asserting his legitimacy, claiming the loyalty of his officials, and setting forth the means and rationale for action in several key areas of government.   DC

King T'aejo: Founding Edict

[From *T'aejo sillok* 1:43a–45a]

The king issued the following edict to all the officials and the people:

The king announces:

It is Heaven which created all the people of the earth, Heaven which ordaines their rulers, Heaven which nurtured them to share life with each other, and Heaven which governed them so as to enjoy peace with one another. There have been both good and bad rulers, and there have been times when people followed their rulers willingly and other times when they turned against them. Some have been blessed with the Mandate of Heaven and others have lost it. This is a principle that has remained constant.

On the sixteenth of the seventh month of the twenty-fifth year in the reign of the Hung-wu Emperor [1392], the Privy Council *[Top'yŏngŭisasa]* and all ranks of officials together urged me to take the throne, saying: "After King Kongmin died leaving no legitimate heir the doom of the Koryŏ dynasty was sealed. Although King Kongyang [1389–1392] was empowered temporarily to take charge of state affairs, he was confused and broke the law, causing many people to rebel and even his own relatives to turn against him, and he was incapable of preserving and protecting the ancestral shrines and institutions. How could anyone restore what Heaven has abandoned? The ancestral shrines and institutions should only be entrusted to one who is worthy, and the throne must not be left vacant for long. People's minds are all looking up to your meritorious achievements and virtue, and you should accept the throne to rectify the situation, thereby satisfying the people's desire."

Fearful that I lack both virtue and capacity to assume the awesome responsibilities, I declined the offer of the throne repeatedly. But I am told that the people's wishes are such that Heaven's will is clearly manifested in them and that no one should refuse the wishes of the people, for to do so is to act contrary to the will of Heaven. Because the people insisted so steadfastly, I yielded finally to their will and ascended the throne. Now that we are at the threshold of a new beginning, I must show abundant grace, and I hereby announce the following policies for the benefit of the people.

As for the civil and the military examinations, I will not abandon one in favor of the other. Let more students be chosen for the Royal Confucian Academy in the capital and the county schools in order to promote scholarship and train men of talent. The original purpose of the examination system was to recruit men of talent for the state. With the practice of calling the examiners "masters" and the candidates "disciples," the system of impartial selection has been replaced by a system of private favors. This does not accord with the original purpose of the law. From now on, the registrar of the Royal Confucian Academy in the capital and the governors of each province will select those students in their schools who are bright in the classics and of good character; they will certify their age, clan, and three ancestors and record the classics they have mastered; and then they will send them to the director of the Royal Confucian Academy. The students will then be examined on their knowledge of the classics, and those who did well on the Four Books and the Five Classics as well as the *Comprehensive Mirror for Aid in Governance [Tzu-chih t'ung-chien]* will be ranked according to the degree of their mastery. Those who pass this first stage of the examination will be sent to the Ministry of Rites for the second stage, where they will be tested on their ability to compose documentary prose *[p'yo]*, memorials *[chang]*, and rhyme-prose *[kobu]*. They will then be examined at the final stage on problem essays *[ch'aeng-mun]*. Of those who are successful in all three stages of examination, thirty-three men will be selected. They will then be forwarded to the Ministry of Personnel for appointment to an office according to their abilities.

The Military Training Administration will be in charge of instruction in military matters. Candidates will be instructed in the seven military classics as well as marksmanship and horsemanship, and they will then be ranked according to their mastery of the classics and their skill as marksmen and horsemen. Thirty-three finalists will be awarded the military degree in the manner of awarding the civil examination degree. Their names then will be sent to the Ministry of War for official appointment.

The cardinal rituals of our state are the rites of capping, marriage, funerals, and ancestor worship. In order for human relations to be harmonized and customs to be rectified, let the Ministry of Rites carefully research the classics and codes, deliberate on past practices, and then establish regulations for the rituals.

We cannot overemphasize the importance of the magistrates, whose duties involve direct dealing with the people. The Privy Council, the Censorate, and the Six Ministries will recommend those whom they know to be just, fair, upright, and capable of appointments as magistrates. After thirty months in office, those whose records are outstanding will be promoted. If any fail to live up to expectations, those who recommended them will bear the blame.

Because of the importance of morals and customs, we should encourage loyal ministers, filial sons, righteous husbands, and faithful wives. Let local officials seek out such people and recommend them for preferential treatment and further advancement and for memorial arches to commemorate their virtuous deeds.

The king should place importance on extending sympathy and providing relief to aged widowers and widows, orphans, and the childless. All local officials should assist those who are hungry and destitute within their jurisdiction and should give them exemption from corvée duties.

Toward the end of Koryŏ, there was no unified system of criminal justice. The Ministry of Punishments, the constabulary, and the detention halls all meted out punishments on their own. These were not always appropriate. Henceforth the Ministry of Punishments will be in charge of the criminal code, litigation, and criminal investigations and punishments. The constabulary, on the other hand, will be in charge of patrolling, catching thieves, and maintaining order. At present, when the Ministry of Punishments renders judgment in a case, the culprit is invariably stripped of his writ of appointment and forced to resign his post, even if the offense is only punishable by flogging, and guilt is attached to his descendants. This is not the way the sage-kings meant it to be.   DC

Admonition to the New King

[From *T'aejo sillok* 1:40a–42b]

The Office of the Inspector-General was one of two main bodies (the other was the Office of the Censor-General) whose functions included remonstrating with the king and pronouncing on morals in general and abuse of public office in particular. The inspector-general was a high-ranking official (Rank 2B), sometimes even a member of the State Council. This document is an admonition to the new king to avoid the evil practices of the past by setting up new procedures. A key element is the repeated concern over the appointment of good men to office, reflecting the early Chosŏn dynasty's critiques of government in the late Koryŏ period. Notable too are the numerous allusions to the Chinese classics, which give authority and legitimacy to the ideas being expressed.   DC

Once again the Inspector-General memorialized the throne:

Your Majesty, responding to the call of Heaven, has accepted the mandate and has now ascended the throne. In the *Book of Documents* it is written: "God dwelling in the great heavens has changed his decree in favor of his eldest son and this great dynasty of Yin. Our king has received that decree. Unbounded is the happiness connected with it, and unbounded is the anxiety. Oh! How can he be other than reverent?"[1]

Reverence is the heart's controlling force and the basis of all things. Thus, whether on such important occasions as serving and offering sacrifices to Heaven or in such small matters as rising, dwelling, eating, and resting, one should never turn away from piety for even a moment. Thus it is our earnest wish that Your Majesty think constantly as if you were with the Lord of Heaven and act as if the Lord of Heaven were present, even in moments of idleness. In dealing with matters of state, you should be even more prudent in your thinking. If you do this, the reverence in your heart will be sufficient to move Heaven, and you will be able to realize the ideal rule.

With this memorial we undertake respectfully to enumerate certain things you should do. We sincerely hope that you will adopt and implement them so that the model of this generation can be emulated by myriad generations.

First, establish rules and laws. One who wishes to rule his state well should not be concerned about safety and peril; rather, he should be concerned with whether the rules and laws are properly established.

Second is an unambiguous system of rewards and punishments. Third is the cleaving to superior men and distancing yourself from inferior men. Truly it is necessary to distinguish between superior men and inferior men. The superior man is one who is honest and holds to principle, not relying on others; who knows how to act with utmost loyalty when in office and how to counsel the sovereign in his weakness when not in office; who is open and fair-minded; who is concerned about the ancestral shrines and institutions and not about himself. The inferior man is one who is wicked and sycophantic; who curries favor to gain acceptance; who usurps authority and abuses it; who claims credit for the accomplishments of others and ingratiates himself with servile flattery; who is concerned solely with his selfish interests without heeding others' opinions. Superior men are hard to find and easy to lose, inferior men are easy to find and hard to get rid of.

Fourth is the willingness to accept remonstrance. The sovereign's majesty is like thunder; his power is as weighty as iron. Is it an easy thing for the minister to brave the thunder and bear the heavy weight to offer his sovereign words as if to cure his ailments? And yet the difference between accepting and rejecting such advice can mean the difference between good fortune and disaster, between profit and loss for the state.

Fifth is rooting out slanderous talk. Sixth is to beware of indolence and dissoluteness. The desire to be in repose in the palace; to feast on fine food; to enjoy the ministrations of your queen and palace women, the pleasures of the hunt, raising dogs and horses; and to amuse yourself with flowers and plants: all these things harm men's disposition and dissipate their will. Therefore, one must exercise caution. For indeed, the Mandate of Heaven is a transient thing.

Seventh is respect for frugality and economy.

Eighth is the shunning of eunuchs. The problem of eunuchs is an old one.

Ninth is the weeding out of unqualified Buddhist clergy. They mingle with ordinary people, using high-sounding words and professing high ideals, bedazzling even scholars and intimidating simple folk with talk of retribution for sin, fostering wasteful habits among the people and encouraging them to forsake their proper occupations. Indeed, nothing is more likely to destroy the state and sicken the people than this. We beseech Your Majesty to round up these Buddhist clerics and examine them carefully on their doctrine and practice. Those who truly know the doctrine and truly practice virtue should be allowed to teach; all the others should be made to let their hair grow out and return to their former occupations.

Tenth is the regulation of access to the palace. The establishment of the palace is meant to enhance the sovereign's power and to define clearly the boundary between the inner and outer courts. We beseech Your Majesty to order the gate guards to prohibit the unauthorized entry of anyone without official position, and especially to spurn shamans who practice women's magic and those who cunningly flatter.

Your ministers believe that trust is the sovereign's greatest asset—for the state is protected by the people, and the people are protected by trust. For this reason, the sage would sooner have done without an army and food to eat than to have done without trust, and that is a profound lesson for later generations and our time as well. If you do not act with trust in attracting superior men and spurning inferior men, the superior will easily become estranged from you, and the inferior will easily find their way into your company. If you do not act with trust in hearing remonstrance and in trying to root out slander, you will find that good advice seems unpleasant to the ear while flattering words will come to influence your decisions. We beseech Your Majesty to keep this trust unwaveringly and firmly, to enforce these points as faithfully as the seasons follow one another, never forsaking the mandate granted you by Heaven above to help you, nor the desires of the officials and the people to have you lead them as their king, so that unbounded peace will prevail for myriad generations.   *DC*

Moving to the New Capital

[From *T'aejo sillok* 6:11a-13a]

Choosing a new location for the capital was an important symbolic step for the new dynasty. The decadence of the final years of Koryŏ encouraged thoughts of a fresh start in a new city, despite the great effort and inconvenience that would attend such a move. Many things had to be taken into account in siting the new city. It had to be defensible, for example, yet accessible by water and road so that officials could travel and taxable commodities could be carried in and out. The lay of the land was important, too, though T'aejo's officials differed in their respect for the laws of geomancy. The Chinese classics had to be consulted in order to determine precedents for moving the capital. And beneath it all were the practical considerations of officials who apparently did not want to leave Songdo, the metropolitan center of Korea, for the undeveloped valley of Hanyang (present-day Seoul). DC

In considering whether to establish the capital here, he had first ordered his officials to scout out the area.

The Director of Treasury Chŏng Tojŏn said: "Since the Three Kingdoms period in our country, our capitals have been Kyerim [Kyŏngju] in the east, Wansan [Chŏnju] in the south, and P'yŏngyang in the north, while in the center there is Songgyŏng [Songdo or Kaesŏng]. Kyerim and Wansan are located in isolated corners of the country, in places too remote for the effective conduct of royal business. P'yŏngyang is too near the northern frontier, and your minister believes it, too, is unsuitable for a capital.

"Your Majesty's rule follows that of the collapsed former dynasty. Because the people's livelihood has not yet recovered and the foundation of the state has not yet been consolidated, it would be better that you first pacify the people and allow them to rest so that they can regain strength. You should select a suitable site for the capital in accordance with the heavenly signs and people's wishes and should wait for a proper time to move. In this way, all will be safe while your dynasty's rule over Chosŏn will be everlasting along with the descendants of your ministers.

"Those who discuss geomancy nowadays are drawing on the experiences of earlier people rather than on their own, just as your minister's words are based on the experiences of earlier people. How, then, can one believe in geomancers and reject the wisdom of Confucian scholars? Your minister's fervent hope is that

Your Majesty will deeply ponder this problem, put the people's welfare first, and only then try divination to determine a new capital, so as to avoid misfortunes."

The next day the king inspected the ancient palace sites of the southern capital and observed the configurations of the mountains. He then asked Yun Sindal and his other companions:

"What about this place?"

Yun replied: "Within the borders of our land, Songdo is the best spot of all, but this is next best. However, it has one regrettable feature: the northwest corner is too low, so the spring water dries up too readily."

The king was pleased and said: "How can there be no deficiencies even in Songdo? As I see the terrain of this place, it seems like a fit location for a royal capital. What is more, it is accessible by water, it is centrally located, and it will also be a convenient place for the people."

The king then spoke to the Royal Preceptor Chach'o, asking: "What do you think?"

Chach'o answered: "There are heights and scenic beauty on all sides here, and the center is level. It is a good place for fortifications and also for a capital. Still, you should consider the opinions of many people before you decide."

The king then ordered his ministers to discuss it, and they returned with a consensus: "If you are determined to move the capital, then this is a good place to move it to."

Ha Yun [1347–1416] alone dissented, saying: "The mountains seem well configured, but from the standpoint of geomancy it cannot be considered good."

Then the king, acting on the advice of his ministers, decided on Hanyang as the capital.   DC

CHAPTER FOURTEEN

Political Thought in Early Chosŏn

The founders of Chosŏn were fully committed to Sung Neo-Confucianism as their guiding creed and endeavored to transform Korea into a Confucian state in which the Ch'eng-Chu tradition would be properly preserved. For the scholar-officials of early Chosŏn, Neo-Confucianism was above all a political philosophy that, grounded in the sociopolitical models of China's antiquity, provided them with reliable and efficient patterns for reforming state and society. They spoke of Neo-Confucianism as "substantial learning" (*sirhak*) that provided not only a new political vision but also answers to the most pressing problems of their time.

Korean Neo-Confucianism recognized the *Great Learning (Ta hsüeh)* — the small treatise that Chu Hsi (1130–1200) had selected as one of the Four Books — as the basic text that outlined a systematic and pragmatic program for moral education as well as political action. The fundamental purpose of scholarship now was to re-create the ideal political order as exemplified by China's sage-rulers, Yao and Shun, and the founders of the Hsia, Shang, and Chou. This connection between scholarship and good rule developed in the course of time into an idealistic imperative of great intensity that ran like a thread through all political thought of early Chosŏn. *MD*

Ruling the New Dynasty

Kwŏn Kŭn (1352–1409) was one of the spiritual founders of Chosŏn Korea. In his treatises and commentaries on the Chinese classics he laid out the basic concepts of Neo-Confucianism and illuminated their relevance for the political as well as the social life of the new dynasty. He emphasized the importance of Confucian learning for activating people's moral nature, a process of self-realization that was to culminate in the development of the proper human relationships between ruler and subject, father and son, elder and younger. One of Kwŏn Kŭn's favorite texts was the *Great Learning*, in which he found an outline for social and political action.

The following memorial (1401) was written after a fire in Such'ang Palace, the royal home of the last Koryŏ kings, in which Yi Sŏnggye had held his enthronement ceremony. Because this fire was interpreted as a warning of Heaven to King T'aejong's young rule (1400–1418), Kwŏn Kŭn pointed out six matters to which the king should pay special attention: loyalty to King T'aejo (1392–1398), administration of state affairs, treatment of officials, attendance at royal lectures, rewarding of loyalty, and performance of state rituals. Kwŏn Kŭn advocated in particular the rehabilitation of his teacher, Chŏng Mongju (1337–1392), who had died as a Koryŏ loyalist. MD

Kwŏn Kŭn: On Royal Action

[From *T'aejong sillok* 1:4b–7b]

On Treating Court Officials

Although the distinction of ruler and minister is ceremonially strict, their relationship must be emotionally intimate. In olden times, the ruler was intimate and close to his high ministers, and he met face to face with his court officials.

Rulers of later generations lived hidden in their palaces, and the ministers they received at court bowed perfunctorily and then retired. Since the feelings of ruler and ministers did not at all match, the wicked and the false deceived their ruler and took pleasure in concealing from him the gains and losses outside the palace and the interests and urgent concerns of the people.

Your servant wishes that from now on Your Majesty would regularly sit in court and receive your ministers in audience all through the day. You should grant an audience to all officials who depart and take leave or come from outside the court, regardless of their rank. If you use warm words to console them and clear questions to draw them out, all your officials will have grateful hearts, and you will learn all about the affairs of the people.

On Attending Royal Lectures

The way of emperors and kings is made bright through scholarship, and the rule of emperors and kings is extensive because of scholarship. From antiquity, those kings who were good even established royal lectures in order to investigate the learning of the sages.

Your servant respectfully wishes that, regardless of the brilliance of your natural talents or the inadequacy of the Confucian scholars, Your Majesty would daily attend the royal lectures and, with unprejudiced mind and humble determination, diligently pursue the studies.

On Rewarding Loyalty

Since antiquity, rulers have certainly rewarded scholars of integrity and rightness as a means to secure the social fabric for myriad generations. In my view, Chŏng Mongju of the former dynasty, as a poor scholar, received T'aejo's special favor of recommendation and thus advanced to high office. Was his heart unwilling to repay T'aejo such favors? With the brilliance of his talents and knowledge was he unaware of the direction in which the Heavenly Mandate and the hearts of the people went? Did he not know that the house of Wang was doomed? Did he not know that his safety was at stake? Even so, he concentrated his mind on what he was doing and did not swerve from his integrity. Therefore he suffered death. That is what is called "even in great emergencies not being deprived of one's principles." Chŏng Mongju died in Koryŏ. Is it utterly impossible to honor him posthumously today?

MD

NEW GOVERNMENT

With his broad erudition and energetic character, Chŏng Tojŏn was a prime mover in the founding process of the new dynasty. In his philosophical works he outlined the Confucian point of view and aggressively turned against Buddhism. He put an end to the Confucians' traditional tolerance of the Buddhist creed and advanced philosophical arguments against it. He also paid close attention to renewing and tightening the governmental structure. Inspired by the *Rites of Chou (Chou li)*, Chŏng Tojŏn wrote the *Administrative Codes of Chosŏn (Chosŏn kyŏngguk chŏn)*, in which he drafted the constitutional outline of the new dynasty. Although he emphasized the ruler's pivotal position in the governing process, he equally envisaged a strong standing for the *ch'ongjae* (prime minister), whose major task was to assist the king at the head of a well-organized administration. He also recognized the importance of the censorial agencies for checking the king as well as for supervising the officialdom. Chŏng Tojŏn's major concern, however, was the building of a government that would function through benevolence rather than force. In this sense he followed the Mencian tradition that eschewed coercion and espoused virtue as the sole means for winning the people's hearts. Chŏng Tojŏn's ideas exerted a lasting influence on the legislative process during the dynasty's first century.   MD

Chŏng Tojŏn: On the Prime Minister

[From *Sambong chip* 7:5a–6a]

The administrative department is the domain of the prime minister. As the functionaries, et cetera, are all subject to the prime minister, administering the educational department also is one of the prime minister's duties. If the prime minister gets the right men, the Six Ministries are well run, and the hundred offices are well regulated. Therefore it is said: "The ruler's task consists in settling for one chief minister." This points to the prime minister.

Above, he assists the king; below, he guides the officials and controls all the people. His task is indeed great! Furthermore, the abilities of rulers differ: some are dull, and some bright; some are strong, and some weak. The prime minister goes along with the ruler's goodness, but corrects his badness; he presents him with the feasible, but withholds from him the wrong. By so doing, he enables the ruler to enter the realm of the Great Mean. Therefore he is called "assistant"; this means that he supports and assists.

All the officials have different tasks, and the people have different occupations. The prime minister treats them fairly so that each does not lose what is proper for him; he treats them impartially so that all gain their proper place. Therefore he is called "chief minister"; this means that he rules and directs.

Only the prime minister knows about the services of the royal consorts and concubines, the duties of the eunuchs, the enjoyments of carriages and horses, of dress and ornaments, the provision of food and drink within the confines of the royal palace. He is an important minister. He is the one the ruler faces with ritual decorum, yet he personally attends to the minutest matters. Is this not trivial? No! The royal consorts, the concubines, and the eunuchs are actually ready for the royal summons. But if the prime minister does not watch over them, they might deceive the king with wickedness and flattery. The carriages and horses, the dress and ornaments, the food and drink are actually for the provision of the royal person. But if the prime minister does not economize, there might be luxurious and lavish expenditures. Therefore the earlier kings established laws and entrusted them all to the prime minister, who uses them for regulating and restraining. Their concern was far-reaching!

The great Confucian of the Sung, Chen Te-hsiu [1178–1235], discussed the task of the prime minister and said: "He corrects himself and rectifies the ruler; he knows the people and tends to the affairs." How excellent are these words! In my opinion, the perfection of self and the rectification of the ruler are the foundation of politics, and knowing the people and administering the affairs are the mechanism of politics. Therefore I have discussed this topic here.   MD

THE KINGLY WAY

A prominent scholar-official of the mid-fifteenth century, Yang Sŏngji (1415–1482) outlined for the teenaged King Tanjong (1452–1455) the essentials of kingly rule. Like his predecessors, Yang Sŏngji emphasized the close correlation between the king's moral stature and the stability and success of his rule. For striking a healthy balance between these two, the selection of capable officials was a king's foremost task. He needed the scholar-officials for his own enlightenment—the pursuit of "right learning" (chŏnghak) required their instruction and explanations. But he needed them equally to carry the message of kingly rule beyond the palace walls. The scholar-officials were thus not only the king's teachers but also the most effective propagandists of the kingly way among the people at large.   MD

Yang Sŏngji: Discussion on the Kingly Way

[From *Nulchae chip* 1:22b–24a]

Your servant has heard that there are three essentials a ruler keeps in mind: humaneness, understanding, and resoluteness. Humaneness means loving and nourishing the people. Understanding means differentiating between good and bad. Resoluteness means keeping inferior men at a distance. There are also three essentials for governing a country: to employ right men, to heed admonitions, and to reward and punish. If one employs the right men, all matters are regulated. If one heeds admonitions, everything good accumulates. If one is trustworthy in rewarding and stern in punishing, the good are encouraged and the bad take warning. And the whole world will exert itself. Ah! Heaven has created the people, but it cannot rule them by itself. Therefore it has entrusted them to the ruler. The ruler cares for the people, but he cannot rule them alone. Therefore he commits them to officials.

Now, in the capital the State Council supervises the hundred officials, and the Six Ministries manage all matters. It is proper to charge those in high positions with supporting and nourishing the royal virtue and those in low positions with aiding and fostering the people's livelihood. For selecting officials, it is necessary to choose the proper men; for collecting taxes and levies, it is necessary to have equal standards; for rites and education, it is necessary to cultivate understanding; for the military administration, it is necessary to motivate to action; for punishments, it is necessary to be impartial and forgiving; for works and repairs, it is necessary to be careful and economical. In all matters of the various offices, it is necessary to be diligent and cautious.

Outside the capital, the governors administer localities, and the local magistrates are in charge of counties. The governor investigates the sufferings of the people and checks the greediness and cruelty of local magistrates. He encourages agriculture in order to enrich the people's livelihood, and promotes schools in order to rectify their customs. When assigning corvée labor, he takes care to be impartial and equitable; when deciding prison sentences, he is determined to be sincere and honest. He promotes what is profitable and does away with what is harmful. It is his task to preserve and care for the people.

The provincial military commanders control separate areas. Each fortification and river station must have adjoining land, and it is necessary to train the soldiers well and make them courageous, to make the weapons and equipment strong and sharp, to maintain the fortresses and embankments well and in good repair, and to keep sufficient provisions. The training must be diligent and the patrolling alert. The commander's task is the raising of troops and the defense of the country.

The Royal Secretariat is the king's mouthpiece, and the censorial agencies are the eyes and ears of the state. The Royal Secretariat issues the royal orders and handles all important matters. The Office of the Censor-General amends deficiencies of the royal orders and corrects omissions. The Office of the Inspector-General screens all offices and scrutinizes the gains or failures of the court and the good or bad actions of the officials. This is its responsibility.

Your Majesty should also put your mind to right learning for making clear the source from which right rule comes forth. You should keep close to the right men for the benefit of your enlightenment. You should engage high officials and widen the channel of memorials. You should act with care every single day and be concerned at the beginning about the end. With high and low you should be in mutual harmony and with capital and countryside in cooperation to maintain forever the peaceful rule of the dynastic ancestors. MD

THE WAY OF PRINCIPLE

At the end of the dynasty's first century, the founders' Confucian vision of a perfect government under a virtuous ruler still remained unfulfilled. Indeed, the century had witnessed Sejo's (1455–1468) usurpation of the throne and Yŏnsangun's (1494–1506) contemptuous and arbitrary rule. The Confucian officialdom itself had lost much of its initial enthusiasm and was bogged down in sterile book learning. Only a relatively small number of scholar-officials continued to pursue the Neo-Confucian dream. Collectively, they became known as the Neo-Confucian literati *(sarim)*. One of them was Cho Kwangjo (1482–1519), who became the recognized leader of an ideological and political restoration movement that centered on the embodiment of the Way *(to)* in government. Emphasizing the value of scholarship for an enlightened rule, Cho had as one of his principal concerns the cultivation of personal virtue as the mainspring of a ruler's transforming influence *(hwa)*. Ruler and scholar were therefore interdependent, and only the ruler's judicious use of the scholar-officials could result in the re-creation of government on the pattern of Yao and Shun, the idealized legendary rulers in China. Cho Kwangjo and his followers espoused these views from the vantage point of the censorial agencies, but, as it had before, such ideological pressure in the end proved counterproductive. Cho Kwangjo became the most prominent victim of the literati purge of 1519. His legacy, however, endured throughout the sixteenth century. MD

Cho Kwangjo: On Problems of the Time

[From *Chŏngam chip* 3:12b–14b]

In our country at the time of King Sejong [1418–1450], rites, music, literature, institutions, and implementations were similar to those of the Chou period. But in the first years of the deposed Yŏnsangun [1494–1506], King Sŏngjong's [1469–1494] coffin had not been long in the memorial chamber when matters in the palace were already deplorable and not one person was able to preserve its integrity. Therefore the scholar-officials all lost their determination and finally were bewildered and confused, but nobody came to their rescue. Because the virtue and benevolence of the dynastic founders were abundant and rich and had penetrated the people's minds, after Your Majesty ascended the throne the people's minds were about to turn toward goodness. Old habits and corrupt customs, however, are difficult to reform all at once. If at this very moment the scholars' mores are not rectified, the people's livelihood is not enriched, and an indestructible basis for many future generations is not established, what will the royal descendants take as a model? Why is it that from ancient times the one who wished to rule was not able to rule well? It is because there were inferior men who took pleasure in slandering others and starting trouble. Your servant says that if Your Majesty's learning is daily progressing toward higher knowledge and brighter insights and you treat your high ministers with greater sincerity, they will not dare make wild statements in front of you and will certainly devote themselves completely to the affairs of the state. If the affairs of the state are not handled by Your Majesty's high ministers, high and low will oppose each other and not find harmony, and good rule will not be achieved.   MD

Cho Kwangjo: On the Superior Man and the Inferior Man

[From *Chungjong sillok* 32:66a–b]

The ruler's entire mind must be brilliantly clear before he is able to recognize the wicked and the upright among men. Since even among inferior men there are some who resemble superior men, there are certain to be inferior men among the officials. If one observes their words and actions, one naturally recognizes whether they are worthy or not. If the ruler, however, does not make an effort to investigate matters and extend his knowledge, he may take a superior man for an inferior man or an inferior man for a superior man. Furthermore, when an inferior man attacks a superior man, he may point at him and call him an inferior man. Or someone may say that a man's words and actions are incongruous, or that he is fishing for fame. A ruler cannot but closely observe such cliquish scholars. Now the ruler should clearly differentiate their kind. If there are wicked men who speak up, he should call them wicked. He should evaluate them and call them either right or wrong. If the judgment of right and wrong emanates from the ruler, the scholars' mores will naturally turn toward what is correct.   MD

ON SAGE LEARNING

Yi Hwang (1501–1570) did not have a brilliant political career in the central government, but his influence on the political thinking at court, exercised from deep in the countryside, was nevertheless considerable. In 1568, during his last sojourn in the capital before his death, he submitted the *Memorial on Six Points Presented in 1568 (Mujin yukcho so)* to King Sŏnjo (1567–1608). This document is one of the most powerful political statements of the Chosŏn dynasty. After reading it, Sŏnjo exclaimed: "These six points are indeed the wise legacy of antiquity, but equally the most urgent matters of our days."

The first two points deal with problems that had become acute because Sŏnjo, at the age of fifteen, had been chosen to succeed his uncle Myŏng-jong (1545–1567), who had died without leaving an heir. They include correct continuation of the royal line, close relations with the two dowager-regents, and guarding against slander. The theme of the third point, here translated in large part, is Sage Learning *(sŏnghak)* as the basis of good rule. It adheres closely to the teachings of Chu Hsi in the *Great Learning* and *The Mean*. The fourth point elucidates the development of the Way *(to)* from antiquity to early Chosŏn, warns against heterodox teachings (Buddhism), and entreats the young king to give the Way a permanent abode in Korea. In the fifth point Yi Hwang emphasizes the importance of trustworthy high officials and the censorial agencies. The last point shows the close connection between recognizing the will of Heaven and the kingly way.

Yi I (1536–1584), who with his older contemporary Yi Hwang dominated the field of Neo-Confucian philosophy in the sixteenth century, did not exhaust his efforts in speculative thinking. He paid equally close attention to the practical problems of his time, and his pronouncements on political, economic, and social issues were widely respected. He did not tire of repeating his fundamental insight, according to which the health and stability of the state rested solely on the peasantry, and he therefore termed the strengthening of the peasants' livelihood the most urgent task of his time.

The *Memorial in Ten Thousand Words* (1574), of which some key passages are translated here, is only one of several important political documents Yi I submitted to King Sŏnjo. It combines Neo-Confucian instruction on kingly rule and popular indoctrination with practical advice on economic, military, and administrative matters. Most significantly, Yi I called for flexibility in policy planning and legislation, and thus distinctly distanced himself from timeworn legal conservatism. For him, too, the basic program of internal cultivation and its application to politics, outlined in Chu Hsi's commentary on the *Great Learning*, remained the foundation of all moral and, by extension, political action. MD

Yi Hwang: Memorial on Six Points

[From *T'oegye chŏnsŏ* 6:42a–46b]

Third: By Esteeming Sage Learning, the Basis of Good Rule Is Built

Your servant has heard that the essential method of the mind, which is part of the learning of the emperors and kings, originated from the Great Shun's order to Yü that said: "The mind of man is precarious. The mind of the Way is barely perceptible. Be discriminating, be single-minded. Hold fast to the Mean."[1]

Shun entrusted the world to Yü with the wish that he should pacify it. Among the words with which he addressed him, none were more urgent than those on government. But Shun's injunctions and admonitions to Yü did not go beyond these words, because he realized that learning and perfect virtue constitute the great foundation of ruling, while discrimination and single-mindedness are the great law of scholarship. If the great foundation of ruling is established with the great law of scholarship, all the governances of the world will emanate from this. Because the plans of the sages of antiquity are like this, even your ignorant servant understands that Sage Learning is the basis of perfect rule and presumptuously addresses Your Majesty on this subject.

Even so, Shun's words only spoke of precariousness and subtlety without giving the reason for them; they only instructed the ruler to be discriminating and single-minded without indicating the method of being discriminating and single-minded. It was very difficult for men of later generations who wanted, on the basis of these words, to know the method exactly and put it into practice. Therefore several sages followed one upon the other, and with Confucius the method became well established. This was the *Great Learning*'s "investigation of things" and "extending of one's of knowledge [understanding]," "being sincere in one's intentions," and "rectifying the mind-and-heart"; and the *Mean*'s manifesting goodness and being sincere with oneself. Thereafter various Confucians successively emerged until Chu Hsi. His theories, which were indeed brilliant, were embodied in his commentaries and questions on the *Great Learning* and *The Mean*. If we now concentrate on these two books and pursue the learning of true knowledge and practice, it is like seeing the sun in the sky upon opening one's eyes, or like walking on the wide path simply by placing one's foot on it.

Regrettably, however, there are few rulers in this world who aspire to this learning. And among those who do aspire to it and are able to make a beginning, few reach the end. Ah! That is the reason why this learning has not been transmitted and government is not like that of old. Yet there is hope that it will become like this!

From the nearness of our own nature and appearance and daily applied human relationships to the myriad things of heaven and earth and the vicissitudes of past and present, everything has in itself the principle of what is and the norm of what must be. This is what is called the Mean of what exists by itself through nature. Therefore, learning must be broad, inquiry accurate, thinking careful, and judgment enlightened. These are the four elements of the extension of knowledge, and among them careful thinking is the most important. What is thinking? It means to search for it in the mind and to obtain it through experience. If one can experience it in the mind and clearly differentiate its principle, if one wishes the inner workings of good and bad and the judgment of rightness and profit, of right and wrong, to be completely exact and free of error, then it is possible to know truly and without doubt the reason for what are called "precariousness" and "subtlety" and the method of being discriminating and single-minded.

Because Your Majesty has already made a beginning in the study of these four elements and set out on this course, your servant hopes that, on the basis of this beginning, you will make an even more sustained effort. The procedure and the items of your study should be based on the details pointed out in Chu Hsi's queries. You should make reverent seriousness your priority and investigate all matters in terms of the reason for their existence and the norm of what they should be. You should ponder this deeply, turn it over in your mind, thoroughly internalize it, and finally reach the ultimate limits of these four elements. If you make such great efforts over a long period of time, one morning, without your realizing it, all problems will dissipate and be solved and there will be a sudden breakthrough to integral comprehension. Then at last you will understand the meaning of the statement that "substance and functions have one source, and there is no gap between the manifest and the hidden."[2] Neither confused by precariousness and subtlety nor bewildered by discrimination and single-mindedness, you will hold fast to the Mean: this is what is called true knowledge.

Your servant wishes also to speak about earnest action. To be sincere in one's intentions is to investigate thoroughly the subtle, even the reality of a single hair. To rectify one's mind is to investigate action and quiescence, even the correctness of one single matter. Cultivating your personal life, don't get trapped in partiality. Regulating the family, don't err in one-sidedness. Be alert and fearful; be watchful when alone. Strengthen your determination without resting. These are the elements of earnest action, and among them mind and intention are the most important. The mind is the heavenly ruler, and the will comes forth from it. If one first makes sincere what comes forth, this sincerity will be sufficient to stop the ten thousand errors. If one rectifies the heavenly ruler, that is, the mind, the whole body will follow its orders, and its movements will all have reality.

Your Majesty has already made a beginning and a start in regard to these various efforts. Your servant hopes that, on the basis of this start, you will make an even more sincere effort. For rules and guidance you should follow the instructions that these two books, *Great Learning* and *The Mean*, hand down, and make reverent seriousness your priority. If at all times and everywhere, in all your thoughts, you are guided by them and remain cautious in all your affairs, the manifold desires will be washed away from the mind, and the Five Relations and all actions will be polished to their very best.

Someone may say: "The learning of emperors and kings is not the same as the learning of scholars and students." But this difference only applies to textual exegesis and laboring over compilation. If one makes reverent seriousness the basis, investigates the principles of all things in order to extend knowledge, and examines oneself in order to practice it—are these not the essentials for making the method of mind subtle and transmitting the learning of the Way? And is there in this respect any difference between emperors and kings and ordinary men?

If you pay attention to this, it will indeed be fortunate!   *MD*

Yi I: Memorial in Ten Thousand Words

[From *Yulgok chŏnsŏ* 5:13b–15b; 24b–25b]

What is called timeliness means being flexible in accordance with time to establish laws and to save the people. Master Ch'eng, when discussing the *Book of Changes,* said that to know time and to recognize the timely circumstances are the great method of learning the *Book of Changes.* He also said: "Change according to time is the constant rule." In general, laws are established according to a particular time; as times change, the laws do not remain the same. Shun followed upon Yao, and appropriately everything remained unchanged, yet he divided the nine provinces into twelve. Yü followed upon Shun, and appropriately everything remained unchanged, yet he changed the twelve provinces back to nine. Was this because sages like to make changes? They did so only in accordance with their time. In general, what can be changed in accordance with a particular time are the laws and institutions. Unchangeable, however, in ancient as well as in present times, are the kingly way, humane government, the three bonds that exist between ruler and minister, father and son, and husband and wife, and the five constants of humaneness, rightness, ritual decorum, wisdom, and trustworthiness. In later generations, when skilled mastery of the Way was no longer to be found, the unchangeable was at times changed, and the changeable was at times adhered to. For this reason the days of political order were generally few, whereas the days of disorder were generally numerous.

Speaking of our eastern region, Korea, there is no textual evidence of Chi Tzu's Eight Rules,[3] and when at the time of the Three Kingdoms, disturbances broke out, the government policies were obliterated. The five hundred years of the former dynasty, Koryŏ, were darkened by the wind and rain of political crises. Arriving at our dynasty, King T'aejo started the dynastic fortunes. King Sejong preserved and advanced them and first used the *Six Codes of Governance (Kyŏngje yukchŏn)*. Under King Sŏngjong the *State Code* [1485] was published, and thereafter, in accordance with time, laws were established and called the *Supplementary Code*. Because sage-king followed upon sage-king, there was appropriately nothing that was not the same; the one used the *Six Codes of Governance,* the other the *State Code*. That these were augmented by the *Supplementary Code* was but an adjustment to the time.

At the beginning of the dynasty, the officials were free to submit their opinions. Institutions were created, but people did not regard them as strange nor was the execution of law interrupted. The people were thus able to rest easy. In contrast, Yŏnsangun was wild and unruly and his expenditures lavish. He changed the tribute laws of the dynastic founders and was daily intent on harming the people and benefiting the royal house. When King Chungjong brought about a restoration, the government should have been made as before, but during the first years those in charge of the state were only ignorant meritorious subjects. Thereupon the worthies of the year *kimyo* [1519] wanted action, but they were falsely accused and destroyed. This was followed by the purge of the year *ŭlsa* [1545], which was even more cruel than the one of [1519]. From then on the Neo-Confucian literati lost heart and regarded an unobtrusive life as good luck. Since they did not dare speak up on state affairs, cunning and powerful groups acted according to their own will and without scruples. What was profitable to them they preserved as old laws; what stood in their way they abolished with new laws. They were solely intent on fleecing the people and fattening themselves. They went so far that the state was daily more hard pressed and the national foundation daily more weakened. Was there anyone who thought about this matter, even if only for an instant?

There are five principles for pacifying the people: first, to open one's sincere mind in order to obtain the sympathy of all subordinates; second, to revise the tribute plan in order to abolish the hardship of coercion and extortion; third, to uphold frugality in order to reverse the trend of extravagance; fourth, to change the selection of slaves for service in the capital in order to relieve the unhappy lot of the public and private slaves; fifth, to revise the military administration in order to strengthen internal as well as external security.

Now I see that Your Majesty's qualifications are impressive: your humanity sufficient to protect the people, your intelligence sufficient to discern cunning, your resoluteness sufficient to decide on sanctions. But Your Majesty's aspiration to become a sage is not firm, and your sincerity to seek right rule is not genuine. Assuming that you cannot reach the level of earlier kings, you withdraw and refer to your own smallness, giving no thought to advancement and development. I do not know what you have experienced to make you like this. If you make a genuine effort toward self-cultivation and put your sincere mind to pacifying the people, you will be able to find worthies and rule with them, you will be able to correct the abuses and salvage the situation.   *MD*

C H A P T E R   F I F T E E N

Culture

Once the dynastic foundation was consolidated, the Chosŏn state attained brilliant achievements in many fields. Respect for education and scholarship was a hallmark of the dynasty. There were many incentives for talented young men to pursue careers in scholarship and government service, since scholars and officials were accorded the highest prestige in Chosŏn society. In 1420, King Sejong organized the Hall of Worthies, where selected scholar-officials were assigned to devote their time to scholarly research. From these studies came a number of important publications on the classics, history, geography, linguistics, law, music, agriculture, astronomy, and medicine. Most important, however, was the invention of the Korean alphabet in 1443.

The early phase of the Chosŏn dynasty was also characterized by brilliant achievements in science and technology. A number of scientific instruments—sundials, clepsydras, armillary spheres, rain gauges—were invented and refined. Moreover, a strong emphasis on the practical application of knowledge to the needs of daily life led to the publication of several manuals for farming as well as medical treatises and compendia of herbal remedies for various diseases. The highly sophisticated advances in book printing developed in Korea at this time easily accommodated these publications.

INVENTION OF THE KOREAN ALPHABET

The invention of the Korean alphabet, called *chŏngŭm* (Correct Sounds), is the crowning achievement of the Chosŏn dynasty. Prior to devising its own writing system, Korea had used Chinese graphs for transcription. But because the Korean language is totally different from Chinese, there were many problems in the use of Chinese graphs in a Korean setting. It was to amend this situation that King Sejong (1418–1450) assembled a group of scholars to devise scripts suitable for the Korean language. Under the personal leadership of the king, after many years of painstaking studies, a phonetic alphabet was finally created in 1443. To assure the practicability and wide use of the newly devised alphabet, King Sejong published a eulogy cycle called *Songs of Flying Dragons (Yongbi ŏch'ŏn ka)* and the translation of a Chinese classic, among other works, using the new script before it was formally proclaimed in 1446.

When the new writing system was officially published, it was called *Correct Sounds to Instruct the People (Hunmin chŏngŭm)*. Consisting of twenty-eight letters—seventeen consonants and eleven vowels—the Korean alphabet is wholly phonetic and capable of transcribing almost any sound. Hailed by modern linguists as one of the most scientific writing systems in the world, the script is extremely simple and very easy to learn. In the twentieth century, this alphabet has been called *hangŭl* (Great Letters).

In publishing the *Correct Sounds to Instruct the People* in 1446, King Sejong wrote a preface explaining his motivation for devising the new writing system, which was followed by a detailed explanation of how the alphabet worked. Chŏng Inji, an official who assisted the king in the invention of the alphabet, then wrote a postscript. The first two selections that follow are King Sejong's preface and parts of Chŏng Inji's postscript.

Although the invention of the Korean alphabet was hailed as a great achievement of the sagely rule of King Sejong, there was a group of scholar-officials, led by Ch'oe Malli (fl. 1419–1444), who strongly opposed the use of Korea's own script. They believed that Korea had long emulated Chinese ideas and institutions and that the adoption of Korea's own writing system would make it impossible to identify Korean civilization with that of China. The third selection is the memorial submitted by Ch'oe Malli offering his reasons against the use of the Korean alphabet.   YC

King Sejong: Preface to *Correct Sounds to Instruct the People*

[From *Hunmin chŏngŭm* 1a]

The sounds of our language differ from those of Chinese and are not easily communicated by using Chinese graphs. Many among the ignorant, therefore, though they wish to express their sentiments in writing, have been unable to communicate. Considering this situation with compassion, I have newly devised twenty-eight letters. I wish only that the people will learn them easily and use them conveniently in their daily life.   YC

Chŏng Inji: Postscript to *Correct Sounds to Instruct the People*

[From *Hunmin chŏngŭm haerye* 26b–29b]

In general, the languages of different countries have their own enunciations but lack their own letters, so they borrowed the Chinese graphs to communicate their needs. That is, however, like trying to fit a square handle into a round hole. How could it possibly achieve its objective satisfactorily? How could there not be difficulties? It is, therefore, important that each region should follow the practices that are convenient to its people and that no one should be compelled to follow one writing system alone.

In the winter of the year *kyehae* [1443], His Majesty, the king, created twenty-eight letters of the Correct Sounds and provided examples in outline demonstrating their meanings. His Majesty then named these letters *Hunmin chŏngŭm*. Resembling pictographs, these letters imitate the shapes of the old seal characters. Based on enunciation, their sounds correspond to the Seven Modes in music. These letters embrace the principles of heaven, earth, and men as well as the mysteries of yin and yang, and there is nothing they cannot express. With these twenty-eight letters, infinite turns and changes may be explained; they are simple and yet contain all the essence; they are refined and yet easily communicable. Therefore, a clever man can learn them in one morning, though a dull man may take ten days to study them. If we use these letters to explain books, it will be easier to comprehend their meanings. If we use these letters in administering litigations, it will be easier to ascertain the facts of a case. As for rhymes, one can easily distinguish voiced and voiceless consonants; as for music and songs, twelve semitones can be easily blended. They can be used whatever and wherever the occasion may be.   YC

Ch'oe Malli: Opposition to the Korean Alphabet

[From *Sejong sillok* 103:19b–22a]

Twentieth day of the second month of the year [1444]. Ch'oe Malli, first counselor in the Hall of Worthies, and his associates offered the following memorial: We humbly believe that the invention of the Korean script is a work of divine creation unparalleled in history. There are, however, some questionable issues we wish to raise for Your Majesty's consideration.

Ever since the founding of the dynasty, our court has pursued the policy of respecting the senior state with utmost sincerity and has consistently tried to follow the Chinese system of government. As we share with China at present the same writing and the same institutions, we are startled to learn of the invention of the Korean script.

Only such peoples as the Mongolians, Tanguts, Jürchens, Japanese, and Tibetans have their own writings. But this is a matter that involves the barbarians and is unworthy of our concern. It has been said that the barbarians are transformed only by means of adopting Chinese ways; we have never heard of Chinese ways being transformed by the barbarians.   *YC*

EDUCATION AND SCHOLARSHIP

Education was one of the principal areas emphasized by the Chosŏn dynasty. Indeed, the Neo-Confucian state of Chosŏn held an almost religious belief that the ideals of Neo-Confucianism could be realized only through education. Thus, from its very beginning, the Chosŏn dynasty set up a well-planned nationwide school system to offer the Confucian education to qualified students. In the capital city of Seoul, a district school was organized in four of the five districts; local schools called *hyanggyo* were established in every county throughout the country; for higher education, the Royal Academy *(Sŏnggyungwan)* was organized in the capital. Usually well endowed by the state, these schools became centers for training future leaders of the government, since all the candidates for the state civil service examinations were drawn from them.

From the mid-sixteenth century on, moreover, private academies, called *sŏwŏn*, were organized in the countryside at the initiative of local scholars and in time became important centers of Confucian scholarship in Korea. The private academies were usually richly endowed through private donations, and they also received a royal charter from the king in the form of a name plaque along with generous grants of books, land, and servants from the government.

The Office of Special Advisers *(Hongmungwan)* was a unique institution in Korea. Originally organized in 1420 by King Sejong as a royal research institute called *Chiphyŏnjŏn* (Hall of Worthies), it was reorganized by King Sejo into the *Hongmungwan* in 1463. Assigned to provide advisory services on all matters dealing with the Confucian classics and literature, this office maintained a library within the palace and offered the royal lecture *(kyŏng-yŏn)* for the king. Thus, its officials had the highest prestige and honor.

The *Administrative Code of Chosŏn (Chosŏn kyŏngguk chŏn)* by Chŏng Tojŏn served as the basic code for the Chosŏn dynasty since its foundation in 1392. The article dealing with the establishment of schools, translated here, describes the structure of the national educational system as envisioned by the dynasty's foremost architect. The description of the Royal Academy is taken from the *Revised and Augmented Gazetteer of Korea (Sinjŭng Tongguk yŏji sŭngnam)*, which was published in 1530. The White Cloud Grotto Academy, organized in 1543 by Chu Sebung, was Korea's first private academy. Fashioned after the renowned White Deer Grotto Academy of Sung China, this academy, later renamed the Sosu Academy, became the model for the hundreds of private academies that subsequently sprang up throughout the country. The description of its foundation is taken from an account given in the *Veritable Records of King Myŏngjong (Myŏngjong sillok)*.

Chŏng Tojŏn: Establishment of Schools

[From *Chosŏn kyŏngguk chŏn* in *Sambong chip* 7:30b]

Schools are the center of teaching and transformation, where the cardinal principles of human relations are further illustrated and men of talent receive training. At the times of the Three Dynasties in ancient China, the laws regarding schools were well prepared. Since the Ch'in and the Han dynasties, despite certain shortcomings in the educational system, there have been few who did not see that schooling was important and that the vigor or decline of the schools was the key to the success or failure of the government. All these characteristics are applicable to the present situation also. Our state has established the Royal Confucian Academy to teach the sons and brothers of the nobility and the officials as well as men of superior talent among the people. The state has also established district schools in the capital city, where instructors are assigned to teach young students. Extending this law to districts, towns, big counties, and counties, the state has organized local schools, where teachers have been assigned to instruct students. In addition, schools for military affairs, law, mathematics, medicine, and foreign languages have been established, and appropriate instructors have been assigned to teach the students enrolled there. In these ways, our educa-tional system has achieved great success. *YC*

Royal Confucian Academy

[From *Sinjŭng Tongguk yŏji sŭngnam* 2:10a–b]

The Royal Confucian Academy, located in the eastern section of Sunggyo district of the capital, is charged with the mission of instructing the Confucian students. The Hall of Illustrating the Cardinal Principles stands north of the Confucian Shrine; to the east of the shrine is the library, and to the north is the Office of Sacrificial Offerings.

Sŏng Kan (1427–1456) wrote the following essay of eulogy for the Hall of Illustrating the Cardinal Principles:

> At daybreak each morning, with the beating of a drum, the headmaster and the instructors of the academy assemble the students in the courtyard. After making a bow to the instructors, the students enter the hall, where lectures and discussions on the classics take place. They study, deliberate, and counsel and assist one another to reach a full understanding of the relationships between ruler and minister, father and son, husband and wife, elder brother and younger brother, and friend and friend. For days and months, they work and rest together as one body to train themselves until they become new men. It is from these students that the future loyal ministers and the future filial sons are produced in prolific number to serve the state and their families. Indeed, never before in the history of our country have we witnessed such a splendid success in nurturing loyal officials and filial sons as we see now. Some people object that since the sage's teachings are many, there is no reason why this hall alone should be called the Hall of Illustrating the Cardinal Principles. To them I say: The relationships between ruler and minister, father and son, husband and wife, elder brother and younger brother, and friend and friend are rooted in the heavenly principle, and hence they are unchanging and everlasting. How can there be any teaching more important than this? *YC*

White Cloud Grotto Academy

[From *Myŏngjong sillok* 10:6a–b]

White Cloud Grotto Academy in P'unggi was founded by the incumbent governor of Hwanghae, Chu Sebung, when he was serving as the magistrate of P'unggi [1543]. All the rules and regulations governing the academy have been modeled after those of the White Deer Grotto Academy of the Great Master Chu Hsi. The academic setup, the library, and the land and food and other supplies have all been richly endowed so that men of talent can further cultivate their potential. Yi Hwang [1501–1570] petitioned the king to grant a charter in the form of a name plaque as well as books, land, and servants. The king granted the charter with the name plaque, books, and two or three additional items, and these grants have encouraged Confucian scholars in the countryside to pursue their scholarship with greater zeal. As for land, the endowment arranged by Chu Sebung is sufficient for the academy to sustain itself, and there are adequate numbers of servants. In order for the Confucian scholars to pursue their scholarship, it is essential that they do so in surroundings of peace and quiet. If the provincial governor or the county magistrate, wishing to exalt their study, prescribes restrictive rules for these scholars, it will deprive them of their freedom and divert them from the proper way of cultivation. There should be no interference from outside.   *YC*

Office of Special Advisers

[From *Sinjŭng Tongguk yŏji sŭngnam* 2:9a–10a]

The Office of Special Advisers is located to the west of the Office of the Royal Secretariat and was formerly called the Hall of Worthies. It also maintains a library. It has the duty of maintaining books for the court and is also entrusted with conducting royal lectures and literary counseling.

During the reign of King Sejo [1455–1468], Yang Sŏngji offered the following advice:

> The practice of safekeeping books started during the time of King Sukchong [1095–1105] of the previous dynasty. One of these collections has books stamped with: "The Royal Collection in the year of *sinsa* [A.D. 1101] of the Fourteenth Ruler of the Koryŏ State"; another collection is stamped with "The Royal Collection of the Koryŏ State." Although it has been 363 years since the time of King Sukchong's reign, these stamps look as if they were stamped yesterday, and the books are readily available to us for reference. It is therefore humbly proposed that we write on the reverse side of each book, in formal characters, "The Royal Collection in the year of *kyemi* [1463] of the Sixth Ruler of the Chosŏn State and the Seventh Year T'ien-shun [1463] of Great Ming," and on the front side, "The Royal Collection of the Chosŏn State" in seal characters. In this way, these books may be known to posterity for myriad generations.   *YC*

The Recruitment Examinations

The Chosŏn dynasty relied mainly on recruitment examinations to select officials to serve in the government. There were three types of examinations—the civil, the military, and the technical—and of these the civil examination was the most important and carried the highest prestige. The civil examination in turn consisted of the lower civil examination, which awarded the graduates either the *saengwŏn* degree for the classics or the *chinsa* degree for literary writings, and the higher civil examination for the *munkwa* degree, which qualified the holder to serve in the government as an official. Normally, all candidates in the civil examinations had to go through three stages of rigorous testing—demonstrating their knowledge in the classics, history, and literature—before the successful candidates were finally selected. For ambitious young men, to become a successful candidate in the higher civil examination was the most coveted honor, and many devoted considerable time and energy in preparing themselves to qualify for such an honor.

The account of the examination scene given here, by Sŏng Hyŏn (1439–1504), describes how the examination was conducted.   *YC*

Sŏng Hyŏn: On the Civil Service Examination

[From *Yongjae ch'onghwa* (Koryŏ taehakkyo ed., 1963), pp. 391–392]

The recruitment examination under the previous dynasty was conducted under the supervision of only two men, the chief examination officer and the deputy examination officer. Because these officials had been appointed in advance, prior to the examination, there were deficiencies in the way it was conducted, leading to the criticism that the successful candidates tended to have been drawn from influential families or from immature scholars. Although the present dynasty continued these deficiencies at the beginning, King Sejong introduced drastic reforms in the examination system.

According to the new system, the Ministry of Personnel at first makes a list of the qualified examiners and presents it to the king, who will in turn select and appoint the examination officers from the list just before the examination. Once appointed, the examination officers go to their respective examination sites. The officials of the Three Offices in charge of registrations assemble all the candidates, and at daybreak each candidate's name is called, one after another, and they are led into the fenced-in examination ground. The inspection officers, standing at the entrance, search each candidate's clothes and writing brush container. If anyone is caught carrying books or notes, he is handed over to arresting officers. If he is arrested before entering the examination site, he is barred for one triennial examination; if he is arrested inside the examination site, he is suspended for two triennial examinations.

Just before sunrise, the examination officers appear on the large platform and take seats under torchlight. Their august appearances resemble those of immortals. The officials of the Three Offices then enter the examination ground, arrange the proper seating of the candidates, and leave. At sunrise, the examination questions are posted. At noon, the examination papers are collected and stamped and then returned to the candidates for further work. As the sun begins to set, with the beating of a drum, the candidates present their papers to the collection officers, who in turn hand them over to the registration officers. These officers then record the matching numbers on both ends of the examination papers and cut them apart—one part has the name of the candidate, now concealed, and the other contains the candidate's answers to the examination questions. The officials responsible for concealing the candidates' identities retire to a separate room carrying with them the portions of the papers with the concealed names. To prevent recognition of candidates' handwriting, the recording officials have the copyists rewrite the candidates' answers in red ink. When the rewriting is finished, the collating officer reads the originals to the assistant collating officer, who checks the copied version to make sure it is accurate. When all these things have been done, the copied versions of the examination papers are given to the readers. Only after these papers have been graded and their rankings decided upon are the officials responsible for concealing the names of candidates allowed to identify the authors of the examination papers.

Moreover, the candidates must go through the oral examination on the classics in three different stages—the preliminary, the middle, and the final. At the end, the points scored at each stage are added up. All the examination processes are supervised not just by one man but by many, and the evaluation of the candidates is conducted not just by one man but by many. Indeed, there is nothing in the state system that is more judicious than the recruitment examination.   YC

COMPILATION OF HISTORY

Few states in world history, it may be said, were as conscious of history as the Chosŏn dynasty. Continuing the long tradition of historical writing in Korea, the Chosŏn dynasty sponsored the compilation of a number of historical works and expended a prodigious amount of energy in producing and preserving historical records.

For historical record keeping, court diarists called *hallim* were appointed to take note of all the activities around the throne, and no official business could be conducted by the king without the presence of a court diarist. Appointed from the cream of the recent graduates of the civil service examination, the court diarists strove to live up to the ideal of "straight brush," recording the activities of the court without fear or favor. After the death of each king, these records as well as the documents of various offices within the central government were assembled for the purpose of compiling the annals called *Veritable Record (sillok)*. Thus, we have the *sillok* for the rule of every king of the Chosŏn dynasty. To safeguard the historical records, the Chosŏn dynasty maintained four separate archives in remote mountainous areas in addition to the central archive in Seoul. Aware that their actions and speeches were being recorded for posterity, the Chosŏn dynasty rulers and their officials often found themselves in a defensive position.

There were two types of historical works: official and private. The official histories were compiled under the auspices of the state; the private histories were written by individual scholars in a private capacity. Both the *History of Koryŏ (Koryŏ sa)* and the *Comprehensive Mirror of the Eastern Kingdom (Tongguk t'onggam)*, whose introductory remarks are translated here, belong to the former category.

The project of compiling the official history of the Koryŏ dynasty in the tradition of China's official dynastic history was started within a few months of the founding of the Chosŏn dynasty in 1392, but it was not completed until 1451 after having undergone several major revisions. Because of its extensive use of primary sources, the *History of Koryŏ* is by far the most important history of the Koryŏ dynasty. The *Comprehensive Mirror of the Eastern Kingdom*, on the other hand, is a general history of Korea from antiquity to the fall of Koryŏ. Published in 1484, the book was perhaps the most widely read book on Korean history among Korean scholars and officials. Because the Chosŏn dynasty was a Neo-Confucian state, the editorial outlook of both the *History of Koryŏ* and the *Comprehensive Mirror of the Eastern Kingdom* strongly reflects the Confucian worldview. That is, history, in addition to recording what happened, also had to provide moral lessons for future generations by praising good deeds and condemning evil acts.

Translated here are the dedication written by Chŏng Inji for the *History of Koryŏ* and the preface by Yi Kŭkton (1435–1503) for the *Comprehensive Mirror of the Eastern Kingdom.*

Chŏng Inji: Dedication of the *History of Koryŏ*

[From *Koryŏ sa, chŏn* 1a–4b]

It is said that when one makes a new ax handle, one examines an old one as a model, and that when one builds a new carriage, one uses an old carriage as a model. That is so that we can learn lessons from the past. Because the rise and fall of various states in history likewise offers lessons of encouragement and warning for the future, we have compiled the *History of Koryŏ* and hereby present it to Your Majesty for your perusal.

The Wang clan rose at the beginning from the state of T'aebong, compelled Silla to surrender, eliminated Later Paekche, and reunited the Three Han under the rule of one family. The new dynasty then turned against Liao, established a respectful relationship with T'ang, maintained deference toward China, and secured our land of Korea. The new government of Koryŏ introduced reforms by eliminating vexing and exploitative rules and regulations and laid the foundation of the state on a grandiose scale. With the institution of the recruitment examination system under King Kwangjong [949–975], Confucian studies began to flourish. With the adoption of various new institutions under King Sŏngjong [981–997], the governing structure of the state was perfected.

Unfortunately, however, the succeeding rulers became lax and confused in their rule, giving rise to powerful individuals who abused their power and even attempted to usurp the sacred throne with the military strength they commanded [*Chŏng proceeds with an account of how the fortunes of the state declined in successive reigns, omitted here.*]

The foundation of the state deteriorated further under the pretenders U [1374–1388] and Ch'ang [1388–1389], until the dynastic fortune finally fell to the true ruler, T'aejo. Our great King T'aejo [1392–1398], with his Heaven-endowed courage and sagacity, renewed and expanded his virtue and achievements, pacified the country with his military might, brought peace and tranquillity to the people, and ascended the throne, thereby inaugurating the new dynasty in response to the new mandate.

King T'aejo believed that even though the dynastic fortune and institutions were in ruin, the history of Koryŏ ought not to be obliterated, and hence he ordered the historians to compile its history in an annalistic style, following the format of the *Comprehensive Mirror for Aid in Governance,* by [the eleventh-century historian of Sung China] Ssu-ma Kuang.

The guidelines for compiling the history follow those of Ssu-ma Ch'ien [c. 145–85 B.C.]. On every issue related to the basic principles, we consulted with His Majesty and abided by his final decision. We avoided the use of the term *pongi* [basic annals] and called it instead *sega* [ruling family] in order to demonstrate our respect for the principle of rectification of names. We downgraded the Sin family members by including them in the biography section to show our harsh condemnation of usurpation. We recorded the loyal and the deceitful officials as well as the evil and the upright individuals under separate categories; we entered various institutions and cultures under their respective classification. We also clarified those parts of the annals of reigns that were confusing and established verifiable chronologies. We traced historical events as fully and clearly as possible and made sure that those aspects that lacked sufficient information were supplemented with additional data.

Only by probing into the past can we be sure of achieving the impartiality of historical writings; only by exhibiting the illustrious mirror of history can we ensure that the consequences of good and evil acts shall not be forgotten by posterity.   YC

Yi Kŭkton: Preface to the *Comprehensive Mirror of the Eastern Kingdom*

[From *Tongguk t'onggam* (Chosŏn kwangmunhoe ed., 1911), *sŏ,* pp. 1–4]

The books of the classics contain the Way and the books of history record events. The classics, as revised and compiled by Confucius, have provided lessons for myriad generations. Moreover, many history books have been written since the times of Ssu-ma Ch'ien and Pan Ku, as each generation thereafter produced historical works, and there are far too many to list them all. The former upright minister Ssu-ma Kuang of Sung China, having assembled a multitude of historical and other books, selected their essentials and compiled the *Comprehensive Mirror for Aid in Governance,* covering the period from the decline of Chou to the end of Five Dynasties. Since then that work has truly become the model for all historians. Based on this book, Master Chu Hsi in turn compiled the *Abridged Essentials (T'ung-chien kang-mu).* All writers since then have abided by the standard set by these two great masters.

In compiling the *Comprehensive Mirror of the Eastern Kingdom,* we examined all the available historical works since the times of the Three Kingdoms as well as various works on Chinese history. We then decided to follow the format of "annals and narratives." We also took the guidelines of the *Comprehensive Mirror for Aid in Governance* as our guide and have eliminated those that are confusing and trivial while preserving the important and essential ones. We have tried to narrate in a straightforward manner the unity and disunity of national strength, the good and weak points in national fortunes, the beneficial and evil rules of kings, and the successful and failed administrations in governing the state for fourteen hundred years. We have been particularly strict in emphasizing the rectification of names, in respecting loyalty and uprightness, in condemning rebels, and in punishing evil and deceitful men in the hope that these will provide lessons for the encouragement and admonition of posterity. As Your Majesty reads this in your leisure hours, we hope that the past history of peace and chaos and the rise and fall of various states will become the constant admonitions of today. If Your Majesty were to exert himself toward the splendid virtue of inquiring into the past, it would indeed be of no small assistance in attaining an exemplary rule.

YC

Printing Books

The invention of movable metallic type can be regarded as one of Korea's most significant contributions to world civilization. Having learned from China the technique of book printing by means of woodblocks, Korea became the first country in the world to develop movable metallic type, as early as the beginning of the thirteenth century. Continuing this tradition, the Chosŏn dynasty frequently undertook book printing projects, constantly improving and refining the technique of typesetting. A recent study has verified the casting of as many as twenty-one different species of type during the fifteenth century alone. The various types cast in Korea are usually identified by the year in which they were cast. For the Confucian state of Chosŏn, book printing was important not only for promoting scholarship but also for striving to realize the ideals of good government. The account translated here indicates the extent of painstaking effort the early Chosŏn state expended in the matter of book printing. YC

Sŏng Hyŏn: On Printing

[From *Yongjae ch'onghwa* (Koryŏ taehakkyo ed., 1963), pp. 456–457]

In the third year, *kyemi* [1403], King T'aejong remarked to the courtiers around him: "If the country is to be governed well, it is essential that books be read widely. But because our country is located east of China beyond the sea, not many books from China are readily available. Moreover, woodblock prints are easily defaced, and it is impossible to print all the books in the world by using woodblock prints. It is my desire to cast copper type so that we can print as many books as possible and have them made available widely. This will truly bring infinite benefit to us." In the end, the king was successful in having copper type cast with the graphs modeled after those of the *Old Commentary on the Book of Odes* and the *Tso Commentary*, and that is how the typecasting foundry became established in our country.

[*Sŏng proceeds with a discussion of different kinds of type and processes of typecasting in different reigns, omitted here.*]

Science and Technology

The early Chosŏn dynasty achieved great success in science and technology. The moving force behind this development was King Sejong, who, equipped with personal knowledge, initiated a number of scientific programs to improve and refine the observation and measurement of various natural phenomena. The king was particularly interested in astronomical matters. Seasonal changes, times of sunrise and sunset, rainfall and drought—all were vitally important for a country whose economy was almost totally dependent upon agriculture. Thus we have elaborate armillary spheres charting constellations, refined rain gauges, and various sundials and clepsydras (water clocks) designed with great scientific sophistication, all made during the reign of King Sejong. Particularly noteworthy is the construction in the year 1434 of an instrument that announced the hours automatically: the *chagyŏngnu* (automatic striking clepsydra). Devised and constructed by a former slave, Chang Yŏngsil (d. 1455), this automatic clepsydra was installed on the grounds of the royal palace to tell the time twenty-four hours a day. (The main parts of a replica of this instrument made in 1536 are still preserved in Seoul.) The *Veritable Records of King Sejong* records in detail how this clepsydra operated and offers other information on the development of science and technology. YC

The Automatic Striking Clepsydra

[From *Sejong sillok* 65:1a–3a]

On the first day of the seventh month [1434], the new clepsydra was put into operation. The king had decided that the old clepsydra was not accurate enough and had ordered the casting of metal parts for a new one.

The king was also worried that the officials in charge of time announcements could not avoid mistakes, so he ordered Chang Yŏngsil of the Palace Guard to construct wooden jacks that would announce the time automatically without human agency.

The king ordered Kim Pin [d. 1455] to make an inscription for it, the preface of which said:

> Among the policies of emperors and kings, none has been more important than the unification of times and seasons. The methods used for the study of these matters have been the armillary sphere, the celestial globe, the sundial, and the clepsydra. Without the sphere and the globe, there could be no study of the motions of the heavens and earth; without the sundial and clepsydra, there could be no measure of the divisions between the days and nights. Over a thousand years, at the correct moment each one will start without any error.
>
> Now, His Majesty's servants, having in mind his profound respect for the Emperor Yao, and imitating the example of the Great Shun, have constructed this new clepsydral apparatus in order to equalize the sundial and the intervals; it is set up in the western part of the palace.
>
> As each hour comes round, the jackwork immortals of the clepsydra respond with the appropriate time-signals. Consulting the celestial globe and the armillary sphere, people find that the time-signals correspond to the movement of the heavens without the slightest mistake. It is really as if the gods and spirits were in charge of it. No one seeing it does not heave a sigh and aver that we Koreans certainly had nothing like this in former times.
>
> The sundial and clepsydra have long been made, but from the time of the legendary sage-emperor Huang-ti on there have been different methods, and only we Easterners have developed and extended the different designs.[1]

Kim Ton: Instruments to Measure Days and Nights

[From *Sejong sillok* 77:7a]

At the beginning of the year [1437], King Sejong had ordered the construction of instruments to measure the days and nights. The king commissioned Kim Ton [1385–1440] to make an inscription, the preface of which said:

> The making of celestial globes and armillary spheres is a high and ancient practice. From the emperors Yao and Shun down to the Han and T'ang dynasties there was no one who did not regard it as a most important thing. The literature about it is to be found in the classics and histories, but as we are far removed from ancient times, the methods have not been handed down in great detail. Now His Majesty reverently took the work of these sages as the capstone of the achievements of antiquity. While resting from the myriad concerns of his duties, he turned his attention to the principles of astronomy and uranographic models. Accordingly, what were of old called armillary spheres, celestial globes, gnomons, simplified instruments, automatic striking clepsydras, small simplified instruments, hemispherical scaphe sundials, horizontal sundials, and plummet sundials, all these instruments have been made without one missing. Such is His Majesty's respect for heavenly knowledge and for the exploitation of earthly things.[2] [*For further information on scientific developments in Sejong's time, see SKC 1:543–545.*]

Invention and Use of Rain Gauges

Because traditional Korea was a predominantly agrarian society, the people's livelihood depended largely on the land, and the state's main source of revenue was the land tax. Since the success or failure of the harvest depended heavily on the amount of rainfall, it was important for the state to keep a correct assessment of this amount. Based on a long tradition of science and technology, an instrument to accurately measure the amount of rainfall was invented in 1442 during the reign of King Sejong. Modern scientists marvel at the rain gauge perfected during Sejong's rule, as it is almost identical to the instruments that are currently in use. The government's effort to establish uniformity in gauging and reporting the amount of rainfall throughout the country is also impressive, but the detailed accounts recorded in the *Veritable Records of King Sejong* are omitted here.

Compilation of Medical Books

Korea has a long tradition of compiling and publishing medical books. The Chosŏn dynasty, from its beginning, devoted considerable time and energy to compiling and publishing a number of medical works in order to bring the latest information on remedies to the people. Conducting exhaustive research into all the available medical books, including those published in China, and undertaking comprehensive collections of the native prescriptions and herbs that had proven effective, the Chosŏn government spared no effort to publish the collections of medical remedies. In 1393, King T'aejo dispatched medical instructors to every province to train medical specialists; in 1397, *Collection of Native Prescriptions to Save Life (Hyangyak chesaeng chipsŏng pang)* was published. During his brilliant reign, King Sejong sponsored the compilation and publication of a comprehensive medical book entitled *Compilation of Native Korean Prescriptions (Hyangyak chipsŏng pang)*. Completed in 1433 after two years of exhaustive research, this work explains some 959 different diagnoses and gives prescriptions for 10,706 different remedies, its material being classified into various specialties such as internal and external medicine and ophthalmology. In addition, the book also covered 1,476 different techniques of acupuncture. In preparing this book, special effort was made to collect remedies that had proven effective in Korean experience. With the compilation of this work, the study of medical science in Korea reached a new milestone. In 1445, King Sejong published another medical work, *Classified Collection of Medical Prescriptions (Ŭibang yuch'wi)*, a medical encyclopedia. Then, after the Japanese invasion of 1592–1598, a monumental work entitled *Exemplars of Korean Medicine (Tongŭi pogam)* was compiled by Hŏ Chun (d. 1615) and published in 1610. Widely admired for its usefulness, it was published in China and Japan as well.

Translated here is part of the preface to *Compilation of Native Korean Prescriptions*, written by Kwŏn Ch'ae (1399–1438) and published in 1433. Noteworthy in this preface is the emphasis on finding proper medicine and remedies based on Korean experiences in the compilation of this collection. YC

Kwŏn Ch'ae: Preface to *Compilation of Native Korean Prescriptions*

[From *Sejong sillok* 60:39b–40a]

Eleventh day of the sixth month of the year [1433]. The *Compilation of Native Korean Prescriptions* has just been completed. Following the royal command, Kwŏn Ch'ae wrote the preface as follows:

> Since the times of the legendary rulers of Shen-nung and Huang-ti in China, there have been medical officers who looked after the illnesses of myriad people. In diagnosing illness and dispensing medicines, the doctor gives remedies appropriate to the nature of each individual case and does not depend solely on one method for all cases. The people in regions separated by one hundred *ri* do not have the same social customs, just as the areas separated by one thousand *ri* do not have the same wind. Just as the plants and trees have favorite places to grow, so do the people have favorites in food and drink, according to their customs. Because of this, the ancient sages at first learned the nature of various plants and respected the characteristics unique to the regions in governing the state.
>
> In the humble opinion of this servant, nothing is more important than humanity in the Kingly Way, and humanity, being ultimately great, is of many different kinds. Now, His Majesty is totally committed to the greatness of the Kingly Way in order to realize virtuous rule in government, and his benevolent rule is fully demonstrated in this project of compiling and publishing a book of medicine for the purpose of promoting the people's welfare. In the past, there were rulers who personally prepared medicine for the benefit of individual patients, receiving accolades from posterity. The compilation of a medical book for wide dissemination, however, brings benefit to millions of people for thousands of generations, and the extent of the benevolence it bestows is great and diverse. From now on, those who suffer from illness may take medicines according to the prescriptions explained in this book to regain their health. And if that allows them to enjoy the normal lifespan given by nature, is not this the result of the benevolent rule of our ruler, who is totally committed to humanity? YC

C H A P T E R   S I X T E E N

Social Life

The establishment of the new dynasty in 1392 ushered in an era of social reform that led to a fundamental restructuring of Korean society. Champions of the Confucian way and vigorous opponents of Buddhism, the scholar-officials surrounding the dynastic founders envisaged a new sociopolitical order rooted in Confucian moral principles. Theirs was an idealistic program that favored the formation of a controlled political elite. Inspired by the models they found in Chinese classical literature, the Confucian legislators laid the groundwork from which the highly structured patrilineal descent groups characteristic of Chosŏn society eventually emerged. New standards of ritual behavior and thinking were to provide the elite with values relevant to private as well as to public life. Their platform of ritual action was the *Family Rites of Chu Hsi (Chu Tzu chia-li)*, the most authoritative ritual manual of the Chosŏn period.

The reforms, although propagated through moral incentives as well as legal sanctions, were slow in taking root, and the dynasty's first two centuries were a distinct transition period. Traditional institutions and beliefs resisted change and were therefore not reformed "in one morning." The acculturation process went through several stages. The first is illustrated by the documents that are presented here.   *MD*

OPPOSITION TO BUDDHISM

The Confucians' rise to power was accompanied by the repression of Buddhism. Mismanagement by the Buddhists was held responsible for the economic and spiritual demise of Koryŏ. According to the Confucians, Buddhism lacked the practical standards necessary for social control and economic prosperity. The first measures against Buddhism taken at the beginning of the dynasty were motivated by economic and military considerations and therefore directed at the institutional foundation of the Buddhist monasteries. The contest for control of the spiritual-religious realm, however, was more difficult because the early kings and the people at large continued to adhere to traditional Buddhist customs and ceremonies. Even King Sejong's attitude toward the religious past was ambivalent, and he opposed "sudden changes." Typically, then, warning voices and bold proposals came from the Hall of Worthies—a research institution founded in 1420 and staffed with young and energetic Confucian scholars—and from activist circles at the Royal Confucian Academy. By exposing the defects and inadequacies of Buddhism as a religion and as an institution, the Confucians were able to propagate, in contrast, the qualities of Confucianism. MD

Yun Hoe: On the Harmfulness of Buddhism

[From *Sejong sillok* 23:27a–b]

Yun Hoe [1380–1436], Deputy Director of the Hall of Worthies, and others submitted the following memorial [in 1424]: We consider the harm of the Buddhists to be prevalent still. Since the Han period the reverence for Buddha has been increasingly fervent, yet neither happiness nor profit has been gained. This is recorded in the historical books, which Your Majesty has certainly perused thoroughly. Must you therefore wait for your ministers to tell you?

We think that of all the heterodox teachings, Buddhism is the worst. The Buddhists live alone with their barbaric customs, apart from the common productive population; yet they cause the people to be destitute and to steal. What is worse than their crimes? Beasts and birds that damage grain are certainly chased away because they harm the people. Yet even though beasts and birds eat the people's food, they are nevertheless useful to the people. The Buddhists, however, sit around and eat, and there has not yet been a visible profit. No rain falls now— it is a year of drought. The public granaries are empty, and as to the livelihood of our people, neither life nor death is guaranteed. And yet the food these Buddhists eat is the same in good years as well as bad. One sees only the people starving, never a monk. One sees only the people dying of starvation, never a monk. They are reckless in daily deceiving and betraying the people. We are indeed concerned about it, and in the past many superior men earnestly pointed out their harm.

MD

Sin Ch'ŏjung: On the Deceitfulness of Buddhism

[From *Sejong sillok* 23:30a–32b]

Sin Ch'ŏjung, a licentiate at the Royal Confucian Academy, and one hundred and one others went to the palace and tendered the following memorial [in 1424]:

Those Buddhists, what kind of people are they? As eldest sons they turn against their fathers; as husbands they oppose the Son of Heaven. They break off the relationship between father and son and destroy the obligation between ruler and subject. They regard the living together of man and woman as immoral and a man's plowing and a woman's weaving as useless.

If those monks were forced to return to their home villages; if they were treated as men fit to join the military; if they were made to settle down in order to increase the households; if we burnt their books in order to destroy their roots and branches; if their fields were requisitioned in order to supply military rations; if their slaves were given to the government in order to distribute them among the offices; if their bronze statues and bells were entrusted to the Offices of Supply in order to mint copper cash; if the utensils they use were handed over to a ceremonial office in order to prepare them for official use; if within the capital the temples of each sect were divided up among the offices without buildings; if the temples outside the capital were all torn down in order to build postal stations and school buildings; if for funerals the *Family Rites of Chu Hsi* were exclusively relied upon,—then, in a few years, the human mind would be corrected and the heavenly principles clear, the households would increase, and the number of soldiers would be complete.

MD

THE ROLE OF RITES

In their effort to transform Korean society into a Confucian society, the Confucians never tired of pointing out the fundamental role of the four rites (*sarye*)—capping, wedding, funeral, and ancestor worship—in this transformatory process. To the Confucian, rites were not an imposition upon human nature. Rather, they activated what was good in a person and thus formed the human mind. If properly observed, they determined the relationships within the domestic sphere and stabilized the social foundation of the public realm. The peace and prosperity of a state were thus guaranteed in proportion to the purity of its ritual life. MD

Sŏng Hyŏn: The Fundamental Role of Rites

[From *Hŏbaektang chip* 10:12a–13b]

Rites must be cultivated. If they are not cultivated, the human mind is unstable, laws and orders are numerous, and the way of good rule cannot emerge. It is comparable to curing a man's sickness: if one tried to remedy it hastily in one morning with poisonous medicine, would his constitution not also be harmed? One should first provide the taste of the five grains; thereafter the body naturally regains vitality, and the sickness disappears.

If a man lives idly and does not have instruction, he is insolent and disorderly and differs but slightly from wild animals. Therefore the sages have made the rites as guidelines so that the one who overshoots them retrenches and adapts himself, and the one who falls short desires to reach them. When a man grows up and is capped, he reaches adulthood. The sages, fearing it might look hasty and ill-prepared, have made the rite of divining the date and the names of the guests, the rite of adding the three things,[1] and the rite of the libation; hereby they cultivated the proper rites. The wedding is the great desire of men; it is the match by which two surnames are joined. Fearing that it might look intimate and be lacking the proper separation of the sexes, the sages have made the rites of betrothal *[napch'ae]*, of asking the name of the bride's mother *[munmyŏng]*, of divining the bride's qualities *[napkil]*, and of sending the wedding gifts *[napp'ye]*; hereby they cultivated the proper rites. The funeral is the final act by which a man is sent off, and a son devotes all his mind to it. Fearing that he might be negligent and incomplete, the sages have made for the son the rites of drinking water and eating gruel, of weeping and mourning; hereby they cultivated the proper rites. Ancestor worship is the communication with the spirit of the deceased. It is the means by which the son pays his gratitude to his parents. Fearing that there might be distance and forgetfulness, the sages have made the rites of presenting offerings and libations to the soul of the deceased; hereby they cultivated the proper rites. People communicate with each other, and visitors come. Therefore the sages have made the rites of entertaining the guests and presenting gifts; hereby they cultivated the proper rites. People get together and feast. Therefore the sages have made the rites of bowing and yielding and exchanging the wine cups.   MD

FUNERARY AND ANCESTRAL RITES

Buddhist and shamanist beliefs and ceremonies that had prevailed in Koryŏ continued to dominate the cult of the dead at the beginning of the Chosŏn dynasty. The Confucians tried to counteract these overwhelming traditions by demanding that the focus of ancestral rituals be shifted away from the Buddhist temple and shaman altar to the *kamyo* or *sadang* (domestic shrine). This necessitated an architectural addition to the Korean house, an innovation not easily accomplished. More important, the institution of domestic shrines introduced an entirely new rhythm into the daily life of Koreans because the continued presence of the ancestors required regular offerings and frequent communication. These ritual tasks were entrusted to the eldest male member of the household. He became the chief officiant for the ancestors, who were his direct lineal forebears. The ancestral shrine in the Confucian model, then, concentrated exclusively on the male descent line, and the participants at the seasonal offerings were all patrilineally related. Women, the ritual practitioners of the past, were excluded from this male domain. The establishment of domestic shrines and the institutionalization of Confucian-style ancestor worship were instrumental in introducing the patrilineal concept into Korean society.   MD

Yi Chi: On the Establishment of Domestic Shrines

[From *T'aejong sillok* 2:21b–22a]

Inspector-General Yi Chi [d. 1414] and others memorialize [in 1401]:

In recent years the state has been concerned about the daily deterioration of customs, and every time Your Majesty issued an edict, you gave priority to the order to establish domestic shrines, wishing the people's virtue to return to wholesomeness. That nobody has yet willingly complied is due to the strength and persistence of the Buddhists' false theories, and there may also be some who do not yet know how to establish domestic shrines.

In our opinion the royal capital is the source of the civilizing influence and the mainstay of good government. If the scholar-officials are ordered to establish shrines first, and the order reaches the rest of society later, would there be noncompliance? Moreover, quarters are cramped within the city walls, and thus it may be difficult to establish shrines. Instead, for convenience, a wooden box may be used to store the spirit tablets in a clean room. Outside the capital, a domestic shrine should provisionally be built at the east side of the government office in each prefecture and district. If those appointed magistrates are eldest sons, they should take the spirit tablets to the place of their appointment; if they are not eldest sons, they should use paper tablets in the district shrines and perform the rites. Whether inside or outside the capital, those in charge of the rites in the domestic shrine should rise at dawn daily, burn incense, and bow twice, and when they go in or out of the house, they should announce this in the domestic shrine. If the ancestral rites follow the *Family Rites* completely in order to give an example to those below, this influence will naturally reach the people without special encouragement. *MD*

Reform of Funerary Practices

[From *Sejong sillok* 76:15b–16a]

The royal edict to the Department of Punishments [in 1437] reads as follows:

Nowadays people of high and low social status commonly compete with each other in upholding wanton ceremonies; they respect and trust shamans and dissipate fortunes. Some mourners visit shaman houses where music is played and the spirit of the dead is feasted. Others go to Buddhist temples and have a service held for the repose of the soul. Still others serve wine and food on the burial day, and host and guests console each other. All strive to outdo one another in lavishness and extravagance. This is indeed something to worry about, because the people's livelihood consequently deteriorates, and the quality of the customs is bound up with this.

From now on the playing of music, the gathering of guests, and the performance of wanton ceremonies for the spirits, as well as visits of mourners to shaman houses to feast the spirit of the dead, or the invitation of guests to pray for the soul's repose, and the serving of wine on funeral days must be clearly and sternly prohibited by the censorial offices in the capital and by the local authorities in the province. *MD*

THE POSITION OF WOMEN

The Confucians' emphasis on the patrilineal descent line had serious consequences for women's relations to men and their position in society. In Koryŏ, it had not been uncommon for an upper-class man to have several wives who were not subject to any social ranking order. In the patrilineal society the Confucians envisioned, however, only one woman, the primary wife, could qualify to become the mother of her husband's lineal heir. Any other women the husband might have were therefore of lesser importance, and the differentiation between main wives and concubines *(ch'ŏch'ŏp)* became one of the sharpest social dividing lines, and the most tragic one, in Korean society.

The union between husband and wife was regarded as the foundation of human morality and the mainspring of the socialization process that extended from the relation between father and son to that between ruler and subject. The main wife was in charge of the domestic sphere *(nae)*, while the husband's domain was the public sphere *(oe)*. The peace and stability of the family were a precondition for the peace and prosperity of the state. Women, although inferior members of society, nevertheless bore the responsibility of providing the government with loyal and capable men.   MD

On Differentiating Between Main Wife and Concubine

[From *T'aejong sillok* 25:13a–b]

The Office of the Inspector-General memorializes [in 1413] as follows:

Husband and wife are the mainstay of human morality, and the differentiation between main wife and concubine may not be blurred. Embodying the great principles of the one hundred kings of the Spring and Autumn period, King T'aejo accentuated the boundary between main wife and concubine [devised by] the scholar-officials and instituted the law of conferring ranks and land on main wives. The distinction between main wife and concubine has thus become clear and the root of human morality straight.

At the end of the former dynasty, the influence of ritual decorum and morality was not pervasive, and the relationship between husband and wife deteriorated. The members of the officialdom followed their own desires and inclinations: some who had a wife married a second wife; others made their concubine their main wife. This has consequently become the source of today's disputes between main wives and concubines.

We have carefully examined the Ming code, which reads: "The one who makes a concubine his main wife while the latter is alive is to be punished with ninety strokes of the heavy bamboo, and the situation must be rectified. Someone who already has a main wife and still gets another one is also to be punished with ninety strokes, and they must separate."   MD

On Treating the Main Wife

[From *Sejong sillok* 30:20a–b]

[In 1425] the Office of the Inspector-General demands the punishment of Yi Chungwi, who maltreated his wife.

The king says: "If we leave such a case untreated, there will be no warning for the future, and this will certainly lead people to throw off all restraint. Each of you should state how he would settle such a matter."

Inspector-General Ko Yakhae [1377–1443] says: "If there is a ranking order of main wife and concubine, the domestic way is straight. If it gets lost, the domestic way is in disorder. If somebody treats his concubine preferentially and does not look after his main wife, he should be punished according to the law."

Minister of Personnel Hŏ Cho [1369–1439] says: "The woman manages the interior of the house; the man manages the exterior. If someone allows his concubine to become the mistress of his household and to dominate his house, not only does the social ranking break down but this also leads to discord among the brothers and estrangement among the slaves. How is it possible to manage a house under such circumstances? It is absolutely necessary to punish the crime of such fellows."

Royal Secretary Kwak Chonjung says: "If someone loves his concubine and estranges his main wife, his property is generally transferred entirely to the concubine's house, leaving the main wife poor and destitute and causing mutual resentment. It is proper to punish such a man severely."

The king agrees and orders to proceed according to the law, so that it is made known. *MD*

Ch'oe Hang: On Remedying the Wedding Rite

[From *T'aehŏjŏng munjip*, "Kiyŏng hoegi," 2.1:30a–37b]

During the Koryŏ dynasty, the customary form of marital residence was uxorilocal—that is, the husband moved into his wife's house. In the eyes of the Confucians this was an objectionable living arrangement because it upset the natural order of male preceding female. The early legislators therefore demanded the reform of the wedding ceremony, which, according to the *Family Rites*, came to a culmination when the bridegroom personally inducted the bride into his own house (*ch'inyŏng*). Tradition proved especially persistent, however, in the native wedding customs, and no Confucian-style wedding ceremony was performed in an upper-class house during the fifteenth century. In this document Ch'oe Hang (1409–1474) encourages a reluctant King Sejong to initiate corrective measures as part of his overall reform policies.

Your servant has respectfully read your policy plan that states that the wedding rite is not easy to change all of a sudden. From this your servant recognizes Your Majesty's sincerity [in trying] to reform this custom and to restore the old ways.

Your servant says: That heaven precedes earth is the principle of hard and soft. That the wife obeys her husband is the principle of yin and yang. Therefore the man makes taking the reins his talent and leads, and the woman makes obedience her task and follows behind. This is the constant principle of heaven and earth and the universal rule of former and present times. If, then, the wedding rite is not correct and the meaning of leading and following not clear, how will the three relationships be correct and the five social constants be in order?

How is it that the abuses of the former dynasty have not been checked and Koryŏ customs continue unchanged? The man enters the woman's house and thereby confuses the meaning of husband and wife. Yang obeys yin and thereby opposes the principle of heaven and earth. Is there not a deficiency in the codes of this well-ruled time?

If, over a long period of time, you enforce strict measures against the wrongs in the decadent women's quarters, people will themselves recognize the quality of the rite and will no longer dare conduct weddings in violation of the proper rites.   *MD*

Prohibition Against Remarriage of Women

[From *Sŏngjong sillok* 82:9b–20a]

Marriage was largely an affair between "two surnames," and, as far as the wife was concerned, it lasted beyond her husband's death. Confucian ideology stressed the woman's devotion to one husband, and this emphasis on the exclusive nature of the marital relationship provided Confucian legislators with the arguments they needed to prohibit the remarriage of women, a custom prevalent during Koryŏ. The lost version of the *State Code* of 1469 apparently barred the sons and grandsons of thrice-married women from advancing into the higher officialdom. The debate of 1477 makes it clear that the majority of the discussants, here represented by Kim Yŏngyu (1418–1494), were in favor of keeping the restriction to third and not extending it to second marriages. King Sŏngjong (1469–1494), who was especially concerned with improving upper-class mores, sided with the minority opinion, here represented by Im Wŏnjun (1423–1500). How sensitive the issue was is documented by the fact that the *State Code* of 1485 did not directly outlaw remarriage but provided that the sons and grandsons of remarried women would not be eligible for civil or military office and would be barred from taking the lower and higher civil service examinations. The ideological and legal implications thus, in fact, made remarriage for a woman impossible.   *MD*

[In 1477] the king orders the members of the highest officialdom to discuss the prohibition against the remarriage of women.

Inspector-General Kim Yŏngyu and others say:

"Now, according to the *State Code* [1469], thrice-married women are listed together with licentious women, and their sons and grandsons are barred from the examinations and cannot receive posts in the censorial and administrative offices. Twice-married women are not mentioned. Generally, statutes are based on fundamental law, and ritual decorum is connected with human feelings. For a woman of a poor and lowly house who on neither side has supportive relatives, it is difficult to keep her chastity when she becomes widowed in early years. If her parents or relatives decide that she should marry for a second time, that does not harm ritual decorum. We think that the law of the *State Code* according to which the sons and grandsons of thrice-married women do not receive high office should be strictly enforced."

Sixth State Councillor Im Wŏnjun and others argue: "A state without strict prohibitions will cause the sons and grandsons of those who lost their integrity to hold important office. Such a practice will then turn into a custom that nobody will consider strange. Under such circumstances there will be women who, even without a master of ceremonies, will obtain a husband on their own initiative. If this is not prohibited, where will it lead? From now on remarriage must be strictly prohibited."

Royal edict to the Ministry of Rites: "The *Record of Rites* says: 'Faithfulness is the virtue of a wife. Once married to her husband, she does not change it during her lifetime.'

From now on, in order to correct the customs, the sons and grandsons of twice-married women will no longer be listed as members of the upper class."

                                                                      MD

Ŏ Sukkwŏn: Critique of Discrimination Against Secondary Sons

[From *P'aegwan chapki* 2:88]

The distinction between main wife and concubine *(ch'ŏch'ŏp)*, instituted at the beginning of the dynasty, had grave consequences for the social status of the concubine's sons *(sŏŏl)*. As far as the main descent line was concerned, they were superfluous members, and, because their mothers usually belonged to the lower strata of society, they were socially despised as well. Historically, the origin of barring them from the examinations and the higher officialdom had been attributed to the personal initiative of Sŏ Sŏn (1367–1433), but it is clear that the structural constraints of strictly lineal considerations caused this social imbalance. Ŏ Sukkwŏn, himself a secondary son, lived under these restrictions in the first half of the sixteenth century.

MD

It is not an old law of our country that the descendants of secondary sons are not allowed to take the civil service examinations and enter the bureaucracy. Since the compilation of the *State Code* [1485], when the barring of secondary sons from office was added for the first time, one hundred years have not yet passed. Between heaven and earth and outside the nine divisions of China there are far more than a hundred territorially based countries, yet such a law has never been heard of. For the sole reason that secondary sons—even when they are the sons of high officials—do not have a proper maternal line, they are barred from office for generations. Even if they have outstanding talents and usable skills, in the end they bow their heads in frustration and die in the countryside. Is it not regrettable that they are valued less than local clerks and sailors?

MD

PROPAGATION OF CONFUCIAN VALUES

The conduct of a ritually pure life was the privilege of the upper class, whose members possessed the necessary learning as well as the economic means to enact the intricate prescriptions of the ritual manuals. They were frequently admonished to set an example with their proper behavior, one that could be emulated by the lower social classes. In addition, books like the *Illustrated Conduct of the Three Bonds (Samgang haengsil to)* were distributed to inculcate in the minds of the uneducated the fundamental Confucian virtues of loyalty, filial piety, and chastity. For easy comprehension the Chinese text was augmented with a Korean rendering, enriched with pictures for each story. Because of its didactic value this book was printed in many versions throughout the dynasty and was undoubtedly instrumental in propagating basic Confucian values among the common people.   MD

Kwŏn Ch'ae: Preface to *Illustrated Conduct of the Three Bonds*

[From *Tong munsŏn* 93:19–21]

Among the five great principles of this world the Three Bonds stand at the very head; in fact the great law of arranging the moral imperatives is the principal source of all human transformation.

In the summer of the year *sinhae* of Hsüan-te [1431], our King Sejong said to his closest ministers: "The Three Dynasties all ruled by illuminating human relations. In later generations their teachings deteriorated, and the people were no longer friendly to each other. The great social relationships between ruler and subject, father and son, and husband and wife were no longer considered innate qualities, and they became steadily more tenuous. There were many, however, with outstanding behavior and great integrity who were not misled by customary practices, but caught the people's attention with their exemplary behavior. I wish to have the most prominent ones selected, their pictures drawn, and their stories compiled and distributed inside and outside the capital so that all the ignorant husbands and wives, by looking at them with sympathy, may be easily stimulated to proper behavior. This, then, will also be a method to transform the people and improve the customs." Thereupon he charged the first counselor of the Hall of Worthies, Sŏl Sun [d. 1435], with the compilation.   MD

Sŏ Kŏjŏng: Preface to the *Genealogy of the Andong Kwŏn*

[From *Andong Kwŏnssi sebo sŏ* 1a–2b]

With the emergence of the concept of patrilineal descent, it became important to be able to document the main as well as the collateral lines of kin that derived their origin from a common apical ancestor. Written genealogies (*chokpo*), while proliferating from the seventeenth century, had begun to be compiled as early as the fifteenth century. The genealogy of the Andong Kwŏn, dated 1476, is one of the first extant examples. Although often only putative, the origin of such prominent descent groups was frequently traced as far back as Silla times. Such written genealogies were, and still are, impressive evidence of lineage consciousness, and only someone with a certified lineage background could hope to maintain a position of prominence in the political, social, and economic life of the country. The preface to the Andong Kwŏn genealogy was written by Sŏ Kŏjŏng (1420–1488), a prominent official and literary figure. After giving a genealogical account ostensibly reaching back to the Silla period, Sŏ proceeds as follows:

I think that in ancient times there was a "clan law" according to which the clan members were arranged in the *chao-mu* order[2] and differentiated on the basis of branch lines so that even one hundred generations of descendants could be identified. After the clan law deteriorated, the genealogical records came into use. To make a genealogy it is necessary to trace the clan back to its very origins and record in detail its developments, to differentiate clearly the various branches, and to specify close and remote relatives. This is also adequate to express mutual respect and harmonious feelings among the clan members and to regulate the human principles.

In Korea, however, there was of old neither clan law nor genealogy; even big families and great descent groups did not have family records. Thus, after several generations the names of the ancestors in the four ascending generations were lost, and their descendants consequently became estranged from each other, looking at one another like strangers in the street. For this reason Kwŏn Che and Kwŏn Nam tirelessly compiled the genealogy, and I made an effort to bring their intention to completion.

Alas! Since antiquity the famous clans and prominent descendants have been quite numerous. Who of those in high office and brilliant positions were not looked up to and respected? Why, then, have they, after only a few generations, declined and disappeared? It is because the foundation of the earlier generations was not firm, and the descendants lost it by sudden arrogance and extravagance.

The Kwŏn have maintained their house over generations with honesty and have made loyalty and filiality their central concern. Could it be that the descendants are not mindful of the efforts with which their ancestors have built up their house? With this I would like to admonish again the descendants of the Kwŏn.   *MD*

Sin Sukchu: House Rules

[From *Pohanjae chip* 13:1a–4b]

Confucian society functioned through the proper observance of the rites (*ye*). Their practice started with the cultivation of the moral potential of the individual and extended to those with whom the individual interacted most closely: his family and relatives. House rules *(kahun)* were aimed at smoothing the relationships within a kin group and spreading a civilizing influence even into the domestic sphere of the house, the women's quarters. They constituted an idealized code of conduct based on the assumption that people have to be constantly encouraged to strive for moral perfection. If the principal members of the family were to observe the rules of proper conduct, it was reasoned, even the domestic slaves could be persuaded to lead moral lives. Prepared by Sin Sukchu (1417–1475) in 1468, "House Rules" preached moral integrity and economic austerity and linked the harmony in the domestic sphere directly to peace and stability in the public realm. These "House Rules," then, contained the essence of the moral capabilities of the Confucian society, which, if properly developed, were the mainstay of the Confucian state.   MD

Rule One: Make the Mind Discerning

Man's mind does not have constancy. If it is trained, it exists; if it is neglected, it vanishes. If the mind does not exist, one looks but does not see; one listens but does not hear. How much more is it like this in the discernment of right and wrong? The mind is the prime minister of the body. In the eye's relationship to color, it is the mind that sees. In the ear's relationship to sound, it is the mind that hears. All the members of the body depend on the mind for functioning. That is why it is the prime minister of the whole body. Therefore, if one wishes to straighten out the members of the body, one should straighten out the mind first.

Rule Two: Be Circumspect in Behavior

If the body is not trained, it is not possible to regulate the house. Why do I say this? If in serving my father I do not exert myself to be filial, my son will do to me as I have done to my father. If in serving my elder brother I am not respectful, my younger brother will do to me as I have done to my elder brother. Therefore, only if I make myself stand on faultless ground will everyone among father and son, elder brother and younger brother, husband and wife, be equally correct. This can be extended to the relationship between ruler and subject and between friends.

Rule Three: Be Studious

One who has narrow ears and eyes can never have a wide mind. For widening eyes and ears nothing is better than reading books. The ways of the sages and worthies are laid out in books. If, once the determination is firm, one progresses step by step and with great care, in the course of time one naturally gets results. The essential of learning lies in gathering up the dissipated mind. If the mind is concentrated, it is naturally brilliant and circumspect, and its understanding is more than sufficient. It is not possible to advance in scholarship without a settled mind. The essence of gathering up one's mind lies solely in seriousness.

For a human being, not to study is exactly like facing a wall. If what has been studied is not vigorously practiced, it is of no use to read even ten thousand volumes. Therefore, when reading the books of sages and worthies, one should search for their minds and incorporate them one by one in oneself.

Rule Four: On Managing a Household

Under present customs father and son and brothers rarely live under one roof. As they establish their own households, each keeps his own slaves, and gradually they become estranged from each other and are no longer on friendly terms. As father and elder brother, one should be patient and forbearing, generous and humane, and not petty and small. As son and younger brother, one should leave the unimportant and think of the important, advance sincerity and be mutually sympathetic, filial, and friendly.

The harm of extravagance is greater than a natural disaster. If a house declines, it is usually because of overspending. Therefore frugality is the first principle in managing a household. This does not mean one should be stingy and avaricious. If the needs of the house are met—the living fed and the dead sent off properly, the needy supported, and emergencies relieved—is this not enough of prosperity?

We and our relatives derive from the same source and split up into branches. Seen by our ancestors, we are all alike. If we are able to establish households thanks to the accumulated good and the extra blessings of our ancestors, we have to be mindful of aiding the poor and sympathizing with the orphans in order to counterbalance the blessings of our ancestors.

Rule Five: On Holding Office

As a high official, one cannot rule independently; one must rely on one's subordinates. The way to treat a subordinate is to extend sincerity in order to employ him. In case of doubt, don't employ him. If employed, don't doubt him. If a man knows that he is doubted, he certainly does not dare to do his best. A high official thus should not have doubts about his subordinates. Once he has a doubtful mind, he cannot but be a bad administrator.

Rule Six: On Instructing Women

The wife is the mate of the master of the house and has the domestic management in her hands. The rise and fall of a house depends on her. Usually people know how to instruct their sons, but do not know how to instruct their daughters. This is misguided.

A wife is loyal and pure, self-controlled, flexible and obedient, and serving others. She minds the domestic realm exclusively and does not concern herself with public affairs.

Above, she serves her parents-in-law; if she is not sincere and respectful, she cannot fulfill her filial loyalty. Below, she treats the slave servants well; if she is not kind and benevolent, she is not able to win their hearts. Only if she is sincere and respectful in serving her superiors and kind and benevolent in treating her subordinates is there complete affection between husband and wife.

Generally, she should also be accomplished in female tasks. If she herself is not diligent, she lacks the capacity to lead her subordinates.   MD

C H A P T E R S E V E N T E E N

Economy

Like most preindustrial societies, the Chosŏn dynasty was predominantly an agrarian state, and land was its main source of wealth and revenue. Thus, the primary emphasis of the state economy was on agriculture. After the drastic land reform of 1390, based on the principle of an equitable redistribution, a great deal of effort was put into increasing the land's productivity. Advanced agrarian methods were introduced from China, and various experiments were conducted, leading to the publication of several manuals of farming. With the use of improved seeds, fertilizer, and irrigation, there was a significant increase in food production in early Chosŏn.

While the Neo-Confucian state of Chosŏn regarded agriculture as the root of all wealth, it treated commerce as an unproductive branch that existed at the expense of farming. Initially, commerce was limited strictly to licensed merchants; but the need to exchange goods for daily life gave rise to periodic markets in rural areas. The government's attempts to circulate paper currency early in the Chosŏn period were not successful, as people continued to use cloth as a medium of exchange. (The use of coins was not accepted widely until after the seventeenth century.) Believing the resources of wealth to be limited, Chosŏn society placed a great deal of emphasis on frugality in expenditure by both the state and individuals.

THE LAND SYSTEM

An equitable distribution of land to all tillers was the ideal of good government in traditional Korea. The disintegration of the land system in the latter period of the Koryŏ dynasty (918–1392) was a main contributing factor to its demise. As the state control over land weakened, the land system in late Koryŏ became chaotic. Ownership of land became concentrated in the hands of powerful families and Buddhist temples and monasteries. This concentration forced more and more people to leave the land, and they were thus reduceded to desperate straits. It was in this situation in 1390 that General Yi Sŏnggye, after dramatically burning all the existing land registration records, carried out a drastic land reform. A member of Yi Sŏnggye's brain trust in founding the new Chosŏn dynasty, Chŏng Tojŏn was one of the masterminds of the 1390 land reform. In the essay translated here, Chŏng Tojŏn depicts the chaotic land system of late Koryŏ (at least partly to justify the reform he helped institute) and offers some basic ideas shaping the new land system, which the Chosŏn dynasty continued to maintain. YC

Chŏng Tojŏn: On Land

[From *Sambong chip* 13:14b–16a]

In ancient times, all the land belonged to the state, and the state then granted land to the people; thus, all the land that the people cultivated had been given them by the state. There was no one who did not receive land, and there was no one who did not cultivate land. Therefore, there was no excessive differentiation between the rich and the poor and between the strong and the weak. Because all the produce from the land went to the state, the state was prosperous. But as the land system began to disintegrate, powerful individuals acquired more and more land. While the land of the rich extended far and wide, the poor had no land even to stand on. The poor thus were forced to lease land from the rich to till. Even though they worked hard and diligently all year round, they still did not have enough to eat. The rich, however, did not cultivate their land and remained idle. Instead, they hired men to work their land and collected more than half of the yield.

His Majesty King T'aejo had personally witnessed the evil effects of this chaotic land situation while he was still a private person and was determined, as one of his future missions, to abolish the private land system. He believed that all the land in the country should revert to the state and should then be given to the people on the basis of a careful account, in order to revive the rectified land system of ancient times. But the old families and the powerful lineage groups, realizing that His Majesty's plan would work against their interests, slandered and obstructed the plan with all the power at their command. His Majesty, however, together with two or three like-minded ministers, investigated the laws of the former dynasties, deliberated about what would be good for the present situation, and surveyed and measured all the land in the country in terms of *kyŏl*.[1] [His Majesty then instituted the land reform in the year 1390.] He established court land, military provision land for state use, and office land for civil and military officials. In addition, off-duty military men residing in the capital as guards for the royal court, widows remaining faithful to their deceased husbands, government workers in the local magistracies, postal station workers, and river ferry workers, as well as commoners and artisans performing public duties, have all been granted land. Although the distribution of land to the people may not have reached the standard set by the ancient sages, the new land law has restored equity and balance. Compared to the evil system of the former dynasty, the new land reform has brought infinite improvement.   YC

PROMOTION OF AGRICULTURE

Fifteenth-century Korea witnessed a dramatic increase in food production as a result of technological advances in agriculture. First, the fallow system, whereby certain portions of land are periodically kept uncultivated, was gradually replaced by a new system of continuous cultivation. This more intensive use of land was made possible largely by the introduction of improved organic fertilizers developed in post-Sung southern China. The second change involved shifting from dry farming to wet farming in rice cultivation. Wet farming at this time involved direct seeding of rice in wet land. The transplantation system that is currently used in Korea was gradually adopted in the three southern provinces during the fifteenth and sixteenth centuries. For this kind of wet farming, it is essential to secure sufficient water. Largely to meet the demands of these changes, King Sejong ordered the compilation of a farm manual, *Straight Talk on Farming (Nongsa chiksŏl)*, which was printed for wide distribution in 1429. Designed to increase productivity, the manual emphasizes four points: the appropriate timing of sowing, the effective use of fertilizers, the need for weeding, and the autumn plowing. As stated in the preface to the manual, the information contained in the book was obtained from actual experimentation carried out by veteran farmers in various regions as well as from various manuals published in Korea and China. The manual provided the practical information and ideas that were suitable to local climate and soil conditions. The preface, translated here, describes the nature of the book and its objectives.

In addition to his brilliant achievements in language, literature, science, and technology, King Sejong vigorously promoted agriculture throughout his thirty-two-year reign. In 1444, the king issued the Edict for the Promotion of Agriculture. As the direct responsibility for overseeing the farmers was in the hands of magistrates, the edict was addressed largely to these officials, outlining what the king expected of them in their dealings with farmers. Noteworthy is King Sejong's strong belief that the effects of natural disaster, such as those caused by drought, could be averted by human effort.

As the eldest son of King Sejong, King Munjong had received a good education and training for Confucian rulership before he succeeded his father in 1450. He remained on the throne for only a little over two years, however, as he died in 1452 at the age of thirty-eight. As the fifth monarch of the Chosŏn dynasty, Munjong continued the brilliant achievements of his father. The progress in agriculture during the fifteenth century necessitated a greater and more efficient use of water. Since the ancient period, reservoirs had been constructed at higher elevations by damming water from mountains and hills, thus allowing a controlled flow of water to farmland below. These reservoirs alone, however, were not sufficient to meet the increasing demands of fifteenth-century agriculture. Thus, there were a number of attempts to devise new methods of irrigation. Both Kings T'aejong and Sejong attempted a wider use of water mills, for example, borrowing ideas from China and Japan, but water mills proved ill suited to Korea's terrain and soil conditions. A new method, however, was more successful and eventually became widely used throughout the country. This method involved drawing water from a river by constructing embankments. For land at higher elevations, the embankment was made at an upper river flow; for lower land, the embankment was constructed along the river to divert small channels of the flow. This irrigation method later came to be called *po*. Although the southern provinces had developed an efficient system of irrigation, the northwestern regions lagged behind. So when a drought struck the two northwestern provinces of Hwanghae and P'yŏngan in 1451, King Munjong issued the edict translated here, emphasizing that human effort can avert natural disasters.   YC

Chŏng Ch'o: Preface to *Straight Talk on Farming*

[From *Sejong sillok* 44:16b]

His Majesty ordered Commissioner Chŏng Ch'o [d. 1434] and other officials to compile *Straight Talk on Farming*. Its preface reads as follows:

Farmers are the roots of all the nations in the world. Since ancient times, all sage-kings have emphasized the importance of farming. When Emperor Shun organized nine officials and twelve magistrates, he placed the greatest importance on the appropriate timing essential for food production. Without farming, it is truly impossible to provide for sacrificial rites and the resources needed to nourish life. Our own King T'aejong at one time ordered the Confucian ministers to select the most useful parts of the old agrarian manuals and to add commentaries in the vernacular script. He then had these printed and distributed widely so that the people would work diligently for agriculture. Continuing the illustrious work of King T'aejong, His Majesty King Sejong has shown particular concern for the people's welfare.

Because climate and soil in different regions are not the same, each area should have its own way of sowing and cultivating, as is appropriate to the region, and they cannot all conform to the old manuals. His Majesty therefore ordered the governors of all the provinces to seek out and interview experienced farmers in various prefectures and counties and to collect information on farming that is based on experiments actually conducted in the region, and [had it] compiled in one book. We then named it *Straight Talk on Farming*.

It is hoped that this book will guide the people to an enriched life so that every household will be well provided for and every individual well supplied.   *YC*

King Sejong: Edict for the Promotion of Agriculture

[From *Sejong sillok* 105:25a–26b]

The people are the root of the state, and food is an indispensable necessity of the people. Because all food and clothing are produced by the farmers, our government must give them foremost priority. When King T'aejo, responding to the call of destiny, inaugurated our dynasty, he first rectified the land system to relieve the people of misery and allow them to enjoy the benefits of agriculture. The ways by which he tried to promote agriculture have been incorporated into laws. King T'aejong, continuing the task, redoubled the efforts to promote agriculture. Apprehensive that the people might not be well informed about the proper ways of sowing and reaping, King T'aejong ordered his officials to translate the books on farming into the vernacular script and to publish and transmit them widely.

I sincerely wish to continue the works of our forefathers. I believe that agricultural matters should be entrusted to those officials who are in intimate contact with the people.

As I examined the sagacious magistrates of the past, I found they were able to achieve good works and bring benefit to the people only through diligence and hard work. In general, men need to be aroused to work hard; when not aroused, they tend to be indolent.

In general, farm families who start early also harvest early, and those who put in more effort reap more. Therefore, the key to agrarian administration lies in not missing the appropriate time and in not depriving the people of their energies. As a man has only one body, his energy cannot be divided; if the government takes people's labor away, how can we exhort them to work hard on the land? Our recent experiment in the year *chŏngsa* [1437], conducted on land behind the palace, has shown that we can avert disaster from drought by means of the maximum use of manpower, as the land produced an abundant crop in spite of bad weather. This experiment has proved clearly that natural misfortune can be overcome by human effort.

In some cases magistrates, ignorant of the appropriate time for plowing and sowing, are concerned only with the duties of exhorting and leading the farmers to plant seeds prematurely, which results in the death of the seeds, thus bringing the farmers to ruin. In other cases magistrates, truly not knowing the proper season, become careless in their calculations, thus losing the opportunity for sowing.

All the officials in my government should embody my entrusted wishes in their duties. They should observe faithfully the ancestral laws for enriching the well-being of the people, should emulate the rules practiced by the former sage officials for promoting agriculture, should investigate widely what may be good for the climate and soil of the region, and should consult the agrarian manual to prepare in advance so as not to be either too early for sowing or too late. Moreover, no one should impose corvée duties upon the farmers that will deprive them of their time. Instead, everyone should devote his mind and effort to guiding the people into attending to agriculture. YC

King Munjong: Edict on Irrigation Works

[From *Munjong sillok* 10:24b–26a]

His Majesty personally composed the following edict for the governors of Hwanghae and P'yŏngan provinces. It reads:

I hear that various means of irrigation are used widely in China and that much of their success is due mainly to the use of water mills. I also hear that the state of Japan takes advantage of irrigation to the extent that a small-scale flood or drought rarely causes farmers to lose their crops, and hence the people have a constant and sufficient supply of food. Our country too has, from ancient times, constructed river dikes to contain water, but still there are places where the advantages of water control are not available.

As I considered the intent of the former kings in the construction of water mills, and as I contemplated day and night the ways to save those people in the northern provinces who have been the victims of this year's misfortune, I came to the conclusion that nothing is more urgent than the work on river embankments and other irrigation. Some may insist that no advantages will come from the construction of new irrigation works. I, however, disagree with this thinking. If we accept the notion that all that can be done has been done by men in the past and that hence there is no room for new considerations, how can there be cotton in our country, which was introduced not long ago, and how can we have the benefit of refined gunpowder, which was not developed until the year *ŭlch'uk* [1445]? There have been many other similar developments in recent years. If we had followed these people, we would not be enjoying the benefit of these things.

When I consulted with the ministers, they all said there is no need to send officials [to oversee agricultural improvements]; instead, they counseled that I should issue a royal edict to the governors of these provinces urging them to promote the reclamation of wetland. You, governors, knowing this situation, should make the villagers understand my intention and guide them in realizing the advantages of wet land. Then there will be some who recognize the advantages and will in turn lead other people so that they too may respond favorably. After meeting and discussing this with the people, you should reclaim as much wet land as possible, either by means of spring water or by constructing river embankments. After carefully investigating whether or not the works are feasible and whether or not the people favor them, you should submit a report to me.

YC

WEALTH AND COMMERCE

The Chosŏn dynasty government in general followed the traditional notion of discouraging commerce. Believing agriculture to be the sole creator of wealth, the Chosŏn Confucianists treated commerce as a nonproductive occupation and regarded merchants as a parasitic element living at the expense of the farmers. Two expressions of these views are translated here.

The first is by Yi I (1535–1584), who, in addition to being known as one of the Chosŏn dynasty's two greatest philosophers of Neo-Confucianism, was a highly respected statesman and enjoyed a distinguished career as a government official. Among his many works on government and individual ethics, *Essentials of the Sages' Learning (Sŏnghak chibyo)* was one of the most popular, read widely by scholars and officials. Written for the king in 1575 as a guide for sagely rule, *Essentials of the Sages' Learning* offers Yi's views on how a ruler should conduct himself and administer the government. In it Yi quotes from former sages as well as adding his own comments and ideas. In the seventh chapter, dealing with economy, parts of which are translated here, Yi emphasizes the importance of economizing in order to protect the country's wealth and promote the well-being of the people. The second passage is part of a memorial submitted by Censor-General Yu Paeksun in 1410.

Yi I: On Economy

[From *Yulgok chŏnsŏ 23:49b–51a*]

Economy in my humble opinion means showing respect for virtue, whereas extravagance is a great evil. If one is economical, one's heart is never dissolute, and one's mind is at ease with anything that may occur. If one is extravagant, one's mind will always seek external things and will never be satisfied, not even for one day. Although the success or failure of one family will affect only a small number of people, a [dynastic] state involves all aspects of the accumulated achievements of the ancestors, in a magnitude that cannot be compared with one family's fortune. There is nothing in the state's treasury that is not produced by the toil and sweat of the people. How dare one carelessly indulge himself in extravagance and dissipate this precious wealth, cause distress among the people, and bring ruin to the achievements of our forefathers?

The former kings of this country ruled the state by means of economy for many generations, and their expenditures were always based on revenues; therefore, the country was affluent and the storehouses were full of surplus. But since the time of Yŏnsangun [1494–1506], the expenditures in the palace have increased extravagantly, and the practices of former rulers have been disregarded. Since then, the court has followed undesirable customs and has so far failed to reform itself. Therefore, the state's expenditures have increased daily. There are at present no unusual luxurious customs being practiced in the palace and no unessential public work projects being carried out within the country; yet the annual revenues cannot support the annual expenditures and the savings accrued under many former kings will be exhausted in the future. If a famine strikes or a war breaks out, we will be utterly helpless. Is this not truly deplorable?

If there is no reform from above, the state will lose its reason for existence. The way to correct this cannot be found in the ordinary rules. Instead, the reform must come from above, with the heart of Emperor Yao, who lived in a house thatched with reeds and used earthen steps. The queen and the court ladies must emulate the Empress Ma of Later Han, who always dressed herself in costumes made of coarse cloth, and must economize by reducing the palace expenditures. If the economizing starts in the palace and the families of scholar-officials become impressed by these practices and accept them, economizing will then spread to the people. Only then can we expect the old detrimental practices to be reformed, the precious wealth to be saved, and people's wealth to grow.   YC

Yu Paeksun: On Commerce

[From *T'aejong sillok* 20:24a–b]

It has been said that farming is the root of government. It has also been said that when too many people pursue the petty occupation of commerce, farming is at the mercy of the marketplace. With sweat and strain, farmers' work is hard and arduous; the more land they cultivate, the greater their hardship. Merchants, on the other hand, merely exchange cheap goods for precious items, thereby gaining twofold profit. Instead of toiling, merchants lead a life of ease and pleasure. It is no wonder therefore that the number of farmers diminishes and that of merchants increases daily. Since one farmer who works on the land feeds ten people, how can the state possibly become affluent and the people have sufficient food if this situation continues? It is requested that from now on all merchants should be required to register with the magistrate office in the capital or in the county where they reside and that, following the ancient practice of taxing idle people, they be required to carry a transit permit to be issued only after they pay two piculs [*sŏk*] of rice for each peddling trip. Anyone who engages in commerce without proper authorization should be reported to the government, whereupon all the merchant's goods would be confiscated—half going to the government and the other half to the person reporting the unauthorized merchant. In this way, we can realize the goal of promoting agriculture and discouraging commerce.   YC

CIRCULATION OF CURRENCY

As the use of currency as a medium of exchange has obvious advantages over other media, in 1401 King T'aejong enacted a law to promote the use of paper money. The people in general, however, were reluctant to use the government-issued paper currency, as they had long been accustomed to the use of five-ply cloth *(osŭngp'o)* as a medium of exchange. This practice created serious problems. At first, the government prohibited the use of *osŭngp'o* in an attempt to encourage the sole use of paper currency. When this measure failed, the government allowed the concurrent use of paper currency and *osŭngp'o*. When that did not work either, King Sejong minted copper coins for circulation in 1424. But the copper coin was not accepted by the public either. Thereafter, for about one hundred years, until the early sixteenth century, the Chosŏn government tried to circulate paper currency without success. Cloth and grain were the more popular media of exchange until the early seventeenth century, when a further growth in commerce gave rise to the general acceptance of metallic coins. The following passages from the *Veritable Records* suggest the motivation for pushing for the circulation of paper and metallic currency and the problems it created.

Efforts to Introduce and Encourage the Use of Paper Currency and Metal Coins

[From *T'aejong sillok* 2:15b–16a; 4:14a–b; *Sejong sillok* 21:17a–b; 31:19b–20a]]

Twenty-first day of the tenth month [in 1401]. The Office of the Inspector-General submitted a memorial requesting abolition of the Office of Currency Management. His Majesty disapproved it. The memorial in summary reads as follows: "Our country has not used paper currency before. People are accustomed to using cloth money and do not like to use paper currency. It is requested that we stop making paper currency and dismiss the officials in the Office of Currency Management."

His Majesty T'aejong summoned Inspector-General Yi Chi [d. 1414] and Third Inspector Pak Ko and stated: "I am always pleased to receive advice that is meant to benefit the people, such as you have submitted. It is, however, my intention to promote the use of paper currency because it is convenient to use."

Pak Ko replied: "How can I, your subject, dare offer opinions that may go against the interest of the people? What the people value are rice and cloth only. In order to promote the use of paper currency, Your Majesty prohibited the use of *osŭngp'o* and has also replaced all the tribute cloth from Kyŏngsang and Chŏlla provinces with rice. These measures have caused incalculable damage to the people. I do not know of any way to produce wealth by means of using paper currency. How can the state possibly have sufficient wealth to spend?" The king stated: "What you are saying is reasonable. Even so, if we continue to use paper currency for a long time, it will be widely accepted in the end."

Twenty-fourth day of the tenth month [in 1402]. The Office of the Inspector-General and Office of the Censor-General offered a joint memorial as follows: "Since ancient times, the rulers have enacted laws and created institutions [that were] based always upon the needs of the people. Emulating the Chinese system, our country printed paper currency in order to make it a valuable item for both public and private use. It is thought that the paper currency will not only bring unlimited advantages to the state but also be convenient to carry and store. When this law was first enacted, all the court officials believed it to be a good law that would enrich the nation and the people.

"But as our people's customs and products are different from those in China, they have no trust in the paper money and regard it as useless. As their worry and doubt increase daily, the price of commodities has been rising with no end in sight. The more strictly the government enforces the currency law, the cheaper the value of the paper currency becomes. At present, the use of paper currency is causing deep resentment as it brings the people no benefit. That it is rejected by the people is manifestly clear. Although the use of paper currency was regarded as a good law in the beginning, it has created serious problems in its implementation. How can we hesitate to revise it? It is humbly requested that Your Majesty look into the heart of the people and order the concerned officials to revise this law."

The king instructed the State Council to discuss this memorial. In the meeting of the Three Offices, the officials were divided on the use of paper currency, but the majority at the same time favored restoration of the use of cloth money.

Sixteenth day of the ninth month [in 1423]. There was a discussion whether or not metallic currency should be minted. When the paper currency was first introduced, one sheet of paper money could buy one peck of rice, and thirty sheets were worth one bolt of cotton cloth. But the value of paper currency has now been greatly diminished, and one sheet of paper money can buy only one-tenth of a peck of rice, and more than a hundred sheets are needed to buy a bolt of cotton cloth. Thus, a joint conference of the State Council and the Six Ministries was held to discuss the question of minting metallic currency to be circulated along with the paper. The Ministry of Taxation then offered a memorial: "Copper coins have been used historically in China. It is requested that in minting coins the weight of ten coins should be made equal to one *yang*, following the standard used by K'ai-yüan coins of T'ang, that each coin should carry an engraving of 'Currency of Korea,' that the Office of Currency Management should handle all matters related to coinage, and that any private individual who mints unauthorized coins should be punished in accordance with the law." His Majesty approved the proposal.

Twenty-sixth day of the second month [in 1426]. Director Pyŏn Kyeryang stated the following before His Majesty: "As a new law of metallic currency has now been formulated, its main purpose is to facilitate the benefit of the people. And yet it contains certain provisions that are excessively hard to implement, and these should be seriously considered. People must not go without food even for a day; yet famines in recent years have made it doubly difficult to obtain food. And now the new law requires all trade to be transacted with metallic currency. The people, however, are accustomed to the old practices and are not willing to use coins. In buying and selling, they do not wish to be paid in coins; they would rather use what they possess to exchange goods in private. Thus, there will be a number of people who will violate the law. A family may consist of one or two, or three or four, or even five to seven members. Yet, if one of them should violate the law, it calls for confiscation of the entire family's property, thus forcing the whole family to starve. This provision is not appropriate. It is humbly requested that the people be allowed to trade either in coins or in goods as they please, so that they can maintain their existence, and that only the payment for redemptions and for government purchases be made in copper currency."

His Majesty replied: "I can see good intentions in your statement. But formulating a new law is meant to demonstrate the government's trust in the people, and how can we amend a law according to people's likes and dislikes? If the metallic currency law is applied only to the government and is not enforced among the people, this is not the way to demonstrate trust in the people. As for the law on metallic currency, we must either do away with it or enforce it. If we are to enforce it, we should not try to amend the law each time there is a dispute.   *YC*

TRADING IN SILVER

Early Chosŏn Korea discouraged the use of gold and silver—partly because of Confucian frugality and partly to avoid Chinese demand for the precious metals. In the year 1542, however, the thirty-seventh year of King Chungjong, the official Japanese envoy brought eighty thousand *yang* (taels) of silver and asked to trade, causing a lengthy controversy at court. At issue was how to reconcile the Confucian purists' insistence that the precious metal had no practical use in daily life with the need to maintain friendly relations with the Japanese. In the end a compromise was reached: a portion of the Japanese silver could be traded.

Question of Allowing Silver in Trade with the Japanese

[From *Chungjong sillok* 98:15a–b; 98:4a]

Twenty-fourth day of the fourth month [in 1542]. The Office of Censor-General offered the following memorial: "In the name of the communication mission, the Japanese envoy brought silver amounting to eighty-thousand *yang* and asked us to trade for it. Although silver is a precious item, people cannot eat or dress with it, and in reality it is of no use. In our country, cotton cloth is widely used and all the people depend on it for their living. To exchange what people depend upon for an item of no practical use will give the Japanese an advantage at our expense. This is extremely undesirable. There is no precedent for the Japanese envoy's bringing silver to our country. If we allow this trade now, they will gain an easy profit and will in future bring twice the present amount. Once this silver trade is open, it will be difficult to comply with the limitless wishes of the Japanese."

Yi Ŏnjŏk [1491–1553] then made the following proposal: "A king should not value things that are brought from afar; he should value only virtue. The rare treasures of gold and silver are not urgently needed for the people's life or for their food or clothing. In principle, they ought to be rejected and should never be accepted. The price of silver in our country is extremely cheap. They will offer the silver to us as a precious item; if we buy it as a cheap item, they will surely be disappointed and might even be angry. Since the silver has already been brought into the capital, we should not reject all of it. Instead, we should allow them to trade only twenty or thirty thousand *yang* at a very high price as a way of mollifying their desire; the remainder of the silver should be turned down with appropriate excuses. This idea seems to be a good way of handling it." The king agreed to accept Yi Ŏnjŏk's suggestion.   YC

DEVELOPMENT OF RURAL MARKETS

Commercial activities under the Chosŏn dynasty were carried out largely by licensed merchants under government supervision. Toward the end of the fifteenth century, however, a new phenomenon began to develop that was eventually to have a far-reaching effect upon the economy and society. This was the rise of *changmun* markets (later *sijang*) at various population centers in all the provinces. Apparently originating in the southwestern province of Chŏlla as a meeting place to exchange goods in times of famine or other economic distress, *changmun* gradually became a popular site for private commercial activities. Fearful that commerce would drain people from farming, the Chosŏn government attempted to suppress the growth of these markets. The government effort, however, was in vain. Once the people began to realize their convenience and usefulness, they flocked to the markets, which were established in virtually every town throughout the country and held regularly at certain periodic intervals, such as every five days. These periodic markets became important centers not only for economic but also for social activities in the rural areas, even down to the present day. The following translations, selected from the *Veritable Records*, offer a picture of the debates within the government on the growth of the markets during their formative years.

Rural Markets

[From *Sŏngjong sillok* 20:16a; 27:4a–b]

Twenty-seventh day of the seventh month [in 1472]. The Minister of Taxation offered the following memorial: "In response to reports that many profit-seeking people gather together at what are now called *changmun* in Muan and other counties of Chŏlla province, such gatherings causing a number of problems for the people, Your Majesty asked the concerned officials to discuss this matter and make a recommendation as to whether these markets should be done away with or allowed to continue. When this minister communicated with the governor of Chŏlla province, Kim Chigyŏng [1419–1485], on this issue, he reported that a large number of people assemble on roadsides in many different counties to open a marketplace twice every month, and that although people trade at the marketplace to obtain what they do not have for what they have, they are abandoning the root of agriculture to seek the branch of commerce. This is causing the price of commodities to rise, thus inflicting a great deal of damage. The governor also reported that he has already instructed all the county magistrates to prohibit markets. It is therefore recommended that Your Majesty issue a further order to the governor to strictly forbid holding markets." His Majesty approved.

Eleventh day of the second month [in 1473]. Sin Sukchu [1417–1475], former chief state councillor, offered his views on currency and markets: "There is only one way to promote a wider use of currency, and that is to open markets and shops in various provinces where people can trade goods with each other. When they trade, they will consider the distances they have to travel and the value of various goods before the transactions. For these transactions, currency will become a necessity, and for the circulation of currency, shops and markets are necessary. In establishing shops and markets, we will not be successful if we do not follow the people's wish.

"In the year *kyŏngin* [1470], when there was a famine, a large number of people gathered in Chŏlla province to open shops and markets, and they called these *changmun*. The people managed to survive the famine only because of these markets. This was truly a good opportunity to develop markets in the countryside. But when the minister of taxation sought opinions of the county magistrates on this matter, all the magistrates, without considering the possible beneficial or harmful effects, wanted to prohibit markets simply on the ground that they had never existed in the past. This is a deplorable attitude of blindly following the old practices."

[From *Myŏngjong sillok* 6:28a]

Twenty-seventh day of the ninth month [in 1547]. Yi Hwang, expositor in the Office of Special Advisers, stated at the morning lecture session before His Majesty: "Markets at various localities are causing many people to seek commerce, and the number of robbers and thieves has also increased. For these reasons, the government had prohibited the markets. But as we are severely afflicted by a bad famine at present, the people have to rely upon markets to trade goods in order to support themselves. If we prohibit markets, how can the people sustain their lives? When there were famines before, no prohibition against markets existed and the people were allowed to help one another to obtain relief. For this years's famine, however, there is a total prohibition against markets, and as a result the people are suffering greatly. I recommend that we do not prohibit markets.   YC

CHAPTER EIGHTEEN

Thought

Neo-Confucianism is the name given by Western scholars to a Confucian revival movement that began about A.D. 1000 in China. After centuries of Buddhist and Taoist predominance, a new Confucian movement creatively synthesized traditional Confucian social and moral concerns with a new metaphysics and spirituality that rivaled the sophistication of the Buddhists and Taoists. Neo-Confucianism subsequently became the predominant intellectual and spiritual tradition throughout East Asia. The first and "orthodox" school of Neo-Confucian thought was that of the great synthesizer Chu Hsi (1130–1200); the second major school was that of Wang Yang-ming (1472–1529), which at times overshadowed Chu Hsi's school in China and Japan. One of the distinctive characteristics of Korea was its consistent and almost exclusive development of the Chu Hsi tradition.

Introduced to the Korean peninsula toward the end of the Koryŏ dynasty, Neo-Confucianism played a central role in the political, intellectual, and spiritual life of the subsequent Chosŏn dynasty. The selections that follow are taken from the works of outstanding Neo-Confucians of the first half of the Chosŏn dynasty. We begin with selections that illustrate the broad outlines of the Neo-Confucian worldview, then consider the practical spiritual concerns inherent in the philosophy.

Kwŏn Kŭn (1352–1409)

Kwŏn Kŭn's *Diagrammatic Treatises for the Commencement of Learning (Iphak tosŏl)* is the earliest extant Korean exposition of Neo-Confucian thought. When it was written in 1390, the Neo-Confucian movement had been gradually gaining strength on the Korean peninsula for over seven decades. Indeed, in just two years the Koryŏ dynasty would be replaced by the Chosŏn dynasty, the only East Asian regime officially founded under Neo-Confucian auspices. The section selected from the *Diagrammatic Treatises* reflects the appropriation of the new learning at this early stage.

Diagrammatic Treatises: Explanation of the First Diagram

[From *Iphak tosŏl* 1:1b–2a]

This first selection is from the text that accompanies the first and most important of Kwŏn's diagrams, entitled "Heaven and Man, Mind and Nature, Are Conjoined as One." The diagram and text are intended as a synthetic presentation of the content of two of the most important works by early Chinese Neo-Confucians, Chou Tun-i's *Diagram of the Supreme Ultimate*, and Chu Hsi's *Commentary on the Great Learning*. The former is the cornerstone of Neo-Confucian metaphysics; the latter presents the essential path of learning or self-cultivation in terms of a metaphysically based structure of the inner life. The scope of this ambitious synthesis illustrates the broad and accurate grasp of this complex system even at this very early date. Its concern with the system of the inner life of the mind and nature foreshadows what was to become the hallmark of Korean Neo-Confucian thought in later centuries.

In the diagram I have respectfully followed the explanations found in Master Chou Tun-i's *Diagram of the Supreme Ultimate* and Master Chu Hsi's *Commentary on the Great Learning* regarding man's mind-and-heart and his nature in order to clarify for students the distinction between principle and material force and between good and evil.

In the coming into being of humans and other creatures, this principle is the same, although their material force has the differences of being penetrating or blocked up, partial or integral. The recipient of integral and penetrating material force becomes a human being; the recipient of partial and blocked-up material force becomes a lesser creature. If we look at this diagram, the circle labeled

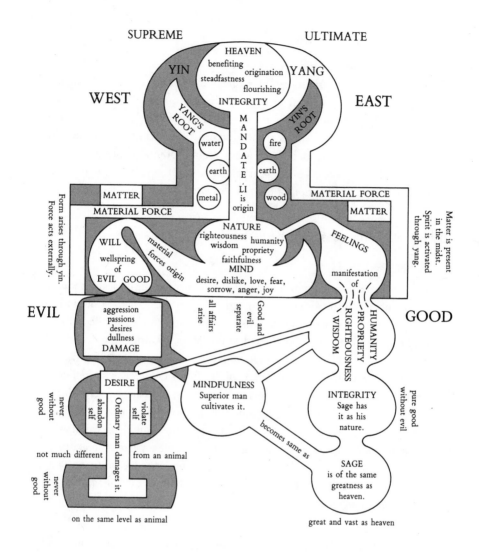

SUPREME   ULTIMATE

YIN   YANG

WEST   EAST

HEAVEN
benefiting
origination
steadfastness
flourishing
INTEGRITY

YANG'S ROOT   YIN'S ROOT

MANDATE LI is origin

water   fire

earth   earth

metal   wood

MATTER   MATERIAL FORCE

MATERIAL FORCE   MATTER

Form arises through yin.
Force acts externally.

Matter is present
in the midst.
Spirit is activated
through yang.

NATURE
righteousness humanity
wisdom propriety
faithfulness
MIND
desire, dislike, love, fear,
sorrow, anger, joy

WILL
wellspring
of
EVIL GOOD

material
forces origin

FEELINGS

manifestation
of

EVIL   GOOD

aggression
passions
desires
dullness
DAMAGE

all affairs
arise

Good and
evil
separate

HUMANITY
PROPRIETY
RIGHTEOUSNESS
WISDOM

DESIRE

MINDFULNESS
Superior man
cultivates it.

INTEGRITY
Sage has
it as his
nature.

never
without
good

abandon
self

violate
self

Ordinary man damages it.

pure good
without evil

becomes same as

SAGE
is of the same
greatness as
heaven.

not much different from an animal

never
without
good

on the same level as animal   great and vast as heaven

"integrity" is the case of one who has received the most refined and penetrating material force and so is a sage; the circle labeled "mindfulness" is one who has received integral and penetrating material force and is an ordinary man; the circle labeled "desire" is one who receives partial and blocked-up material force and is like a subhuman creature; beneath it is the level of animals. Those who receive material force that is even more partial and blocked-up become grass and trees. In this respect a representation of the transformative production of the myriad creatures is likewise included here.

Indeed in the inexhaustible transformation and productive activity of heaven and earth, the past ones rest and the coming ones continue the process. Human beings and beasts, plants and trees, have myriad shapes and forms, each with its own correct nature and mandate, all flowing forth from the midst of the single Supreme Ultimate. And there is nothing in the world outside the compass of this nature; therefore the *Mean* says: "It is only he who is possessed of the most complete sincerity that can exist under heaven, who can give his nature its full development. Able to give its full development to his own nature, he can do the same to the nature of other men. Able to give their full development to the natures of creatures and things, he can assist the transforming and nourishing powers of heaven and earth."[1] Ah! This is indeed the ultimate!   MK

Sŏ Kyŏngdŏk (1489–1546)

During the first century of the Chosŏn dynasty, Neo-Confucianism developed in Korea along two distinct lines. One group was actively involved in government service; these worked mainly to transform the political and social institutions of Korea in the light of ideal Confucian models. The second group stayed in the countryside, avoiding the turmoil of the court and devoting themselves to study, self-cultivation, and teaching.

Sŏ Kyŏngdŏk, better known by his pen name, Hwadam, represented the second group. He endured poverty in order to live an undisturbed life of study and teaching. His thought bears the mark of the early period of wide-open investigation and speculation before Neo-Confucian thought had taken on an orthodox, public face in Korea. He is famous for elaborating a philosophy that is an emphatic monism of *ki*, or material force, in pronounced contrast to the dualism of *i* and *ki* characteristic of the school of Chu Hsi, the orthodoxy of both China and Korea. Sŏ Kyŏngdŏk took great pride in his independence and originality, but historians note a marked similarity between his ideas and those of the early Chinese Neo-Confucian Chang Tsai (1020–1077). Although only a slender volume of Sŏ's writing has survived, he is generally considered one of the three outstanding thinkers of the Chosŏn dynasty. The two brief pieces that follow illustrate the character of his ideas.

The Theory of the Great Void

[From *Hwadam chip* 2:14b–15a]

The Great Void is empty and yet not empty. The void is identical with material force. The void is inexhaustible and all-embracing; material force is likewise inexhaustible and all-embracing. If it is called the void, how can it be called material force? When the void is in repose, it is the substance of material force. Coagulation and disintegration are its functions. If one knows that the void is not really empty, one cannot call it nonbeing. Lao Tzu says: "Being is born from nonbeing."[2] He did not know that the void is identical with material force. It is also said: "The void can produce material force."[3] That is not so. If one says that the void produces material force, then there would exist no material force before it was produced, and the void would be something dead. If material force did not already exist, from what could it be produced? Material force has no beginning and no birth. Not having a beginning, how can it end? Not having birth, how can it become extinct? Lao Tzu speaks of nothingness, the Buddhists speak of annihilation. That is because they do not know the source of principle and material force. How could they know the Tao?

Discussion on Life and Death, Ghosts and Spirits

[From *Hwadam chip* 2:15a–16a]

The translucent uniformity and pure emptiness of material force originate at the beginning of the Great Void's moving and giving rise to yang, quiescing and giving rise to yin. When the gradual intensification of its coagulation has reached its saturation point, it becomes heaven and earth and us men. The disintegration of man is just the disintegration of his outward form and spiritual component; the translucent uniformity and pure emptiness of the coagulation actually never disintegrate, but dissolve into the translucent uniformity and pure emptiness of the Great Void and are identical with the one material force. As for the coagulation and disintegration of consciousness, it is only a matter of relative duration and speed. Even if the disintegration is very fast it is a matter of days or months, as in the case of the most insignificant entities.

But what does it mean to say one's material force in the end also does not disintegrate? Since material force in its translucent uniformity and pure emptiness never had a beginning, it never has an end. This is why principle and material force are utterly mysterious. If scholars could apply themselves and reach this point, they would for the first time fully perceive the incompletely transmitted subtle meaning of the thousand sages. Though the material force of a piece of incense or a candle seems to disintegrate before our eyes, its remaining material force in the end never disintegrates. How could one speak of complete annihilation?   MK

Yi Ŏnjŏk (1491–1553)

Neo-Confucian thought, however speculative it may sound, had as its essential rationale the grounding of a practical system of moral and spiritual self-cultivation. In the early Chosŏn dynasty, however, development was not necessarily even; before a common and "orthodox" consensus on the interpretation of basic concepts was formed, there was room for a misconstruing of certain ideas in a way that led in the direction of quietistic Buddhist forms of self-cultivation. Neo-Confucians spoke of the mind as having two basic conditions: that of being active and that of being quiescent. Self-cultivation addressed to the latter condition amounted to a kind of meditation practice often referred to as "quiet sitting." This condition, understood as the mind-and-heart being in serene union with the Supreme Ultimate or the Tao, the inner nature of all things, could easily be construed as superior to the active involvement of everyday life.

One must understand that the "Supreme Ultimate" or "Tao" in the Neo-Confucian context refers to the fundamental inner pattern that existed precisely as a guide to inform and direct *activity*. When the full import of the theoretical framework is grasped, it is clear that there is no place for meditative quiet to become an end in itself or to be given preference over active moral cultivation. A famous series of letters by Yi Ŏnjŏk to Cho Hanbo (Manggidang) attacked Cho's quietistic orientation and explained the orthodox meaning of "the Supreme Ultimate and Ultimateless." These letters mark the coming to maturity of Chosŏn Neo-Confucianism in these matters.

Third Letter to Manggidang

[From *Hoejae chip* 5:17b–19b]

Although your letter says you have not been mired in theories regarding trance for years, it seems that your old habituation in these matters has not yet been put off. Therefore your discussion is excessive regarding the most extreme and mysterious aspects of moral principle, but it is deficient when it comes to the essential practice of thoroughly embodying the Way in personal conduct. You present vast and empty themes that have nothing to do with practical down-to-earth lessons in what is proper. This I cannot bring myself to accept.

I have heard that Master Chu Hsi has said: "The Way is the principles or patterns we should follow in dealing with everyday affairs; these are all present in our mind-and-heart as the characteristics of our nature. There is no creature that does not have this pattern and no time when it is not so."[4] From ancient times to the present the discussion of the substance of the Way comes to this, and it cannot be more perfectly presented.

I would like to explicate this a bit further. The Way in its Great Origin proceeds from heaven and spreads to the Three Ultimates, Heaven, Earth, and Man. In all the universe there is nowhere one can go where there is no ongoing activity of this Way; there is not a creature that does not embody this Way. As for the form it takes in man, the greater elements are the primary relationships between ruler and subject, father and son, husband and wife, elder and younger; the lesser elements are the appropriate measure regarding activity and quiet, food and rest, coming forward to serve in office or retiring, rising and declining. This goes to the extent that each case of speaking or keeping silent, each frown or smile, has its own proper norm. One cannot part from it for the slightest moment or deviate from it by a hair's breadth. There is nothing that is not the wondrousness of this principle.

If one sees it as diversified in its varied functioning, it seems so complexly and minutely divided that one could hardly grasp its essential points; it has such myriad forms and types that it seems one could never make a unity. Nevertheless the original substance by which this is so is nothing but the undivided Heavenly Mandate, which constitutes our nature and is present in our mind-and-heart. When the feelings of joy and anger, sorrow and pleasure, have not yet been aroused, the perfect genuineness of our mind-and-heart is quiet and unmoved: this is what is described as the wonder of the non-finite, and the Great Foundation of the universe consists in this. Therefore one should always apply oneself to preserving and nurturing it so that the Great Foundation may be established and serve as the master of our interaction with others and the myriad changing developments of life. Then what issues from the aroused mind-and-heart will be perfectly measured, and one will have attained to being right whenever one acts.

Nevertheless at the moment of the subtle incipient activation of the mind-and-heart there is the conflict of heavenly principle and selfish human desire, and a hair's breadth of carelessness interrupting the process may result in an error of a thousand miles. At this point one must bring even greater mindfulness and caution to bear! In the terms Chang Nan-hsien [1133–1180] used to describe this, one must preserve one's inborn good nature in quiescence in order to nurture the foundation of activity; one must exercise discernment in activity so that it will manifest what was preserved in quiescence; only then will nothing escape.

If one deals with things in this way, there will not be the slightest interruption in the constant clarity of the mind-and-heart, and it will not be beclouded by selfish desire for things. Then the establishment of the Great Foundation will daily become more firm, and, furthermore, at the subtle incipience of interaction in response to things there will not be a bit of selfish desire mixed in. As a result, one's response will be a pure manifestation of moral principle. From one's individual mind-and-heart and one's own person to the handling of the countless affairs and things of the world, there will be nothing inappropriate, and in carrying out one's activities there will never be a transgression.   MK

YI HWANG (1501–1570) AND THE SAGE LEARNING

Yi Hwang, better known by his pen name T'oegye, was born of a modest *yangban* lineage and lived for most of his life near Andong. His father died when he was still an infant, but his mother eked out a meager living for seven sons and a daughter through agriculture and sericulture. With the help of an uncle, Yi Hwang received an education, and showed promise enough to enter the Royal Confucian Academy in Seoul in 1523. After passing the two lower-level exams for the civil service in 1527 and 1528 and the final examinations in 1534, he spent fifteen years in routine official service before, on his retirement in 1549, he could pursue his scholarly interests, attract many students, and win fame as the leading Korean proponent of Chu Hsi's teaching.

Among many important writings that would gain Yi Hwang not only a large following among generations of Koreans but the high respect of Confucian scholars in Tokugawa period Japan and warm tributes later from Chinese scholars in the twentieth century, are his *Essentials of Chu Hsi's Correspondence* and his *Comprehensive Record of Sung, Yüan, and Ming Neo-Confucianism*, both demonstrating his capacity for scholarly research and astute criticism, as well as his *Record of Self-Reflection*, manifesting his efforts at intense moral and spiritual self-cultivation.

Worthy of special note is Yi Hwang's involvement in the most celebrated controversy in Korean Neo-Confucian history, the Four-Seven Debate, which he carried on in correspondence with a younger colleague. In it Yi Hwang broke new ground in the metaphysically based psychological theory of the Ch'eng-Chu school, which set the Korean intellectual agenda for generations to come. Highly technical and philosophically sophisticated, it does not lend itself to summary treatment here. (Interested readers should consult *SKC* 1: 613–614.)

The Ten Diagrams is Yi Hwang's last great work, as well as his best known and most popular writing. Generations of students have appreciated the clarity and brevity with which it presents the essential framework of, and linkages among, Neo-Confucian metaphysics, psychological theory, moral conduct, and spiritual discipline.

In content it focuses on the central theme of Neo-Confucian teaching: Sage Learning as a theory of human nature and practice of self-cultivation. In form it carries on the tradition of lectures to the ruler (or heir apparent) by Ch'eng I, Chu Hsi, and Chen Te-hsiu, known as the "Learning of the Emperors and Kings" or "Classics Mat Lectures," which were adopted by the Chosŏn dynasty court. When Yi Hwang retired from this function in 1568, he left this concise summation of his teachings for King Sŏnjo.

Ten Diagrams on Sage Learning

The basic format is a diagram accompanied by a text from one or more of the Neo-Confucian masters with additional commentary by Yi Hwang. Here space considerations compel further abridgement of Yi Hwang's already concise exposition; only four of the actual diagrams, and only some of the text and commentary, are reproduced—yet enough, we hope, to make each of the ten topics comprehensible. For a full exposition, see Bibliography under Kalton, *Ten Diagrams*.

Section 1: Diagram of the Supreme Ultimate

This chapter presents Chou Tun-i's *Diagram of the Supreme Ultimate* and his *Explanation of the Diagram of the Supreme Ultimate*. These works, as interpreted by Chi Hsi, became the cornerstone of Neo-Confucian metaphysical thought; here we find the essential framework for under-standing both man's place in the universe and the process by which he achieves his ultimate perfection and fulfillment—matters which are taken up at length in the remainder of this work. Two of the most important Chinese compilations of Neo-Confucian thought, the *Chin ssu lu* and the *Hsing-li ta ch'üan* begin with the same work. Yi Hwang abridges Chu Hsi's analysis of the graphics of the *Diagram of the Supreme Ultimate* and incorporates it as a gloss into the diagram itself.

1. Diagram of the Supreme Ultimate

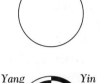

◯ This represents the Supreme Ultimate and the Indeterminate. That is [it gives rise to] yin and yang, but this indicates that in its fundamental substance there is no admixture of yin and yang

◎ This represents how ◯ moves and produces yang, quiesces and produces yin. The ◯ in the center represents their fundamental substance. ☽ is the root of ☾ ; ☾ is the root of ☽ .

This represents how yang by its change and yin by its union therewith produces Water, Fire, Wood, Metal and Earth

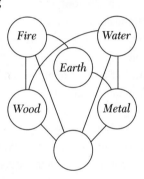

Yang   Yin

Action   Quiet

Fire   Water

Earth

Wood   Metal

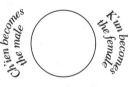

Ch'ien becomes the male   *K'un becomes the female*

The production and transformation of all creatures

☿ represents how the Indeterminate and yin and yang and the Five Agents wonderously unite and are without separation.

◯ This represents how by the transformations of material forces Ch'ien becomes the male and K'un becomes the female.

Male and female each have their own natures, but are the one Supreme Ultimate.

◯ This represents how all things evolve and are produced by transformations of form.

Each thing has its own nature but all are the one Supreme Ultimate.

The Indeterminate and also the Supreme Ultimate: The Supreme Ultimate through activity produces yang. Activity having reached its limit, there is quiescence. Through quiescence [the Supreme Ultimate] produces yin. When quiescence reaches its limit there is a return to activity; thus activity and quiescence each in turn becomes the source of the other. In this way the distinction between yin and yang arises and the two modes are established. Yang changes and yin corresponds, and thus are produced Water, Fire, Wood, Metal, and Earth; these Five Agents are harmoniously arrayed, and the four seasons proceed in their course.

The Five Agents are the one yin and yang; yin and yang are the one Supreme Ultimate; the Supreme Ultimate is fundamentally Indeterminate. But in the production of the Five Agents, each has its own nature.

The reality of the Indeterminate and the essence of the two modes [i.e., yin and yang] and the Five Agents wondrously unite and consolidate. *Ch'ien* [Heaven] constitutes the male element and *K'un* [Earth] constitutes the female element. These two forces by their interaction transform and produce the myriad creatures. The myriad creatures produce and reproduce, and so change and transformation go on without end.

Man alone, however, receives [the Five Agents] in their highest excellence and so is endowed with the fullest spiritual potential. His physical form is produced and his spirit manifests intelligence. His fivefold nature is stirred [in response to external phenomena] and acts; thus the distinction of good and evil arises and human affairs take place.

The Sage properly orders these [affairs] according to the mean, correctness, humaneness, and rightness, taking quiet as the essential; in this way he establishes the ultimate standard for man. Therefore the Sage "with respect to Heaven and Earth is at one with their character, with respect to the sun and moon is at one with their brilliance, with respect to the four seasons is at one with their order, and with respect to the spirits is at one with the good fortune and the misfortune [which they mediate]." The superior man in cultivating these qualities enjoys good fortune, while the inferior man in violating them suffers misfortune.

YI HWANG'S COMMENTS

This diagram and its accompanying explanation are both the work of Chou Lien-hsi [Tun-i]. Yeh Ping-yen spoke of this diagram as follows: "It takes the words of the Appended Remarks [of the *Book of Changes*], 'The *Book of Changes* has the Supreme Ultimate; this produced the Two Modes; the Two Modes produced the Four Forms,' and expands and clarifies their meaning. The only difference is that the *Book of Changes* speaks in terms of the hexagrams and their lines, while the *Diagram* speaks in terms of the creation and transformation [of the physical universe]." Master Chu called it "the great fountainhead of moral principle" and again referred to it as "the source of proper understanding of the Way through all ages."

This diagram has been placed at the very beginning of this work for the same reason that its explanation was placed at the beginning of [Chu Hsi's] *Reflections on Things at Hand.* That is, one who would learn to be a sage should seek the beginning here in this [diagram] and apply his efforts to the practice of [what is presented in] such works as the *Elementary Learning* and the *Great Learning.*

Master Chu in discussing the Indeterminate and yet the Supreme Ultimate says: "If one does not say 'Indeterminate,' then the Supreme Ultimate would become the same as a single thing and would not suffice as the root of the ten thousand transformations; if one does not say 'Supreme Ultimate' then the Indeterminate would be confused with a quiescent emptiness and would not be able to serve as the root of the ten thousand transformations." Ah! Ah! This saying can be said to perfectly encompass the matter in every respect. [From *T'oegye chŏnsŏ* I:16:04b]

Section 2: Diagram of the Western Inscription

The *Western Inscription* is the work of Chang Tsai (1020–1077), and it stands with the *Diagram of the Supreme Ultimate* as one of the most fundamental documents of the Neo-Confucian tradition. It puts flesh and blood on the bare bones of metaphysics, reflects on Heaven and Earth as the common parents of all creatures; stemming from a single common origin, all of creation is therefore a single body, and all people form a single great family.

CHANG TSAI'S *WESTERN INSCRIPTION*

Ch'ien [Heaven] is called the father and *K'un* [Earth] is called the mother. I, this tiny being, am commingled in their midst; therefore what fills all between Heaven and Earth is my body, and that which directs Heaven and Earth is my nature.

All people are from the same womb as I, all creatures are my companions. The Great Ruler is the eldest son of my parents, and his great ministers are the household retainers of the eldest son. By honoring those who are advanced in years, I carry out the respect for age which is due my aged, and by kindness to the solitary and weak, I carry out the tender care for the young which should be paid to my young. The Sage is at one with the character [of Heaven and Earth], and the wise man is of their finest [stuff]. All persons in the world who are exhausted, decrepit, worn out, or ill, or who are brotherless, childless, widowers, or widowed, are my own brothers who have become helpless and have none to whom they can appeal.

To maintain [our awe of Heaven] at the proper time is to show the respect of a son; to feel joy [in what Heaven allots] without anxiety is to exemplify filial piety in its purity. Deviation from [the will of Heaven] is called a perverse disposition; doing injury to humanity *[jen]* is called villainous. One who promotes evil is lacking in [moral] capacity; he who fulfills his bodily design [by doing good] resembles [his parents, Heaven and Earth]. Understanding the transformations [of the universe] is being skillful in carrying forward [one's parents'] activities; exhaustively plumbing the spiritual is being good at perpetuating their intentions. He who even in the recesses of his house does nothing shameful will bring no shame; he who is mindful and fosters his nature will not be negligent.

Wealth, honor, good fortune, and abundance have as their aim the enrichment of our lives. Poverty, meanness, grief, and sorrow serve to discipline us so as to make us complete. In life I shall serve [my parents, Heaven and Earth] compliantly and in death I shall be at peace.

YI HWANG'S COMMENTS

The above inscription is the work of Master Chang Heng-ch'ü [Tsai]. At first it was entitled *Correcting Obstinacy;* Master Ch'eng [I] changed it to *Western Inscription.* Ch'eng Lin-yin made this diagram of it. The learning of the sages consists in the seeking of humanity. It is necessary to deeply inculcate in oneself the intention [of becoming humane], and then understand that one makes up a single body with Heaven and Earth and the myriad creatures. To truly and actually live this way is what is involved in becoming humane. One must personally get a taste [of this experience]; then he will be rid of the problem [of thinking that] it is something so vast as to be unobtainable and also will be free from the mistaken notion that other things are identical with himself, and the inner dispositions of his mind-and-heart will thus become perfect and complete. Thus Master Ch'eng says, "The meaning of the *Western Inscription* is exceedingly perfect and complete; it is the substance of humanity." And again, "When one has fully attained to this, he will be a sage."

PRINCIPLE AS OBJECTIVE NORM AND SUBJECTIVE IDENTITY

Principle, or, in more traditional terms, the Way, serves as the objective norm of the way things should be, and as we have seen in the *Western Inscription,* the unity of principle establishes an objective, cosmic ground for an ethics of unselfishness in human relationships. But Yi Hwang notes that the *Inscription* should not be read in a merely objective, nonpersonal sense.

There is a world of difference between looking at principle as something objective, "out there," and realizing that it is actually the substance of one's own being, the heart of one's own identity. The first section of the *Western Inscription* brings this out naturally because filial piety is fundamentally based on a proper understanding of one's own identity. But systematically it is broadly founded on the metaphysics of principle, which locates principle both in the realm of objective norms and in one's own nature as the substance or basis of personal consciousness and identity. Yi Hwang's emphasis here on the absolute necessity of a personal grasp and personal experience runs throughout his discussion of study and the investigation of principle. In this framework, understanding the universe and what is proper in the conduct of affairs is also, ultimately and most urgently, a matter of understanding oneself.

[Chang Tsai] employs the terms people use to refer to their own persons; all who read this work should neither consider these ten [first-person pronouns] as references to the self of Heng-ch'ü, nor put them off as referring to the self of others: they must all be seen as indications of one's personal responsibility for what is one's own affair. Only then will one be able to grasp how the *Western Inscription* is fundamentally a formulation of the substance of humanity. Heng-ch'ü also regards humanity as something that, although [it means] being as one body with Heaven and Earth and all creatures, must nevertheless first come from the self as its fundamental source and master; one must attain a personal realization of the interrelatedness of the self and others in the unity of principle. When the disposition of commiseration which penetratingly fills the heart flows forth, unblocked by anything and with nothing which it does not encompass, then this finally is the true substance of humanity. If one does not understand this principle and just broadly considers humanity as a matter of Heaven and Earth and all creatures being as a single body, then what is called the substance of humanity will be something vast and distant. What connection will there be with one's own body and mind? [From *T'oegye chŏnsŏ* I:7:50a–b]

Section 3: Diagram of the Elementary Learning

The *Elementary Learning* is a compilation of 386 passages, a little more than half of which are drawn from the classics and the remainder from the writings of outstanding Confucians of the postclassical period, including a

Diagram of the Elementary Learning

Establishing Instruction

Establishing instruction in womb nurture, fostering and rearing

Establishing instruction: the Small and the Great the beginning and the end

Establishing instruction: the 'three matters' and the 'four skills'

Establishing instruction: master and disciple giving and receiving

Clarifying Relationships

Clarifying affection between father and son

Clarifying righteousness between ruler and minister

Clarifying distinction between husband and wife

Clarifying order between elder and younger

Clarifying intercourse between friends

Making One's Person Mindful

Clarifying the essential skills of dealing with inner dispositions

Clarifying the norms of proper decorum and dignity

Clarifying regulations regarding clothing

Clarifying proper moderation in food and drink

Examining Ancient Examples

ESTABLISHING INSTRUCTION

CLARIFYING RELATIONSHIPS

MAKING ONE'S PERSON MINDFUL

Fine Sayings

Expanding on establishing instruction

Expanding on clarifying relationships

Expanding on making one's person mindful

Fine Deeds

Actual practice of establishing instruction

Actual practice of clarifying relationships

Actual practice of making one's person mindful

liberal selection from the early Sung dynasty Confucians. Its purpose was to present the most fundamental teachings and values of the Confucian tradition for the instruction of the young; it includes extensive materials dealing with the Five Relations, which constitute the core of traditional Confucian ethical teaching.

This work became the gateway to serious study for generation upon generation of Confucian scholars. In Korea it was considered virtually one of the classics, and from the first decades of the Chosŏn dynasty its memorization became a prerequisite for admittance to the lowest level of the civil service examinations. The high point of its importance was reached in the generation immediately preceding Yi Hwang's, when it became a symbol of the distinctive moral seriousness of the burgeoning Neo-Confucian movement. Kim Koengp'il (1454–1504), one of the foremost scholars and teachers of that period, made it his boast that he devoted himself exclusively to the *Elementary Learning* until he was thirty years old and was a member of a club of prominent scholars and officials dedicated to maintaining and practicing the principles taught in it.

Although the *Elementary Learning* is generally attributed to Chu Hsi, the actual compilation was done at his direction by one of his disciples, Liu Ch'ing-chih (1139–1189); Chu Hsi himself then rearranged it, added a few passages, and wrote a preface and an introduction for it. His introduction constitutes the main portion of the text which accompanies this diagram.

This chapter is much concerned with the relationship of the *Elementary Learning* and the *Great Learning*, which is the topic of the next chapter. It is concerned with Chu Hsi's view of the character of the learning process and the interrelated nature of its two stages, the elementary learning in which the young are engaged and the "great" or "adult" learning pursued by young adults (see below, Commentary, first section). The two texts, the *Elementary Learning* and the *Great Learning* stand for these two stages.

CHU HSI'S "INTRODUCTION TO THE SUBJECT MATTER OF THE *ELEMENTARY LEARNING*"

Origination, flourishing, benefiting, and firmness are the constant characteristics of the Way of Heaven; humaneness, rightness, ritual decorum, and wisdom are the [inherent] guidelines of human nature; in all of these, from the very beginning there is nothing which is not good. Thus like a verdant growth the Four Beginnings are stirred and move in response [to external phenomena] and appear.

Loving one's parents, reverencing one's older brother, being loyal to one's ruler, and showing respect to elders is called "holding to one's inborn nature"; [such conduct] is in accord [with one's natural dispositions], not forced.

But only the sage possesses the full, vigorous perfection of the inborn nature [in its pure, original condition]; without the slightest bit [of further perfection] being added to it, all goodness is already there in its fullness. The ordinary man is foolish and ignorant; the desire for things beclouds his vision and causes his inborn good qualities to decline, and he is thus content to do violence to himself and throw himself away. The sages, pitying this [miserable condition], set up schools and established teachers in order to fertilize the roots and make the branches arrive at their full growth.

The method in *Elementary Learning* was to have them sprinkle water and sweep [the hall], answer and respond [to questions], act filially in their homes and obediently when abroad, and to see to it that in their actions there would be no violation [of the rites]. With what energy was left from this, they recited poetry, read books, sang songs, and danced, so that in all their thoughts there would be no transgression [of the proper norm].

As for exhaustively investigating principle and cultivating one's person [in this way], that was the matter for more advanced learning [i.e., it was taken up in schools for young adults]. [With the pursuit of such learning] the bright Imperative would shine forth; there would come to be no distinction between one's interior dispositions and external conduct; virtue would become lofty and one's accomplishments would broaden, and one would finally recover the original [perfection of human nature].

It was not due to some peculiar deficiency in the ancients [that such schooling was necessary]. How can we think that we now are more perfect [and have no need of it]? A great length of time has passed; the sages have perished, the classics have been damaged, and instruction has become lax. The rearing of the young lacks a proper foundation, so as adults they just become the more given over to corrupt luxury. The villages no longer have good customs; the times are without men of fine talent; greed dizzies men and entangles them, and deviant teachings set up a great clamor.

Fortunately the inborn good nature of man will not perish as long as Heaven lasts; therefore I have collected together what has been heard of old, that it may serve to enlighten generations to come.

COMMENTS FROM CHU HSI'S *QUESTIONS AND ANSWERS ON THE "GREAT LEARNING" (TA-HSÜEH HUO-WEN)*

Master Chu said: "In learning, that which is great and that which is elementary certainly have their differences. Nevertheless, as far as the Way is concerned, it is one and that is all. Thus if when one is young he does not verse himself in it through *Elementary Learning,* he will not have the good means to recover his errant mind-and-heart and foster the good qualities of his nature in order to lay the foundation for the *Great Learning.* And when one is an adult, if he does not advance to *Great Learning,* he will not have the means to discern moral principle and put it into practice in actual affairs, and thus receive the fulfillment of *Elementary Learning.*

YI HWANG'S COMMENTS

Formerly there was no diagram of the *Elementary Learning;* I have used its table of contents to make this diagram, which is meant to be paired with the diagram of the *Great Learning.* I have also quoted Chu Hsi's general discussion [of the relationship of] *Great Learning* and *Elementary Learning* which appears in his *Questions and Answers on the Great Learning* in order to show the general nature of the approach to applying one's efforts as it relates to these two. For *Elementary Learning* and *Great Learning* are mutually interdependent and complementary; in this respect they are one and yet two, two, and yet one. Therefore in the *Questions and Answers* they can be encompassed in a single discussion, and these two diagrams can be taken together as mutually completing one another.

In sum, the Confucian way of learning is that in order to ascend to lofty heights one must begin with the lowly, to travel afar one must begin with what is near. Indeed, to begin from the lowly and near certainly is a slow process. But apart from it, whence comes the lofty and distant? In applying one's efforts to gradual advancement one attains what is lofty and distant without parting from what is lowly and near; it is in this that it is different from Buddhist and Taoist learning. [From *T'oegye chŏnsŏ* I:19:26b]

Section 4: Diagram of the Great Learning

The *Great Learning,* though of ancient origin, is very much a Neo-Confucian creation. It was buried in obscurity as the forty-second chapter of the voluminous *Record of Rites,* and attracted little notice until it was taken up by the Ch'eng brothers and Chu Hsi; it subsequently became a classic in itself, its every phrase committed to memory by generation upon generation of Confucian scholars. Crucial to this development was the metaphysics of *li* originated by the Ch'eng brothers. When read in a traditional context, the *Great Learning* seems to be a rather conventional treatise on self-cultivation for rulers and noblemen. But when interpreted in the light of the philosophy of *li,* it takes on an entirely new dimension of meaning, pointing out a path of self-cultivation that incorporates the new philosophy and leads to the ultimate perfection of sagehood.

The original text of the *Great Learning* as found in chapter 42 of the *Record of Rites* is undivided. Chu Hsi divided the work into one chapter of "text," which outlines the essential steps of self-cultivation, and ten chapters of "commentary." The text he ascribed to Confucius himself, with the chapters of commentary being attributed to one of his leading disciples, Tseng Tzu. This ascription of authorship gave the *Great Learning* the highest possible pedigree of authority, though it rested only on the dictum of Chu Hsi.

THE "TEXT," OR FIRST CHAPTER, OF THE *GREAT LEARNING*

The Way of great learning consists in manifesting illustrious virtue, renewing the people, and abiding in the highest good.

Only after one knows wherein to abide can [one's will] have an established direction; only after one has an established direction can one be tranquil; only after one is tranquil can one have peaceful repose; only after one has peaceful repose can one deliberate; only after deliberation can one attain [the highest good].

Things have their roots and their ends; affairs have their beginning and their completion. Knowing what comes first and what comes last will bring one close to the Way.

The ancients who wished to make illustrious virtue manifest throughout the world would first bring order to their states; those who wished to bring order to their states would first regulate their families; those who wished to regulate their families would first cultivate their own persons; those who wished to cultivate their persons would first rectify their minds; those who wished to rectify their minds would first make their intentions sincere; those who wished to make their intentions sincere would first extend their knowledge; the extension of knowledge consists in the investigation of things.

When things are investigated, knowledge is extended; when knowledge is extended, the intention becomes sincere; when the intention becomes sincere, the mind is rectified; when the mind is rectified, one's person is cultivated; when one's person is cultivated, the family will be regulated; when the family is regulated, the state will be ordered; when the state is well-ordered, the world will be tranquil.

From the Son of Heaven down to the common man, all must regard cultivation of their persons as the root and foundation. There has never been a case when the root is in disorder and the end is nonetheless well-ordered; there never has been a case in which that which is carefully nurtured wastes away, or that which is negligently tended flourishes.

COMMENTS FROM CHU HSI'S *QUESTIONS AND ANSWERS ON THE* "GREAT LEARNING"

Someone asked: "How does one apply himself to the practice of mindfulness [reverent seriousness]?"

Master Chu said: "Ch'eng I spoke of it as 'concentrating on one thing and not departing [from it],' and again in terms of being 'well-ordered and even-minded, grave and quiet'.

Once the mind is established in this condition, one may proceed with this state of mind to pursue the investigation of things and the extension of knowledge, and thereby exhaustively comprehend principle as it is present in things and affairs; that is what is meant by "honoring the good inborn qualities of one's nature and following the path of inquiry and study." One may proceed with this state of mind to make his intentions sincere and rectify his mind, and thereby cultivate his person; that is what is meant by "first establish that which is greater, and the lesser will not be able to take it away." One may proceed in this state of mind to regulate the family, and properly order the state, and thereby attain even to making the whole world tranquil; that is what is meant by "Cultivate your own person in order to give ease to the people; make much of reverence [in your own person] and the world will enjoy tranquillity." All of this shows that one cannot absent himself from the practice of mindfulness for a single day. That being the case, how can the one word, "mindfulness," but be the essence of both the beginning and the completion of sage learning?

YI HWANG'S COMMENTS

Above is the first chapter of the writing handed down in the Confucian school. Kwŏn Kŭn, who was an official in the early years of this dynasty, made the diagram of it. The text of the first chapter is followed by a quotation from the *Questions and Answers on the Great Learning*'s general discussion of the meaning of *Great Learning* and *Elementary Learning*.

It is not only the explanation of these two, however, which should be seen in combination; all of the eight diagrams which precede and follow them should also be seen in relation to these two diagrams. The two diagrams which precede these deal with the ultimate [framework]: seeking out the foundation, broadening and perfecting it, embodying Heaven, and totally fulfilling the Way. They present the ultimate goal and the basic foundation of *Great Learning* and *Elementary Learning*. The six diagrams that follow deal with applying one's efforts: understanding the good, making one's person sincere, exalting virtue, and broadening self-cultivation. They represent the field [of the application] of *Great Learning* and *Elementary Learning*, that which is to be worked upon.

In what one investigates, sometimes one meets with complexities and intricacies that using all one's strength one cannot get through, or sometimes one's nature happens to have a blind spot on the matter and it is difficult to force illumination and break it open. Then one ought to set the matter aside and approach another and investigate it. In this way, investigating one way and then another, there is an accumulation which deepens and ripens; the mind naturally gradually clears, and the actuality of moral principle gradually becomes manifest to one's eye. Then if one again takes up what one formerly could not successfully investigate and reflects on it, combining it for consideration and comparison with what one has already successfully investigated, while one hardly is aware of what is happening, they will interact at the same time to produce enlightenment and understanding regarding what had not been investigated [successfully]. This is the flexible approach to the investigation of principle; it does not mean that when an investigation is not successful one just puts it aside [for good]. [From *T'oegye chŏnsŏ* I:14:21a]

Section 5: *Diagram of Rules of the White Deer Grotto Academy*

This chapter uses the rules Chu Hsi established for the White Deer Grotto Academy to show that the Five Relations are not only the foundation, but the sum and substance of all learning, the object toward which all study and practice are ultimately devoted.

In his comments, Yi Hwang narrates the story of Chu Hsi's refounding of the White Deer Grotto Academy and mentions the official support it had earlier received from Emperor T'ai-tsung (960–976). Yi Hwang viewed such private academies as ideal institutions for Neo-Confucian learning, and was anxious to see them spread in Korea; for this, he felt, official royal sanction and support were essential. Hence there is a special point in his including this material in a document he hopes will be repeatedly perused by the king. Yi Hwang's comments in the fifth section discuss his role in obtaining royal support for private academies in Korea and the important role they subsequently came to play in Chosŏn dynasty society.

YI HWANG'S COMMENTS

The above rules were made by Master Chu to be posted for the students of the White Deer Grotto Academy. The grotto was on the southern side of K'uang-lu Mountain in the northern part of Nan-k'ang prefecture. During the T'ang dynasty, Li Po [fl. c. 810], while living there in retirement, raised a white deer which followed him about, and the grotto was named accordingly. During the Southern T'ang [937–975] an academy was established there and named the State School

DIAGRAM OF THE RULES OF THE WHITE DEER GROTTO ACADEMY

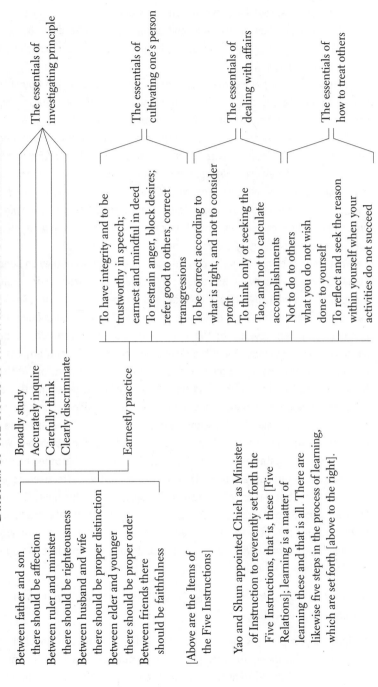

Broadly study
Accurately inquire
Carefully think
Clearly discriminate

— The essentials of investigating principle

Earnestly practice

To have integrity and to be trustworthy in speech; earnest and mindful in deed

To restrain anger, block desires; refer good to others, correct transgressions

— The essentials of cultivating one's person

To be correct according to what is right, and not to consider profit

To think only of seeking the Tao, and not to calculate accomplishments

— The essentials of dealing with affairs

Not to do to others what you do not wish done to yourself

To reflect and seek the reason within yourself when your activities do not succeed

— The essentials of how to treat others

Between father and son there should be affection

Between ruler and minister there should be righteousness

Between husband and wife there should be proper distinction

Between elder and younger there should be proper order

Between friends there should be faithfulness

[Above are the Items of the Five Instructions]

Yao and Shun appointed Chieh as Minister of Instruction to reverently set forth the Five Instructions, that is, these [Five Relations]; learning is a matter of learning these and that is all. There are likewise five steps in the process of learning, which are set forth [above to the right].

[Kuo-hsiang]; it always had several hundred students. Emperor T'ai-tsung [960–976] of the Sung showed his favor and encouraged the academy by bestowing books and giving an official rank to the head of the academy, but since then it had fallen into decay and ruin.

[Yi Hwang's note:] The above five diagrams are based upon the Way of Heaven, but their application consists in manifesting proper human relationships and devoting one's effort to the cultivation of virtue.

[*Serious Neo-Confucian learning focused on mindfulness as central, and while this self-possessed, recollected state of mind encompassed both active and tranquil periods, it could best be cultivated initially in a relatively quiet and secluded environment, which came to be looked upon as the ideal circumstance, if not the absolute prerequisite, for serious application to learning. Yi Hwang championed the private academies because he saw them as the ideal institutional counterpart of the Neo-Confucian theory of self-cultivation.*]

What could they get from the private academies? Why were they so honored by China? Scholars who dwell in retirement in order to pursue their resolve, the group of those who investigate the Tao and verse themselves in learning, frequently become wearied and distressed by the world's noisy wrangling and pack up their books and escape to the broad and relaxed countryside or the quiet solitude of the seashore, where they can sing and recite [verses on] the Way of the former sage-kings, or be quiet and look into the moral principle of the world in order to nurture their virtue and ripen their humanity, regarding this as their pleasure. Therefore they are pleased to go to a private academy. They see that the national academies and district schools are located within the walls of the capital or local towns; on the one hand these [schools] are encumbered with the restrictions and obstacles of school regulations, and on the other they present temptations to turn toward other things. How could their effectiveness be compared with [that of the private academies]! Considered in this light, it is not only scholars' pursuit of learning which is strengthened by private academies; the state's attainment of wise and talented men [to serve in government] will certainly by this means far surpass what could be accomplished through those [state and district schools]. [From *T'oegye chŏnsŏ* I:9:5b]

Section 6: Diagram of the Saying "The Mind Combines and Governs the Nature and the Feelings"

This chapter presents the basic elements of Neo-Confucian psychological theory. In this theory the metaphysical concepts that describe the universe are likewise applied so as to elucidate the composition and functioning of the human psyche. The subject is complex, but the description of the psyche has immediate bearing upon how one approaches the practical task of self-cultivation.

The essence of the matter is this: that which includes both principle and material force and combines and governs the nature and the feelings is the mind; and the moment of the nature's issuance as feelings is the subtle wellspring of the whole mind, the pivot of ten thousand transformations, the separation point of good and evil. If one who pursues learning is truly able to recollect himself through maintaining mindfulness and does not confuse principle with human desires but brings the greatest caution to bear on this matter; and if his application to the composure [of his mind] and the nurturing [of his nature] before the mind is aroused is profound and he is likewise well-versed in the exercise of reflection and discernment after it is aroused; and if he accumulates truth and is constant in his effort for a long time and does not stop—[if all this is so,] then the learning of sagehood characterized as "being refined [discriminating] and undivided, holding fast the mean," and the method of cultivating the mind wherein it is composed in substance and [accurately] responsive in function, need not be sought elsewhere, but will all be attained in this.

Section 7: Diagram of the Explanation of Humaneness

From the earliest times, humanity, *jen*, has been the virtue of all virtues in the Confucian tradition. Confucius used the term to signify the highest perfection, the epitome of all human excellence. Mencius says, "*Jen* is to be human," that is, it is the full perfection of the human being as such. The Neo-Confucians preserved this heritage concerning *jen*. But their philosophy of principle explicated a vision of the ultimate unity of man and the universe, and a new description of man's inner life had developed from the application of the categories of substance and function to describe the relationship of the nature and the feelings in the life of the mind-and-heart. This new framework invited a new inquiry into the meaning of *jen*: How can *jen* be thought of as a cosmic quality in which man participates? What does it mean to say that *jen* is the substance of the mind? Addressing such questions brought a profound new development in the way of understanding *jen* that moved decisively beyond traditional formulations.

TEXT OF THE DIAGRAM

Master Chu says: "Humanity is the mind of Heaven and Earth whereby they produce and give life to creatures," and this is what man receives as his own mind. Before [this mind] is aroused, the four virtues are complete within it, and humanity alone encompasses all four; thus it permeates and fosters these virtues as an integral whole, unifying and controlling them all. What is spoken of as "the nature to grow" and the principle of love is the substance of humanity.

When [the mind] is aroused and interacts [with things], the Four Beginnings are manifested, and commiseration alone runs throughout all four; thus it entirely flows throughout and permeates all of them, and comprehends them all. What is spoken of as the feelings of the nature and the manifestation of love is the function of humanity.

Speaking generically, the condition before [the mind] is aroused is that of substance, and the condition after it is aroused is that of function. Speaking specifically, humanity is substance and commiseration is function. Impartiality is that whereby one embodies humaneness, as illustrated in the saying [of Confucius], "To overcome oneself and return to the rites is to be humane." For if one is impartial, then he will be humane; if he is humane, he will be loving. Filial piety and respectfulness are functions [of humanity], and empathy is the means whereby it is extended to others [in practice]. As for [the equation of humanity with] conscious awareness, [consciousness] is what is involved in the exercise of wisdom.

CHU HSI'S "TREATISE ON *JEN*"

And again he says: "The mind of Heaven and Earth has four characteristics: they are origination, flourishing, benefiting, and firmness, and origination runs throughout all. As they move in rotation, we have the cycle of spring, summer, fall, and winter, and the generative force of spring runs throughout all. Therefore in the mind of man there are likewise four characteristics: they are humaneness, rightness, ritual decorum, and wisdom, and humanity encompasses them all. When these issue forth as function, they become the feelings: they are love, respect, a sense of what accords with the rite, and a sense that distinguishes [right and wrong]; commiseration runs throughout all of these."

For humanity's constituting the Way consists in the fact that the mind [i.e., disposition] of Heaven and Earth to produce and give life to creatures is present in everything. Before the feelings are aroused, this [disposition] is already integrally present as substance, and when they are aroused its function is inexhaustible. If one can in truth embody and preserve it, [one will find that] the wellspring of all good and the foundation of all activity is entirely present within it. This is why the teaching of the Confucian school always urges those who would pursue learning to seek after humanity with unflagging diligence.

In the words [of Confucius] there is the saying, "To overcome oneself and return to the rites is to be humane." This means that if one is able to overcome and expel all of one's self-centeredness and return to the principle of Heaven, then the substance of this mind [i.e., humanity] will be present everywhere and the function of this mind will be always operative.

[Confucius] again has said, "When dwelling at home be respectful; when handling affairs be mindful; in your relationships with others be loyal." This is how one preserves this mind. Again it is said, "Be filial in serving parents," "Be respectful in serving elder brothers," and "Be empathetic in dealing with others." This is how this mind is put into practice.

But what is this mind of which we speak? In Heaven and Earth it is the inexhaustible disposition to produce and give life to creatures; in men it is the warm love for others and the disposition to benefit all creatures. It encompasses the four virtues and runs throughout the Four Beginnings.

Someone said: "Master Ch'eng [I] said, 'Love is a feeling and humanity is the nature; thus one may not regard humanity as love.' In view of what you have said, is this incorrect?"

I [Chu Hsi] say: "Such is not the case. What Master Ch'eng said has to do with applying the term *humanity* to the active manifestation of love, while in my discussion I apply the term to the principle of love. For when it comes to the feelings and the nature, although their spheres are not the same, nonetheless they communicate as an interconnected system of veins, each having its own place. How could they ever be separated and cut off as if having nothing to do with one another? I am distressed nowadays that students just recite the words of Master Ch'eng without seeking out their intention, and so come to speak of humanity as something distinctly separate from love."

YI HWANG'S COMMENTS

The above explanation of humanity is that given by Chu Hsi, and he also made the diagram to go with it. In explaining the Way of humanity there is nothing more that could be said. The commentary section of the *Great Learning* says, "One who is a [true] ruler abides in humanity." If Your Majesty wishes to seek out what the ancient emperors and rulers handed down concerning the wondrous manner in which the mind embodies humanity, its meaning is exhaustively present here.

I venture to say that the great virtue of Heaven and Earth is to produce and give life. Between Heaven and Earth there is a dense multitude of living creatures; whether they be animals or plants, large or small, they are all compassionately covered and loved by Heaven. How much more is this the case when it comes to the likes of us humans, who are the most spiritual and are as the mind of Heaven and Earth! Although Heaven has this mind it is not able itself to manifest it, but must especially favor the most sagacious, wise, and excellent, one whose virtue can unite spirits and men, and make him ruler, entrusting him with the duty of looking after [the people] in order to put its humane and loving governance into practice. [From *T'oegye chŏnsŏ* I:6:34a]

Section 8: Diagram of the Study of the Mind

From Yi Hwang's youth Chen Te-hsiu's *Classic of the Mind-and-Heart* was one of the most important and formative influences on him. In the supplemented and annotated edition that circulated widely in Korea and was used by Yi Hwang, the *Hsin-ching fu-chu (Simgyŏng puju)*, this diagram and its explanatory text are inserted immediately before the first chapter with the following note: "This diagram of Ch'eng [Fu-hsin]'s exhausts the wonders of the study of the mind-and-heart, and what it discusses likewise suffices to manifest the essence of the study of the mind-and-heart." Thus it serves as both an introduction and a summation to the *Classic of the Mind-and-Heart*. Yi Hwang, who remarks that he has always "loved this diagram," uses it here in a similar fashion, making it an introduction to and summation of Neo-Confucian ascetical doctrine, the method of cultivating one's mind-and-heart, which is the central concern of the *Classic*.

Chen Te-hsiu's *Classic of the Mind-and-Heart* and Ch'eng Fu-hsin's "Diagram of the Study of the Mind-and-Heart" both witness the vigor with which this aspect of Chu Hsi's teaching was developed during the Yüan dynasty (1279–1368). Yi Hwang's constant emphasis upon the centrality of mindfulness is a faithful reflection of Chu Hsi, but it is also an unmistakable reflection of the influence of Chen's *Classic*.

YI HWANG'S COMMENTS

Ch'eng Fu-hsin collected together the terms in which the sages and wise men have discussed the study of the mind and made the above diagram of them. His categorically distinguishing and arranging them in corresponding pairs is complex but not tiresome, for by this means he shows that the system of the mind-and-heart in sage learning is likewise complex, and one must apply diligent effort to all these aspects.

[The lower half of the diagram] is arranged in an order that proceeds from the top to the bottom; it is meant as a schematic presentation [of the process of self-cultivation] simply in terms of what is shallower and what more profound, what is less mature and what more mature. Since this is its approach, it does not mean to depict the stages and steps of the process in the temporal order of prior and

8. Diagram of the Study of the Mind

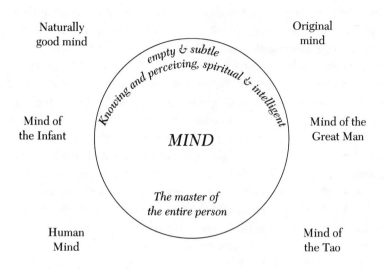

Naturally
good mind

Original
mind

*empty & subtle
and perceiving, spiritual & intelligent
Knowing*

Mind of
the Infant

MIND

Mind of the
Great Man

*The master of
the entire person*

Human
Mind

Mind of
the Tao

Be discerning
Select the good

Watchful
when alone

Be Undivided
Hold to it firmly

Cautious and
apprehensive

Overcome and
return

Grasp and
preserve

The mind is
present

MINDFULNESS

The master of the mind

The mind
exercises thought

Recovering the
errant mind

Nurturing the
mind

The mind
is rectified

Exhaustively
realized mind

At forty the
mind is not moved

At seventy can
follow inclinations

posterior, as [does the *Great Learning* in speaking of] extending knowledge to the utmost, making the will sincere, rectifying the mind, and cultivating one's person.

The six types of mind arranged above, below, and to the right and left of the "mind" circle simply describe how there is a particular point to each of the ways in which the sages and wise men talk about the mind. It is like this: because of its fundamental goodness it is called the "naturally good mind"; because of its original possession of goodness it is called the "original mind"; because it is simple and without any artificiality, and nothing more, it is called the "mind of the infant"; because it is simple and without any artificiality and is able to comprehend all changes totally, it is called the "mind of the great man"; because it is produced through the psychophysical component, it is called the "human mind"; and because it has its origin in the moral imperative which constitutes the nature, it is called the "Tao Mind." Since the "naturally good mind" and the "original mind" have very similar types of meaning, they are placed in correlation to each other at the top on the left and right; the "mind of the infant" and the "mind of the great man" and the "human mind" and the "Tao Mind," because their fundamental terminology involves a mutual contrast, are arranged in pairs to the left and right of the middle and bottom respectively. [From *T'oegye chŏnsŏ* I:14:35b]

The human mind is the foundation of [selfish] human desires. Human desires are the flow of the human mind; they arise from the mind as physically conditioned. The sage likewise cannot but have [the human mind]; therefore one can only call it the human mind and cannot directly consider it as human desire. Nevertheless human desires in fact proceed from it; therefore I say it is the foundation of human desires. The mind ensnared by greed is the condition of the ordinary man who acts contrary to Heaven; therefore it is termed "human desire" and called something other than "human mind." This leads one to understand that such is not the original condition of the human mind; therefore I say it is the "flow" of the human mind. Thus the human mind is prior and [selfish] human desire come later; the former is correct and the latter is evil. [From *T'oegye chŏnsŏ* I:40:9b–10a]

In general, although the study of the mind-and-heart is complex, one can sum up its essence as nothing other than blocking [selfish] human desires and preserving the principle of Heaven, just these two and that is all. All the matters that are involved in blocking human desires should be categorized on the side of the human mind, and all that pertain to preserving the principle of Heaven should be categorized on the side of the Tao Mind.

The intent of Ch'eng Lin-yin's "Diagram of the Study of the Mind-and-Heart" is truly like this. [From *T'oegye chŏnsŏ* I:37:28b]

Section 9: Diagram of the Admonition for Mindfulness Studio

Mindfulness stands at the heart of Chu Hsi's teaching as it is understood by Yi Hwang, and in this chapter Yi Hwang presents the text which served as his own source of inspiration, constant reflection, and self-examination. The *Admonition* approaches mindfulness topically, presenting its various applications to activity and quiet, to external deportment and internal attitudes.

THE ADMONITION FOR MINDFULNESS STUDIO

Properly order your clothing and cap and make your gaze reverent; recollect your mind and make it abide, as if you were present before the Lord on High. The appearance of the feet must be as if they were heavy, the disposition of the hands respectful.

When you go abroad, behave to everyone as if you were meeting an important guest; preside over affairs as if presiding at a sacrifice. Always cautious and fearful, never venture to slacken. Stop up your mouth like the opening of a bottle, and guard your intentions as you would a city wall. Always reverent and sincere, never venture to treat anything frivolously.

When you encounter some affair attend only to it; do not set off about something else. Because of two [matters to be dealt with] do not divide your mind into two; because of three do not divide your mind into three. Let your mind be undivided as it watches over the myriad changes. If one should falter for a single moment, selfish desire will put forth ten thousand shoots.

THE CENTRALITY OF MIND AND ITS CULTIVATION

The mind is the foundation of all affairs and the nature is the origin of all good; therefore when the former Confucians discussed learning they unfailingly regarded "recovering the errant mind" and "nurturing the virtuous nature" as the very first thing to which one must apply oneself as the means whereby one fulfills one's fundamental constitution. This they regarded as the foundation for fulfilling the Way and developing the full extent of one's virtue; as for the essence of the way to apply one's effort, what need is there to seek it in anything else?

The application of concentrating on one thing runs throughout both the active and quiet states, while the field of caution and apprehension is entirely in the not-yet-aroused state. Neither of these can be omitted. And regulating the exterior in order to nurture the interior is an even more urgent matter.

For beginning students nothing is better than devoting one's practice to being "properly ordered and controlled, grave and quiet." In this there is no place for searching after [a particular mental condition] or trying to manage [the mind] in a particular way; it is just a matter of establishing oneself in accord with the fixed norm [*literally, "square, compass, and ink-line"*] being cautious and watchful in the hidden, secluded places [where one is not observed], and not allowing the mind-and-heart to get away the least bit. Then, after practicing this for a long time, one naturally becomes "always bright and alert," one naturally does "not allow a single thing [to have hold on the mind]"—and this without the least problem in regard to being either negligent [on the one hand] or trying to help [it grow on the other]. [From *T'oegye chŏnsŏ* II: *Ŏnhaeng nok* 1.14b–15a]

Thus the *Book of Odes* speaks of reverence for the Way of Heaven, saying:

> *Reverence it, reverence it!*
> *Heaven is lustrous,*
> *Its Mandate is not easy!*
> *Do not say it is lofty and high above;*
> *Ascending and descending,*
> *It watches daily over your affairs.*

For with regard to the issuing forth of the principle of Heaven, there is nothing in which it is not present and no time that it is not so. If in one's daily conduct there is a slight deviance from the principle of Heaven and one slips into following [selfish] human desire, that is not how one reverences heaven. [From *T'oegye chŏnsŏ* II: *Ŏnhaeng nok* 3.22a–b]

Section 10: Diagram of the Admonition on "Rising Early and Retiring Late"

The *Admonition on "Rising Early and Retiring Late"* depicts the practice of mindfulness in the context of the fluctuating rhythm of the daily routine. This chapter, by describing a well-lived day, gives us a concrete picture of the life-style that is the ideal embodiment of this kind of self-cultivation. Accounts of Yi Hwang's own life when he finally managed to escape from holding office bear a close resemblance to what is presented here, and in 1560 he wrote: "*The Admonition on 'Rising Early and Retiring Late'* fully expresses the way of pursuing learning. Although I have not been able personally to carry it out [fully], it is what I wish to practice."

TEXT OF THE *ADMONITION*

When the cock crows and you awake, thoughts gradually increase their pace; at this time how can one but compose oneself and bring order to them? Sometimes reflect on your past faults; at others follow out what has been newly apprehended. With proper order and sequence, lucidly ponder this matter in silence.

The foundation being thus established, as day breaks, rise, brush your teeth, comb your hair, and don your robes and cap. Then, sitting erect, compose your body and recollect your mind, making it as luminous as the rising sun; become solemn and silent, ordered and even, empty and lucid, still and undivided.

Then open your books and enter the presence of the sages and wise men; Confucius is seated, Yen Hui and Tseng Tzu attend before and behind. Personally and reverently attend to the words of the sage Master; carefully going over and reconsidering the questions and discussions of the disciples, settle them [in your own mind].

When some matter arises, respond to it; then you may experience [what you have been learning] in actual practice. The clear Mandate will shine forth; keep your attention constantly upon it. When the matter has been responded to and is finished, be as you were before, with your mind clear and calm. Recollect your spirit and dispel distracting thoughts.

Over the cyclic alternation of activity and quiet, the mind alone presides; it should be possessed in quiet and discerning in activity. Do not allow it to become divided into two or three. In the time left over from reading, from time to time take a swim to relax your mind and refresh and nourish your feelings and nature.

As the sun sets one tends to slacken, and a dull spirit easily comes upon one; purify, refresh, order, and settle yourself, reinvigorating your mind. When the night is far gone, go to bed, lying with your hands at your sides and your feet together; do not let your mind wander in thought, but make it return to abide [in repose]. Nurture it in the restorative atmosphere of the night; after Steadfastness there is a return to Origination.

Be mindful of the matter at hand, industrious day and night.

YI HWANG'S COMMENTS

Indeed, the uninterrupted flow of the Way throughout the affairs of daily life is such that there is nowhere one can go that it is not present; thus there is not a single foot of ground in which principle is absent. What place is there that one may cease his diligence? And [the Way] does not pause for the least instant; thus there is not a moment's time in which principle is absent. What time is there that one must not apply oneself?

That is how, in harmony with the alternation of quiescence and action and in accord with the time and the place, one carries to the utmost the complementary practices of preserving and nurturing [one's innate, good dispositions in quiescence] and exercising reflection and discernment [in action]. When one is finally able to conduct oneself in this manner, there will be no topic which is neglected, and so there will not be "a hair's breadth disparity"; there will be no time of day which is not attended to, so one will not "falter for a single moment." One must advance in both respects in unison; in this lies the essence of becoming a sage.

Kim Sŏngil] asked about Master Yen-p'ing [Li T'ung]'s theory of quiet-sitting. Master [Yi Hwang] said: "Only after [practicing] quiet-sitting can one's mind and body become recollected and moral principles finally all come together and be anchored. If one's form and bones are heedlessly relaxed and without restraint, then the body and mind are darkened and disordered and moral principle no longer has a place to which to gather and be anchored. Therefore Kao-t'ing [Chu Hsi] quiet-sat facing Master Yen-p'ing for an entire day, and after he had parted from him likewise did so on his own."

In general, the way one should pursue learning does not take into account the presence or absence of affairs [to be dealt with] or the presence or absence of intention; one should only regard mindfulness as the primary thing, and then neither action nor quiescence will miss the norm. Before thoughts have arisen the substance of the mind will be empty and clear and its foundation deep and pure; after thoughts have arisen moral principle will be clearly manifest and [selfish] desire will recede and be cut off. The problem of a confused and disordered [state of mind] will gradually diminish in proportion as one accumulates [practice] and comes closer to becoming fully accomplished. This is the essential method. But now if one does not concern oneself with this and instead regards the spontaneous arising of thoughts as one deals with affairs and interacts with others as what is permissible, then he will want to be absolutely without thought when there is no affair to be dealt with. If one regards having [deliberate] intentions and thoughts as a hindrance to the mind, this means one would have to be like a sage who has no [deliberate] intentions or thoughts; then there would be no hindrance to the mind. Wanting to cut off thoughts is close to [Taoist] sitting in forgetfulness; being without [deliberate] intention or thought, furthermore, is not something that one who is less than a great wise man can approach. I fear this is all wrong. What's more, as for what has been said about there being a self-centered intent as soon as there is [deliberate] thought, that is certainly true if one is speaking with regard to someone whose original nature has been ensnared and submerged. But if one considers it in terms of moral principle, how can the arising of self-centered intentions be considered the fault of [deliberate] thought? Mencius says, "The office of the mind is to think. If one thinks one apprehends [what is right]; if one does not exercise thought, one does not attain it." This means that the arising of self-centered intentions in ordinary people is in fact due to their not exercising thought. [From *T'oegye chŏnsŏ* I:28:17a–b]   MK

Yi I (1536–1584)

Yi I (Yulgok) rivals Yi Hwang for the position of foremost philosopher of the Chosŏn dynasty. He was a great statesman and theorist of government as well as a metaphysical thinker of rare perceptiveness and clarity. In the decade after Yi Hwang's death, Yi I resurrected the position finally abandoned by Ki Taesŭng in the Four-Seven Debate and further developed it in debate with his friend Sŏng Hon (1535–1598).

Yi Hwang and Ki Taesŭng had argued the question in terms of two sets of feelings: the purely good Four Beginnings and the sometimes good and sometimes evil Seven Feelings. In this selection Yi I refers instead to the "Tao Mind" and the "Human Mind," classical terms that likewise referred to normative and good inclinations versus those of a more dubious sort. The basic question—whether or not this differentiation is founded upon different modal relationships of principle and material force—remains the same, however.   MK

Letter to Sŏng Hon

[From *Yulgok chŏnsŏ* 10:11a-18a]

There is a single thread running through both the explanation of principle and material force and the explanation of the Human Mind and the Tao Mind. If one has not comprehended the meaning of the Human Mind and the Tao Mind, it amounts to not comprehending principle and material force. If one has already clearly understood the inseparability of principle and material force, then one can extend that to an understanding of the fact that the Human Mind and Tao Mind do not have a twofold origin. Only if there is something not yet comprehended about the relationship between principle and material force might one perhaps regard them as separate, with each occupying its own distinct place. And thus one might also then question whether in the case of the Human Mind and the Tao Mind there might be two distinct origins.

Principle is above forms; material force is on the level of form. The two cannot be separated from each other. If they cannot be separated, then their issuance as function is single and one cannot speak of them as mutually possessing issuing functions. If one says they mutually possess issuing functions, that would mean that when principle issues as function, material force at times might not be right with it, or that when material force issues as function, there might be times when principle is not right with it. In that case the relation of principle and material force would admit of both separation and conjunction and prior and posterior. Activity and tranquillity would have a commencement; yin and yang would have a beginning. The error in all this is indeed anything but small!

But principle is nonactive; rather it is material force that has concrete activity. Therefore in the case of feelings that emerge from the original nature and are not disrupted by our physical constitution, they are classed on the side of principle. Those that, although at the beginning emerging from the original nature, are then disrupted by the physical constitution are classed on the side of material force. One cannot get by without such propositions. That which accounts for the original goodness of man's nature is principle; but if it were not for material force, principle, being nonactive, would have no issuance. Then as for the Human Mind and the Tao Mind, are they not indeed both rooted in principle? It is not a matter of the outgrowth of the Human Mind already standing in contrast to principle in the mind-and-heart in the state before it is aroused. The wellspring is single but its outpouring is dual; how could Master Chu not have understood this? It's just that the kinds of expression used to clarify the matter for others all have their own particular focus.

Master Ch'eng said: "It's not correct that good and evil are in the nature as two contrasting items, each with its own emergence."[5] Indeed, good and evil are two distinct things; still there is no rationale whereby they stand in contrast in the mind and both emerge separately. How much more is this so in the case of principle and material force, which are inseparably intermixed. How could there be a rationale whereby they stand in contrast and mutually give issuance? If Master Chu actually thought that principle and material force have as function mutual issuances that could be contrasted with one another and each emerges on its own, then that would mean that Master Chu is also mistaken. But one who could make such an error could not be a Master Chu!

As for developing the terminology of "Human Mind" and "Tao Mind,"[6] how did the sage have any alternative? Principle in its original condition is definitely perfectly good, but it mounts material force to issue as function, and this is where good and evil diverge. If one only sees that it mounts material force and involves both good and evil and does not understand principle in its original condition, then that amounts to not knowing the Great Foundation. If one only sees principle's original condition and does not understand its mounting on material force to issue as function—a condition that may develop into evil—then that is like mistaking the bandit for a son. Therefore the sage was concerned about this matter and categorized the feelings that directly follow from our normative nature in its original conditions as the "Tao Mind" in order to get people to preserve, nurture, and develop it to the fullest extent. The feelings that are disrupted by the effects of our physical constitution and are unable to be the direct consequence of our normative nature in its original condition he categorized as the "Human Mind" in order to get people to examine the excess or deficiency involved in such feelings and moderate them accordingly.

That which moderates them is the Tao Mind. Indeed, concrete form is a part of the nature with which we are endowed by Heaven. As for the Human Mind, how is it likewise not good? But its negative connotation is from its involving excess or deficiency and devolving into evil, that is all. If one is able to develop the Tao Mind to its fullest extent and moderate the Human Mind, making the proclivities that attend our physical constitution each follow its proper norm, then whether in activity or tranquillity, speech or deeds, there will be nothing that is not of our normative nature in its original condition.

As for something that cannot be separated from a vessel and has ceaseless activity, water is just the thing. Thus water is just the metaphor for principle. The original clarity of water is like the nature's original goodness. The difference between a clean and a dirty vessel is like the differentiation of the physical nature. When the vessel moves, the water moves—which is like material force issuing and principle mounting it. The vessel and the water move together; there is no difference between the vessel's moving and the water's moving. Nor is there a difference in the issuance of material force and principle, as suggested by the mutual issuance theory. When the vessel moves, the water necessarily moves; the water never moves of itself. Principle is nonactive; it is material force that has activity.

The psychological endowment of a sage is perfectly pure, and his nature is in integral possession of its substance without a single bit of the self-centeredness of selfish human desires. As for the issuance of this nature, therefore, "he can follow his heart's desire without transgressing the norm,"[7] and the Human Mind is likewise the Tao Mind. It's like a perfectly clean vessel filled with water: since there is not a speck of dirt, when it moves and the originally clear water is poured out and flows forth, it remains entirely clear water.

As for the worthy, although his psychophysical endowment is pure, it has not escaped a slight admixture of turbidity. Therefore it must be supplemented by the application of further cultivation before it regains the full perfection of the original nature. As for its issuance, there is that which is the direct consequence of the original nature and is not disrupted by the physical constitution. There is also that which, although it issues from the nature, is also affected by the physical constitution; but although the physical constitution has some effect, the Human Mind submits to what is mandated by the Tao Mind. Therefore the appetites for food and sexual pleasure also stay on the right track. It is like a vessel filled with water that is basically clean but has not escaped a slight bit of dirt inside: there must be further cleansing before the water regains its original clarity. As for its movement, therefore, sometimes there is clear water that pours out, and the dirt has not yet moved. There are other cases when although clean water comes out, the dirt has already been moved, and so the dirt must be stopped and not allowed to become mixed in, and then the outpouring water can keep its clarity.

One who has no semblance of his original perfection has a psychophysical endowment that has a lot of the turbid and little of the clear in it, much that is impure and little that is pure. The original condition of the nature is overwhelmed, and, moreover, there is no application made to cultivate and perfect it. What issues forth in such a case is for the most part due to the physical constitution; here the Human Mind is in control. Intermittently the Tao Mind emerges mixed in with the Human Mind, but the person does not know how to discern and preserve it, so he consistently gives himself over to the self-centered proclivity of his physical constitution.

When this reaches the point of one's being conquered by the feelings, concupiscence burns hotly, and the Tao Mind is reduced to the Human Mind. It is like an unclean, filthy vessel filled with water: the muddy water has lost its original clarity, and there is moreover no effort to cleanse it. As for its movement, muddy, roiled water comes forth, and one sees no evidence of its having been clean water. There are occasions when the mud has not yet been roiled up and suddenly clear water comes out for a moment, but in the blink of an eye the mud is again roiled up, so that what was clear again becomes turbid, and what flows forth is all dirty water.

The nature is originally good, but due to influence of the imperfect psychophysical endowment at times it devolves into evil. To regard evil as not the original condition of the nature is permissible; to say that it is not based on the nature is impermissible. The water is originally clear, but owing to the roiling up of the mud it ends as a turbid outflow. One may regard the turbidity as not the original condition of water, but one cannot say that the turbid outflow is not that of water. The middle sort of person's nature falls between that of the worthy and the person who bears no semblance to his original condition. One can understand it by following it out along these lines.

Principle's inseparability from material force is really like the water's being inseparable from the vessel. Now if you would say they mutually have issuances as function, then that would mean that sometimes the vessel would move first and the water would follow and move, sometimes the water would move first and the vessel would follow and move. How in the world could there be a rationale for this?

And if one uses the metaphor of a man mounted on a horse, then the man is the nature and the horse is the psychophysical constitution. The horse's temperament may be docile and good or it may be unruly: this represents the differences of clarity and turbidity, purity and impurity, in the psychophysical endowment. When they go out the gate, sometimes the horse follows the will of the rider and goes out, sometimes the rider leaves it to the horse and goes out. When the horse follows the will of the rider and goes out, it is classed on the side of the man; that is the Tao Mind. When the man leaves it to the horse and goes out, it is classed on the side of the horse; that is the Human Mind. The road in front of the gate is the road of things and affairs as it ought to be traversed. When the rider has mounted the horse but not yet gone out the gate, there is no commencement or sign of either the man's leaving it to the horse or the horse's following the will of the man: this is the same as there originally being no outgrowths of the Human Mind and the Tao Mind that stand in contrast to one another.

The vital forces of the sages are the same as those of other men: when they are hungry, they desire to eat; when thirsty, they wish to drink; when cold, they want clothing; when they itch, they want to scratch. They likewise are not free from such matters. Therefore the fact that even a sage must have the Human Mind is like the situation of having a horse that has a perfectly docile temperament: Will there not be times when the rider goes forth leaving it to the horse? But the horse is so submissive to the rider's will that it does not wait for the reins to control it but of itself follows the proper road. That is what is meant by the sage's "following the desires of his heart without transgressing the norm,"[8] and the Human Mind's being also the Tao Mind.

In the case of ordinary persons, their psychophysical endowment is not perfectly pure, so when the issuance of the Human Mind is not controlled by the Tao Mind it devolves into evil. It is like the rider who goes forth leaving it to the horse and not using the reins for control, so the horse has its way and does not traverse the proper road.

In this line of comparison, there is the case of a horse of the most unruly temperament. Even though the rider tries to control it with the reins, it bucks continually and inevitably runs off into wild groves and thickets of thorns. This is the case of a turbid and impure psychophysical endowment in which the Human Mind is in control and the Tao Mind is covered over and obscured. When the temperament of the horse is so unruly, the horse bucks continually and will not stand quietly for even a moment. This is the condition of the man with a dark and confused mind-and-heart who has never established the Great Foundation.

Even if it is an unruly horse, if by chance it happens to stand still, then, while it is standing still, there is no difference between it and the docile, good horse. This is like the situation of the ordinary man whose mind-and-heart is dark and confused; even though he has not established its substance, there is by chance a period when his mind-and-heart is not yet aroused. At that moment its clear and pure substance is no different from that of a sage.

From this kind of comparison, how can the explanation of the Human Mind and the Tao Mind, and the matter of focusing on principle or focusing on material force, be anything but clear and easy to understand? If one wants to apply it to the mutual issuance thesis, it would be like the man and the horse being in different places when they have not yet gone out the gate and the man mounting the horse after they go out. In some cases the man might go out and the horse follow him; in others the horse might go out and the man follow. The terminology and the rationale both go wrong, and it becomes meaningless. A man and a horse can be separate from one another, however, so the comparison is not quite as close as that of the vessel and water. But water also has concrete form, and in this respect likewise is not comparable to principle, which is formless. Similes must be looked at flexibly; one must not get mired down in them.

Concerning the psychophysical nature man receives at birth, there are certainly some cases in which good and evil are already determined. Therefore Confucius said that at birth men's natures are close to being the same, but by the habituation of practice they become far different from one another. And again he said: "The highest kind of wise man and the worst kind of fool do not change."[9] But that is not a matter of the original condition of the fool's nature, but the consequence of his darkness and confusion; hence this cannot be called the equilibrium of the as-yet-unaroused condition of the mind. The not-yet-aroused condition is the nature in its original condition. If there is darkness and confusion, then material force has already disrupted the nature. Therefore one cannot say this is the substance of the nature.

Mencius said: "When bad government prevails in the kingdom, princes of small power are submissive to those of great, and the weak to the strong. This is the rule of Heaven."[10] Indeed not taking into account the greatness or smallness of virtue but only taking small or great in terms of strength and weakness as that which determines victory or defeat, how could that be the original natural condition! It's just that he is speaking in terms of power, that is all. If power works that way, then the principle is also that way, and so he calls it "natural."

That being the case, if a certain evil man manages to preserve his life, one may say that such is not the original nature of principle. But if one says it is solely the product of material force and has nothing to do with principle, then it is wrong. Where in the world is there any material force apart from principle?

The wonder that is principle and material force is difficult to understand and also difficult to explain. Principle has only a single wellspring; material force likewise has only a single wellspring. Material force is evolvingly active and becomes diversified and even; principle likewise acts evolvingly and becomes diversified and uneven. Material force does not part from principle; principle does not part from material force. That being the case, principle and material force are a unity. Where can one see any difference? *MK*

CHAPTER NINETEEN

Buddhism

One of the most important changes from the Koryŏ to the Chosŏn dynasty was the shift from sponsoring Buddhism to the Confucianization of the state through the adoption of Neo-Confucianism, based in particular on the writings of Chu Hsi. Generally, Confucian rulers, except King Sejo (1455–1468) and Queen Dowager Munjŏng (1501–1565), who acted as a regent to the young King Myŏngjong from 1545 until her death in 1565, attempted to suppress all beliefs and practices other than those of Chu Hsi regarding the nature and patterns of government, society, and people. Thus, as Confucianism enjoyed unreserved governmental patronage, Buddhism was continuously suppressed and even persecuted. Eminent Buddhist monks made efforts to defend Buddhism against attacks from the Confucian view and to find ways to reconcile and integrate their views with Confucianism. Although the Confucians' main critical arguments against Buddhism were based on ethical issues, in fact the government's policy was more concerned with economics.

In 1393, King T'aejo confiscated the property of a great many monasteries and turned the land over to the state. In 1405, King T'aejong abolished the clerical posts of *wangsa* (royal preceptor) and *kuksa* (national preceptor). In 1406 the number of temples was reduced to 242, and the number of sects was reduced to seven. The number of monks who could live in any given temple was set by the government. Most temples lost their tax-exempt status, and the number of temple attendants was strictly limited. In 1424, King Sejong decreed that the number of temples in the country be limited to thirty-six and that the seven remaining sects be amalgamated into two authorized schools, the Sŏnjong (Meditation school) and Kyojong (Doctrinal school). In 1492, during the rule of Sŏngjong, the law providing for the ordination of monks was rescinded, and all monks were under pressure to return to lay status. During the reign of Yŏnsangun (1494–1506), many temples and Buddhist images were destroyed, and the protective umbrella of state recognition of Buddhism was withdrawn. The monk examinations and ranks disappeared. Under King Chungjong (1506–1544) the Buddhist department in the state examination system was abolished, and the destruction or appropriation of Buddhist property increased.

In response, some Buddhist thinkers tried to vindicate Buddhism against Confucian criticisms or attempted to find grounds for reconciliation with Confucianism. The most famous of these thinkers are Kihwa (1376–1433), Pou (1515–1565), and Hyujŏng (1520–1604). It is notable that all three had studied Confucianism before becoming Buddhist monks, and thus had the knowledge and confidence to compare Confucianism with Buddhism. They played a leading role in their times and occupy prominent positions in the history of Chosŏn Buddhism. In general, however, the survival of Buddhism under the Chosŏn dynasty during the period of suppression and persecution should be attributed mostly to the efforts of those monks who devoted themselves to continued study and practice in remote mountain monasteries and to the pious support of lay Buddhists, including both ordinary people and women of the upper class. *JW*

KIHWA (1376–1433)

Kihwa was one of the eminent Meditation masters who advocated reconciliation among religions in the early Chosŏn dynasty and left behind a number of writings, commenting on Buddhist scriptures and attempting to reconcile Buddhism with Confucianism. The *Treatise on Manifesting Rightness* (*Hyŏnjŏng non*), translated here, compares Buddhist principles and their function in the world with Confucianism in order to defend Buddhism against attacks from Confucians and to seek reconciliation. *JW*

Treatise on Manifesting Rightness

[rom *Hanguk pulgyo chŏnsŏ* 7:217a–225b]

That of which the essence is neither being nor nonbeing, but which pervades both being and nonbeing, and that of which the origin is neither past nor present, but which pervades past and present, is the path.

The causes of being and nonbeing are embedded in one's true nature and emotions. The causes of past and present are embedded in birth and death. One's true nature is originally without emotions, but emotions arise as a result of true nature's becoming deluded. Emotions give rise to the obstruction of wisdom. Thoughts are transformed, and the essence becomes differentiated. Therefore, myriad things are formed, and birth and death begin.

As for emotions, they include defilement and purity, good and evil. Purity and goodness are what give rise to saints; defilement and evil are what produce ordinary people. Therefore, we should know that if emotions do not arise, then neither ordinary people nor saints will be able to flourish.

A bodhisattva is one whose nature may already be enlightened, but whose emotions have not yet completely disappeared. Therefore making the claim that "an enlightened one has emotions" in reference to bodhisattvas—how much more true is this for the two-vehicle adherents of śrāvakas and pratyekabuddhas! All three-vehicle adherents still have emotions, so how much more do humans, heavenly beings, and various other beings.

The enlightenment of a buddha is complete, and there is nothing that his wisdom does not include. His purity is consummate, and his emotional troubles have already disappeared. Therefore discussion about emotions cannot be applied to a buddha. That is why everyone is called a sentient being except a buddha.

In my view, the ultimate point of the *Tripiṭaka* is only that it causes people to leave emotions and manifest their true nature. Emotions arise in one's true nature like clouds rising in a vast sky. Abandoning emotions and manifesting one's true nature is like clouds' opening and manifesting the great blue sky.

Emotions are light and emotions are weighty, just like clouds that are light and clouds that are thick. Clouds differ in lightness and thickness, but they are the same in blocking the light of the sky; emotions can be distinguished as light and weighty, but they are the same in obstructing the light of one's true nature.

When clouds rise, the sun and moon withhold their light, and the world becomes darkened; when clouds open, the light pervades a thousand world-systems and brightens the vast universe. By comparison, Buddhism is like the fresh wind that clears away the floating clouds. Those who want an expansive view but dislike the fresh wind are deluded; those who want pure peace between themselves and others but dislike our path of Buddhism are lost.

If one teaches people to rely on Buddhism and cultivate it, their minds can be accomplished and righteous; their bodies can be accomplished and cultivated; they can manage their homes; they can rectify the state; and the whole world can be at peace.

In general, the five abstentions[1] and the ten wholesome deeds[2] are the barest minimum in our teaching. Originally these were established for the people with the lowest capacities. Nevertheless, if anyone practices these well, then it is not only good for oneself but also beneficial for others. If there is benefit from these minimal practices, how much more would arise from the four noble truths[3] and the twelvefold chain of dependent origination![4] How much more from the six perfections![5]

Confucianism regards the five constants[6] as pivotal to the practice of the Way. The five abstentions that are taught by the Buddha are identical to the five constants taught by the Confucians: no killing means humaneness; no stealing means rightness; no sexual misconduct means ritual decorum; no drinking intoxicants means wisdom; no lying means trustiworthiness.

But when it comes to the means Confucians use for instructing people when they do not practice virtue, they govern by means of punishment. Therefore, it is said: "If the people are led by laws, and one seeks to give them uniformity by punishments, they will try to avoid the punishment but have no sense of shame. If they are led by virtue, and one seeks to give them uniformity by the rules of ritual decorum, they will have the sense of shame and moreover will become good."[7] But for persons who are not saintly, it is not possible to "be led by virtue, and [for] uniformity to be given them by the rules of ritual decorum." Therefore, it is said: "Completing the study of them by silent meditation, and securing the faith of others without the use of words, depended on their virtuous conduct."[8] "If the people are led by laws, and one seeks to give them uniformity by punishments," one cannot avoid having rewards and punishments. Therefore, it is said that rewards and punishments are the powerful handle of the state.

"Completing the study of them by silent meditation, and securing the faith of others without the use of words" is truly our Buddha's method of transformation, in addition to displaying cause and effect. When people are taught by means of rewards and punishment, their lack of transgression will be on the surface only and that is all. But when people are taught by means of cause and effect, their minds will become obedient. In today's world, we can see with our own eyes such development taking place. Why? If you motivate people to do good using rewards and prohibit people from evil using punishment, then one who abstains from evil does so out of a feeling of fear and dread, and one who does good does so out of an interest in being rewarded. Therefore, compliance with the teaching is merely superficial and not heartfelt obedience.

Our Buddha's teachings are only concerned with how to make people follow the function of the Way without distinction between lay people and monks. This means that people do not have to shave their hair or wear different robes to practice the Way. Therefore, it is said, "Freeing people from their bonds through skillful methods is expediently called *samādhi*"; it is also said, "There is no precise dharma named the Supreme Enlightenment."[9] The Buddha's mind is like that. How can his way be considered narrow? If you lack the power of patience, however, it is difficult to live in the mundane world without contamination or to attain the Way while living at home. Therefore the Buddha taught people to leave their homes in order to have them cultivate the practice of radical detachment.

Now, human beings receive their birth from their parents and owe their survival to the state. Filial piety at home and loyalty to the state are proper duties for a subject and a son. Marriage and memorial services for ancestors are also the great principles of men's cardinal relationships. Without marriage, the principle of reproduction may be annihilated; without memorial services, the tradition of ancestor worship may be extinguished. But to fulfill completely the duties of loyalty and filial piety as a subject and as a son is difficult. To remain married while maintaining rightness till the end of one's life, to perform ancestor worship with heart and soul, and to abide in perfect purity are also difficult. If one scrupulously keeps his office while at the same time remaining totally dedicated to loyalty and filial piety, and if one continuously upholds rightness and abides in perfect purity until his death, he will not only not lose his good name while he is alive but will also gain rebirth as a human being after death. This is a result of adhering to the unchangeable way of the principle.

Most people attempt to obtain fame only; very few try to restrain themselves from passion. Most people only want rebirth as a human being and find it difficult to free themselves from endless transmigration. Passion is the root cause of transmigration; lust is the immediate cause of birth. For those people who are no longer in a position to avoid ties to their wives and children, can they possibly cut themselves off from passion? If they cannot remove themselves from passion, can they possibly free themselves from transmigration? If one wants to be free from transmigration, one should first eliminate passion; if one wants to eliminate passion, one should first leave one's wife and children; if one wants to leave one's wife and children, one must abandon the mundane world. If one does not abandon the mundane world, one cannot leave one's wife and children, nor can one eliminate passion and be free from transmigration.

In the case of Śākyamuni, our original master, when he dwelled in the Tuṣita Heaven, he was called Prabhapala, Guardian of Illumination Bodhisattva. When he descended from the Tuṣita Heaven to the palace of the king Suddhodana in ancient India, he was named Siddhartha, Goal Achieved. How can we say that he was a person who had no power of fortitude? We can say that the sun was ashamed and its light was so faint, and the supreme heaven was ashamed and was cleansed through him. Although he had been involved in passion, he had never been contaminated by it. Wishing to be an exemplar for future generations, he, an ideal prince of the great king, acted in an unfilial way and left the palace without informing his parents and entered the Himalayas. There he practiced difficult asceticism without regard for his life. With fortitude he concentrated on meditation without disturbance. Having extinguished completely his emotional ties and attained clearly the true enlightenment, he returned to his native place to greet his father and ascended into heaven to visit his mother in order to preach the dharma and save them both. This is how the sage adapts to circumstances as occasions demand. His virtue has spread throughout the world and later generations, and has caused the future generations throughout the world to call his parents "the father and mother of the great sage" and to use his family name as their surname. Also those who have entered the homeless life are called offspring of Śākyamuni. How can you not say that this is great filial piety?

Moreover, monks never neglect their prayers for the king and the state at the daily ritual services in the morning and evening. How could this not be called loyalty? Whereas the rulers promote virtue by conferring honors and emoluments and prohibit evil by punishing crimes, we Buddhists instruct people that good deeds bring happiness and evil deeds bring disaster. Therefore those who learn Buddhism will naturally withdraw from evil thoughts and develop good intentions. Although the Buddhists do not confer honors as rewards or awe the people with punishment, our Buddha's teachings cause the people to be transformed. Is this not assisting the king and the state?

Of the three religions [Buddhism, Confucianism, and Taoism], it is Buddhism that is capable of transforming the people without having recourse to conferring honors. This is because of the influence that people feel from the great sageliness and great compassion of the Buddha. The sage ruler Shun "loved to question others, and to study their words, though they might be shallow. He concealed what was bad in them, and displayed what was good."[10] The sage ruler Yü "did homage to the excellent words."[11] If Shun and Yü had encountered the teachings of the Buddha, how could they not have taken refuge in their beauty? *JW AND YC*

KIM SISŬP (1435–1493)

Kim Sisŭp is renowned for syncretizing Buddhism and Confucianism. In *On No-Thought (Musa)*, Kim, writing under his pen name of Ch'ŏnghanja, comments on Buddhist practices of his time, criticizes those idle Meditation practitioners who were not sincere in their meditation while pretending to be transcendent, and insists on a syncretic approach to Buddhist practices within a secular life of Confucian perspective. *JW*

On No-Thought

[From *Maewŏltang chip* 16:1a–2b]

Ch'ŏnghanja said: "When ancient men practiced the Way, they devoted every moment of their time as if it were precious and never indulged in idleness. But people nowadays are indolent and give no thought to it [sc. the Way], nor are they anxious about it all day; when can they attain enlightenment?" A guest took issue with this and stated: "The Way is by nature without thought and without anxiety. To think and to be anxious are delusions. Can one think and be anxious while practicing the Way?"

Ch'ŏnghanja said: "That which has no thought or anxiety is the essence of the Way. To be anxious with great care and not to be idle are the essentials of its practice. We see all the time in our worldly affairs that neglecting to be anxious leads to the destruction of myriad things. If such is the case, how can one attain the true Way of no delusion through idleness? Therefore, Chi-wen of the state of Lu thought over three times before acting.[12] Confucius set up the 'Nine Items of Thoughtful Consideration.'[13] Tseng Tzu kept a reminder: 'One attains only through anxiety.' Confucius had a precept for profound anxiety. Unless one is an innately intelligent person who does not need to exert himself, how can it be possible for one not to think? The dispositions of men are not the same; some are stupid and ignorant, and some are bright and intelligent. If one is not diligent and steadfast, how can one become equal to superior sages? One must think and be anxious studiously and meticulously, and one must train daily and discipline oneself monthly until one attains the realm of enlightenment by oneself. Only thereafter can one say that, in the Way, there is no thought and anxiety." *JW AND YC*

HYUJŎNG (1520–1604)

Hyujŏng is generally regarded as the greatest monk of the Chosŏn dynasty. Most of the eminent masters of modern Korean Buddhism trace their dharma lineage back to him. Although he studied the Confucian classics at the Royal Academy in Seoul, he became a Buddhist monk at the age of nineteen. Having passed the monk examination in 1552, he was appointed director of the Doctrinal school and then director of the Meditation school in 1555. In 1557 he retired to the mountains until 1592, when Japan invaded Korea. Despite his religious beliefs and age—he was then seventy-two—he organized and led a militia, largely composed of Buddhist monks, to repel the invaders. Because of his successful military exploits, he has become a legendary folk hero even to this day. He is also known as Sŏsan Taesa (Great Master of the Western Mountain).

Surrounded by the hostile environment of the Neo-Confucian orthodoxy of the Chosŏn state, Buddhism was placed in the unenviable position of having to justify its teachings as compatible with the dominant state ideologies. In the *Mirror of Three Religions (Samga kwigam)*, Hyujŏng attempted to show that the three religions, Confucianism, Taoism, and Buddhism, were ultimately not divergent in transmitting the truth and that the ultimate messages they convey are basically the same. The section on Buddhism in the *Mirror of Three Religions* is often published separately as *Mirror for Meditation Students (Sŏnga kwigam)* and is one of the most widely read Buddhist texts in Korea. See *SKC* 1:659–663 for the text. Abstracting key passages from various scriptures and adding his own commentaries, Hyujŏng compiled *Mirror for Meditation Students* as a guide for the practitioners of meditation. *Secrets of Meditation and Doctrine (Sŏn Kyo Kyŏl)* was also compiled by Hyujŏng on behalf of his disciple Yujŏng (1544–1610). In these two works and many others, Hyujŏng tried to unify the Meditation school and the Doctrinal school in an attempt to revitalize Buddhism in Korea.

JW

Secrets of Meditation and Doctrine

[From *Hanguk pulgyo chŏnsŏ* 7:657b–658a]

The students of meditation nowadays say: "Meditation is our master's dharma." The students of doctrine say: "Doctrine is our master's dharma." For one dharma, there are two different claims, and so they argue, pointing at a deer and calling it a horse. Alas! Who can solve this problem? Nevertheless, meditation is the mind of the Buddha and doctrine is the words of the Buddha. Doctrine is what reaches wordlessness from words, whereas meditation is what reaches wordlessness from wordlessness. What reaches from wordlessness to wordlessness cannot be named, and hence it is arbitrarily called mind. Not knowing its reason, people say that it can be learned by studying and can be obtained by thinking. This is indeed pitiful. People of the Doctrinal tradition say, "In the doctrine, there is also meditation," and quote the phrase: "It emerges not from the śrāvaka [disciple] vehicle, not from the pratyekabuddha vehicle, not from the bodhisattva vehicle, and not from the Buddha vehicle." But this is merely an initiatory phrase for the beginners of meditation; and it is not the real principle of meditation.

The teachings the World-Honored One gave during his life are like casting three types of compassionate nets into the sea of birth-and-death in the triple worlds. By using a small net, shrimps and bivalves are caught (as the Hīnayāna teachings do for human beings and heavenly beings). By using a medium net, bream and trout are caught (as the teachings of the Middle Vehicle for pratyeka-buddhas). By using a big net, whales and sea tortoises are caught (as the complete and sudden teachings for the Mahāyāna people). It is as if they were being placed altogether on the other shore of nirvana. This is the arranged order of the Doctrinal tradition.

Among those in the sea, there is one extraordinary being whose mane is like red fire, whose claws are like an iron lance, whose eyes shoot sunlight, and whose mouth spits a thunderstorm. When it turns its body over, the sky is filled with white waves, mountains and rivers are shaken, and the sun and the moon are darkened. It transcends the realms of the three kinds of nets, ascends straight up to the blue clouds, and pours out the sweet dew of the compassionate dharma to save all beings (exactly like the capacity of the patriarchs' teaching transmitted outside the doctrine). This is the difference between meditation and the doctrine.

This dharma of meditation was especially transmitted to our Buddha, the World-Honored One, by the patriarch Chingwi,[14] and is not the stale words of ancient buddhas. Nowadays, among those who erroneously transmit the goal of meditation, some consider the gate of "sudden and gradual" enlightenment the correct lineage; some take the teaching of "complete and sudden" enlightenment to be the essential vehicle; some cite non-Buddhist scriptures to explain the secret meaning of meditation; some frivolously play with karmic consciousness as being the fundamental dimension of meditation; some regard mental light and shadow as the real self; and some even commit unrestrained actions, like the blind wielding a stick and the deaf shouting without remorse or shame. What is their true mind? How can I dare talk about these transgressions of slander against the dharma?

I say that what is transmitted outside the doctrine cannot be known by studying nor be grasped by thinking. Only after thoroughly devoting one's mind to the extent that its way is totally cut off can it be known. Only after the realization is reached willingly can it be obtained. Can it be obtained by thinking? Can it be obtained by deliberation? It is, it can be said, like a mosquito trying to bite the back of an iron ox.

We are now in the last days of the world, and many practitioners are ill equipped for the special transmission outside the doctrine. Therefore, they only value the "complete and sudden approach" to make people see, listen, believe, and understand the use of the Way to produce seeing, hearing, belief, and understanding. They do not value the shortcut approach that has no principles, no meanings, no mind, no words, no taste, and no pattern for searching out a foundation and for breaking the black bucket of ignorance. In this situation, what can we do? Now the masters should face the practitioners of meditation all around the world and use the blade of the wisdom sword to cut through to what is essential. You should not try to bore a hole; instead you should invoke directly the living words of the original shortcut approach to lead them to self-awakening and self-enlightenment. This is the way the religious masters deal with the people. Seeing students who are not making progress, if you immediately try to steer them through preaching, it will cause no small damage to their vision. If a master of meditation violates this dharma in his practice, even though his teaching of dharma may lead to a showering of heavenly flowers, it will be like a lunatic running around at the fringe. If students of meditation believe this dharma of the shortcut approach, then even though they may yet have to achieve enlightenment in this life, they will not be taken to bad places by evil karma upon their death; instead, they will immediately enter the correct path toward enlightenment.

In the past, Ma-tsu's one shout caused the deafness of Po-chang and enabled Huang-po's tongue to spill out. This is the origin of the Lin-chi tradition. You must select the orthodox lineage of meditation. Since your spiritual vision has been clear, I am telling you this in detail. In the future, do not fail to meet the expectations of this elderly monk. If you fail to live up to this elderly monk's expectations, you fail to meet a great obligation owed to the buddhas and patriarchs. Think carefully; think carefully.   *JW AND YC*

N O T E S

1. *Origins of Korean Culture*

1. Diminutive horses that one could ride "without mishap under the lowest branches of a fruit tree." See Edward H. Schafer, *The Golden Peaches of Samarkand* (Berkeley: University of California Press, 1963), p. 68.

2. *The Rise of the Three Kingdoms*

1. The biography of Wen Yen-po in *Chiu T'ang shu* 61:2360 reads:

    Wen Yen-po was transferred to the post of vice-director of the Secretariat [*chung-shu shih-lang*] and enfeoffed as duke of Hsi-ho Commandery. At that time Ko[gu]ryŏ sent an envoy with tribute of local products. The Eminent Founder [T'ai-tsu] said to his ministers: 'Between name and fact, principle demands that there be perfect correspondence. Ko[gu]ryŏ declared its vassalage to Sui, but in the end fended off Emperor Yang: what kind of vassal have we here? In our respect for the myriad things we have no desire to be overbearing or lofty; but since we are in possession of the terrestrial vault, it is our task to bring all men together in harmony: why then must we let them declare their vassalage just to exalt and magnify themselves? Let a rescript be drawn up setting forth our concerns in this matter!' Yen-po stepped forward and said, 'The territory east of the Liao was the state of Chi Tzu [Kija] under the Chou, and under the house of Han was Hsüan-t'u Commandery. Thus, prior to Wei and Chin it was nearby and inside the imperial domain: we should not now let it off without a declaration of vassalage. Besides, if we were to contend with Koguryŏ about rites, what would the barbarians of the four quarters have to look up to? Moreover, the Middle Kingdom's attitude toward the barbarians should be like that of the sun toward the planets. In the order of things our downward gaze should favor all the barbarians in equal measure, without any question of demeaning or exalting.' The Eminent Founder thereupon rescinded his order." MR

3. The Introduction of Buddhism

1. One of the sixteen *samādhi* mentioned in the chapter "The Bodhisattva Fine Sound," in Leon Hurvitz, trans., *Scripture of the Lotus Blossom of the Fine Dharma* (New York: Columbia University Press, 1976), p. 303.

2. It was believed that the sphex wasp carried away the young of the *ming-ling* and raised them as its own, and thus Hyŏngwang is urged to nurture others in the dharma (*Book of Odes* 196, Legge 3:334).

3. *Chou i (SPTK)* 1:3a (Legge, *Yi King*, Sacred Books of the East 16 [Oxford: Clarendon, 1882], p. 411).

4. Ninth year of Queen Sŏndŏk, rather than the fifty-eighth year of Kŏnbok, which did not exist.

5. Monks *(bhikṣu)*, nuns *(bhikṣunī)*, laymen *(upāsaka)*, and laywomen *(upāsikā)*.

6. Monks, nuns, male novices *(śramanera)*, female novices *(śramaṇerikā)*, and female postulants *(śikṣamānā)*.

7. Four classes of arhats, pratyekabuddhas, and buddhas.

8. Avalokiteśvara is meant.

9. Gods, dragons, yakṣas (supernatural beings), gandharvas (musician demigods), asuras (titans), garuḍas (mythical birds), kinnaras (mythical beings), and mahoragas (great serpents).

4. Consolidation of the State

1. Marquis of P'ing-chin and chancellor under Emperor Ching; *Shih chi* 112:2949–2953 (Burton Watson, *Records of the Grand Historian*, 2:219–225).

2. Marquis of P'ing-yang and prime minister under Emperor Hui; *Shih chi* 54:2021–2031 (Watson 1:421–426).

3. An upright official who served both the Northern Chou (557–581) and Sui dynasties (581–618). He died at the age of sixty-eight. His biographies in the *Pei shih* 75 and *Sui shu* 62 do not mention the words to which Ch'oe alludes.

4. *Han Shu* 71:3039–40. For the translation and commentary on T'ao Ch'ien's poem, "In Praise of the Two Tutors Surnamed Shu," see James R. Hightower, *The Poetry of T'ao Ch'ien* (Oxford: Clarendon Press, 1970), pp. 215–219.

5. *The Rise of Buddhism*

1. Voidness of characteristics, voidness of voidness, and voidness of both.

2. Fixed wisdom (= integrative wisdom), unfixed wisdom (= sublime-observation wisdom), nirvana wisdom (= perfection in action wisdom), ultimate wisdom (= great perfect mirror wisdom).

3. Of buddhahood: the fruition buddha who is endowed with all meritorious qualities (= reward body); the *tathāgatagarbha* buddha (= dharma body); and the form buddha (= transformation body).

4. The rules of conduct and deportment; the cultivation of all wholesome dharmas; aiding all sentient beings.

5. The path to enlightenment is all-embracing; enlightenment is attained by correct understanding; one enters enlightenment by not differentiating concentration from wisdom.

6. Empty-space liberation; adamantine liberation; *prajñā* liberation.

7. Abiding on the equal-enlightenment state for one hundred, one thousand, or ten thousand aeons.

8. The dharma, reward, and transformation bodies.

9. Existence in the realms of sense desire, subtle form, and formlessness.

10. To avoid unwholesome states that have not yet arisen; to overcome unwholesome states that have already arisen; to develop wholesome states that have not yet arisen; to maintain wholesome states that have already arisen.

11. Concentration of will, mind, effort, and investigation.

12. Wŏnhyo explains that these are four powers inherent in the mind's original enlightenment and act as the conditions for the observation of the three moral codes given above. The four powers are (1) the tranquil aspect of original enlightenment, which is distinct from all the defilements and acts as the condition for the perfection of the rules of conduct and deportment; (2) the wholesome aspect of original enlightenment, which conforms with all the wholesome faculties and acts as the condition for the cultivation of all wholesome dharmas; (3) the compassionate aspect of original enlightenment, which does not abandon any sentient being and acts as the condition that prompts one to help all sentient beings; (4) the wisdom aspect of original enlightenment, which is separate from any mundane characteristic and acts as the condition for freeing the mind from any attachment to the phenomenal characteristics of the three types of moral conduct so that they will conform with thusness. VS, p. 370c25–28; KSGN 3:991a3–b14.

13. Of cause, effect, path, and extinction.

14. Form, feeling, perception, impulse, consciousness.

15. The fifty evils are another unusual listing found in VS. The consciousness aggregate (*vijñānaskandha*) includes eight evils — the eight consciousnesses — as do both the feeling and perception *skandhas*. The impulse *skandha* possesses

nine evils: eight associated with mind and one dissociated from it. The form *skandha* possesses seventeen evils: the four primary elements and the thirteen derivative forms. These make a total of fifty evils. *KSGN* 2:981b25–c3.

16. Faith, exertion, mindfulness, concentration, wisdom.

17. The development of the five spiritual faculties into potent forces.

18. Voidness of—the three existences, the six destinies, the characteristics of dharmas, the characteristics of names, and mind and consciousness.

19. Faith, consideration, cultivation, practice, relinquishment.

20. Gods, humans, animals, hungry ghosts, and denizens of hell.

21. Giving, morality, patience, exertion, concentration, and wisdom.

22. Eye, ear, nose, tongue, body, mind.

23. Mindfulness, investigation of dharmas, exertion, joy, serenity, concentration, equanimity.

24. A peculiar classification unique to VS. The term appears in VS as "great matrix of meaning," which the sutra elucidates as follows: "great" means the four great elements of earth, air, fire, and water; "meaning" refers to such lists as the aggregates, elements, and senses; "matrix" means the original consciousness (*mūlavijñāna*); VS, p. 372a21–23. Wŏnhyo interprets these as contemplations on the four gross phenomena (the four great elements), as well as the contemplation of three subtler categories of dharmas (the aggregates, and so forth), making a total of seven meanings. These contemplations lead to the destruction of the beginningless seeds of conceptual proliferation (*prapañca*) within the *mūlavijñāna*; *KSGN* 3:988a4–8, 998c2–11.

25. The aspect of suchness in one mind and the aspect of arising and ceasing in one mind.

26. The number 108 is frequently used to indicate abundance.

27. Stanley Weinstein, "A Biographical Study of Tz'u-en," *Monumenta Nipponica* 15 (1959–1960): 119–149, especially p. 147.

28. Reading *Chen* for *Cheng*.

29. Three natures: imaginariness (*parikalpita*), dependency (*paratantra*), and perfection (*parinispanna*).

30. *Chieh shen-mi ching* (T. 16, no. 676) 2:697a23–b8.

31. Robert Buswell would like to thank Professor Alan Sponberg for his detailed suggestions. The translation benefited greatly from his valuable advice.

32. Nangnang: the Chinese colony founded during the Han dynasty along the central coast of the Korean peninsula.

33. The sixth of the fallacies of the inferential reason. It is normally used to describe that type of fallacy in which two distinct, yet equally valid, reasons lead to contradictory results.

34. The first three elements (*dhātu*) are visual form (*rūpa*), the eye (*cakṣu*), and eye consciousness (*cakṣurvijñāna*).

35. Dharmapāla explains that emptiness is equivalent to the imaginary aspect of dharmas, while nonemptiness refers to the perfected and dependent natures of dharmas.
36. Existence, nonexistence, both, neither.
37. Or Sunje in SGYS 4:202.

7. Local Clans and the Rise of the Meditation School

1. Sunji places this section in the context of a hypothetical exchange between master and disciple; I summarize only the gist of the discussion.

8. Early Koryŏ Political Structure

1. A statement made out of false modesty and not out of true conviction.
2. According to SGSG 12:121, in King Hyogong's second year (898), over thirty towns in P'aesŏ and Hansan (Seoul) surrendered to Kungye, who then made Songak (Kaesŏng) his headquarters.
3. See SGSG 12:121, King Hyogong's fifth year.
4. There is a discrepancy here as the third year is 899, but *kyŏngsin* year is 90.
5. In Silla *ach'an* was the sixth highest in the seventeen-grade official rank system, and as such could be attained only by men of head-rank six or higher.
6. SGYS 1:29 notes that in this year, Kungye called his country Koryŏ.
7. Because Later Liang (907–923) was founded by Chu Ch'üan-chung, it is called Chu-Liang, as in SS 50:453.
8. *Taeach'an* was the fifth-highest Silla rank, attainable only by a man of *kol* status.
9. Except for the year, all dates in the text are given according to the lunar calendar.
10. Yao and Shun are two mythical Chinese leaders who exemplified the classical ideal of the model ruler.
11. The remainder of this translation is from Hahm Pyong-Choon, *The Korean Political Tradition and Law: Essays in Korean Law and Legal History* (Seoul: Hollym, 1967), pp. 47–51, with minor changes.
12. *Chou i* (SPTK) 4:1a (Legge, *Yi King*, p. 238).
13. Legge 1:295.
14. James Legge, *Li Ki* (Oxford: Oxford University Press, 1885), 1:400.
15. "Meritorious subjects" was the title given to the civil and military officials who received recognition for exceptionally meritorious service at times of dynastic foundation or political crisis. They occupied high office and were rewarded with land and slaves. More than two thousand were so honored by the founder of Koryŏ.
16. *Yüeh-ling* (monthly ordinances) sets forth month by month the annual events to be conducted by the government in accordance with the seasonal order of the year.

17. The gentleman has four daily routines. In the morning, he attends to government affairs; during the day, he seeks advice; in the evening, he refines government ordinances; and at night he takes care of his health.

18. *Analects* 2:25 (Legge 1:147).

19. Legge 5:218–219.

20. During the period of division in China between the Han and T'ang (c. A.D. 700–600), Hou Ching (502–552) revolted against the Liang kingdom and attempted to establish himself as an emperor of Han.

21. Chu I (482–548) was a chief minister of Liang.

22. The highest titular office, often conferred on a high-ranking official in recognition of unusual contributions to the dynasty.

23. Ki Hongsu (1148–1210) and Ch'a Yaksong (d. 1204) were prominent military officials under Ch'oe Ch'unghŏn, whose high-handed military rule saw a serious erosion in the bureaucratic administration of the government dominated by Confucian literati.

24. What follows here in the original text is Yi Chibaek's memorial on the same subject, which is found in translation in ch. 12 of this book.

9. Koryŏ Society

1. Over time the nine classics were given slightly different formulations, which included the *Book of Documents*, *Book of Odes*, *Book of Changes*, and three ritual works—the *Rites of Chou*, *Ceremonial*, and *Record of Rites*—and the *Spring and Autumn Annals* and its commentaries. These works were later supplemented with four other books: *Analects*, *Mencius*, *Great Learning*, and *Doctrine of the Mean*. The three histories are *Historical Records (Shih chi)*, *History of the Former Han (Han shu)*, and *History of the Later Han (Hou Han shu)*.

2. Minister of public works under the first T'ang emperor, Kao-tsu.

3. Rose to be prime minister in the early T'ang dynasty.

4. It was a practice at that time for the royal family and nobility to marry their close kindred. Such marriages were common in the early period of Koryŏ, less common in the middle period, and taboo from the 14th century on.

5. The Three August Sovereigns were Fu-hsi, Shen-nung, and Huang-ti. The mythical five ancient Chinese emperors begin with Huang-ti and end with Yao and Shun.

6. A man of the Later Wei dynasty who was known for his filial piety.

7. Known as one of the twenty-four most filial sons throughout Chinese history.

8. The three texts comprise *Rites of Chou (Chou li)*, *Ceremonial (I li)*, and *Record of Rites (Li chi)*.

9. A candidate *(hyanggong chinsa)* recommended by his district to sit for the examination.

10. Son of Chancellor Kim Injon (d. 1127).
11. *Sanwŏn tongjang*, a position given to a person of provincial origin.

10. *Military Rule and Late Koryŏ Reform*

1. One *tu* in modern times equals 316 cubic inches, or about 5,180 cubic centimeters.
2. These are ritual, music, archery, chariot driving, calligraphy, and mathematics.
3. One *yang* in modern times equals 1.325 ounces, or 37.564 grams.
4. One *kan* equals 5 feet 5 inches, or 180 centimeters.
5. Though phrased in the first person, this quotation is a paraphrase of the original statement found in the *Doctrine of the Mean* (Legge 1:411).
6. In 1343, Yüan removed and exiled King Ch'unghye (1330–1332 and 1339–1344) because of his licentious and cruel behavior. He died in 1344 while en route to exile.
7. The *choŏp* (ancestral occupation) and *kubun* (pension) land, though originally granted by the state, became hereditary, whereas most other state land grants did not.
8. One *mu* equals approximately 6,600 square feet, or 590 square meters in modern times; 6.6 *mu* is about one acre, or 0.4 hectare.

11. *Buddhism: The Ch'ŏnt'ae and Chogye Schools*

1. Generality and particularity; identity and difference; integration and distinction.
2. Where the Buddha preached the sixty-chapter version of the *Flower Garland Scripture.*
3. Each resides in all; all reside in one; one resides in all; and all reside in all.
4. Ten different aspects of the Flower Garland theory of the unimpeded interpenetration of all phenomena.
5. Fa-tsang's five divisions of the scholastic teachings: Hīnayāna; Mahāyāna inception teachings; Mahāyāna final teachings; sudden teachings; complete teachings.
6. The fundamental meditative subjects in the Flower Garland school: true emptiness; unimpeded interpenetration of principle and phenomena; all-embracing interfusion.
7. Alluding to *Analects* 17:7 (Legge 1:321).
8. The five pervasive causes and effects were a hermeneutical device for explicating the *Flower Garland Scripture.*
9. The *kyŏl* is a unit of land measurement varying according to the quality of the land and equaling from 61 to 138.3 acres, or 24.4 to 55.3 hectares.
10. The eighth rank in the nine-rank Buddhist hierarchy. A monk of this rank can be appointed abbot of a temple.
11. One *pu* equals 5 feet, or 150 cm.

12. The posts are called *changsaeng p'yo*, or "longevity posts." They posts had a religious function as shamanistic guardians of the area and were also boundary markers indicating the distance from various places.

13. Pyŏngong (1178–1234), also known as Hyesim, was Chinul's successor and a major leader of Meditation under the rule of the Ch'oe house.

14. Chingong (d. 1252), also known as Ch'ŏnjin, was the third national preceptor at Songgwang Monastery.

15. *The Platform Scripture* is the collection of sermons delivered by Hui-neng (638–713), the sixth patriarch of the Ch'an school in China.

16. Adapted from a verse attributed to the Fourth Ch'an Patriarch Upagupta.

17. The four benefactors are those to whom one is beholden for one's spiritual progress. The lists vary: teacher, parent, ruler, supporters; parents, sentient beings, ruler, the three treasures (the Buddha, his teachings, and his order).

18. This phrase is commonly attributed to Ma-tsu Tao-i (709–788).

19. The instruction given by Nan-ch'üan P'u-yüan (748–835) that brought Chao-chou T'ung-shen (778–897) to awakening.

20. Te-shan Hsüan-chien (780–865), a fifth-generation successor in the T'ien-huang branch of the Ch'ing-yüan Hsing-ssu lineage.

21. Lin-chi I-hsüan (d. 866) was the founder of the Lin-chi school of the mature Ch'an tradition.

22. "Groped for our heads" is an allusion to the story of Yajñadatta, who one day woke up thinking he had lost his head and went wildly about the city trying to find it. It is used as an image of the ignorant person who has always had the enlightened nature but assumes in his delusion that he has lost it.

23. Alluding to the Parable of the Burning House from the *Lotus Scripture* (*T.* 9, no. 262) 2:12c–13c.

24. Kāśyapa was the Buddha whose advent immediately preceded that of the Buddha of the present age, Śākyamuni.

25. Verses by later masters in the Meditation school that attempted to point the student to the essential feature in a meditation topic *(kongan)*.

26. Ch'oe Hongyun (d. 1229) was a civil official in early thirteenth-century Koryŏ.

27. Analects 9:4 (Legge 1:217).

28. The sobriquet of the Sung literatus Chang Shang-ying (1043–1121).

29. *Analects* 4:15 (Waley, *The Analects of Confucius*, p. 105).

30. *Analects* 4:8 (Waley, p. 103).

12. *Popular Beliefs and Confucianists*

1. These religious festivals date from early in the dynasty.

2. Hyŏndo (Hsüan-t'u in Chinese) Commandery, originally established as one of the four Han commanderies, is variously thought to have been located in northern Korea or in Manchuria. Here the name may be used to mean Korea in general.

3. Chinhan, an ancient term for the southern region of the Korean peninsula, may here refer to Silla during the Later Three Kingdoms period.
4. Source unidentified.
5. Early T'ang monk, also known as Chang-tsui.
6. *Shang Shu* 10:6a and 11:4b (Legge 3:490 and 539).
7. Yao, Shun, and Yü, the legendary founder of the Hsia, were sage rulers. T'ang was the founder of the Shang dynasty (1751–1112 B.C.). Wen, Wu, Ch'eng, and K'ang were the first four kings of the Chou dynasty (c. 1122–256 B.C.) in China.
8. A Taoist adept of Sung Hui-tsung's reign (1101–1125) in China.
9. One *mal* equals 18 liters, or 19 quarts.
10. The Two Directorates were the Chancellery *(Munha sŏng)* and the Security Council *(Milchik sa)*.
11. Known in Korean as *Yanghyŏn-go*, this fund supported students at the Royal Confucian Academy.
12. *Mencius* 2A:6 (Legge 2:202).
13. *Analects* 15:8 (Legge 1:297).
14. *Mencius* 2A:2 (Legge 2:189).
15. *Mencius* 4B:21 (Legge 2:327).

13. Founding the Chosŏn Dynasty

1. *Shang shu (SPTK)* 8:13b (Legge 3:425).

14. Political Thought in Early Chosŏn

1. *Shang shu* 2:4a–b (Legge 3:61–62, with minor changes).
2. This is a quotation from Ch'eng I's preface to the *Commentary to the "Book of Changes [I ch'uan]."*
3. According to the *Book of Documents*, Chi Tzu refused to acknowledge the sovereignty of King Wu, the founder of Chou (Legge 3:320). Chi Tzu (Kija) thus became the second legendary founder of Korea and made his "Eight Rules" the basis of his rule.

15. Culture

1. Translation taken from Joseph Needham et al., *The Hall of Heavenly Records: Korean Astronomical Instruments and Clocks, 1380–1780* (Cambridge: Cambridge University Press, 1986), 17–18, 23–26.
2. Ibid., pp. 18–19.

16. Social Life

1. The three things are the topknot *(sangt'u)*, the headband *(manggŏn)*, and the hat *(kat)*.
2. The *chao-mu* order was used in ancient China to arrange the spirit tablets in the ancestral hall.

17. Economy

1.   *Kyŏl* is a unit of land measurement based on acreage as well as soil fertility.

18. Thought

1.   *Doctrine of the Mean* 22 (Legge 1:415–416).
2.   *Tao Te Ching* 40.
3.   Paraphrase of *Huai-nan Tzu (SPPY)* 3:1a.
4.   *Commentary on the "Doctrine of the Mean"* 1:2.
5.   *I-shu (SPPY)* 1:7b.
6.   The terms originated in the *Book of Documents* (Legge 3:61, with minor changes), a famous passage that reads: "The mind of man is precarious. The mind of the Way is subtle. Be discriminating, be single-minded. Hold fast to the Mean!"
7.   *Analects* 2:4 (Legge 1:147).
8.   Ibid.
9.   *Analects* 17:3 (Legge 1:318).
10. *Mencius* 4A:7 (Legge 2:296).

19. Buddhism

1.   No killing, no stealing, no sexual misconduct, no lying, and no drinking intoxicants.
2.   The strictures against killing, stealing, sexual incontinence, lying, gossiping, harsh speech, flattery, coveting, hating, and delusion.
3.   All existence is suffering; suffering is caused by selfish craving; the eradication of selfish craving brings about the cessation of suffering and enables one to attain nirvana; and there is a path by which this eradication can be achieved, namely, the discipline of the eightfold path.
4.   Ignorance, action, consciousness, name and form, six sense organs, contact, sensation, desire, attachment, existence, birth, and old age and death.
5.   Giving, morality, patience, effort, concentration, and wisdom.
6.   Humaneness, rightness, ritual decorum, wisdom, and faithfulness.
7.   *Analects* 2:3 (Legge 1:146).
8.   Legge, *Yi King*, p. 378.
9.   *Chin-kang po-jo po-lo-mi ching* (T. 8, no. 235) 749b14–15.
10. *Doctrine of the Mean* 6 (Legge 1:388).
11. *Shang shu* 2:6a (Legge 3:66).
12. *Analects* 5:19 (Legge 1:180).
13. *Analects* 16:10 (Legge 1:314).
14. Legendary teacher of Śākyamuni.

BIBLIOGRAPHY

Beal, Samuel. *Buddhist Records of the Western World*. London: Truebner, 1884. Reprint, New York: Paragon, 1968.

Best, Jonathan W. "Tales of Three Paekche Monks Who Traveled Afar in Search of the Law." *Harvard Journal of Asiatic Studies* 51, no. 1 (1991): 139–197.

Buswell, Robert E., Jr. *The Formation of Ch'an Ideology in China and Korea: The Vajrasamādhi-Sūtra—A Buddhist Apocryphon*. Princeton: Princeton University Press, 1989.

———. *The Korean Approach to Zen: The Collected Works of Chinul*. Honolulu: University of Hawaii Press, 1983.

Chan, Wing-tsit, trans. *Reflections on Things at Hand: The Neo-Confucian Anthology Compiled by Chu Hsi and Lü Tsu-ch'ien*. New York: Columbia University Press, 1967.

Chang, Garma C. C. *The Buddhist Teaching of Totality: The Philosophy of Hwa Yen Buddhism*. University Park: Pennsylvania State University Press, 1971.

Edgerton, Franklin. *Buddhist Hybrid Sanskrit Dictionary*. New Haven: Yale University Press, 1953.

Fung, Yu-lan. *A History of Chinese Philosophy*. Trans. Derk Bodde. Princeton: Princeton University Press, 1953.

Guenther, Herbert V. *Philosophy and Psychology in the Abhidharma*. Berkeley: Shambhala, 1976.

Hahm Pyong-Choon. *The Korean Political Tradition and Law*. Seoul: Hollym, 1967.

Henthorn, William. *Korea: The Mongol Invasions*. Leiden: E. J. Brill, 1963.

Hurvitz, Leon. "Chih-i (538–597): An Introduction to the Life and Ideas of a Chinese Buddhist Monk." *Mélanges chinois et bouddhiques* 12 (1962).

——. *Scripture of the Lotus Blossom of the Fine Dharma.* New York: Columbia University Press, 1976.

Inaba Shōju. "On Chos-grub's Translation of the *Chieh-shen-mi-ching-shu.*" In *Buddhist Thought and Asian Civilization: Essays in Honor of Herbert V. Guenther on his Sixtieth Birthday*, ed. Leslie S. Kawamura and Keith Scott, 105–113. Emeryville, Calif.: Dharma Publishing, 1977.

Jan, Yüan-hua. "Tsung-mi: His Analysis of Ch'an Buddhism." *T'oung Pao* 58 (1972): 1–50.

Karlgren, Bernhard. *The Book of Odes.* Stockholm: Museum of Far Eastern Antiquities, 1950.

——. "Legends and Cults in Ancient China," *Bulletin of the Museum of Far Eastern Antiquities* 18 (1946): 206–344.

Lai, Whalen. "The *Chan-ch'a ching*: Religion and Magic in Medieval China." In *Chinese Buddhist Apocrypha*, ed. Robert E. Buswell, Jr., 175–206. Honolulu: University of Hawaii Press, 1990.

Lau, D. C. *Lao Tzu: Tao Te Ching.* Harmondsworth: Penguin, 1963.

Lee, Ki-baik. *A New History of Korea.* Trans. Edward W. Wagner with Edward J. Shultz. Cambridge: Harvard University Press, 1984.

Lee, Peter H. et al., ed. *Sourcebook of Korean Civilization.* Vol. 1. New York: Columbia University Press, 1993.

Legge, James. *The Chinese Classics.* 5 vols. Hong Kong: Hong Kong University Press, 1960.

——. *Li Ki.* 2 vols. Sacred Books of the East 27–28. Oxford: Oxford University Press, 1885.

——. *Yi King.* Sacred Books of the East 16. Oxford: Clarendon Press, 1882.

Liao, W. K., trans. *Complete Works of Han Fei Tzu.* London: Probsthain, 1959.

MacDonell, Arthur A. *Brhad-devata.* Harvard Oriental Series 5–6. Cambridge: Harvard University Press, 1904–1905.

Makra, Mary Lelia, trans. *The Hsiao Ching.* New York: St. John's University Press, 1961.

Needham, Joseph et al. *The Hall of Heavenly Records: Korean Astronomical Instruments and Clocks, 1380–1780.* Cambridge: Cambridge University Press, 1986.

Schafer, Edward H. *The Golden Peaches of Samarkand: A Study of T'ang Exotics.* Berkeley: University of California Press, 1963.

Seo, Kyung-bo. *A Study of Korean Zen Buddhism Approached Through the Chodangjip.* Seoul: Poryŏngak, 1973.

Takakusu, Junjirō. *Amitayurdhyana sūtra.* Sacred Books of the East 49. Oxford: Clarendon, 1894.

——. *The Essentials of Buddhist Philosophy.* Honolulu: University of Hawaii Press, 1949.

Thurman, Robert. *The Holy Teaching of Vimalakīrti*. University Park: University of Maryland Press, 1976.

Vaidya, P. L.., ed. *Gandavyuha sutra*. Buddhist Sanskrit Texts No. 5. Darbhanga: Mithila Institute, 1960.

Waley, Arthur. *The Analects of Confucius*. London: Allen & Unwin, 1949.

———. *The Book of Songs*. London: Allen & Unwin, 1954.

———. *The Way and Its Power: A Study of the Tao Te Ching and Its Place in Chinese Thought*. New York: Grove Press, 1958.

Watson, Burton. *The Complete Works of Chuang Tzu*. New York: Columbia University Press, 1968.

———. *Records of the Grand Historian*. 2 vols. New York: Columbia University Press, 1961; rev. ed. in 3 vols., 1993.

Watters, Thomas. *On Yuan Chwang's Travels in India, 629–645* A.D. 2 vols. London: Royal Asiatic Society, 1904.

Wayman, Alex and Hideko Wayman. *The Lion's Roar of Queen Śrīmālā*. New York: Columbia University Press, 1974.

Weinstein, Stanley. "A Biographical Study of Tz'u-en." *Monumenta Nipponica* 15 (1959–1960): 119–149.

Yampolsky, Philip B. *The Platform Sutra of the Sixth Patriarch*. New York: Columbia University Press, 1967.

Yi T'aejin. "The Socio-Economic Background of Neo-Confucianism in Korea of the Fifteenth and Sixteenth Centuries." *Seoul Journal of Korean Studies* 2 (1989): 39–63.

INDEX

OTHER WORKS IN THE COLUMBIA ASIAN STUDIES SERIES
Translations from the Asian Classics

Major Plays of Chikamatsu, tr. Donald Keene 1961

Four Major Plays of Chikamatsu, tr. Donald Keene. Paperback ed. only. 1961; rev. ed. 1997

Records of the Grand Historian of China, translated from the Shih chi of Ssu-ma Ch'ien, tr. Burton Watson, 2 vols. 1961

Instructions for Practical Living and Other Neo-Confucian Writings by Wang Yang-ming, tr. Wing-tsit Chan 1963

Hsün Tzu: Basic Writings, tr. Burton Watson, paperback ed. only. 1963; rev. ed. 1996

Chuang Tzu: Basic Writings, tr. Burton Watson, paperback ed. only. 1964; rev. ed. 1996

The Mahābhārata, tr. Chakravarthi V. Narasimhan. Also in paperback ed. 1965; rev. ed. 1997

The Manyōshū, Nippon Gakujutsu Shinkōkai edition 1965

Su Tung-p'o: Selections from a Sung Dynasty Poet, tr. Burton Watson. Also in paperback ed. 1965

Bhartrihari: Poems, tr. Barbara Stoler Miller. Also in paperback ed. 1967

Basic Writings of Mo Tzu, Hsün Tzu, and Han Fei Tzu, tr. Burton Watson. Also in separate paperback eds. 1967

The Awakening of Faith, Attributed to Aśvaghosha, tr. Yoshito S. Hakeda. Also in paperback ed. 1967

Reflections on Things at Hand: The Neo-Confucian Anthology, comp. Chu Hsi and Lü Tsu-ch'ien, tr. Wing-tsit Chan 1967

The Platform Sutra of the Sixth Patriarch, tr. Philip B. Yampolsky. Also in paperback ed. 1967

Essays in Idleness: The Tsurezuregusa of Kenkō, tr. Donald Keene. Also in paperback ed. 1967

The Pillow Book of Sei Shōnagon, tr. Ivan Morris, 2 vols. 1967

Two Plays of Ancient India: The Little Clay Cart and the Minister's Seal, tr. J. A. B. van Buitenen 1968

The Complete Works of Chuang Tzu, tr. Burton Watson 1968

The Romance of the Western Chamber (Hsi Hsiang chi), tr. S. I. Hsiung. Also in paperback ed. 1968

The Manyōshū, Nippon Gakujutsu Shinkōkai edition. Paperback ed. only. 1969

Records of the Historian: Chapters from the Shih chi of Ssu-ma Ch'ien, tr. Burton Watson. Paperback ed. only. 1969

Cold Mountain: 100 Poems by the T'ang Poet Han-shan, tr. Burton Watson. Also in paperback ed. 1970

Twenty Plays of the Nō Theatre, ed. Donald Keene. Also in paperback ed. 1970

Chūshingura: The Treasury of Loyal Retainers, tr. Donald Keene. Also in paperback ed. 1971; rev. ed. 1997

The Zen Master Hakuin: Selected Writings, tr. Philip B. Yampolsky 1971

Chinese Rhyme-Prose: Poems in the Fu Form from the Han and Six Dynasties Periods, tr. Burton Watson. Also in paperback ed. 1971

Kūkai: Major Works, tr. Yoshito S. Hakeda. Also in paperback ed. 1972

The Old Man Who Does as He Pleases: Selections from the Poetry and Prose of Lu Yu, tr. Burton Watson 1973

The Lion's Roar of Queen Śrīmālā, tr. Alex and Hideko Wayman 1974

Courtier and Commoner in Ancient China: Selections from the History of the Former Han by Pan Ku, tr. Burton Watson. Also in paperback ed. 1974

Japanese Literature in Chinese, vol. 1: Poetry and Prose in Chinese by Japanese Writers of the Early Period, tr. Burton Watson 1975

Japanese Literature in Chinese, vol. 2: Poetry and Prose in Chinese by Japanese Writers of the Later Period, tr. Burton Watson 1976

Scripture of the Lotus Blossom of the Fine Dharma, tr. Leon Hurvitz. Also in paperback ed. 1976

Love Song of the Dark Lord: Jayadeva's Gītagovinda, tr. Barbara Stoler Miller. Also in paperback ed. Cloth ed. includes critical text of the Sanskrit. 1977; rev. ed. 1997

Ryōkan: Zen Monk-Poet of Japan, tr. Burton Watson 1977

Calming the Mind and Discerning the Real: From the Lam rim chen mo of Tsoṇ-kha-pa, tr. Alex Wayman 1978

The Hermit and the Love-Thief: Sanskrit Poems of Bhartrihari and Bilhaṇa, tr. Barbara Stoler Miller 1978

The Lute: Kao Ming's P'i-p'a chi, tr. Jean Mulligan. Also in paperback ed. 1980

A Chronicle of Gods and Sovereigns: Jinnō Shōtōki of Kitabatake Chikafusa, tr. H. Paul Varley 1980

Among the Flowers: The Hua-chien chi, tr. Lois Fusek 1982

Grass Hill: Poems and Prose by the Japanese Monk Gensei, tr. Burton Watson 1983

Doctors, Diviners, and Magicians of Ancient China: Biographies of Fang-shih, tr. Kenneth J. DeWoskin. Also in paperback ed. 1983

Theater of Memory: The Plays of Kālidāsa, ed. Barbara Stoler Miller. Also in paperback ed. 1984

The Columbia Book of Chinese Poetry: From Early Times to the Thirteenth Century, ed. and tr. Burton Watson. Also in paperback ed. 1984

Poems of Love and War: From the Eight Anthologies and the Ten Long Poems of Classical Tamil, tr. A. K. Ramanujan. Also in paperback ed. 1985

The Bhagavad Gita: Krishna's Counsel in Time of War, tr. Barbara Stoler Miller 1986

The Columbia Book of Later Chinese Poetry, ed. and tr. Jonathan Chaves. Also in paperback ed. 1986

The Tso Chuan: Selections from China's Oldest Narrative History, tr. Burton Watson 1989

Waiting for the Wind: Thirty-six Poets of Japan's Late Medieval Age, tr. Steven Carter 1989

Selected Writings of Nichiren, ed. Philip B. Yampolsky 1990

Saigyō, Poems of a Mountain Home, tr. Burton Watson 1990

The Book of Lieh Tzu: A Classic of the Tao, tr. A. C. Graham. Morningside ed. 1990

The Tale of an Anklet: An Epic of South India—The Cilappatikāram of Iḷaṅkō Aṭikaḷ, tr. R. Parthasarathy 1993

Waiting for the Dawn: A Plan for the Prince, tr. and introduction by Wm. Theodore de Bary 1993

Yoshitsune and the Thousand Cherry Trees: A Masterpiece of the Eighteenth-Century Japanese Puppet Theater, tr., annotated, and with introduction by Stanleigh H. Jones, Jr. 1993

The Lotus Sutra, tr. Burton Watson. Also in paperback ed. 1993

The Classic of Changes: A New Translation of the I Ching as Interpreted by Wang Bi, tr. Richard John Lynn 1994

Beyond Spring: Tz'u Poems of the Sung Dynasty, tr. Julie Landau 1994

The Columbia Anthology of Traditional Chinese Literature, ed. Victor H. Mair 1994

Scenes for Mandarins: The Elite Theater of the Ming, tr. Cyril Birch 1995

Letters of Nichiren, ed. Philip B. Yampolsky; tr. Burton Watson et al. 1996

Unforgotten Dreams: Poems by the Zen Monk Shōtetsu, tr. Steven D. Carter 1997

The Vimalakirti Sutra, tr. Burton Watson 1997

Japanese and Chinese Poems to Sing: The Wakan rōei shū, tr. J. Thomas Rimer and Jonathan Chaves 1997

A Tower for the Summer Heat, Li Yu, tr. Patrick Hanan 1998

Traditional Japanese Theater: An Anthology of Plays, Karen Brazell 1998

The Original Analects: Sayings of Confucius and His Successors (0479—0249), E. Bruce Brooks and A. Taeko Brooks 1998

The Classic of the Way and Virtue: A New Translation of the Tao-te ching *of Laozi as Interpreted by Wang Bi,* tr. Richard John Lynn 1999

The Four Hundred Songs of War and Wisdom: An Anthology of Poems from Classical Tamil, The Puranāṇūṟu, eds. and trans. George L. Hart and Hank Heifetz 1999

Original Tao: Inward Training (Nei-yeh) *and the Foundations of Taoist Mysticism,* by Harold D. Roth 1999

Lao Tzu's Tao Te Ching: A Translation of the Startling New Documents Found at Guodian, Robert G. Henricks 2000

The Shorter Columbia Anthology of Traditional Chinese Literature, ed. Victor H. Mair 2000

Mistress and Maid (Jiaohongji) by Meng Chengshun, tr. Cyril Birch 2001

Chikamatsu: Five Late Plays, tr. and ed. C. Andrew Gerstle 2001

The Essential Lotus: Selections from the Lotus Sutra, tr. Burton Watson 2002

Early Modern Japanese Literature: An Anthology, 1600—1900, ed. Haruo Shirane 2002

The Sound of the Kiss, or The Story That Must Never Be Told: Pingali Suranna's Kalapurnodayamu, tr. Vecheru Narayana Rao and David Shulman 2003

The Selected Poems of Du Fu, tr. Burton Watson 2003

Far Beyond the Field: Haiku by Japanese Women, tr. Makoto Ueda 2003

Just Living: Poems and Prose by the Japanese Monk Tonna, ed. and tr. Steven D. Carter 2003

Han Feizi: Basic Writings, tr. Burton Watson 2003

Mozi: Basic Writings, tr. Burton Watson 2003

Xunzi: Basic Writings, tr. Burton Watson 2003

Zhuangzhi: Basic Writings, ed. and tr. Burton Watson 2003

Modern Asian Literature

Modern Japanese Drama: An Anthology, ed. and tr. Ted. Takaya. Also in paperback ed. 1979

Mask and Sword: Two Plays for the Contemporary Japanese Theater, by Yamazaki Masakazu, tr. J. Thomas Rimer 1980

Yokomitsu Riichi, Modernist, Dennis Keene 1980

Nepali Visions, Nepali Dreams: The Poetry of Laxmiprasad Devkota, tr. David Rubin 1980

Literature of the Hundred Flowers, vol. 1: *Criticism and Polemics,* ed. Hualing Nieh 1981

Literature of the Hundred Flowers, vol. 2: *Poetry and Fiction,* ed. Hualing Nieh 1981

Modern Chinese Stories and Novellas, 1919 1949, ed. Joseph S. M. Lau, C. T. Hsia, and Leo Ou-fan Lee. Also in paperback ed. 1984

A View by the Sea, by Yasuoka Shōtarō, tr. Kären Wigen Lewis 1984

Other Worlds: Arishima Takeo and the Bounds of Modern Japanese Fiction, by Paul Anderer 1984

Selected Poems of Sō Chōngju, tr. with introduction by David R. McCann 1989

The Sting of Life: Four Contemporary Japanese Novelists, by Van C. Gessel 1989

Stories of Osaka Life, by Oda Sakunosuke, tr. Burton Watson 1990

The Bodhisattva, or Samantabhadra, by Ishikawa Jun, tr. with introduction by William Jefferson Tyler 1990

The Travels of Lao Ts'an, by Liu T'ieh-yün, tr. Harold Shadick. Morningside ed. 1990

Three Plays by Kōbō Abe, tr. with introduction by Donald Keene 1993

The Columbia Anthology of Modern Chinese Literature, ed. Joseph S. M. Lau and Howard Goldblatt 1995

Modern Japanese Tanka, ed. and tr. by Makoto Ueda 1996

Masaoka Shiki: Selected Poems, ed. and tr. by Burton Watson 1997

Writing Women in Modern China: An Anthology of Women's Literature from the Early Twentieth Century, ed. and tr. by Amy D. Dooling and Kristina M. Torgeson 1998

American Stories, by Nagai Kafū, tr. Mitsuko Iriye 2000

The Paper Door and Other Stories, by Shiga Naoya, tr. Lane Dunlop 2001

Grass for My Pillow, by Saiichi Maruya, tr. Dennis Keene 2002

For All My Walking: Free-Verse Haiku of Taneda Santō with excerpts from His Diary, tr. Burton Watson 2003

Studies in Asian Culture

The Ōnin War: History of Its Origins and Background, with a Selective Translation of the Chronicle of Ōnin, by H. Paul Varley 1967

Chinese Government in Ming Times: Seven Studies, ed. Charles O. Hucker 1969

The Actors' Analects (Yakusha Rongo), ed. and tr. by Charles J. Dunn and Bungō Torigoe 1969

Self and Society in Ming Thought, by Wm. Theodore de Bary and the Conference on Ming Thought. Also in paperback ed. 1970

A History of Islamic Philosophy, by Majid Fakhry, 2d ed. 1983

Phantasies of a Love Thief: The Caurapañcāśikā Attributed to Bilhaṇa, by Barbara Stoler Miller 1971

Iqbal: Poet-Philosopher of Pakistan, ed. Hafeez Malik 1971

The Golden Tradition: An Anthology of Urdu Poetry, ed. and tr. Ahmed Ali. Also in paperback ed. 1973

Conquerors and Confucians: Aspects of Political Change in Late Yüan China, by John W. Dardess 1973

The Unfolding of Neo-Confucianism, by Wm. Theodore de Bary and the Conference on Seventeenth-Century Chinese Thought. Also in paperback ed. 1975

To Acquire Wisdom: The Way of Wang Yang-ming, by Julia Ching 1976

Gods, Priests, and Warriors: The Bhṛgus of the Mahābhārata, by Robert P. Goldman 1977

Mei Yao-ch'en and the Development of Early Sung Poetry, by Jonathan Chaves 1976

The Legend of Semimaru, Blind Musician of Japan, by Susan Matisoff 1977

Sir Sayyid Ahmad Khan and Muslim Modernization in India and Pakistan, by Hafeez Malik 1980

The Khilafat Movement: Religious Symbolism and Political Mobilization in India, by Gail Minault 1982

The World of K'ung Shang-jen: A Man of Letters in Early Ch'ing China, by Richard Strassberg 1983

The Lotus Boat: The Origins of Chinese Tz'u Poetry in T'ang Popular Culture, by Marsha L. Wagner 1984

Expressions of Self in Chinese Literature, ed. Robert E. Hegel and Richard C. Hessney 1985

Songs for the Bride: Women's Voices and Wedding Rites of Rural India, by W. G. Archer; eds. Barbara Stoler Miller and Mildred Archer 1986

The Confucian Kingship in Korea: Yŏngjo and the Politics of Sagacity, by JaHyun Kim Haboush 1988

Companions to Asian Studies

Approaches to the Oriental Classics, ed. Wm. Theodore de Bary 1959

Early Chinese Literature, by Burton Watson. Also in paperback ed. 1962

Approaches to Asian Civilizations, eds. Wm. Theodore de Bary and Ainslie T. Embree 1964

The Classic Chinese Novel: A Critical Introduction, by C. T. Hsia. Also in paperback ed. 1968

Chinese Lyricism: Shih Poetry from the Second to the Twelfth Century, tr. Burton Watson. Also in paperback ed. 1971

A Syllabus of Indian Civilization, by Leonard A. Gordon and Barbara Stoler Miller 1971

Twentieth-Century Chinese Stories, ed. C. T. Hsia and Joseph S. M. Lau. Also in paperback ed. 1971

A Syllabus of Chinese Civilization, by J. Mason Gentzler, 2d ed. 1972

A Syllabus of Japanese Civilization, by H. Paul Varley, 2d ed. 1972

An Introduction to Chinese Civilization, ed. John Meskill, with the assistance of J. Mason Gentzler 1973

An Introduction to Japanese Civilization, ed. Arthur E. Tiedemann 1974

Ukifune: Love in the Tale of Genji, ed. Andrew Pekarik 1982

The Pleasures of Japanese Literature, by Donald Keene 1988

A Guide to Oriental Classics, eds. Wm. Theodore de Bary and Ainslie T. Embree; 3d edition ed. Amy Vladeck Heinrich, 2 vols. 1989

Introduction to Asian Civilizations
Wm. Theodore de Bary, General Editor

Sources of Japanese Tradition, 1958; paperback ed., 2 vols., 1964. 2d ed., vol. 1, 2001, compiled by Wm. Theodore de Bary, Donald Keene, George Tanabe, and Paul Varley

Sources of Indian Tradition, 1958; paperback ed., 2 vols., 1964. 2d ed., 2 vols., 1988

Sources of Chinese Tradition, 1960, paperback ed., 2 vols., 1964. 2d ed., vol. 1, 1999, compiled by Wm. Theodore de Bary and Irene Bloom; vol. 2, 2000, compiled by Wm. Theodore de Bary and Richard Lufrano

Sources of Korean Tradition, 1997; 2 vols., vol. 1, 1997, compiled by Peter H. Lee and Wm. Theodore de Bary; vol. 2, 2001, compiled by Yŏngho Ch'oe, Peter H. Lee, and Wm. Theodore de Bary

Neo-Confucian Studies

Instructions for Practical Living and Other Neo-Confucian Writings by Wang Yang-ming, tr. Wing-tsit Chan 1963

Reflections on Things at Hand: The Neo-Confucian Anthology, comp. Chu Hsi and Lü Tsu-ch'ien, tr. Wing-tsit Chan 1967

Self and Society in Ming Thought, by Wm. Theodore de Bary and the Conference on Ming Thought. Also in paperback ed. 1970

The Unfolding of Neo-Confucianism, by Wm. Theodore de Bary and the Conference on Seventeenth-Century Chinese Thought. Also in paperback ed. 1975

Principle and Practicality: Essays in Neo-Confucianism and Practical Learning, eds. Wm. Theodore de Bary and Irene Bloom. Also in paperback ed. 1979

The Syncretic Religion of Lin Chao-en, by Judith A. Berling 1980

The Renewal of Buddhism in China: Chu-hung and the Late Ming Synthesis, by Chün-fang Yü 1981

Neo-Confucian Orthodoxy and the Learning of the Mind-and-Heart, by Wm. Theodore de Bary 1981

Yüan Thought: Chinese Thought and Religion Under the Mongols, eds. Hok-lam Chan and Wm. Theodore de Bary 1982

The Liberal Tradition in China, by Wm. Theodore de Bary 1983

The Development and Decline of Chinese Cosmology, by John B. Henderson 1984

The Rise of Neo-Confucianism in Korea, by Wm. Theodore de Bary and JaHyun Kim Haboush 1985

Chiao Hung and the Restructuring of Neo-Confucianism in Late Ming, by Edward T. Ch'ien 1985

Neo-Confucian Terms Explained: Pei-hsi tzu-i, by Ch'en Ch'un, ed. and trans. Wing-tsit Chan 1986

Knowledge Painfully Acquired: K'un-chih chi, by Lo Ch'in-shun, ed. and trans. Irene Bloom 1987

To Become a Sage: The Ten Diagrams on Sage Learning, by Yi T'oegye, ed. and trans. Michael C. Kalton 1988

The Message of the Mind in Neo-Confucian Thought, by Wm. Theodore de Bary 1989